MOSAICS

FOCUSING ON ESSAYS

MOSAICS

FOCUSING ON ESSAYS

Kim Flachmann
California State University, Bakersfield

Jane Maher
Nassau Community College

Elizabeth H. Campbell
GMI Engineering & Management Institute

Nancy Johnson
University of New Orleans

D.B. Magee
Texas Christian University

Prentice Hall
Upper Saddle River, NJ 07458

Library of Congress Cataloging-in-Publication Data

Mosaics : focusing on essays / Kim Flachmann . . . [et al.].
    p. cm.
   Includes index.
   ISBN 0-13-272907-5
   1. English language—Rhetoric. 2. English language—Grammar.
  3. Report writing. I. Flachmann, Kim.
  PE1408.M698 1997
  808'.042—dc21   97-12338
                                     CIP

Editor-in-Chief: Charlyce Jones-Owen
Acquisitions Editor: Maggie Barbieri
Editorial Assistant: Joan Polk
Development Editor: Victoria Nelson
Director of Production and Manufacturing: Barbara Kittle
Project Manager: Maureen Richardson
Manufacturing Manager: Nick Sklitsis
Prepress and Manufacturing Buyer: Mary Ann Gloriande
Creative Design Director: Leslie Osher
Interior Design: Circa 86
Cover Design: Ximena Tamvakopoulos
Illustrator: Circa 86
Marketing Manager: Rob Mejia
Copyeditor: Kathryn Graehl
Proofreader: Helena DeKeukelaere

This book was set in 10.5/12 Goudy by Digitype and was printed and bound by Courier Companies, Inc. The cover was printed by Phoenix Color Corp.

Credits appear on pages 495–496, which constitute a continuation of the copyright page.

 © 1998 by Prentice-Hall, Inc.
Simon & Schuster/A Viacom Company
Upper Saddle River, NJ 07458

Printed in the United States of America
10 9 8 7 6 5 4 3 2 1

ISBN 0-13-272907-5

Prentice-Hall International (UK) Limited, London
Prentice-Hall of Australia Pty. Limited, Sydney
Prentice-Hall Canada Inc., Toronto
Prentice-Hall Hispanoamericana, S.A., Mexico
Prentice-Hall of India Private Limited, New Delhi
Prentice-Hall of Japan, Inc., Tokyo
Simon & Schuster Asia Pte. Ltd., Singapore
Editora Prentice-Hall do Brasil, Ltda., Rio de Janeiro

CONTENTS

3

OBSERVING   61

READING AND WRITING FOR A REASON

4 EXPLAINING   111

READING AND WRITING FOR A REASON

5 INVESTIGATING   158

READING AND WRITING FOR A REASON

6

RESTATING   211
READING AND WRITING FOR A REASON

7

ANALYZING 273

READING AND WRITING FOR A REASON

Students everywhere must learn to respond to the varying intellectual demands made on them throughout the college curriculum so that they have the best possible chance of succeeding in higher education. One extremely important part of this process is being able to analyze ideas and think critically about issues in many different subject areas. **Mosaics: Focusing on Essays** is the third in a series of three books that teaches the basic skills so necessary to all good academic writing. By focusing on eight primary purposes for writing in each book, this series illustrates how the companion skills of reading and writing are parts of a larger process that moves back and forth through the tasks of prereading/reading, prewriting/writing, and revising/editing. In other words, the **Mosaics** series shows how these tasks are integrated at every stage of the writing process.

ASSUMPTIONS

This text is based on the following fundamental assumptions:

1. Thinking, reading, and writing are intricately related.
2. Students learn best from discovery and experimentation rather than from instruction and abstract discussion.
3. Students must be able to transfer their writing skills to all their college courses.
4. Students profit immeasurably from studying models of both professional and student writing.
5. Students perform better in college when they learn to think critically and analytically.
6. Students learn both individually and collaboratively.

HOW THIS BOOK WORKS

This book begins with a general introduction to the writing process (Chapter 1) outlining the scope and sequence of the volume. The eight chapters that follow are each divided into three carefully integrated sections:

Reading and Writing for a Reason

Tips for Revising

Tips for Editing

Reading and Writing for a Reason. Each chapter focuses on one of the eight primary purposes for writing: recalling, observing, explaining, investigating, restating, analyzing, persuading, and problem solving. The purpose is explained and then featured in a professional essay and a student essay before the readers are asked to compose an essay of their own.

- *Learning from Published Writers* focuses on a provocative professional essay with a controlled reading level in order to introduce students to a specific purpose for writing. Each essay was chosen for its high interest and moderate readability level and serves as a springboard in form and content for the rest of the chapter.

- *Learning from Your Peers* walks students through the writing process using an actual student essay. Your students witness the development of a student essay that moves through the general recursive tasks of thinking, planning, developing, organizing, drafting, revising, and editing. The revised draft is printed in each chapter with the student changes highlighted.

- *Writing Your Own Essay* asks students to compose their own essays focusing on the purpose they have just studied. Following a brief review of the highlights of the chapter and the composing process, students are given four writing topics to choose from. After they draft, revise, and edit their essays, students are then asked some specific questions that require them to pause and reflect on their own composing process before they start another chapter.

Tips for Revising and Tips for Editing. The second and third sections of each chapter, Tips for Revising and Tips for Editing, can be taught by themselves or in conjunction with the first section. The revising sections focus on effective essays; they progress from fairly simple to more complex revision strategies. The editing sections then serve as brief but thorough reference guides to grammar and usage; they move from the most basic usage and syntactic problems to more sophisticated writing conventions. The strategies in these sections are integrated into the first part of each chapter. In addition, the Tips for Revising and Tips for Editing include instruction and focused exercises (on both the sentence and paragraph levels) that are drawn from the professional and student essays featured in the chapter. Each Tips section begins with a checklist summarizing the tasks to be covered and ends with collaborative work for individual, small group, or entire class projects.

The specific skills taught in the three main sections of this third book in the **Mosaics** series are listed here so that you can see in abbreviated form how this particular book works:

Chapter	Reading and Writing	Tips for Revising	Tips for Editing
1	Introduction		
2	Recalling	Essays	Words/Phrases/Clauses

Chapter	Reading and Writing	Tips for Revising	Tips for Editing
3	Observing	Thesis/Introductions	Sentence Structure
4	Explaining	Development	Fragments/Run-ons
5	Investigating	Organization	Agreement
6	Restating	Coherent Essays	Verbs/Nouns/ Pronouns/Modifiers
7	Analyzing	Levels of Generality	Punctuation/Mechanics
8	Persuading	Effective Essays	Diction/Spelling
9	Problem Solving	Conclusions	Successful Sentences

UNIQUE FEATURES

Several unique and exciting features separate this book from other basic writing texts:

1. It moves students systematically from personal to academic writing.
2. It gives student writing the same attention as professional writing.
3. It illustrates all aspects of the writing process.
4. It integrates reading and writing throughout the text.
5. It teaches revising and editing through the student essays in each chapter.
6. It features culturally diverse reading selections that are of high interest to students.

THE MOSAICS SERIES

All three books in the *Mosaics* series (*Focusing on Sentences in Context, Focusing on Paragraphs in Context,* and *Focusing on Essays*) introduce the writing process as a unified whole and ask students to begin writing full essays in the very first chapter. The Tips for Revising sections, however, change the emphasis of each book: The first book highlights sentence structure, the second book paragraph development, and the third the composition of essays. The books also differ in the length and level of their reading selections, the complexity of their writing assignments, the degree of difficulty of their revising and editing strategies, and the length and level of their student writing samples. Each volume moves from personal to more academic writing in various disciplines throughout the curriculum.

The books are fully integrated in two significant ways: (1) The revising and editing strategies for each chapter are integrated into the demonstration of the writing process in the first part of each chapter, and, in turn, (2) the Tips for Revising and Tips for Editing draw examples and exercises from the professional and student essays in the first section of each chapter. This constant cross-reference and repetition of ideas and skills in different contexts throughout each chapter will help students grasp the basic procedures and potential power of the entire writing process.

Ultimately, each book in the **Mosaics** series portrays writing as a way of thinking and processing information. One by one, these books encourage students to discover how the "mosaics" of their own writing process work together to form a coherent whole. By demonstrating the interrelationship among thinking, reading, and writing on progressively more difficult levels, these books promise to help prepare your students for success in college throughout the curriculum.

ACKNOWLEDGMENTS

We want to acknowledge the support, encouragement, and sound advice of several people who have helped us through the development of the **Mosaics** series. First, Prentice Hall has provided guidance and inspiration for this project through the wisdom of Maggie Barbieri, Senior Editor of Developmental English; the insights of Vicki Nelson, Development Editor; the diligence and clairvoyance of Maureen Richardson, Project Manager; the hard work and patience of Fred Courtright, Permissions Editor; and the common sense and organization of Joan Polk, Administrative Assistant for Developmental English. Also, this book would not be a reality without the insightful persistence of Phil Miller, President of the Humanities Division at Prentice Hall.

In addition, we are especially grateful to the following reviewers who have guided us through five years of the development of this book: Lisa Berman, Miami-Dade; Patrick Haas, Glendale Community College; Jeanne Campanelli, American River College; Dianne Gregory, Cape Cod Community College; Clara Wilson-Cook, Southern University at New Orleans; and Thomas Beery, Lima Technical College.

We want to give very special thanks to Kelly McClain, who served as head research assistant on all three books; to Rebecca Juarez, who has truly blossomed as a research assistant; to Patti Sarr, who did an exceptional job coordinating the accompanying *Instructor's Resource Manual;* and to Susanne Christensen, who supported this project in a variety of important ways.

We also want to express our gratitude to our students, from whom we have learned so much about the writing process, about teaching, and about life itself.

Finally, we owe a tremendous personal debt to the people who have lived with this project for the last five years; they are our closest companions and our best advisors: Michael, Christopher, and Laura Flachmann; Pat Maher; Russ Campbell; Joe Blandino; and Matt Kobler. To Michael Flachmann, we owe special thanks for the valuable support and feedback he has given us through the entire process of creating this series.

MOSAICS

FOCUSING ON ESSAYS

The Writing Process

How do I know what I think until I see what I say?
—E. M. FORSTER

The simple act of using the written word to communicate makes a writer. Whether we use writing to list what we need when we shop, to send a message to a friend, to fulfill an assignment in school, or to earn a living, we are all part of a community of writers.

Any piece of writing more formal than a grocery list, however, is usually the result of a sequence of activities that seems on the surface to have nothing directly to do with the act of writing itself. This sequence of activities is called **the writing process,** and learning to follow this process to write essays is what this book is all about.

GETTING STARTED

To begin with, you should be aware of the many choices involved in the writing process. Though all writers are different, some general principles apply to everyone—students and professional writers alike. Before you can begin the process of composing an essay, you need to set aside a time and place for your writing, gather supplies, and establish a routine.

A Time and Place to Write

In her famous *A Room of One's Own,* Virginia Woolf argues that all writers have a basic need for space, privacy, and time. You need to set up your own place that suits your needs as a writer, and it should be a place where you are not distracted or interrupted. You should also set aside a special time for your writing tasks and plan to do nothing else in that time period. The dog's bath will wait until tomorrow; the kitchen appliances don't have to be polished today; drawers can be cleaned and organized some other time; the dirt on the car won't turn to concrete overnight.

(These are all some of the activities that writers confess they have done to put off the inevitable beginning.)

Even if you are lucky enough to have a private study area, you may find that you still need to make some adjustments. You may decide to unplug your phone during the time you spend on your composition assignments. Or you may discover that tuning your radio to an all-night jazz station helps you shut out noises from other parts of the house but doesn't distract you in the way talk shows and rock music do. (One well-known biographer owns a "white noise" machine that he cannot write without.) The first general principle for all writers is logical: *Find a place that is comfortable where distractions can be kept to a minimum.*

Writing Equipment and Supplies

Some writers use a legal pad and a pencil to get started on a writing task; some use typewriters or word processors. Some people work best at a desk in a straight chair, while others relax in a big armchair or on a bed. Ernest Hemingway and Virginia Woolf both wrote standing at a big desk, but Woolf used pen and ink for her early drafts, whereas Hemingway worked on a typewriter. The biographer with the white noise machine types on the battered portable typewriter that H. L. Mencken, a famous journalist of the 1920s, used to write his reports and essays. If you find you are most comfortable with your computer, you may want to use it even for your prewriting and early drafts. The next general principle remains the same for all writers and for all writing tasks: *Gather your supplies before you begin work.* Who knows what great idea might escape while you search for a pen that writes, scour the house for paper, or try to find a formatted disk?

Journal Keeping

The word *journal* means "a place for daily writing." The southern novelist Frances Newman kept a purple leather notebook with her at all times. (It had to be purple, and it had to be real leather.) In this little notebook she recorded ideas, snatches of conversation, dreams, and descriptions of people, places, or objects that caught her attention. According to Newman, her last novel developed entirely from a brief description she jotted down of the figure of a young man in Michelangelo's mural on the ceiling of the Sistine Chapel.

Even though most people aren't as particular as Newman about the type of notebook they write in, journal keeping is a very popular activity. For your life as a writer, you will find a personal journal to be an invaluable tool. Now, with the advent of notebook-sized computers, your journal can even be electronic. Just be sure to back up computer entries fairly often so you don't run the risk of losing everything in a power failure or through some other unforeseen problem. Also, you may need to print hard copies to take with you to class.

A good way to establish the habit of journal writing is to use your journal for answering the questions that accompany the readings in this text. You can also jot down in your journal ideas and plans for essays as they occur to you. In addition, you can do all your prewriting activities in your journal. It is much easier to keep up with a notebook than to keep track of assorted scraps of paper. You might want to buy a loose-leaf binder or a notebook divided into several sections so that different types of entries can have their own place.

Keeping a section of your journal private is also a good idea. Sometimes, when you think on paper or let your imagination loose, you don't want to share the results—yet these notes can be very important in finding a subject to write about or developing a topic.

Now that you've chosen your time and place for writing, your writing tools, and your journal, you're ready to embark on your own writing process. In the course of this journey, you'll discover your own preferences and routines as you begin to recognize yourself as a writer.

PREWRITING

Many students are surprised by the fact that a number of vital steps come during the writing process before the act of putting words down on paper. When we speak of **prewriting,** we mean those activities that help us explore a subject, generate ideas about it, settle on a specific topic, establish a purpose, and analyze the audience for an essay. Your reading assignment and journal entries are a first step in this direction. Many writers use one or more of the following activities as an early step to stimulate their thinking in their writing process. You may find that one suits your writing process better than others, or a combination of two or more may work best for you.

Thinking

Thinking is your initial stage of exploration. It's a time to let your mind run free over the material you have to work with. Here are some activities that promise to stimulate your best thoughts:

- *Rereading* Sometimes a good way to jump-start your thinking and writing process is to reread the professional essay in each chapter, along with your notes, your underlining, and your journal entries. Together these might give you new insights into your topic.

- *Listing* Many writers find it helpful to jot down a list of ideas about possible essay topics or ideas for expanding a chosen topic. (See pp. 69–70 for an example.)

- *Freewriting* Writing freely about anything that comes to your mind is the way to *freewrite*. The act of writing itself usually makes writers think of other ideas. (See p.70 for an example.)

- *Brainstorming* Like freewriting, *brainstorming* draws on free association. You can brainstorm alone, with a friend, or, best of all, with a group. Regardless of the method, write down *all* your ideas; the act of writing itself often leads to more ideas. (See p. 69 for an example.)

- *Clustering* Clustering lets you map your ideas as fast as they come into your mind. To cluster, take a sheet of blank paper and write a key word, phrase, or sentence in the center of the page, and draw a circle around it. Next, write down and circle any more ideas you have, and connect them with lines to the thoughts they came from. This exercise usually lasts two or three minutes. (See p. 71 for an example.)

- *Discussing* Run your ideas by friends and classmates; often they'll have a perspective on your topic — or understand your problems in locating a topic — that will put you on an entirely new path.

- *Questioning* Journalists and many other writers routinely ask questions to generate ideas on a topic. Using some type of questioning technique can help you avoid omitting important details. Most often, the questions used to generate ideas and details on a topic are the five *w*'s and one *h*: *Who, What, Why, When, Where,* and *How*.

Planning

Planning an essay involves making some important decisions about the composition you are about to create:

- What **content** (person, event, object, etc.) do you want to focus on?
    Each of your essays should *focus* on a set of related details or ideas. Although this focus will become clearer to you as you write, you should try to make some general, preliminary decisions about your content before you begin to draft an essay. Such a commitment on your part will make your essays coherent and unified; it will also help you detect any irrelevant material.

- What is your **purpose?**
    Your purpose is your *reason for writing* an essay. Purposes for essays in this text range from the personal through the practical to the persuasive. Your purpose could be to explore your own knowledge or feelings on a topic, to share information on a subject, to find ways to solve a problem, or to persuade a reader to share your views on a controversial issue.

- Who is your **audience?**
    Your audience consists of the *people for whom your message is intended*. The more you know about the people you are trying to reach with your message, the more likely you will succeed. With information about your audience, you can tailor your comments toward them so you have a good chance of convincing them to see your topic the way you do.

- What **point of view** will you take toward your subject?
    Point of view is your *perspective on a topic*. For example, are you for

or against capital punishment? Did a specific event you are writing about make you happy or sad? Once you choose a stance toward your topic, you should keep that point of view for the entire paper. A single perspective will bring consistency to your essays.

When you answer these four questions, you begin to make some commitments to the direction your essay will take. To help you prepare for making these decisions in your own writing, the questions after each professional essay in this book ask you to deal with these four issues every time you read.

Developing

After you decide on a focus, purpose, audience, and point of view for your essay, you need to expand your ideas to their fullest in your work. You are now ready to develop some specific topics that will make up the bulk of your essay. You may want to go back to the questions you used during your planning stage and use them as a starting point.

Organizing

After you generate some ideas on a topic, you need to plan the best way of presenting your ideas. What should come first? What next? Would a different way of organizing your ideas achieve your purpose better?

In the early paragraphs of an essay, you should supply your audience with the facts they will need to understand the essay's purpose in order to create a context for what they are about to read. By providing answers to basic questions the readers might have (*Who, What, Why, When, Where,* and *How*) or explaining the facts surrounding a particular event, you enable your audience to share your viewpoint as fully as possible.

Then, organize your material in a way that will be most interesting to your audience. What's the most striking detail or fact about your topic? You might want to start with that. What meaning or significance does the topic have for you? You might want to end with that. Remember that those aspects of your topic that interest you are what you are most likely to write about effectively.

PUTTING WORDS ON PAPER

Drafting

When you have a basic plan of organization in mind, you are ready to start writing. **Drafting,** as you may have guessed, means writing out a first draft. At this point, you have been working both by yourself and in class, thinking, planning, developing, and organizing your ideas on your essay topic. You may want to spread out your class notes, your journal, and your clusters or lists. One more good suggestion is to write out your main idea at the top of the page or computer screen to guide you in writing your essay.

Now you're ready to write a working draft of your essay in complete sentences—no more lists and circles. As you write, try to keep a steady flow of words going. Put as much as you can on paper, but don't let worries about style, grammar, or spelling distract you; you'll deal with those details in the next two steps of the writing process. For now, just keep writing.

Revising

As you may already suspect, the process of writing is not finished with your first draft. In writing, you revise your work to make it stronger and better. **Revising** means "seeing again," and that is exactly what you try to do—see your essay again from as many different angles as possible. Sometimes others help with the process; other times you will be on your own. To revise, a writer needs some distance from his or her first draft. Ideally, you should put your draft aside for at least a day before you begin revising it.

Revision is a task that focuses on improving content and organization. (Editing, the last step, focuses on correcting grammar and spelling.) Your main goal in revising is to make sure that the purpose of your essay is clear to your audience and that your main ideas are supported with enough details and examples. In addition, you should check to be sure your organization is logical. Using the checklist in the Tips for Revising section in every chapter of this book will help you establish your own revising strategies.

If you are able to obtain feedback from your classmates in the first stages of your writing process, you may decide they have some helpful ideas you want to use in your revision. You may actually want to draw up a list of revision notes before you go through your draft. Here is a sample revision checklist with references to specific chapters for more information:

Checklist for Revising

✓ Does this essay have an interesting **title** (Chapter 2)?
✓ Is the **main idea** clear (Chapter 3)?
✓ Does the writer focus on his or her **purpose** throughout the essay (Chapter 8)?
✓ Is each main idea in a separate **paragraph** (Chapter 8)?
✓ Does the writer need to **add** anything (Chapter 4)?
✓ Does the writer need to **delete** any unnecessary details (Chapter 8)?
✓ Does the writer need to **rearrange** any of the ideas (Chapters 5 and 8)?
✓ Does the essay have a satisfactory **conclusion** (Chapter 9)?

The Tips for Revising section supplies you with detailed explanations and exercises to refer to if you need more information on any of these specific revision strategies.

Editing

After you revise, the final step in the writing process is **editing.** In this stage, you read your essay slowly and carefully to make sure no errors in grammar, mechanics, or spelling have slipped into your draft. Each chapter in this book includes focused guidelines for editing in a Tips for Editing section along with detailed explanations and exercises demonstrating these guidelines. Following is a general Checklist for Editing with references to specific chapters for further information.

Checklist for Editing

✓ Has the writer written **complete sentences** throughout the essay (Chapter 4)?
✓ Do the subjects of sentences **agree** with their verbs (Chapter 5)?
✓ Has the writer used **punctuation** correctly and effectively (Chapter 7)?
✓ Has the writer observed conventional rules for **mechanics** (Chapter 7)?
✓ Has the writer used **words** correctly (Chapter 8)?
✓ Has the writer checked the **spelling** of words (Chapter 8)?

You should use the material in the Tips for Editing sections as a reference guide in the same way you use a dictionary as a resource for spelling and defining words.

HOW TO USE THIS BOOK

Often, good writing is inspired by good reading. To ensure that you experience the full potential of each of the eight writing purposes this book presents—recalling, observing, explaining, investigating, restating, analyzing, persuading, and problem solving—every chapter after this one opens with a writing sample from a published writer. To focus your reading experience, you will do prereading and postreading activities that help you understand the strategies these published writers have used to compose their essays.

Besides reading and analyzing a professional essay, you will also follow the writing process of a fellow student and watch two drafts of his or her essay take shape through the use of specific drafting, revising, and editing strategies. The steps in the process of writing any essay constantly overlap, but you will find that developing a systematic approach to writing is important to your growth as a writer. To this end, observing the activities and thoughts of someone at your level of development will help you shape your own writing process.

After you read and study each chapter's professional and student writing samples, you'll be ready to put the process together in your own essay. The questions before and after the professional selection will help you dissect each essay and understand how it works. In addition, as you follow the writing process of another student, you will absorb ideas to work with as well as options for giving those ideas shape. All these reading and writing activities will move you closer to producing an essay of your own. After reviewing what you've learned so far in the chapter, you will be ready to tackle your own writing tasks.

You can choose from a list of four assignments. One assignment allows you to design your own topic; the other three assignments provide a purpose and audience in more specific, focused writing topics. Your instructor may assign one or more of these tasks so you can demonstrate your ability to use the contents of each chapter.

As you establish your own writing process, you'll probably be aware that not everything you're doing matches up exactly with the writing process as it is outlined here or even with what the student writer does in the book. Don't be alarmed. Part of the pleasure of writing is learning to trust your own instincts and let them create a ritual for you. Like someone learning to swim, however, you will want to be able to hold on to the edge of the pool when you feel yourself sinking—and that's the kind of security the framework of the writing process is meant to provide as you make your way through its various phases: *thinking, planning, developing, organizing, drafting, revising,* and *editing.*

After you have revised and edited the first draft of your paper, you will produce a final draft to submit to your instructor. Even now, however, there is still more to the process. The last section in every chapter presents a list of questions that help you reflect on your writing and your own writing process so you can learn from each writing experience:

1. What was most difficult about this assignment?
2. What was easiest?
3. What did I learn about this type of writing by completing this assignment?
4. What did I learn about my own writing process from this assignment—how I prepared to write, how I wrote the first draft, how I revised, and how I edited?

Answering these questions in your journal will give you a perspective on each of your writing tasks that you will find valuable in applying to future assignments.

As you make your way through the following eight chapters, you may find yourself returning to this chapter to reread the description of the writing process. Doing this can serve as a productive prewriting strategy for the writing topics each chapter presents. As you develop your own writing process, you may also want to modify or experiment with parts of your writing ritual. Let this chapter be your guide in charting new directions for yourself, and let the professional and student writers you encounter in the following pages be your inspiration as you set out on your journey.

 THE WRITING PROCESS

THINKING   Generate as many ideas on your subject as you can in as many different ways as possible: rereading, listing, freewriting, brainstorming, clustering, discussing, and questioning.

THE WRITING PROCESS (CONTINUED)

PLANNING   Begin to give your ideas shape by deciding on your approach to your topic (your content, your purpose, your audience, and your point of view). Make a list of points you want to include in your essay.

DEVELOPING   Add more details on three or four specific, focused topics that you have chosen from your list of general points.

ORGANIZING   Organize your material in a way that will be most interesting to your audience.

DRAFTING   Write a working draft of your essay in complete sentences.

REVISING   Consulting the Tips for Revising, revise your first draft for meaning, development, and organization.

EDITING   Consulting the Tips for Editing, edit your draft for grammar and correctness.

Recalling

Reading and Writing for a Reason

**One writes out of one thing only—one's own experience.
Everything depends on how relentlessly one forces from this
experience the last drop, sweet or bitter, it can possibly give.**
                                                    JAMES BALDWIN

Recalling is the act of writing about something we remember: something we did, something that happened to us, a person or object that is important to us, or an exciting period in our lives. People who write their autobiographies reminisce about their entire lives. Recalling a shorter period or just one incident, however, is usually a far more manageable and satisfying task. In *The Art and Craft of Memoir* William Zinsser explains that writing about a particular time or incident enables the writer to achieve "a focus that isn't possible in autobiography." Recalling is a "window into a life."

Recalling, however, is not simply writing down exactly what happened during a given time period; that would be a boring exercise both for the writer and the reader. Recalling means first determining why the event, person, or incident that you choose to write about has **significance** for you: Did it teach you a lesson about life? Did it make you realize the value of someone in your life? Did it make you think that you should change something about yourself or your lifestyle? An event can also be significant if it can help your readers recognize or remember something similar that happened to them. Recalling helps writers and readers alike discover that, despite the fact that people differ in many ways, as human beings we share many common experiences.

The following paragraph (from a book called *Deaf in America*) was written by a deaf woman recalling what it was like to be left alone at a residential school for deaf students when she was very young. The story is significant because, although most of us are not deaf, we can still identify with the fear all children have of being separated from their parents as well as the pain all parents endure when they must leave their children.

I asked again where we were going but she [my mother] gave no reply. For the first time I began to feel a sense of fear and foreboding. I stole glances at her face, but it was immobile and her eyes were fixed on an un-seen place somewhere ahead. We rode for a long time, and then we stopped and found ourselves in front of an enormous building. We walked into the building, and once inside I was immediately struck by a medicinal, institutional smell.

   This did not look like a hospital or like any other building I had seen before. My mother bent down, turned me toward her, and said: "This is where you will get your education. You will live here for a while. Don't worry, I will see you again later." Then she couldn't seem to say any more. She hugged me quickly, gave me a kiss, and then, in-explicably, left.

By recalling this painful incident, the writer shares with her readers a significant in-cident in her life, one that she will never forget. Because of its power and signifi-cance, her readers will probably remember it for a very long time as well.

LEARNING FROM PUBLISHED WRITERS

So that you can better understand how to write about something that occurred in your own life, you may find it helpful to read the following recollection by a pub-lished writer. Written by Lynda Barry, it describes an event that occurred during a particularly painful period of her life. It is significant that Barry tells us about the importance of drawing in her childhood because today she is a famous and suc-cessful cartoonist; many of her cartoons have appeared in *The New Yorker,* one of the most prestigious magazines in the United States. This recollection, titled "The Sanctuary of School," was originally published in *The New York Times* in January 1992.

Before You Read

Focusing Your Attention

Before you read this recollection, take a few moments to respond to the following questions in your journal:

   1.   In the essay you are about to read, the writer describes a person who had a lasting impact on her. Do you think you have ever had such an important impact on someone that he or she would write an essay about you? Have you had such an im-pact on more than one person? Who are these people? What would they say about you in their recollections?

   2.   Can you recall a time in your life when you felt particularly lonely or afraid? Write down as many facts, impressions, and memories as you can remember about that period of your life.

Expanding Your Vocabulary

Here are some words and their meanings that are important to your understanding of the essay. You might want to review them before you begin to read.

"**nondescript** [not distinctive or interesting] portable classrooms" (paragraph 7)

"looking across **Rainier Valley** [a beautiful mountain range located in the state of Washington]" (paragraph 8)

Lynda Barry

The Sanctuary of School*

I was 7 years old the first time I snuck out of the house in the dark. It was winter, and my parents had been fighting all night. They were short on money and long on relatives who kept "temporarily" moving into our house because they had nowhere else to go.

My brother and I were used to giving up our bedroom. We slept on the couch, something we actually liked because it put us that much closer to the light of our lives, our television.

At night when everyone was asleep, we lay on our pillows watching it with the sound off. We watched Steve Allen's mouth moving. We watched Johnny Carson's mouth moving. We watched movies filled with gangsters shooting machine guns into packed rooms, dying soldiers hurling a last grenade, and beautiful women crying at windows. Then the sign-off finally came, and we tried to sleep.

The morning I snuck out, I woke up filled with a panic about needing to get to school. The sun wasn't quite up yet, but my anxiety was so fierce that I just got dressed, walked quietly across the kitchen, and let myself out the back door.

It was quiet outside. Stars were still out. Nothing moved, and no one was in the street. It was as if someone had turned the sound off on the world.

I walked the alley, breaking thin ice over the puddles with my shoes. I didn't know why I was walking to school in the dark. I didn't think about it. All I knew was the feeling of panic, like the panic that strikes kids when they realize they are lost.

1

2

3

4

5

6

*Lynda Barry, "The Sanctuary of School" from the *New York Times* (January 5, 1992), "Educational Life" section.

That feeling eased the moment I turned the corner and saw the **7** dark outline of my school at the top of the hill. My school was made up of about 15 nondescript portable classrooms set down on a fenced concrete lot in a rundown Seattle neighborhood, but it had the most beautiful view of the Cascade Mountains. You could see them from anywhere on the playfield, and you could see them from the windows of my classroom—Room 2.

I walked over to the monkey bars and hooked my arms around the **8** cold metal. I stood for a long time just looking across Rainier Valley. The sky was beginning to whiten, and I could hear a few birds.

In a perfect world, my absence at home would not have gone un- **9** noticed. I would have had two parents in a panic to locate me, instead of two parents in a panic to locate an answer to the hard question of survival during a deep financial and emotional crisis.

But in an overcrowded and unhappy home, it's incredibly easy for **10** any child to slip away. The high levels of frustration, depression, and anger in my house made my brother and me invisible. We were children with the sound turned off. And for us, as for the steadily increasing number of neglected children in this country, the only place where we could count on being noticed was at school.

"Hey there, young lady. Did you forget to go home last night?" It **11** was Mr. Gunderson, our janitor, whom we all loved. He was nice and he was funny and he was old with white hair, thick glasses, and an unbelievable number of keys. I could hear them jingling as he walked across the playfield. I felt incredibly happy to see him.

He let me push his wheeled garbage can between the different **12** portables as he unlocked each room. He let me turn on the lights and raise the window shades, and I saw my school slowly come to life. I saw Mrs. Holman, our school secretary, walk into the office without her orange lipstick on yet. She waved.

I saw the fifth-grade teacher, Mr. Cunningham, walking under the **13** breezeway eating a hard roll. He waved.

And I saw my teacher, Mrs. Claire LeSane, walking toward us in a **14** red coat and calling my name in a very happy and surprised way, and suddenly my throat got tight and my eyes stung and I ran toward her crying. It was something that surprised both of us.

It's only thinking about it now, 28 years later, that I realize I was **15** crying from relief. I was with my teacher, and in a while I was going to sit at my desk, with my crayons and pencils and books and classmates all around me, and for the next six hours I was going to enjoy a thoroughly secure, warm, and stable world. It was a world I absolutely relied on. Without it, I don't know where I would have gone that morning.

Mrs. LeSane asked me what was wrong, and when I said "Nothing," she seemingly left it at that. But she asked me if I would carry her purse for her, an honor above all honors, and she asked if I wanted to come into Room 2 early and paint.   **16**

She believed in the natural healing power of painting and drawing for troubled children. In the back of her room there was always a drawing table and an easel with plenty of supplies, and sometimes during the day she would come up to you for what seemed like no good reason and quietly ask if you wanted to go to the back table and "make some pictures for Mrs. LeSane." We all had a chance at it—to sit apart from the class for a while to paint, draw, and silently work out impossible problems on 11 × 17 sheets of newsprint.   **17**

Drawing came to mean everything to me. At the back table in Room 2, I learned to build myself a life preserver that I could carry into my home. . . .   **18**

By the time the bell rang that morning, I had finished my drawing, and Mrs. LeSane pinned it up on the special bulletin board she reserved for drawings from the back table. It was the same picture I always drew—a sun in the corner of a blue sky over a nice house with flowers all around it. . . .   **19**

 ## Questions for Critical Thinking

Thinking Critically About Content

1. Notice the way in which the writer describes herself and her brother as "children with the sound turned off" and their environment "as if someone had turned the sound off on the world." Is this an effective image? Why? What effect does it have on you? What does it tell you about Lynda Barry's childhood?

2. Why do you think the writer used warm and vivid details to describe the arrival of school employees (paragraphs 11 through 16)? What effect does this description have on you, compared with the description she gave of her home life?

Thinking Critically About Purpose

3. What do you think Barry's purpose is in writing this recalling essay? Explain your answer.

4. In your opinion, why doesn't the writer tell us more about her parents' problems?

THINKING CRITICALLY ABOUT AUDIENCE

5. What readers do you think would most understand and appreciate this recollection?

6. Did this essay make you compare your own childhood to Lynda Barry's?

THINKING CRITICALLY ABOUT POINT OF VIEW

7. Describe in a complete sentence the writer's point of view in this essay.

8. Write a paragraph explaining the ways in which this essay would be different if it were written by Lynda Barry's parents.

LEARNING FROM YOUR PEERS

Recalling is an activity we all do naturally every day in both speaking and writing. We learn from recalling, especially when we write, because it helps us understand our past and make better decisions in the future. It helps us understand ourselves and learn from our own experiences. Although recalling comes to all of us naturally, writing about our memories follows a specific process that can help you in all of your writing assignments. To master this process, we are going to follow the writing process of a student named Tommy Poulos in response to the following writing assignment.

Tommy's Writing Assignment: Recalling

This is the topic Tommy's instructor assigned:

You have probably had many experiences that had predictable outcomes: getting a driver's license, graduating from high school, landing a first job. Most of us, though, have had events in our lives that were not so predictable: the car broke down on the way to a job interview; our date for the prom got sick at the last minute; our family needed financial help and we had to delay our schooling. Write a recalling essay about an experience that did not turn out the way you thought it would.

Tommy goes through the process as outlined in Chapter 1: *thinking, planning, developing, organizing, drafting, revising,* and *editing.*

Thinking

After thinking about his assignment, Tommy starts listing all the places that were important in his childhood: his school, his church, the neighborhood stores, the family restaurant, the playground, his favorite shortcuts through the neighbors' yards, and the treehouse his brothers built in the backyard. In his mind's eye, he recreates all the places he was most familiar with.

Then Tommy lists some events that happened at those places. He tries to list all the "firsts" in his life. He thinks of his first day of school, but he cannot remember any details. He remembers his first communion, but he cannot think of anything unusual about it. He recalls going to the shops in his neighborhood to buy new clothes for school. He remembers his first haircut at George's Barber Shop, which was right down the street from his family's restaurant. He realizes that many hours of his childhood were spent in the restaurant because his parents, grandparents, aunts, uncles, and cousins were all connected with it in some way.

Next Tommy lists the events he associates with the restaurant. All the adults spent every day cooking, cleaning, and setting up the booths for business. When he was old enough, he learned to fold napkins and sort silverware. Tommy realizes that his happiest memories were from his preschool days when he had no responsibilities. As long as he did not get into trouble, he was free to explore anything and everything in the restaurant. Suddenly, Tommy remembers the time he was accidentally locked in the restaurant's walk-in freezer. He smiles to himself as he thinks about how funny that incident was and still is. It has become a story that is repeatedly told at family gatherings and has been embellished over the years.

Planning

Tommy begins to jot down the main points of the story:

> I thought I was a world-class explorer. There was no place I could not go--upstairs, downstairs, inside, outside. That made me feel I could climb mountains and walk on the moon. But I had done it all, and I was getting bored. So one day I looked for a new challenge. There it was--the walk-in freezer. The rest of the story was inevitable.
>
> I got stuck inside. Everything got stuck. My feet got stuck--they were bare. I thought I was going to freeze to death. No one could hear me because the doors were too thick. I thought I would never get out.

Tommy takes his short summary to class the next day, and his peer response group tells him that it sounds like it can be developed into a good essay. They ask him the following questions:

How old were you?

How long were you trapped in the freezer?

How did you get out?

Were you punished?

Did you get frostbite?

Did you ever go into the freezer again?

Developing

The next day, Tommy gets out his journal and looks at the questions from his group. He starts writing about his experience again, this time adding answers to the group's questions as he goes:

How old were you? I was five years old, and I thought I was a real adventurer, on a par with astronauts and mountain climbers.

How long were you trapped in the freezer? I was in the freezer long enough to get very scared and very cold. I definitely thought I was going to die. I was very tired because I had worked my little body so hard trying to get the door open. And for what? Vegetables. That was the worst part. All that effort to get in, and only frozen vegetables as a reward. I had flopped my body in every direction, trying to get that door open.

How did you get out? I got out when my grandfather came to the rescue. Everyone had been looking for me, but he found me and gave me some ouzo and wrapped me in a blanket.

Were you punished? I didn't get punished because everyone was so happy to find me alive. Just before they found me, they were about to call the police.

Did you get frostbite? I did practically get frostbite on my feet because I went in there with bare feet.

Did you ever go into the freezer again? It took me a long time to even think of going in the freezer again. I must have been at least 12 before I would go in alone.

Organizing

During the next class, Tommy's peer response group tells him that he is ready to start organizing his essay. Tommy goes to the library with his journal and looks over his notes. He starts a rough outline of the points he wants to include in his essay:

1. I was no ordinary kid--I was a true adventurer.

2. The restaurant was my private domain. I could go anywhere and be anything. My only limit was my imagination.

3. One morning, the walk-in freezer's unexplored mysteries compelled me to enter this forbidden territory.

4. I forced my way into the freezer with all my might, swinging my body from the enormous handle.

5. Once I was inside, there were only vegetables.

6. Worse, my feet stuck to the floor. (The restaurant floors had just been mopped and my bare feet were wet when I went into the freezer.)

7. I started to feel frozen--my eyes, my lungs, my nose, my feet. It felt like needles were poking into my body from all directions.

8. Suddenly praying became more important than exploring.

9. Finally, grandfather came to the rescue.

These points help Tommy decide how to organize his essay. He thinks that readers need to know something about his personality to make his story understandable. He decides to emphasize his adventurous spirit at the beginning of the essay. Then he will develop the essay in chronological order, ending with his rescue.

As he writes, he continues to add details and comparisons that emphasize the dramatic nature of the event.

Drafting

Here is the draft that Tommy wrote.

Tommy's Essay: First Draft

Main Idea: Once my desire for adventure as a child got me into a little more trouble than I was prepared for.

Tentative Title: "The Ice Box"

One day, I was at my family's restaurant. I considered myself to be a world-class adventurer and was always searching for undiscovered and uncharted territory. This morning, I was in a mood to find even larger booty. My adventurous soul was burning with curiosity. I had an urgent need to go "where no man had gone before."

I made a quick tour of the restaurant. Streaking through the kitchen in my bare feet, I tried to keep from slipping on the newly mopped tile floor. Suddenly, my destination loomed in front of me: the huge silver walk-in freezer, the only spot in the restaurant my father had strictly forbidden me to enter. I wondered what lay beyond that heavy door. I was determined to conquer the freezer's unexplored mysteries. Gathering all of my courage, I stretched to reach the huge latch that separated me from the hidden treasures within. Whatever stood in my way would be conquered. I climbed up on some boxes stacked nearby and leaped onto the handle like a frog attacking some forlorn fly. Nothing happened. But I was not going to be defeated. I changed strategies and started flapping my body back and forth like a trout on a line. My pride would not let me give up. Suddenly I felt a cool breeze, and the massive door creaked and opened just wide enough for my scrawny body to slip through the crack. Success! Tommy the Conqueror had landed! If I'd had a flag, I would have planted it on that hard, cold, metallic floor.

I looked around me, searching for the promised bounty within this forbidden metal chamber. Hurriedly trying to absorb all that was around me was tough. I scanned the boxes and bags stacked around the walls, looking for my private gold mine, but all I could see were vegetables. Drat! I hated vegetables. All that work, and what was my reward? Broccoli, cauliflower, and spinach. I didn't even like Popeye. Now what was I going to do? My big adventure had been ruined, so I turned toward the door just as it slammed shut. I tried to pick up my feet and run toward the door, but I could not move. My bare feet had frozen to the floor. I forced them up, only to see chunks of my skin permanently attached to the freezer floor. Letting out a helpless whimper, I unashamedly called for my mommy. I felt helpless. But crying for my mom wasn't the answer. I made my way to the door and pushed with all my might. I threw myself against the door latch, but it didn't budge. I started kicking and screaming, but still nothing happened. There was only silence and the surrounding cold. I decided to sit down on a box of frozen spinach to await my doom. I started to realize that I would soon become as cold and stiff as the multitude of vegetables that stared back at me. I realized there was nothing I could do except wait.

Suddenly, the cooling unit for the freezer kicked on. The air became even colder and drier. I felt pain everywhere. My stupid curiosity had done me in.

I started to pray. Surely I was too young to die. I was too innocent to have been given so harsh a punishment by God. I questioned how God could kill such a young, well-meaning child. While my mind was becoming unfocused, my body was starting to seem like a distant memory. I tried to cuddle my numb legs with my stiff arms. I hoped for the best, but expected the worst. Once I shut my eyes, I awaited my untimely death.

Suddenly, there was a *swoosh* as the gigantic door swung open. My grandfather's eyes met mine. His stern look vanished as he swept me into his arms and rescued me from the frozen tomb. He wrapped me in towels from the kitchen and took me to his office where he quickly poured a shot of ouzo, a Greek liqueur. After he touched it to my frozen lips, I swallowed it reflexively, feeling the warmth of its vapors spreading through my mouth and down to my stomach. The air in the heated office burned the frozen skin on my arms and legs and face. I didn't care because I was so relieved that the numbness was starting to leave my body and I had been brought back to life. My grandfather held me on his lap and kissed my forehead. Then he carried me around and let everyone know that the adventurer had returned. My whole family had a good laugh at my expense, and I had new respect for my father's warnings. I won't say that this adventure was my last, but it certainly was my most memorable.

Revising

Tommy has finally finished the first draft of his essay, but he knows that the work of revising lies ahead. At this point, his instructor wants the class to focus on the various aspects of an essay. The instructor explains that studying the separate parts of an essay will make the whole essay stronger and more effective.

Tommy reviews the Checklist for Recognizing an Essay at the beginning of the Tips for Revising section of this chapter. His instructor explains to the class that revising means focusing on content, not grammar—concentrating on making the components of the essay work well together. Tommy reads the Tips for Revising and completes the assigned exercises. The revising tasks in this chapter involve identifying the basic parts of an essay, analyzing the structure of certain paragraphs, and then sometimes writing alternative paragraphs for specific essays. Tommy learns that he can change the emphasis in a paragraph and even in an essay by including different information and organizing it in different ways.

Returning to his draft, Tommy makes sure that each paragraph is fully developed and correctly placed in his essay. He finds that his meaning is hindered in some cases by paragraphs with missing parts and in other cases by paragraphs that are out of place. He tries to remedy both problems in his revision.

 ## COLLABORATIVE WORK

PEER GROUP ACTIVITY

After you read the portions of the Tips for Revising your instructor assigns, turn to Tommy's first draft (pp. 18–20), and complete the following tasks in small groups:

A.   Put brackets around the introduction (for a definition, see pp. 31–32) and conclusion (for a definition, see pp. 35–36). Then underline the thesis statement.

B.   Underline the topic sentences in Tommy's body paragraphs.

Compare the brackets and underlining your group recorded with the marks your instructor will show you. Where do your marks differ from your instructor's? What do you need to review before writing your own essay?

CLASS ACTIVITY

As an entire class, look at the underlined portions of Tommy's revised draft (pp. 23–26) to see how he changed each sentence.

A.   Did you identify the **revision** problems that Tommy corrected?

B.   Do you think his changes are good ones? Discuss his changes.

Editing

Now that Tommy has made sure that his essay has all the parts it needs, he knows he must do some final editing and proofreading before handing in his essay. His instructor tells the students that this section of the chapter gives them a working knowledge of basic grammar terms to use for the rest of the course. So Tommy shifts his focus from the content of his essay to specific points of grammar. He reads the Tips for Editing section in this chapter to learn about verbs, nouns, pronouns, adjectives, adverbs, prepositions, conjunctions, interjections, phrases, and clauses. After he finishes the assigned exercises, he takes the questions in the Checklist for Editing Words, Phrases, and Clauses one by one and revises his draft according to these guidelines.

COLLABORATIVE WORK

PEER GROUP ACTIVITY

After you read the portions of the Tips for Editing your instructor assigns, turn to Tommy's first draft (pp. 18–20), and complete the following tasks in small groups:

A.   Label as many of these parts of speech as your instructor assigns:

1.   Five nouns (N) (for a definition, see p. 41)

2.   Five pronouns (pro) (for a definition, see pp. 42–44)

3.   Five action verbs (V) (for a definition, see p. 39)

4.   Five adjectives (adj) (for a definition, see pp. 145–46)

5.   Five adverbs (adv) (for a definition, see p. 47)

6.   Five prepositions (prep) (for a definition, see pp. 48–49)

7.   Five conjunctions (conj) (for a definition, see pp. 50–51)

8.   Five interjections (interj) (for a definition, see p. 52)

B.   Put five phrases (for a definition, see pp. 53–54) in parentheses.

C.   Label the subjects (S) and verbs (V) of five clauses (for definitions, see pp. 57–59); then mark these clauses as independent (ind) or dependent (dep).

Compare the marks your group recorded with those your instructor will show you. Where do your marks differ from your instructor's? What do you need to review before writing your own essay?

CLASS ACTIVITY

As an entire class, look at the underlined portions of Tommy's revised draft (pp. 23–26) to see how he changed each sentence.

A.   Did you identify the **editing** problems that Tommy corrected?

B.   Do you think his changes are good ones? Discuss his changes.

Tommy's Revised Essay

/"The Ice ~~Box~~/" Chamber

~~One day, I was at~~ It was an early Saturday morning at my home away from home, my family's restaurant. I was five years old, and I had been to every nook and cranny of our house and restaurant. I considered myself to be a world-class adventurer and was always searching for undiscovered and uncharted territory. I felt it was my mission to search attics, closets, basements, and dark hallways that held abandoned treasures. It was not unusual to find pennies, nickles, dimes, and even quarters under the restaurant booths. To adults, this was spare change. To me, it was comic book money, and I searched for it every morning without fail. This particular morning, though, I was in a mood to find even larger booty. My adventurous soul was burning with curiosity. I had an urgent need to go "where no man had gone before." Before my adventure was over, I would discover more than stray coins; I would learn the meaning of caution.

I made a quick tour of the restaurant. Streaking through the kitchen in my bare feet, I tried to keep from slipping on the newly mopped tile floor. I scampered through the storerooms like a running back through the defense. I whizzed past the silvery blur of kitchen equipment as fast as my short, stocky legs would carry me. Suddenly, my destination loomed in front of me: the huge silver walk-in freezer, the only spot in the restaurant my father had strictly forbidden me to enter. I wondered what lay beyond that heavy door. I was determined to conquer the freezer's unexplored mysteries. Gathering all of my courage, I stretched to reach the huge latch that separated me from the hidden treasures within. I grasped that latch as if it were my

lifeline. I jumped and swayed feverishly, willing that door to open and
let me in. I twisted and jerked, I leaped and turned, all to no avail.
Since I was ready to give up, I sat down on the moist floor, panting
and feeling my sore muscles. After a short rest, I steeled myself for
another try. I was not going to fail. Whatever stood in my way would
be conquered. I climbed up on some boxes stacked nearby and leaped
onto the handle like a frog attacking some forlorn fly. Nothing
happened. But I was not going to be defeated. I changed strategies and
started flapping my body back and forth like a trout on a line. My
pride would not let me give up. Suddenly I felt a cool breeze, and the
massive door creaked and opened just wide enough for my scrawny
body to slip through the crack. Success! Tommy the Conqueror had
landed! If I'd had a flag, I would have planted it on that hard, cold,
metallic floor.

I looked around me, searching for the promised bounty within
this forbidden metal chamber. Hurriedly trying to absorb all that was
around me was tough. I scanned the boxes and bags stacked around
the walls, looking for my private gold mine, but all I could see were
vegetables. Drat! I hated vegetables. All that work, and what was my
reward? Broccoli, cauliflower, and spinach. I didn't even like Popeye.
Now what was I going to do? My big adventure had been ruined, so I
turned toward the door just as it slammed shut. I tried to pick up my
feet and run toward the door, but I could not move. My bare feet had
frozen to the floor. I forced them up, only to see chunks of my skin
permanently attached to the freezer floor. Letting out a helpless
whimper, I unashamedly called for my mommy. I felt helpless. But
crying for my mom wasn't the answer. I made my way to the door
and pushed with all my might. I threw myself against the door latch,
but it didn't budge. I started kicking and screaming, but still nothing
happened. There was only silence and the surrounding cold. I decided
to sit down on a box of frozen spinach to await my doom. I started to

realize that I would soon become as cold and stiff as the multitude of vegetables that stared back at me. I realized there was nothing I could do except wait.

Suddenly, the cooling unit for the freezer kicked on with a loud roar. The air became even colder and drier. I felt pain everywhere. My lungs felt like there were hundreds of needles poking at them in all directions. I could feel my nostrils sticking together. My eyes hurt. I moved to the other corner of the freezer, hoping it would be slightly warmer than the corner near the cooling unit, but there was no improvement. My stupid curiosity had done me in.

I started to pray. Surely I was too young to die. I was too innocent to have been given so harsh a punishment by God. I questioned how God could kill such a young, well-meaning child. While my mind was becoming unfocused, my body was starting to seem like a distant memory. I tried to cuddle my numb legs with my stiff arms. I hoped for the best, but expected the worst. Once I shut my eyes, I awaited my untimely death.

Suddenly, there was a *swoosh* as the gigantic door swung open. My grandfather's eyes met mine. His stern look vanished as he swept me into his arms and rescued me from the frozen tomb. He wrapped me in towels from the kitchen and took me to his office where he quickly poured a shot of ouzo, a Greek liqueur. After he touched it to my frozen lips, I swallowed it reflexively, feeling the warmth of its vapors spreading through my mouth and down to my stomach. The air in the heated office burned the frozen skin on my arms and legs and face. I didn't care because I was so relieved that the numbness was starting to leave my body and I had been brought back to life. My grandfather held me on his lap and kissed my forehead. Then he carried me around and let everyone know that the adventurer had returned.

My whole family had a good laugh at my expense, and I had learned a valuable lesson. The minutes that had seemed like hours in the freezer taught me a new respect for my father's warnings. I won't say that this adventure was my last, but it certainly was my most memorable.

WRITING YOUR OWN RECALLING ESSAY

So far, you have observed a professional writer and a fellow student at work trying to express an idea, impression, or experience from the past that was significant to them. As you read the published essay and followed the writing process of another student from first to final draft, you absorbed ideas and ways of giving those ideas a form of their own. These reading and writing activities have prepared you to write your own essay focusing on a recollection that is meaningful to you.

What Have You Discovered?

Before you begin your own writing task, let's review what you have learned in this chapter so far:

- Recalling is the act of writing about something you remember.
- The event, person, or incident in a recollection should have significance for you.
- Recalling helps writers and readers alike discover that they share many common traits and experiences.
- To present your recollection effectively, you need to organize your ideas.
- To help you shape your essay, you should learn as much as possible about your readers.
- Before you write a draft, you need to decide on a point of view toward your subject.
- After you write a draft, you should revise your essay for meaning and organization.
- After you revise your essay, you should edit its grammar, usage, and sentence structure.

Your Writing Topic

Choose one of the following topics for your recalling essay:

1.   In "The Sanctuary of School," Lynda Barry recalls the way her school and her teachers provided a sanctuary, a place where she could escape from the problems of home. Write an essay in which you recall a place, a person, or an event that made you feel safe, secure, valued, and welcome.

2.   Your old high school has asked you, as a graduate, to submit an essay to the newsletter, recalling a job or volunteer experience that you enjoyed. The editors want to inform current high school students about options for volunteer and paid work. Your purpose is to try to convince the current high school students that the job you had is worth looking into.

3.   Your college class is putting together a collection of essays paying tribute to people who encouraged them to go to college. You decide to submit an essay. Who actually gave you the courage and determination to pursue your education—a teacher, a relative, a supervisor at work? Was there a memorable event or conversation that helped you decide to continue your schooling? Your essay should focus on that person's influence on your life.

4.   Create your own recalling topic (with the assistance of your instructor), and write an essay about it.

When you have selected one of these topics, you should begin to work through the writing process in the same way Tommy did. (You may find his experience helpful in giving you ideas.) This time your purpose is to write your own recalling essay. If some steps occur out of order, that adjustment is probably part of your personal writing ritual. Follow your instincts, and let them mold your own writing process. But make sure you've worked through all the stages to your final draft.

 YOUR WRITING PROCESS

THINKING   Generate as many ideas on your subject as you can in as many different ways as possible: rereading, listing, freewriting, brainstorming, clustering, discussing, and questioning.

PLANNING   Begin to give your ideas shape by deciding on your approach to your topic (your content, your purpose, your audience, and your point of view). Make a list of points you want to include in your essay.

DEVELOPING   Add more details on three or four specific, focused topics that you have chosen from your list of general points.

ORGANIZING   Organize your material in a way that will be most interesting to your audience.

DRAFTING   Write a working draft of your essay in complete sentences.

YOUR WRITING PROCESS (CONTINUED)

REVISING Consulting the Tips for Revising in this chapter (pp. 29–37), revise your first draft for meaning, development, and organization—paying special attention to recognizing and developing specific components in your essay.

EDITING Consulting the Tips for Editing in this chapter (pp. 38–60), edit your draft for grammar and correctness—paying special attention to your use of words, phrases, and clauses.

Turn in your revised draft to your instructor.

Some Final Thoughts

When you have completed your own essay, answer these four questions in your journal:

1. What was most difficult about this assignment?
2. What was easiest?
3. What did I learn about recalling by completing this assignment?
4. What did I learn about my own writing process from this assignment—how I prepared to write, how I wrote the first draft, how I revised, and how I edited?

Recognizing an Essay

Checklist for Recognizing an Essay

✓ Does the essay have a catchy **title?**
✓ Does the essay have an interesting **introduction** that contains a clear **thesis statement?**
✓ Does each **body paragraph** contain a **topic sentence** and enough **supporting details?**
✓ Does the **conclusion** wrap up the essay?

From Jay Leno, with his passion for classic automobiles, to your neighbor, with her collection of matchbook covers, many people share the hobby of collecting things. Collectors, especially those who specialize in antiques, learn to identify objects by their distinctive features. For example, a person who collects coins looks for a date and a mint mark. These two items give the collector information about the age and place of origin of the coin, both of which are important in establishing its value.

Basic Features

Recognizing an essay over other types of writing is a bit like becoming a collector. Although essays may differ a great deal in design, organization, and content, they share certain identifying features that distinguish them from other types of writing. At the simplest level, how an essay looks on the page tells its audience "Here's an essay!" An essay usually has a title that names its broad subject. Many longer, more complex essays also have subtitles. When essayists move from one topic to another, they indicate this shift by indenting a new paragraph. Most essays have a *thesis* that is either stated or implied in the *introduction*, several *body paragraphs* explaining or supporting that thesis, and a *conclusion*.

In content, essays are *nonfiction* as opposed to short stories, poetry, or drama; that is, they deal with real-life subjects rather than made-up ones. Most essays concentrate on one specific subject and focus on a single purpose. For an essay to be successful, most writers choose methods of development that both suit their purpose and appeal to the audience they hope to persuade or inform. The most common purposes for essays are represented in the titles of the chapters for this book: recalling, observing, explaining, investigating, restating, analyzing, persuading, and problem solving. A successful essay gets the reaction from the readers that its author hopes for—whether this response is to appreciate a special scene, identify with someone's grief, or leap to action over a controversial issue.

Title

Like the date and mint mark on a coin or the picture on a baseball card, your title is the first feature of your essay an audience looks for. A **title** is a phrase, usually no more than a few words, that you place at the beginning of your essay. Usually a title gives a hint about the subject, the purpose, or the focus of your essay. For example, the main title we chose for this book, *Mosaics*, reflects the way we view the writing process—many bright pieces logically connected to complete a picture. In other words, that title expresses in capsule form this textbook's purpose, which is to guide writers in fitting the separate pieces of their ideas into a single meaningful whole for their audiences. The title of this chapter, however, is a straightforward naming of its contents: "Recalling." In this chapter, Lynda Barry's title, "The Sanctuary of School," tells readers that her essay's broad subject will be schools but also hints through the word *sanctuary* that the writer has a positive attitude toward her school experiences.

Besides suggesting an essay's purpose, a good title catches an audience's attention or "hooks" the readers so they want to read more. For instance, the essay title "A Nation at Risk" in Chapter 5 catches readers' attention so that they want to find out exactly *how* our nation is at risk.

When Tommy Poulos was composing his recalling essay about his terror at getting locked in a walk-in freezer, he titled his essay "The ice Box." Later, a classmate he was working with asked Tommy, "Wasn't it more like a room than a box?" After thinking it over, Tommy revised his working title so that it was specific and catchy. Then he revised its punctuation and capitalization:

First Draft: "The ice Box"

Revision: The Ice Chamber

Note that essay titles should not be in quotation marks unless they are actually quoted words. Only when you refer to a title do you use quotation marks. All words in titles (except articles and prepositions) should begin with capital letters, and titles need no closing punctuation mark.

Exercise R2-1

List three other titles Lynda Barry might have given "The Sanctuary of School."

Exercise R2-2

List three other titles for Tommy's recalling essay, "The Ice Chamber."

Exercise R2-3

Read the following titles and decide whether they will catch readers' attention or provide hints about the essay's subject and the author's position on the subject. Some may contain errors in capitalization or punctuation.

1. "Legalize Drugs? Not on Your Life."
2. "The Story of an Hour"

3. "What I did on my summer vacation"
4. "Nixon."
5. "Why I came to College"

Exercise R2-4

Write three titles for your recalling essay: (1) one that gives a hint of your subject, (2) one that gives a hint of your purpose, and (3) one that gives a hint of your focus. Make each title as catchy as you can.

Introduction and Thesis

Your first or **introductory paragraph** should both explain your topic and stimulate your audience's interest. The introduction of an essay captures the reader's interest, gives necessary background information, and contains a thesis statement. This paragraph essentially tells the reader what the essay is going to cover without going into detail or discussing any specific items.

The thesis statement is the sentence (or sentences) in your introduction that focuses your readers' attention on the main idea you will develop in the body of your essay. It provides a contract of sorts for what will follow. Usually the final sentence in the introduction, it outlines the writer's purpose and position on the essay's subject. Just as a topic sentence is the controlling idea of a body paragraph, the thesis statement provides the controlling idea for an entire essay.

To lead up to the thesis statement, the sentences at the beginning of the introductory paragraph first need to stimulate your readers' interest. Some effective ways of catching your audience's attention and giving necessary background information are (1) to furnish a description; (2) to tell a story that relates to your topic; (3) to give a revealing fact, statistic, or definition; or (4) to offer an interesting comparison. Always make sure your introduction gives your readers any information they may need to follow your train of thought.

The following paragraph introduces Lynda Barry's essay "The Sanctuary of School." In this introduction, she sets the scene at home and places herself in the midst of her parents' problems. The first sentence, about sneaking out of the house, serves as the thesis statement of the essay. Though the thesis statement is usually the last sentence in an introductory paragraph, this thesis is effective because of its simplicity, its mysteriousness (it doesn't tell us very much), and its unexpected placement at the beginning of the paragraph:

> **I was 7 years old the first time I snuck out of the house in the dark.**
> It was winter, and my parents had been fighting all night. They were short on money and long on relatives who kept "temporarily" moving into our house because they had nowhere else to go.

Barry has set the scene to help her audience focus on her life as a child and has given us the basic information we need to move ahead in her essay.

As Tommy looked over his first draft, he decided that his introduction left too many questions in his readers' minds:

First Draft: One day, I was at my family's restaurant. I considered myself to be a world-class adventurer and was always searching for undiscovered and uncharted territory. This morning, I was in a mood to find even larger booty. My adventurous soul was burning with curiosity. I had an urgent need to go "where no man had gone before."

Tommy has given no information about what day it was, how old he was, why he searched for adventure at the restaurant, and what he learned. Tommy's revised introduction, however, answers most of the questions in his reader's mind. He also adds a thesis statement at the end of the paragraph.

Revision: ~~One day, I was at~~ **It was an early Saturday morning at my home away from home,** my family's restaurant. **I was five years old, and I had been to every nook and cranny of our house and restaurant.** I considered myself to be a world-class adventurer and was always searching for undiscovered and uncharted territory. **I felt it was my mission to search attics, closets, basements, and dark hallways that held abandoned treasures. It was not unusual to find pennies, nickles, dimes, and even quarters under the restaurant booths. To adults, this was spare change. To me, it was comic book money, and I searched for it every morning without fail.** This **particular** morning, **though,** I was in a mood to find even larger booty. My adventurous soul was burning with curiosity. I had an

Thesis Statement: urgent need to go "where no man had gone before." **<u>Before my adventure was over, I would discover more than stray coins; I would learn the meaning of caution.</u>**

Tommy's audience now has more information about his subject and a framework for the remainder of his essay.

Exercise R2-5

Write an alternate introduction for "The Sanctuary of School." Then underline your thesis statement.

Exercise R2-6

Suggest two alternative thesis statements for Tommy Poulos's essay.

Exercise R2-7

Write a title, an introductory paragraph, and a thesis statement for the following topics.

1. My favorite chore
2. My favorite room
3. What I like best about college
4. What I like least about college
5. The best thing about being a kid

Exercise R2-8

Read the following paragraph and prepare a list of questions and suggestions for revision that you would offer the writer.

I have a strenuous but rewarding job. Sometimes, I wonder why I do it. I work long hours and I am often tired. But some things make up for these problems.

Body Paragraphs

Following the introductory paragraph, an essay includes several **body paragraphs** that support and explain the essay's thesis. Indenting and starting a new paragraph gives your readers important information. They know you are moving from your introduction and thesis to a topic that explains your thesis or from one topic that supports your thesis to another.

A body paragraph usually begins with a topic sentence, and the remainder of the sentences in the paragraph support or explain that topic sentence. For example, paragraph 3 of Lynda Barry's essay "The Sanctuary of School" begins with a topic sentence followed by sentences that fill in the details for her audience:

> **At night when everyone was asleep, we lay on our pillows watching it [TV] with the sound off.** We watched Steve Allen's mouth moving. We watched Johnny Carson's mouth moving. We watched movies filled with gangsters shooting machine guns into packed rooms, dying soldiers hurling a last grenade, and beautiful women crying at windows. Then the sign-off finally came, and we tried to sleep.

Barry's topic sentence states the controlling idea of this paragraph—watching late-night TV with her brother. The sentences that follow support her topic sentence with details about the shows and images they saw.

As Tommy looked back over his first draft, he decided that paragraph 4 could be improved if he added more details:

First Draft: Suddenly, the cooling unit for the freezer kicked on. The air became even colder and drier. I felt pain everywhere. My stupid curiosity had done me in.

Revision: Suddenly, the cooling unit for the freezer kicked on **with a loud roar**. The air became even colder and drier. ~~I felt pain everywhere.~~ **My lungs felt like there were hundreds of needles poking at them in all directions. I could feel my nostrils sticking together. My eyes hurt. I moved to the other corner of the freezer, hoping it would be slightly warmer than the corner near the cooling unit, but there was no improvement.** My stupid curiosity had done me in.

Exercise R2-9

Underline the topic sentence in paragraph 7 of Lynda Barry's essay (p.13), and list the details in this paragraph that support or explain the topic sentence.

Exercise R2-10

Study the changes in paragraph 2 of Tommy's revised draft (pp. 23–24). Then, list the supporting details that help his audience share his experience.

Exercise R2-11

Fill in the blanks of the topic sentences below so they apply to you, and supply supporting details for each of them.

1. My favorite restaurant, _____ , serves great food at reasonable prices.

2. I chose _____ as a hobby because _____ .

3. My favorite time of day is _____ .

4. I would rather listen to _____ music than

_____ music.

5. I admire _____ more than anyone else I know.

Exercise R2-12

Revise the following paragraph so that it has a clear topic sentence and enough supporting details.

I participate in a very important activity in my free time. This activity makes me feel good about myself. I wouldn't trade this activity for any other that I can think of.

Conclusions

A **concluding paragraph** is the final paragraph in an essay. It can wrap up an essay in several ways: It can summarize the main ideas, highlight the most important issue, ask a question that provokes thought on the part of the reader, predict the future, of-fer a solution to a problem, or call the reader to action. It can also do a combination of these tasks. For example, Lynda Barry ends "The Sanctuary of School" with a reference to the teacher posting one of her drawings, a gesture of acceptance that was important to her. We also learn the details of the drawing that was dis-played:

> By the time the bell rang that morning, I had finished my drawing, and Mrs. LeSane pinned it up on the special bulletin board she reserved for drawings from the back table. It was the same picture I always drew — a sun in the corner of a blue sky over a nice house with flowers all around it.

As Tommy studied his essay, he decided that his conclusion was combined with his last body paragraph:

First Draft: Suddenly, there was a *swoosh* as the gigantic door swung open. My grandfather's eyes met mine. His stern look vanished as he swept me into his arms and rescued me from the frozen tomb. He wrapped me in towels from the kitchen and took me to his office where he quickly poured a shot of ouzo, a Greek liqueur. After he touched it to my frozen lips, I swallowed it reflexively, feeling the warmth of its vapors spreading through my mouth and down to my stomach. The air in the heated office burned the frozen skin on my arms and legs and face. I didn't care because I was so relieved that the numbness was starting to leave my body and I had been brought back to life. My grandfather held me on his lap and kissed my forehead. Then he carried me around and let everyone know that

Conclusion: the adventurer had returned. My whole family had a good laugh at my expense, and I had new respect for my father's warnings. I won't say that this adventure was my last, but it certainly was my most memorable.

In his revision, Tommy separated the two paragraphs and added more details to his conclusion to emphasize what he learned from the experience:

Revision: My whole family had a good laugh at my expense, and I had **learned a valuable lesson. The minutes that had seemed like hours in the freezer taught me a** new respect for my father's warnings. I won't say that this adventure was my last, but it certainly was my most memorable.

Now Tommy's essay concludes on a strong note that makes his point clear; he learned a valuable lesson about listening to his father's warnings. Also, he predicts that in the future he will be more cautious but still adventurous.

Exercise R2-13

Write an alternative concluding paragraph for Lynda Barry's essay (pp. 12–14). Explain the changes you made.

Exercise R2-14

Write an alternative concluding paragraph for Tommy Poulos's revised essay (pp. 23–26). Explain the changes you made.

Exercise R2-15

For each of the topics here, write a conclusion that either summarizes the main ideas, high-lights the most important issue, asks a question that provokes thought on the part of the reader, predicts the future, offers a solution to a problem, or calls the reader to action.

1.   The Future of Computer Technology

2. Political Campaigns: A Problem for the United States
3. The World in 2050
4. The Value of a College Education
5. How to Study for an Exam

COLLABORATIVE WORK

After writing a draft of your own recalling essay, exchange papers with a classmate, and do the following tasks:

A. Write two alternative titles for the essay.

B. Note any questions you have after reading the introduction.

C. Underline the thesis statement. Does it clearly identify the purpose of the essay? If not, can you suggest revisions?

D. Put a check mark by any body paragraphs that need more details or explanations.

E. Does the conclusion wrap up the essay effectively? Write down any suggestions you have for improving the conclusion.

Then return the paper to its writer, and use the information in this section to revise your draft.

Words, Phrases, and Clauses

Checklist for Editing Words, Phrases, and Clauses

✓ Are the verbs mainly **action verbs?**

✓ Do the sentences include **nouns** that name specific persons, places, things, or ideas?

✓ Do the **pronouns** replace nouns that are clearly identified?

✓ Are the **adjectives** vivid and close to the words they modify?

✓ Do the **adverbs** clearly give additional information about verbs, adjectives, and other adverbs?

✓ Does each **preposition** have an object?

✓ Does each **conjunction** connect two words, phrases, or clauses?

✓ Do **interjections** express strong feelings?

✓ Do **noun phrases** contain a good variety of nouns and adjectives?

✓ Do **prepositional phrases** contain a preposition that connects a noun or pronoun to the rest of the sentence?

✓ Do **verb phrases** consist of four words or fewer, and are main verbs easily identifiable?

✓ Does each sentence contain at least one **independent clause?**

✓ Does each **independent clause** contain at least one subject and one verb?

✓ Is each **dependent clause** connected to a main clause?

Making grammatical elements in sentences work well together is much like coaching the members of a good athletic team. The team members know how to play the sport individually, but they must be especially aware of their roles in relation to one another when they play as a team.

Using words, phrases, and clauses is similar to working with members of a team; their success depends on how effectively you put them together and how well they work in relation to one another. One misused word or phrase can often mean your sentence doesn't communicate or succeed.

Words: Identifying Parts of Speech

Since you were a toddler, you've been using words to communicate a wide variety of messages. Now that you're in college, you'll draw on your knowledge of words to write reports, reviews, summaries, essays, and research papers that fulfill assignments and inform your readers about an array of subjects.

To use words most effectively—and to meet your instructors' expectations and standards—you need to know more than simply a word's definition. You should also know how a word functions—in other words, what role the word fulfills in helping you craft a complete sentence that communicates effectively. Particularly, you need to know how words relate to each other, forming phrases and clauses that eventually produce well-organized essays. If you use words wisely, with careful attention to these building blocks of our language, your essays will send clear, concise, creative messages that leave a lasting impression with your readers.

Verbs

Without verbs, the English language would be dull, boring, and downright dead. Because verbs are the part of speech that tells what happens, they are extremely important words and call for careful usage.

Basically, verbs come in two types: *action* and *linking.* An **action verb,** which tells what someone or something does, can be either transitive or intransitive. A **transitive verb** connects someone or something (the subject) performing the action with someone or something (the direct object) receiving the action. In Tommy's revised recalling essay, several statements depend on transitive action verbs:

DO

Transitive Verbs: I **grasped** that *latch* as if it were my lifeline.

DO

I **hated** *vegetables.*

DO

The air in the heated office **burned** *the frozen skin* on my

arms and legs and face.

An **intransitive verb** still features a subject performing an action, but the action has no receiver. These sentences from Tommy's first draft rely on intransitive verbs:

Intransitive Verbs: Tommy the Conqueror **had landed**!

Nothing **happened**.

My bare feet **had frozen** to the floor.

Unlike both transitive and intransitive verbs, **linking verbs** do not show action. They simply express a state of being. The most common linking verbs are the forms of *be: am, is, are, was, were, being,* and *been.* Other often-used linking verbs include *feel, seem, grow, look, remain, smell, sound, taste,* and *turn.* As the term implies, linking verbs connect the subject with another word that describes or renames the subject. Here are some examples from Tommy's first draft:

Linking Verbs: I **was** *too innocent* to have been given so harsh a

punishment by God.

I **felt** *helpless.*

The air **became** even *colder* and *drier.*

Some verbs can either show action or link words, depending on the sentence:

Action Verb:	Tommy **grew** a tomato *plant* in his dorm room.
Linking Verb:	Tommy **grew** *irritated* when his boss ignored him.

Exercise E2-1

Underline the main verbs in each of the following sentences from Lynda Barry's essay "The Sanctuary of School." Then label each as transitive, intransitive, or linking.

1. We slept on the couch, something we actually liked because it put us that much closer to the light of our lives, our television.
2. We watched Steve Allen's mouth moving.
3. I walked the alley, breaking thin ice over the puddles with my shoes.
4. I stood for a long time just looking across Rainier Valley.
5. I felt incredibly happy to see him.

Exercise E2-2

List the verbs in each of the sentences in paragraphs 5 and 6 of Tommy's revised essay (pp. 25–26), and label each as transitive, intransitive, or linking.

Exercise E2-3

Fill in each blank in the following paragraph with a verb. Then label each verb as transitive, intransitive, or linking.

My psychology professor (1) _____ entertaining, to say

the least. You never (2) _____ what she will do to get her

point across to her students. On rare occasions she (3) _____

for most of the class period, and when she does, she usually adds some humorous

stories or anecdotes. Usually she (4) _____ some sort of

visual aid, whether it be a video, a transparency, or a short demonstration.

She also (5) _____ around the room, which helps keep our

attention. Sometimes she (6) _____ us in small groups so

we can discuss topics. I (7) _____ one class when she

made us sit in a big circle and take turns asking questions about our reading

assignment. That (8) _____ different. In fact, she

(9) _____ different from my other instructors. Most of them

just (10) _____ .

Exercise E2-4

Write sentences using the following verbs as indicated.

1.   smelled (transitive)
2.   smelled (linking)
3.   vote (transitive)
4.   delivers (intransitive)
5.   appears (linking)

Nouns

You probably remember that a **noun** names a person, place, thing, or idea. To use nouns most effectively, however, you need to know more about them so that you can choose the noun that expresses exactly what you mean.

First, nouns are either *common* or *proper*. Whereas **common nouns** refer to a member or members of a general group (*boy, car, building*), **proper nouns** indicate a specific member of the group (*Tommy, Mustang, Superdome*). Note that proper nouns begin with capital letters.

Nouns can also be grouped as either *concrete* or *abstract*. **Concrete nouns** denote things that can be seen or touched (*friend, Brian, computer, pizza, stereo*). **Abstract nouns** indicate concepts, feelings, or qualities that cannot be seen or touched (*gratitude, jealousy, confidence, Christianity, Reaganomics*).

Two additional types of nouns are *collective* and *compound*. **Collective nouns,** which can be common or proper, refer to a unit or group (*herd, army, team, faculty, United States, Senate*). **Compound nouns** are composed of two or more words and may appear in one of three ways: one word (*notebook, basketball*), two words (*high school, vice president*), or hyphenated (*father-in-law, jack-of-all-trades*).

One way to identify a noun is to place *a, an,* or *the* before the word. If the phrase communicates sensibly, you have found a noun (*a date, an offer, the textbook*). Also, look for markers such as characteristic endings of nouns: *-age* (*homage*); *-ance* (*defiance*); *-ation* (*determination*); *-dom* (*kingdom*); *-er* (*mover*); *-ence* (*persistence*); *-ery* (*finery*); *-ice* (*cowardice*); *-ism* (*Judaism*); *-ist* (*jurist*); *-ity* (*humility*); *-ment* (*department*); *-ness* (*kindness*); *-ship* (*kinship*); *-sion* (*persuasion*); and *-tion* (*partition*).

Exercise E2-5

Under the "Noun" column, list the nouns in paragraph 9 of "The Sanctuary of School" by Lynda Barry (p. 13). Then indicate the noun's categories by placing an X in the appropriate columns. Use the following examples as a guide.

Noun	Common	Proper	Concrete	Abstract	Collective
street	X		X		
Madonna		X	X		
team	X		X		X

T I P S   F O R   E D I T I N G

Exercise E2-6

List the nouns in paragraph 3 of Tommy's revised recalling essay (pp. 24–25). Then place an X in the appropriate columns for each noun, as in the chart in Exercise E2-5.

Exercise E2-7

Complete each sentence in the following paragraph by supplying a noun in each blank.

One of my best (1) _____ was on a talk show recently.

She just picked up the phone and called (2) _____ after

she saw an ad about celebrity look-alike makeovers. Of course,

(3) _____ wanted to be made over to look like

(4) _____ , her favorite (5) _____ .

Anyway, after two different (6) _____ called her, she was

approved for the show. Since we live close to (7) _____ ,

we drove to the taping, which was on a (8) _____ . I was

able to go with her because that's my day off. I must say she has more

(9) _____ than I do because (10) _____

asked some rather embarrassing questions about her supposed obsession.

Exercise E2-8

Write sentences using each of the following words.

1. radio station
2. dreamland
3. lady-in-waiting
4. allegiance
5. Pledge of Allegiance

Pronouns

Pronouns give nouns a rest. You can use pronouns in sentences to avoid repeating nouns. The noun that a pronoun replaces or refers to, its **antecedent,** usually precedes the pronoun, either in the same sentence or in a previous sentence. Look at this sentence from Tommy's revised draft, which uses three pronouns:

Pronouns: **I** grasped that latch as if **it** were **my** lifeline.

I, it, and *my* are personal pronouns, the largest pronoun category. *It* is a pronoun that replaces the noun *latch,* which is its antecedent. *I* and *my* refer to the writer. The following chart lists the four types of personal pronouns.

Personal Prounouns

Subject	Object	Possessive (Pronoun)	Possessive (Adjective)
he	him	his	his
she	her	hers	hers
it	it	its	its
I	me	mine	my
you	you	yours	your
we	us	ours	our
they	them	theirs	their

Besides personal pronouns, several other types of pronouns function as "noun replacers":

- **Reflexive pronouns** end in *-self* and refer to the subject: *herself, himself, itself, myself, ourselves, themselves, yourself, yourselves.*

  Tommy gave **himself** a much-needed break from studying.

- **Intensive pronouns** end in *-self* and emphasize their antecedents: *herself, himself, itself, myself, ourselves, themselves, yourself, yourselves.*

  Tommy **himself** paid off his Visa bill.

- **Demonstrative pronouns** identify nouns without naming them: *this, that, these, those.*

  Those are the best.

- **Interrogative pronouns** ask a question: *what, which, who, whom, whose.*

  Who gave Tommy a ride home?

- **Indefinite pronouns** refer to a vague antecedent, one that cannot be clearly identified: *all, another, any, anybody, anyone, anything, each, either, everybody, everyone, everything, more, most, neither, no one, nobody, none, nothing, one, some, somebody, someone, something.*

  We usually believe **anything** Tommy tells us.

- **Relative pronouns** connect or relate a group of words that cannot stand alone to the rest of the sentence: *that, what, whatever, which, whichever, who, whoever, whom, whomever, whose*.

  Tommy decided to do **whatever** he wanted.

  The letter **that** Tommy received was from the financial aid office.

- **Reciprocal pronouns** are made up of two words: *each other, one another*.

  Tommy and Jackie gave **each other** quizzes after a long night of studying.

Exercise E2-9

List the pronouns and their antecedents (if they can be determined) in paragraphs 10 through 12 of Lynda Barry's "The Sanctuary of School" (p. 13).

Exercise E2-10

List the pronouns and their antecedents (if they can be identified) in paragraph 3 of Tommy's first draft (pp. 19–20).

Exercise E2-11

Fill in each blank with a pronoun that will complete the sentence. Then identify each pronoun by type.

(1) _____ says that the unemployment rate is going down nationwide, but in our town (2) _____ is not the case. Last week when the local employment agency took applications for jobs at a new manufacturing plant, lines were long. (3) _____ stretched for almost a block, causing some people to wait for hours. News reports said that the job applicants amused (4) _____ by talking, sharing reading material, and giving (5) _____ encouragement. One job seeker said (6) _____ had spent the night in (7) _____ van so (8) _____ could be first in line. I hope that I never have to put (9) _____ through such an ordeal to get a job. But even with a college education, (10) _____ is guaranteed a place in the work force.

Exercise E2-12

Write sentences using the following pronouns.

1. ourselves
2. anybody
3. whoever
4. them
5. one another

Adjectives

Writers use adjectives to give more specific information about nouns and pronouns. For example, Tommy's paper "The Ice Chamber" is not just an essay but a *recalling* essay. It doesn't just tell a story—it recounts a *vivid, frightening* story. Thus, most of the adjectives in the essay are descriptive adjectives supplying details that make the writing more colorful and interesting (a *world-class* adventurer, the *silvery blur* of kitchen equipment).

The most common adjectives are the **articles** *a, an,* and *the.* They are called *limiting adjectives* and indicate specific nouns:

> A student in **the** front row brought our English teacher **an** apple on **the** day of the final.

Notice that *an* (rather than *a*) is used when the next word begins with a vowel (*an apple*).

As you learned earlier in this chapter, pronouns can sometimes function as adjectives. In fact, words in five of the six pronoun categories can do double duty, falling into the following adjective classifications:

- **Possessive:** *his, her, its, our, their*

  > Tommy paid **his** library fine yesterday so he could check out books for **his** research paper.

- **Demonstrative:** *this, that, these, those*

  > **Those** books are Tommy's, and **these** books are mine.

- **Indefinite:** *all, any, each, more, some*

  > I think that **all** students need to take a class in study skills.

- **Interrogative:** *what, which, whose*

  > **Which** problem were you not able to solve?

* **Relative:** *which, whichever, whatever*

> Tommy plans to sign up for **whatever** classes are still available.

Other adjective categories include **proper adjectives,** which are formed from proper nouns and capitalized (The *Louisiana* coastline has been slowly eroding over the years). **Cardinal adjectives** are used in counting (Tommy has *three* tests next week), and **ordinal adjectives** identify a noun's position in a series (Tommy made a 98 on his *second* history test). All these adjectives either describe or limit the words they modify. If chosen carefully, adjectives can make writing clear, interesting, and vivid.

Exercise E2-13

List the adjectives (including articles) in paragraphs 7 through 9 of "The Sanctuary of School" (p. 13).

Exercise E2-14

List the adjectives (including articles) in paragraph 2 of Tommy's Poulos's first draft (p. 19).

Exercise E2-15

Complete each of the sentences in the following paragraph by supplying one or more adjective in each blank.

I remember my (1) _____ day of high school. Since

it was such a (2) _____ day, all the seniors decided

to wear (3) _____ outfits. We chose to dress in a

(4) _____ theme because we thought we could come

up with some really (5) _____ clothes. Everyone followed

through and arrived at school (6) _____ minutes early for

a (7) _____ meeting. We went over the day's activities,

which included a (8) _____ skit outside during

(9) _____ period and presenting our class gift to the

school, which was a (10) _____ tree.

Exercise E2-16

Write sentences using the following words as adjectives.

1. elaborate
2. sparkling

3. required
4. energizing
5. Italian

Adverbs

Adverbs share describing qualities with adjectives. Instead of modifying nouns and pronouns, however, **adverbs** modify verbs, adjectives, or other adverbs, telling *when, where, why, how, how much, how often,* and *to what extent.*

Adverbs can be classified in the following categories:

- **Adverbs of manner** often end in *-ly* and describe *how* something is done:

  Tommy **solemnly** studied for his test.

- **Adverbs of time** indicate *when, how long,* or *how often* something takes place:

  Tommy studied for his test **yesterday**.

- **Adverbs of place** tell *where* something occurs:

  Tommy studied **somewhere** in the library.

- **Adverbs of degree** indicate *how much* or *how little.* These adverbs include the intensifiers *so, too,* and *very.*

  Tommy, who is **very** concerned about his grades, **generally** studies **too much** for each test.

Exercise E2-17

Identify the adverbs in paragraphs 15 through 17 of "The Sanctuary of School" (pp. 13–14) by Lynda Barry.

Exercise E2-18

List each of the adverbs in paragraph 3 of Tommy Poulos's first draft (pp. 19–20).

Exercise E2-19

Fill in each blank with an adverb that will make the sentence complete.

I wish that I knew something about cars because every time I need repair work

it's (1) _____ expensive. The last time I took my car to the shop I got (2) _____ upset when I got the bill. The mechanic

had (3) _____ told me the bill would be $232 for replacing my

radiator. But when I picked up the car (4) _____ , he said

the charge was $298! I (5) _____ asked him why the bill

was (6) _____ high. He said that they had to replace a couple of

extra hoses that were (7) _____ leaking. I asked him

why they didn't call to tell me about the extra charges. He said they

(8) _____ call customers when the extra charges will be at least

$100 over the estimate. I told him (9) _____ didn't agree with

the company's policy. Then I wrote a check and (10) _____ left.

Exercise E2-20

Write original sentences using the following words as adverbs.

1. eternally
2. meekly
3. away
4. later
5. somewhat

Prepositions

Writers use **prepositions** to show the relationship between words, more specifically the relationship of a noun or pronoun that follows a preposition to another word in the sentence. The group of words that begins with a preposition and ends with a noun or pronoun is called a **prepositional phrase.** (For more on prepositional phrases, see pp. 55–56.) Look at these sentences with prepositions from the first paragraph of Tommy's revised recalling essay:

Prepositions: It was an early Saturday morning **at** my home away **from**

home, my family's restaurant.

I was five years old, and I had been **to** every nook and

cranny **of** our house and restaurant.

At, from, to, and *of* are four of the most common simple prepositions. Prepositions can also be made up of more than one word (*according to, on top of*). Following is a list of common prepositions for easy reference:

Common Prepositions				
about	before	except for	next to	through
above	behind	for	of	throughout
according to	below	from	off	to
across	beneath	in	on	toward
after	beside	in addition to	onto	under
against	besides	in back of	on top of	underneath
along	between	in case of	out	unlike
along with	beyond	in front of	out of	until
among	by	in place of	outside	up
apart from	by means of	inside	over	upon
around	concerning	in spite of	past	up to
as	despite	instead of	prior to	with
as for	down	into	regarding	within
at	during	like	since	without
because of	except	near		

Exercise E2-21

List the prepositions in paragraphs 11 through 13 of "The Sanctuary of School" by Lynda Barry (p. 13).

Exercise E2-22

List the prepositions in paragraph 2 of Tommy Poulos's first draft (p. 19).

Exercise E2-23

Supply a preposition in each blank to complete the sentences in the following paragraph.

One (1) _____ the scariest times (2) _____ my life was when I rode my first roller-coaster. I don't remember the coaster's name, but it looked monstrous (3) _____ my ten-year-old eyes. The tracks seemed to disappear (4) _____ the sky and then plunged downward (5) _____ the ground in loops of twisting, curving steel. My brother was riding with me. As he stood (6) _____ me in line, he kept telling me stories (7) _____ roller-coaster disasters, gruesome tales that I'm sure he made up. But I believed him then, and butterflies raced (8) _____ my stomach. Nevertheless, I was determined to conquer the coaster monster. As the carnival worker helped us

(9) _____ our seats, I briefly panicked. But before I knew it, I was sitting (10) _____ my hands with my eyes closed, praying the ride would be finished soon.

Exercise E2-24

Write sentences using the following prepositions.

1. except
2. past
3. behind
4. among
5. on top of

Conjunctions

While prepositions show relationships between words, **conjunctions** join words or groups of words. Conjunctions fall into one of two general categories, *coordinating* or *subordinating.*

Coordinating conjunctions connect individual words and groups of words of equal importance. There are only seven coordinating conjunctions: *for, and, nor, but, or, yet,* and *so.* Notice how Tommy uses coordinating conjunctions in the following sentences from paragraph 1 of his revised essay:

> **Coordinating Conjunctions:**   It was not unusual to find pennies, nickels, dimes, **and** even quarters under the restaurant booths.
>
> I was five years old, **and** I had been to every nook **and** cranny of our house **and** restaurant.

A **correlative conjunction** is a special kind of coordinating conjunction. Correlatives are used in pairs: *either . . . or, neither . . . nor, both . . . and, not . . . but, not only . . . but also, whether . . . or.* Look at this sentence from Tommy's journal:

> **Correlative Conjunctions:**   **Either** I would go "where no man had gone before," **or** I would go nowhere.

Subordinating conjunctions connect two clauses—groups of words that have their own subject and verb—that are not equal in importance. A subordinating conjunction connects a dependent clause to an independent clause that completes the meaning of the dependent clause. Together, dependent and independent clauses form complete thoughts. (For more information on dependent clauses, see pp.

58–59; for more information on independent clauses, see p. 58.) Look at this sentence from Tommy's essay.

Subordinating Conjunction: **If** I'd had a flag, I would have planted it on that hard, cold, metallic floor.

Familiarize yourself with the subordinating conjunctions that appear in the following list.

Common Subordinating Conjunctions

after	even though	though
although	how	unless
as	if	until
as if	in order that	when
as long as	since	whenever
as soon as	so	where
as though	so that	wherever
because	than	whether
before	that	while
even if		

Exercise E2-25

List the conjunctions in the first five paragraphs of "The Sanctuary of School" by Lynda Barry (p. 12).

Exercise E2-26

List the conjunctions in paragraphs 5 and 6 of Tommy Poulos's revised recalling essay (p. 25).

Exercise E2-27

Fill in the blanks in the following paragraph with subordinating conjunctions to make each thought complete. You may have to add punctuation marks.

(1) _____ students decide on majors, they should do some homework. My friend Julie went to the library (2) _____ she found a wealth of information about interior design and architecture, two of her interests. (3) _____ she read the books and articles she found, Julie decided that architecture would be best for her (4) _____ her earning potential would be greater. Samir, another friend of mine, took

the Meyers-Briggs test (5) _____ he declared a major.

(6) _____ he's a student worker in the career counseling

office, Samir knew all about the test. It asks questions about a person's interests

(7) _____ possible careers can be isolated.

(8) _____ the test results said that Samir should be a teacher,

he is still planning to major in engineering (9) _____ he can't

pass calculus. Then he may have to seriously consider a teaching career, a bridge

(10) _____ he hopes he never has to cross.

Exercise E2-28

Write original sentences using the following conjunctions.

1. not only . . . but also
2. yet
3. until
4. wherever
5. as long as

Interjections

When you want to express emotion, particularly shock or surprise, you can use an interjection—words such as *aha, hallelujah, hell, hey, goodness, my, oh, ouch, well,* or *wow* or expressions such as *oh no, good grief,* or *for heaven's sake.* When you express mild emotion, place a comma after the interjection. Use an exclamation point after an interjection that indicates strong emotion.

Interjections: **Oh,** I think Tommy is a pretty good guy.
                     Oh! You almost scared me to death!

Exercise E2-29

List the interjections in Tommy Poulos's revised recalling essay (pp. 23–26).

Exercise E2-30

Write sentences using the following words and expressions as interjections.

1. aha
2. wow
3. my goodness
4. well
5. ouch

Phrases

Writers put together words to form **phrases,** groups of words that perform a variety of functions. Even though they cannot stand alone as sentences, phrases provide additional details that help complete a sentence. There are five types of phrases: verb phrases, verbal phrases, noun phrases, prepositional phrases, and absolute phrases.

Verb Phrases

A **verb phrase** is composed of the sentence's main verb plus any helping verbs that assist the main verb in expressing action or state of being. The most common helping verbs are *be, am, is, are, was, were, being, been, have, has, had, do, did, can, may, must, might, shall,* and *will.* Note the verb phrases in these sentences from paragraph 2 of Tommy's revised draft:

Verb Phrases: I **was determined** to conquer the freezer's unexplored

mysteries.

Tommy the Conqueror **had landed**!

Verbal Phrases

Unlike verb phrases, verbal phrases cannot serve as the main verbs in sentences. Rather, a **verbal phrase** is a group of words that begins with a *verbal,* a verb form that begins with *to* (*to roam*) or ends in *-ing* or *-ed* (*roaming, roamed*). The verbal then functions in the sentence as a noun, an adjective, or an adverb.

A **participial phrase** is a verbal phrase that functions as an adjective. A participial phrase may begin with either a present participle (verb + *-ing*) or a past participle (verb + *-d, -ed, -en, -t,* or *-k*):

Present Participle: *Driving* **to work this morning,** Tommy had a flat tire.

Past Participle: *Worn* **out,** *beaten,* **and** *dejected,* **the team got on the bus for the long ride home.**

Another kind of verbal phrase is a **gerund phrase,** a present participial phrase that functions as a noun.

Gerund Phrases: *Driving* **45 miles to work every day** gets tedious.
Some people like *driving* **to work**.

An **infinitive phrase** is composed of an infinitive (*to* + a verb) plus any objects or modifiers that go with it. Infinitive phrases can function as nouns, adjectives, or adverbs:

Infinitive Phrases: *To live* happily ever after is everyone's fairy tale.

Her wish **to live** happily ever after probably won't be granted.

Tommy lay down **to take** a short nap.

Exercise E2-31

Underline the verb phrases in each of the following sentences from "The Sanctuary of School."

1.   We watched movies filled with gangsters shooting machine guns into packed rooms, dying soldiers hurling a last grenade, and beautiful women crying at windows.
2.   I walked over to the monkey bars and hooked my arms around the cold metal.
3.   In a perfect world my absence at home would not have gone unnoticed.
4.   But in an overcrowded and unhappy home, it's incredibly easy for any child to slip away.
5.   The high levels of frustration, depression, and anger in my house made my brother and me invisible.

Exercise E2-32

List each verbal phrase and its type in paragraph 3 of Tommy Poulos's first draft (pp. 19–20).

Exercise E2-33

Complete the following paragraph by supplying verb phrases and verbal phrases in the blanks.

Last Saturday night I got an unexpected night off from work. I

(1) _____ (verb phrase) a boring night at the restaurant. But it

seems that few people wanted (2) _____ (infinitive) at the

China Gardens on a cold January evening. (3) _____ (participial

phrase) I called up my friend Betsy. We (4) _____ (verb phrase)

about going to a new dance club that stayed open until 3 a.m. But as I told her the

good news, our brains started (6) _____ (gerund phrase).

We began (7) _____ (gerund phrase). Finally, after

about five minutes of talking, Betsy was pretty insistent that she wanted
(8) _____ (infinitive phrase). I (9) _____
(verb phrase) for something a little more upbeat. (10) _____
(participial phrase), I felt a little disappointed that I had given in. But little did I
know that my disappointment would soon turn to excitement as Betsy and I began
our big adventure.

Exercise E2-34

Write two sentences with verb phrases, two sentences with participial phrases, two sentences with infinitive phrases, and two sentences with gerund phrases. Underline the verb phrases, and circle the verbal phrases.

Noun Phrases

A **noun phrase** usually begins or ends with a noun and includes adjectives that describe the noun. As a single unit, the phrase functions as a noun. Look at these examples from paragraph 1 of Tommy's revised recalling essay:

> **Noun Phrases:**   To me, it was **comic book money**, and I searched for it
> **every morning** without fail.
> **My adventurous soul** was burning with curiosity.

An **appositive phrase** is a special type of noun phrase that identifies or renames another noun, pronoun, or noun phrase. The appositive phrase comes immediately before or after the word or phrase it modifies. Look at these examples from Tommy's revised essay:

> **Appositive Phrases:**   It was an early Saturday morning at my **home** away from
> home, *my family's restaurant*.
> **Tommy** *the Conqueror* had landed!

Prepositional Phrases

Earlier in this chapter you learned how prepositions show relationships between words. A **prepositional phrase** begins with a preposition and ends with a noun or pronoun (its object). Modifiers between the preposition and the object help complete the phrase's meaning.

A prepositional phrase functions as a unit, serving as either an adjective or an adverb. Look at these examples from Tommy's revised essay:

Prepositional Phrases:

I made a quick tour **of the restaurant**.

I whizzed past the silvery blur **of kitchen equipment** as fast as my short, stocky legs would carry me.

Since I was ready to give up, I sat down **on the moist floor**, panting and feeling my sore muscles.

I climbed up **on some boxes** stacked nearby and leaped **onto the handle like a frog** attacking some forlorn fly.

Exercise E2-35

List the noun phrases in paragraph 17 of "The Sanctuary of School" (p. 14).

Exercise E2-36

List the prepositional phrases in paragraphs 4 and 5 of Tommy Poulos's first draft (p. 20), and label them as either adjectives or adverbs.

Exercise E2-37

Fill in each blank with an appropriate phrase to complete the sentences in the following paragraph.

(1) _____ (noun phrase) must be one of the best places to live (2) _____ (prepositional phrase). It has many attractions (3) _____ (prepositional phrase), such as good schools and a low crime rate. It also has many offerings (4) _____ (prepositional phrase). When I was visiting there, I found (5) _____ (noun phrase) that had lots of people enjoying themselves. (6) _____ (noun phrase) lives there, and he thinks there's no better place.

(7) _____ (noun phrase) might be better, but I heard it's really expensive. For example, if you go out (8) _____ (prepositional phrase), you should be prepared to spend (9) _____ (prepositional phrase). That's too much (10) _____ (prepositional phrase).

Exercise E2-38

Write ten sentences, including at least one prepositional phrase in each. Underline each prepositional phrase, and circle each noun phrase.

Absolute Phrases

An **absolute phrase** consists of a noun or pronoun (usually followed by a participle) and any additional modifiers; it is not connected to a specific word in the rest of the sentence but, instead, refers to the entire sentence. These examples will help explain:

Absolute Phrases:	Tommy's face had a glazed look, **his eyes staring blankly into space**.
	The sale having ended yesterday, the store's employees took a break today.

Exercise E2-39

Underline the five absolute phrases in the following paragraphs.

The defendant took the witness stand, his hands sweating profusely. As he settled himself in the chair, his mother closed her eyes and prayed, her back bent forward, her eyes closed in silence.

This was the moment the prosecutor had been waiting for. He rose from his table, squared his shoulders, and stared at the defendant. He took slow, measured steps toward the witness stand, his breath coming in an easy rhythm. The defendant shifted nervously, anticipation building as he waited for the prosecutor to speak.

Exercise E2-40

Write sentences using the following absolute phrases.

1. roads glazed with ice
2. mouths open in amazement
3. the employees having voted to strike
4. fans screaming at the top of their lungs
5. clothes torn to shreds

Clauses

Like phrases, **clauses** are groups of related words. But clauses include both a subject and a predicate (the main verb plus any words that complete the verb's meaning). There are two types of clauses: independent or main and dependent or subordinate.

Independent Clauses

An **independent clause** makes a complete statement and can stand alone as a sentence because it has a subject and a predicate. In fact, every sentence must contain at least one independent clause, as these examples from Tommy's first draft illustrate:

	Subject	Predicate
Independent clauses	I	made a tour of the restaurant.
	My pride	would not let me give up.
	The air in the heated office	burned the frozen skin on my arms and legs and face.

Dependent Clauses

A **dependent clause** also contains a subject and a predicate. But it cannot stand alone as a complete sentence because it begins with a word that makes it dependent. The words that begin dependent clauses are subordinating conjunctions, such as *since, although,* and *because,* and relative pronouns, such as *who, which,* and *that.* (See p. 51 for a list of subordinating conjunctions and p. 44 for a list of relative pronouns.) The dependent clause, then, relies on the independent clause for its meaning, as the following examples from Tommy's revised draft illustrate:

Dependent Clause: **Since** I was ready to give up

Paired with Independent Clause: **Since I was ready to give up**, I sat down on the moist floor, panting and feeling my sore muscles.

Dependent Clause: **that** held abandoned treasures

Paired with Independent Clause: I felt it was my mission to search attics, closets, basements, and dark hallways **that held abandoned treasures**.

As a unit, a dependent clause functions as either a noun, an adjective, or an adverb. Look at the following sentences from Tommy's revised essay, which contain dependent clauses:

Noun Clauses: I wondered **what lay beyond that heavy door**. (I wondered *what?*)

Whatever stood in my way would be conquered. (*What* would be conquered?)

Adjective Clauses: Hurriedly trying to absorb all **that was around me** was

tough.

I started to realize that I would soon become as cold and

stiff as the multitude of vegetables **that stared back at**

me.

I grasped that latch **as if it were my lifeline**.

Adverb Clause: **If I'd had a flag**, I would have planted it on that hard, cold,

metallic floor.

Exercise E2-41

In the following sentences from "The Sanctuary of School," underline the independent clauses, and circle the dependent clauses.

1. They were short on money and long on relatives who kept "temporarily" moving into our house because they had nowhere else to go.
2. All I knew was the feeling of panic, like the panic that strikes kids when they realize they are lost.
3. It was Mr. Gunderson, our janitor, whom we all loved.
4. I could hear them jingling as he walked across the playfield.
5. But she asked me if I would carry her purse for her, an honor above all honors, and she asked if I wanted to come into Room 2 and paint.

Exercise E2-42

List the dependent clauses in the last paragraph of Tommy Poulos's first draft (p. 20). Then label each clause as a noun, an adjective, or an adverb.

Exercise E2-43

Complete the following paragraph by adding an independent or dependent clause in each blank.

(1) _____ (dependent clause), I plan on moving

away from Mississippi. Don't get me wrong. I like my home state, but

(2) _____ (independent clause). I've traveled a bit to

different parts of the country. I really liked Arizona (4) _____

(dependent clause). My family spent two weeks there (5) _____

(dependent clause). (6) _____ (independent clause), who is

my favorite relative besides my grandparents. I guess I liked the weather and the

scenery the best. Since I'm from Mississippi, (7) _____
(independent clause). I also like Miami. Last spring five friends and I went there for
spring break. It was a blast (8) _____ (dependent clause).
We particularly liked Miami Beach with its art deco hotels and buildings, and
(9) _____ (independent clause).
(10) _____ (dependent clause), I'll always call
Mississippi home.

Exercise E2-44

*Write sentences with dependent clauses, using the following subordinating conjunctions and
relative pronouns. Then underline the dependent clauses, and label each as a noun, an adjective, or an adverb. Finally, circle each independent clause.*

1. which
2. until
3. although
4. whoever
5. as long as

COLLABORATIVE WORK

After you revise your recalling essay, exchange papers with a classmate, and do the
following tasks:

A. Read the essay slowly, circling any words that seem to be used incorrectly.

B. Choose one paragraph and label each phrase: verb, verbal, noun, prepositional,
or absolute.

C. Select a different paragraph, and underline and label each independent and dependent clause.

Then return the paper to its writer, and use the information in this section to edit
your draft.

Observing

Reading and Writing for a Reason

**One of life's quiet excitements is to stand somewhat apart
from yourself and watch yourself softly becoming the author
of something beautiful.**

NORMAN MACLEAN

If you were asked to write down everything happening around you right at this moment, without looking up from the paper you were writing on, how much would you be able to record? Your answer would reflect how observant you are and what kinds of details you notice. Some people would notice the type of earrings worn by a stranger who just rushed by; some wouldn't even know whether the person they spent the last hour with *was* wearing earrings.

Observing isn't limited, however, to what people see. Good observers use all their senses: seeing, hearing, touching, smelling, even tasting. To write a clear, accurate, interesting observing essay, you must, of course, use your senses to gather the material you will need—facts, details, descriptions, and impressions. But simply observing and recording all the material you gather isn't enough. When you write an observation, you cannot simply *tell* your reader what you saw; you must *show* your reader. You must use your writing skills to recreate what you observed, to help your readers see, feel, hear, taste, and understand as if they were there. Your ultimate goal in writing an observing essay is to use your words to give your readers an experience as close to yours as possible.

In an autobiographical novel titled *A Death in the Family*, writer James Agee describes meeting for the first time his 103-year-old great-great-great-grandmother when he was a small child. Through his vivid and detailed observations, Agee helps his readers actually *see* her ancient body and come as close as possible to his experience.

> Her hands crawled in her skirts: every white bone and black vein showed through the brown-splotched skin; the wrinkled knuckles were like pouches; she wore a red rubber guard ahead of her wedding ring. . . .
> Her temple was deeply sunken as if a hammer had struck it, and frail as a fledgling's belly. Her skin was crosshatched with the razor-fine slashes

of innumerable square wrinkles and yet every slash was line smooth; her ear was just a fallen intricate flap with a small gold ring in it; her smell was faint yet very powerful, and she smelled like new mushrooms and old spices and sweat. . . .

Notice how Agee uses his senses to describe his aged relative: what he saw, touched, and smelled. And in describing these extraordinary sensations, he helps the reader "see" the old woman almost as clearly as he did.

Of course, it would be counterproductive for writers to observe—and record—everything about a person, place, incident, or situation. The result would be nothing but an endless, confusing account of everything they saw, heard, smelled, tasted, or touched. Therefore, writers must focus on one dominant impression—that is, the one feeling or message they are trying to relay to their readers. As a writer, you must decide which details to include and which details to eliminate, so that your readers are left with a single dominant impression rather than a collection of confusing impressions. Notice that James Agee's entire observation serves the purpose of helping readers realize the incredible age of the woman—every detail contributes to that single dominant impression.

Observations are not written so that readers can simply share your experience. They are written so that readers can understand the impact a specific observation had on you: how it changed you or maybe helped you discover something about yourself, about other people, about society, or even about the world.

LEARNING FROM PUBLISHED WRITERS

The following observing essay was written by N. Scott Momaday, a Kiowa Indian who was born in Lawton, Oklahoma, in 1934. Much of Momaday's writing is dedicated to discovering the history, rituals, and beliefs of his ancestors, who were almost destroyed as a result of the settlement and conquest of North America by European immigrants. The lifestyle of the Kiowa is so special and so different from that of most Americans that it is hard for us to imagine now. But Momaday brings this culture to life through his exquisite and powerful observations and descriptions.

Before You Read

Focusing Your Attention

Before you read this observation essay, take a few moments to respond to the following questions in your journal:

1. Think of a place or an object that is special to your family or culture. What are your main impressions of the place or object? Write down as many descriptive words and phrases as you can—using all your senses—to bring it to life for someone who has never seen it.

2. In the last paragraph of his essay, N. Scott Momaday describes his beloved grandmother in the "postures that were peculiar to her": standing by the stove, sitting at a window, going out, praying. Think of a very special relative or friend who is either dead or far away, and make a list of the "postures" or positions in which you think of him or her in your memory.

Expanding Your Vocabulary

Here are some words and their meanings that are important to your understanding of the essay. You might want to review them before you begin to read.

"A single **knoll** [small rounded hill or hilltop]" (paragraph 1)

"the prairie is an **anvil's** [hard, flat block of iron used by metalsmiths to hammer on] edge" (paragraph 1)

"to **writhe** [twist in pain] in fire" (paragraph 1)

"at last **infirm** [weak, unhealthy]" (paragraph 2)

"in **alliance** [having a formal agreement] with the **Comanches** [another Native American tribe]" (paragraph 3)

"warfare was **preeminently** [mainly] a matter of **disposition** [mood]" (paragraph 3)

"the grim, **unrelenting** [persistent, not giving up] advance" (paragraph 3)

"they abandoned their crucial **stores** [food and equipment] to **pillage** [stealing]" (paragraph 3)

"the **affliction** [pain] of defeat" (paragraph 3)

"ancient **nomadic** [having no fixed residence, roaming] spirit" (paragraph 4)

"my **pilgrimage** [a trip with special meaning or purpose]" (paragraph 5)

"the inland slope of the Rockies is **luxuriant** [lush and rich]" (paragraph 7)

"the **dark lees** [sheltered, unlit sides] of the hills" (paragraph 7)

"oldest **deity** [god] ranging after the **solstices** [two dates of the year, when the sun is furthest north or south of the equator; often celebrated as sacred]" (paragraph 7)

"they **veer** [turn, swerve] southward to the **caldron** [large kettle for boiling] of the land" (paragraph 7)

"**engender** [cause] an awful quiet" (paragraph 8)

"the Kiowas have **kinsmen** [relatives or allies]" (paragraph 8)

"however **tenuous** [uncertain] their well-being" (paragraph 8)

"a **wariness** [suspicion] in her, and an ancient **awe** [feeling of wonder and respect]" (paragraph 9) "to **consummate** [to bring to completion] the ancient sacrifice" (paragraph 9)

"to **impale** [pierce with a stick or spear] the head of a buffalo bull" (paragraph 9)

"to **disperse** [scatter or separate] the tribe" (paragraph 9)

"she bore a vision of **deicide** [killing a god]" (paragraph 9)

"a high and **descending** [lowering] pitch" (paragraph 10)

N. Scott Momaday

The Way to Rainy Mountain*

A singe knoll rises out of the plain in Oklahoma, north and west of the Wichita Range. For my people, the Kiowas, it is an old landmark, and they gave it the name Rainy Mountain. The hardest weather in the world is there. Winter brings blizzards, hot tornadic winds arise in the spring, and in summer the prairie is an anvil's edge. The grass turns brittle and brown, and it cracks beneath your feet. There are green belts along the rivers and creeks, linear groves of hickory and pecan, willow, and witch hazel. At a distance in July or August the steaming foliage seems almost to writhe in fire. Great green and yellow grasshoppers are everywhere in the tall grass, popping up like corn to sting the flesh, and tortoises crawl about on the red earth, going nowhere in the plenty of time. Loneliness is an aspect of the land. All things in the plain are isolate; there is no confusion of objects in the eye, but *one* hill or *one* tree or *one* man. To look upon that landscape in the early morning, with the sun at your back, is to lose the sense of proportion. Your imagination come to life, and this, you think, is where Creation was begun.   1

I returned to Rainy Mountain in July. My grandmother had died in the spring, and I wanted to be at her grave. She had lived to be very old and at last infirm. Her only living daughter was with her when she died, and I was told that in death her face was that of a child.   2

I like to think of her as a child. When she was born, the Kiowas were living the last great moment of their history. For more than a hundred years they had controlled the open range from the Smoky Hill River to the Red, from the headwaters of the Canadian to the fork of the Arkansas and Cimarron. In alliance with the Comanches, they had   3

---

*N. Scott Momaday, "The Way to Rainy Mountain" from *The Way to Rainy Mountain*. Reprinted with the permission of the publishers.

ruled the whole of the southern Plains. War was their sacred business, and they were among the finest horsemen the world has ever known. But warfare for the Kiowas was preeminently a matter of disposition rather than of survival, and they never understood the grim, unrelenting advance of the U.S. Cavalry. When at last, divided and ill-provisioned, they were driven onto the Staked Plains in the cold rains of autumn, they fell into panic. In Palo Duro Canyon they abandoned their crucial stores to pillage and had nothing then but their lives. In order to save themselves, they surrendered to the soldiers at Fort Sill and were imprisoned in the old stone corral that now stands as a military museum. My grandmother was spared the humiliation of those high gray walls by eight or ten years, but she must have known from birth the affliction of defeat, the dark brooding of old warriors.

Her name was Aho, and she belonged to the last culture to evolve   **4** in North America. Her forebears came down from the high country in western Montana nearly three centuries ago. They were a mountain people, a mysterious tribe of hunters whose language has never been positively classified in any major group. In the late seventeenth century they began a long migration to the south and east. It was a journey toward the dawn, and it led to a golden age. Along the way the Kiowas were befriended by the Crows, who gave them the culture and religion of the Plains. They acquired horses, and their ancient nomadic spirit was suddenly free of the ground. They acquired Taime, the sacred Sun Dance doll, from that moment the object and symbol of their worship, and so shared in the divinity of the sun. Not least, they acquired the sense of destiny, therefore courage and pride. When they entered upon the southern Plains, they had been transformed. No longer were they slaves to the simple necessity of survival; they were a lordly and dangerous society of fighters and thieves, hunters and priests of the sun. According to their origin myth, they entered the world through a hollow log. From one point of view, their migration was the fruit of an old prophecy, for indeed they emerged from a sunless world.

Although my grandmother lived out her long life in the shadow of   **5** Rainy Mountain, the immense landscape of the continental interior lay like memory in her blood. She could tell of the Crows, whom she had never seen, and of the Black Hills, where she had never been. I wanted to see in reality what she had seen more perfectly in the mind's eye, and traveled 1500 miles to begin my pilgrimage.

Yellowstone, it seemed to me, was the top of the world, a region of deep lakes and dark timber, canyons and waterfalls. But, beautiful as   **6** it is, one might have the sense of confinement there. The skyline in all directions is close at hand, the high wall of the woods and deep cleavages of shade. There is a perfect freedom in the mountains, but it belongs to the eagle and the elk, the badger and the bear. The Kiowas reckoned their stature by the distance they see, and they were bent and blind in the wilderness.

Descending eastward, the highland meadows are a stairway to the plain. In July the inland slope of the Rockies is luxuriant with flax and the buckwheat, stonecrop, and larkspur. The earth unfolds, and the limit of the land recedes. Clusters of trees, and animals grazing far in the distance, cause the vision to reach away and wonder to build upon the mind. The sun follows a longer course in the day, and the sky is immense beyond all comparison. The great billowing clouds that sail upon it are shadows that move upon the grain like water, dividing light. Farther down, in the land of the Crows and Blackfeet, the plain is yellow. Sweet clover takes hold of the hills and bends upon itself to cover and seal the soil. There the Kiowas paused on their way; they had come to the place where they must change their lives. The sun is at home on the plains. Precisely there does it have the certain character of a god. When the Kiowas came to the land of the Crows, they could see the dark lees of the hills at dawn across the Bighorn River, the profusion of light on the grain shelves, the oldest deity ranging after the solstices. Not yet would they veer southward to the caldron of the land that lay below; they must wean their blood from the northern winter and hold the mountains a while longer in their view. They bore Tai-me in procession to the east.

A dark mist lay over the Black Hills, and the land was like iron. At the top of a ridge, I caught sight of Devil's Tower upthrust against the gray sky as if in the birth of time the core of the earth had broken through its crust and the motion of the world was begun. There are things in nature that engender an awful quiet in the heart of man; Devil's Tower is one of them. Two centuries ago, because they could not do otherwise, the Kiowas made a legend at the base of the rock. My grandmother said: *Eight children were there at play, seven sisters and their brother. Suddenly the boy was struck dumb; he trembled and began to run upon his hands and feet. His fingers became claws, and his body was covered with fur. Directly there was a bear where the boy had been. The sisters were terrified; they ran, and the bear after them. They came to the stump of a great tree, and the tree spoke to them. It bade them climb upon it, and as they did so it began to rise into the air. The bear came to kill them, but they were just beyond its reach. It reared against the tree and scored the bark all around with its claws. The seven sisters were borne into the sky, and they became the stars of the Big Dipper.* From that moment, and so long as the legend lives, the Kiowas have kinsmen in the night sky. Whatever they were in the mountains, they could be no more. However tenuous their well-being, however much they had suffered and would suffer again, they had found a way out of the wilderness.

My grandmother had a reverence for the sun, a holy regard that **9** now is all but gone out of mankind. There was a wariness in her, and an ancient awe. She was a Christian in her later years, but she had come a long way about, and she never forgot her birthright. A a child she had been to the Sun Dances; she had taken part in those annual rites, and by them she had learned the restoration of her people in the presence of Tai-me. She was about seven when the last Kiowa Sun Dance was held in 1887 on the Washita River above Rainy Mountain Creek. The buffalo were gone. In order to consummate the ancient sacrifice—to impale the head of a buffalo bull upon the medicine tree—a delegation of old men journeyed into Texas, there to beg and barter for an animal from the Goodnight herd. She was ten when the Kiowas came together for the last time as a living Sun Dance culture. They could find no buffalo; they had to hang an old hide from the sacred tree. Before the dance could begin, a company of soldiers rode out from Fort Sill under orders to disperse the tribe. Forbidden without cause the essential act of their faith, having seen the wild herds slaughtered and left to rot upon the ground, the Kiowas backed away forever from the medicine tree. That was July 20, 1890, at the great bend of the Washita. My grandmother was there. Without bitterness, and for as long as she lived, she bore a vision of deicide.

Now that I can have her only in memory, I see my grandmother **10** in the several postures that were peculiar to her: standing at the wood stove on a winter morning and turning meat in a great iron skillet; sitting at the south window, bent above her beadwork, and afterwards, when her vision failed, looking down for a long time into the fold of her hands; going out upon a cane, very slowly as she did when the weight of age came upon her; praying. I remember her most often at prayer. She made long, rambling prayers out of suffering and hope, having seen many things. I was never sure that I had the right to hear, so exclusive were they of all mere custom and company. The last time I saw her, she prayed standing by the side of her bed at night, naked to the waist, the light of a kerosene lamp moving upon her dark skin. Her long, black hair, always drawn and braided in the day, lay upon her shoulders and against her breasts like a shawl. I do not speak Kiowa, and I never understood her prayers, but there was something inherently sad in the sound, some merest hesitation upon the syllables of sorrow. She began a high and descending pitch, exhausting her breath to silence; then again and again—and always the same intensity of effort, of something that is, and is not, like urgency in the human voice. Transported so in the dancing light among the shadows of her room, she seemed beyond the reach of time. But that was illusion; I think I knew then that I should not see her again.

 ## Questions for Critical Thinking

Thinking Critically About Content

1. How much of this essay is about the writer's grandmother? How much of this essay is about the land on which his grandmother's tribe lived? Could the author have written about his grandmother *without* observing the land? Explain your answer.

2. Why does the writer tell us so much about his ancestors' history?

Thinking Critically About Purpose

3. What do you think N. Scott Momaday's purpose is in writing this essay?

4. After reading this essay, do you have a different impression or a deeper understanding of the Kiowa tribe's culture? Explain your answer.

Thinking Critically About Audience

5. Can you imagine a particular audience for whom this essay would be most interesting? Describe that audience.

6. How does the writer enable his readers to understand the way in which his grandmother was both simple and wise? Explain your answer.

Thinking Critically About Point of View

7. Does the author use objective, precise, scientific descriptions, or does he rely more on subjective, emotional descriptions? What effect does his style of description have on you?

8. Write a paragraph describing and explaining which senses, details, and images you would use to tell about a person or place that is important or sacred to you.

LEARNING FROM YOUR PEERS

The act of observing naturally makes us more aware of the day-to-day elements of the world around us. By looking intently at commonplace objects or people, we may begin to see patterns that we did not previously see. Writing about these patterns forces us to be even more keenly aware of our environment and the people around us. In response to this observation assignment, we are going to follow the writing process of a student named Alison Winthrop.

Alison's Writing Assignment: Observing

This is the topic Alison's instructor assigned:

Observe an event or activity that is familiar to you. Look at people and places you see every day, and describe them in an essay so that others can see them as fully and vividly as you do.

Alison goes through the process as outlined in Chapter 1: *thinking, planning, developing, organizing, drafting, revising,* and *editing.*

Thinking

Alison's class brainstorms for this assignment by writing on the board a list of possible places and activities. This is their list:

Eating lunch at the campus cafeteria

Jogging around the track

My family reading the Sunday newspaper

Children playing in the park

Having breakfast at Sam's Diner

Working a shift at the local fast-food franchise

Working at the car wash

Watching my brother wash and polish his beloved truck

Watching my sister watch videos with her girlfriends

Watching my son play in the sandbox

Going to the grocery store

Bagging orders of groceries for eight hours

Working the midnight shift at the convenience store

Working at the copy center

> Sitting in the library
>
> Being stalled in a traffic jam

Planning

That evening Alison starts freewriting on her computer. This is what she writes:

> My life is pretty boring. No reason to emphasize that now, is there? Let's see, what's the most interesting boring thing I do? Go to the mall. Who would want to admit that? Social life has been a drag lately—school and all.
>
> Well, what do I see when I go to the mall? I seem to have spent an extraordinary amount of money on cappuccino (extra whipped cream, please) lately. What possible reason do I have for sitting there and staring at people and pretending that I'm deep in thought?
>
> Could it be? Yes! I'm observing. That's what I'm doing. See, all this time I thought I was wasting my life, procrastinating, putting off work until a more convenient time. And here I was observing all the time. Whattya know!
>
> For instance, I remember that couple last Saturday. He with whipped cream and strawberries, she with granola and fruit chunks. People who shouldn't even try to develop a relationship. And then there was the couple going to the rock festival—he in baggy shorts, she in a black lace cocktail dress. Miscommunication? Let's imagine that conversation:
>
> He: I've been wanting to ask you out for a long time, and I finally got a pair of concert tickets for Saturday night.
>
> She: Oh, I'd be delighted to go to a concert with you.
>
> Hah! Little did they know. Maybe they are still together and laughing about it.

Developing

Alison looks over her notes the next day and thinks that she needs to open up her topic to more possibilities. She knows that she has several observations in her notebook from previous trips to the mall, but she does not want to give the impression that she spends her life sitting in the food court drinking cappuccino. She browses through notes that she has made in her writer's notebook over the last several months and realizes that she often watches people.

She also has notes about the people she observed at an outdoor concert series. These notes are very similar to the observations she made at the mall. She decides to ask her instructor if she can group these observations into one essay about people-watching—her favorite activity.

Her instructor tells her to recall as many observations as she can and then work on organizing her material to find out if she has enough for an essay. So Alison takes a few minutes to cluster ideas related to her topic and see where it takes her.

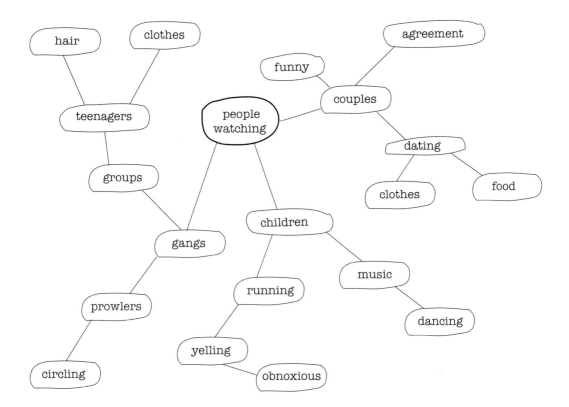

Organizing

Alison lists some people-watching categories on her computer and jots down some notes under each one. This is what her categories look like after she lists some ideas from her writer's notebook:

Mall trolling:

Teens on the prowl

People who like food better than other people

Kids mesmerized by decorations

Concerts in the park:

The trained dancers, showing off their skills

Mr. Jogging Shorts/Ms. Black Lace Cocktail Dress

Food people vs. beer people

Little people:

Natural-born musicians

Starry-eyed marvelers

Cute-as-a-button types

Kids who come off as brats because their parents try too hard to control them

Alison looks at her lists and decides that she can copy her descriptions from her writer's notebook onto the computer. She follows the categories she has just listed above, adding introductory material and transitions as she goes along. Since she is working on the computer, she does not have to plan the sequence in detail before she starts writing.

Drafting

Here is the essay that Alison wrote.

Alison's Essay: First Draft

Main Idea: I like watching people in crowds and imagining what they are thinking and doing during their days.

My favorite activity is watching people in crowds. I can spend an entire day looking at how people are dressed and watching the way they interact with each other. Outdoor concerts and street fairs are some of the best places to watch people without fear of being discovered. Another place that almost anyone can go to watch people is the local mall.

Couples of all ages are always fun to watch. I think I can always pick out the ones on a first date because they do not seem comfortable with each other. One may be dressed in a business suit; the other may be wearing jeans and an old T-shirt. Others have lived and shopped together so long that they look like bookends out for a stroll. At one outdoor concert that I attended recently, a man and woman who had obviously been taking dancing lessons were all dressed up, and as soon as the music started, they showed off their steps. Their obvious enjoyment of their new skills was appreciated by dozens of people. The crowd applauded them as heartily as they did the musicians. There was another couple who fell into the first-date category. She was dressed for a symphony concert in a black cocktail dress and high heels. Her hair was freshly styled, and her make-up was perfect. She even carried a sequined bag. He was dressed for the outdoor concert they were attending: running shoes, T-shirt, and baggy shorts. You could call him casual. It would be interesting to know if they ever had a second date.

At the concerts some people come for the beer, and some come for the food. The beer drinkers often bring their own coolers. Then they secretly drink one beer after another. However, no matter how secretive they are, their drinking begins to show because they begin to lose their coordination and look a little bleary-eyed after a while. The people who come for the food make a great ceremony of getting the perfect sandwich or the most delectable dessert. They can be quite obsessive, so they always stand out in a crowd. I was close enough recently to eavesdrop on a man and woman who were obviously on a first date. The woman asked the man some questions about his interests and hobbies, but the man didn't respond. He was unable to answer because his attention was completely focused on the sublime mountain of ice cream, whipped cream, and strawberries that was rapidly being transferred from his dish to his mouth. He kept saying, "You should really try some of this." He was a glutton. What do you think she did? She kept refusing and changing the subject while her fork fiddled with the small pile of granola and fruit chunks on her own plate. I suspect that that was their first and last date, but you never know.

I also like to watch children at these events. Running around and climbing and jumping and chasing each other, some of them just give me fits. Others really listen to the music and cannot resist swaying and dancing to the rhythms. At the mall some of them are amazed and wide-eyed with wonder at the seasonal decorations. Meanwhile, others whine and beg for all the latest offerings in consumer land. Some of their parents are tolerant, but others try so hard to control their children that they make themselves and everyone around them miserable.

Another common sight in these places is gangs of teenagers. I call them prowlers, and they deserve this name. You might expect to see variations in appearances, but they usually travel in same-sex groups that dress alike. There is almost always a group of teenage girls who have gone to great lengths to appear casual, coincidentally wearing the same makeup and hairstyles. There is a group of teenage boys who betray their interest in the girls by acting nonchalant and uninterested, their combs peeking out of the back pockets of their jeans. The two groups often circle the crowd in opposite directions so they can look for subtle signs of acceptance before anyone makes a move on the other group. Sometimes the boys and girls make contact; however, usually it's a standoff with no one making a move.

If I am feeling very brazen in these settings, I will take out a small notebook and a pen and write down my impressions of these people. They probably see me as an eccentric loner, but I plan to write a novel about my hometown one of these days. Perhaps I will include that adorable child with the red curly hair and the denim cap with the sunflower on it or that sulky-looking young woman with her arm in a cast. Perhaps she fell while she was having a fight with her boyfriend. Maybe she was trying to rescue the neighbor's cat from a tree, or maybe she has an incurable disease of the bone marrow. As you can see, I never get tired of watching people and trying to imagine what their lives are like. If they ever close the mall in my hometown, I will just have to drive until I find another one.

Revising

Alison has methodically completed a draft of her essay on crowds. When she goes to class the next day, Alison learns that the instructor wants the students to continue working on their introductions and believes they are ready to look at ways they can expand and vary the opening paragraphs of their essays. The instructor emphasizes how important it is for writers to catch their readers' attention and to introduce their topics as accurately as possible at the beginning of an essay. Alison now understands that a writer must go back to the introduction and make it fit the completed draft.

First, Alison reviews the Checklist for Writing Thesis Statements and Introductions at the beginning of the the Tips for Revising in this chapter. Then she reads the Tips for Revising and does the assigned exercises. Alison learns that most introductions can be made clearer and more interesting. In her own essay, for example, she thinks she can do a better job of introducing and narrowing her topic. Alison approaches her revision determined to develop her introduction as effectively as possible.

 ## COLLABORATIVE WORK

PEER GROUP ACTIVITY

After you read the portions of the Tips for Revising your instructor assigns, turn to Alison's first draft (pp. 72–75), and complete the following tasks in small groups:

A. Put a caret (^) at points in the introduction where you think Alison needs to furnish more interesting information.

B. Write out your suggestions for making her thesis statement more accurately represent the entire essay.

C. Put an X by the thesis if it is not the first or last sentence in the introduction.

Compare the marks your group recorded with those your instructor will show you. Where do your marks differ from your instructor's? What do you need to review before writing your own essay?

CLASS ACTIVITY

As an entire class, look at the underlined portions of Alison's revised draft (pp. 76–79) to see how she changed each sentence.

A. Did you identify the **revision** problems that Alison corrected?

B. Do you think her changes are good ones? Discuss her changes.

Editing

Now that Alison has rewritten her introduction, she needs to do some final editing and proofreading of her entire essay before handing it in. In class, the instructor explains that a working knowledge of basic sentence structure is a necessity for effective writing. Alison reads this chapter's Tips for Editing to learn about subjects, predicates, direct objects, and indirect objects as well as several types of sentences she can create. After she finishes the exercises her instructor has assigned, she sets out to apply this information to her own writing.

 ## COLLABORATIVE WORK

PEER GROUP ACTIVITY

After you read the portions of the Tips for Editing your instructor assigns, turn to Alison's first draft (pp. 72–75), and complete the following tasks in small groups:

A.   Label every subject S and every verb V. (For definitions, see pages 89 and 92.)

B.   Label each clause (or subject-verb set) as either independent, if it can stand alone, or dependent, if it is introduced by a relative pronoun or subordinating conjunction. (For definitions, see pp. 58 and 59.)

Compare the marks your group has recorded with those your instructor will show you. Where do your marks differ from your instructor's? What portions of the Tips for Editing do you need to review before writing your own essay?

CLASS ACTIVITY

As an entire class, look at the underlined portions of Alison's revised draft (pp. 76–79) to see how she changed each sentence.

A.   Did you identify the **editing** problems that Alison corrected?

B.   Do you think her changes are good ones? Discuss her changes.

Alison's Revised Essay

Crowds

My favorite activity is watching people in crowds. I can spend an

entire day looking at how people are dressed and watching the way they interact with each other. Outdoor concerts, ~~and~~ street fairs, and malls are some of the best places to watch people without fear of being discovered. ~~Another place that almost anyone can go to watch people is the local mall.~~ People-watching is a bit like searching for treasures in a secondhand store. One day a small child (about six years old) caught my eye, and I ended up following him and his mother through the entire mall. The stores they stopped in and the purchases they made gave me a lot of information about their personalities. I spend as much free time as possible people-watching, always looking for the most conspicuous characters, imagining what they are thinking and what their lives are like. Some of my best people-watching discoveries have been couples, concertgoers, children, and teenagers on the prowl.

Couples of all ages are always fun to watch. I think I can always pick out the ones on a first date because they do not seem comfortable with each other. One may be dressed in a business suit; the other may be wearing jeans and an old T-shirt. Others have lived and shopped together so long that they look like bookends out for a stroll. At one outdoor concert that I attended recently, a man and woman who had obviously been taking dancing lessons were all dressed up, and as soon as the music started, they showed off their steps. Their obvious enjoyment of their new skills was appreciated by dozens of people. The crowd applauded them as heartily as they did the musicians. There was another couple who fell into the first-date category. She was dressed for a symphony concert in a black cocktail dress and high heels. Her hair was freshly styled, and her make-up was perfect. She even carried a sequined bag. He was dressed for the outdoor concert they were attending: running shoes, T-shirt, and baggy shorts. You could call him casual. It would be interesting to know if they ever had a second date.

At the concerts some people come for the beer, and some come for the food. The beer drinkers often bring their own coolers. Then they secretly drink one beer after another. However, no matter how secretive they are, their drinking begins to show because they begin to lose their coordination and look a little bleary-eyed after a while. The people who come for the food make a great ceremony of getting the perfect sandwich or the most delectable dessert. They can be quite obsessive, so they always stand out in a crowd. I was close enough recently to eavesdrop on a man and woman who were obviously on a first date. The woman asked the man some questions about his interests and hobbies, but the man didn't respond. He was unable to answer because his attention was completely focused on the sublime mountain of ice cream, whipped cream, and strawberries that was rapidly being transferred from his dish to his mouth. He kept saying, "You should really try some of this." He was a glutton. What do you think she did? She kept refusing and changing the subject while her fork fiddled with the small pile of granola and fruit chunks on her own plate. I suspect that that was their first and last date, but you never know.

I also like to watch children at these events. Running around and climbing and jumping and chasing each other, some of them just give me fits. Others really listen to the music and cannot resist swaying and dancing to the rhythms. At the mall some of them are amazed and wide-eyed with wonder at the seasonal decorations. Meanwhile, others whine and beg for all the latest offerings in consumer land. Some of their parents are tolerant, but others try so hard to control their children that they make themselves and everyone around them miserable.

Another common sight in these places is gangs of teenagers. I call them prowlers, and they deserve this name. You might expect to see variations in appearances, but they usually travel in same-sex groups that dress alike. There is almost always a group of teenage girls who have gone to great lengths to appear casual, coincidentally wearing the same make-up and hairstyles. There is a group of teenage boys who betray their interest in the girls by acting nonchalant and uninterested, their combs peeking out of the back pockets of their jeans. The two groups often circle the crowd in opposite directions so they can look for subtle signs of acceptance before anyone makes a move on the other group. Sometimes the boys and girls make contact; however, usually it's a standoff with no one making a move.

If I am feeling very brazen in these settings, I will take out a small notebook and a pen and write down my impressions of these people. They probably see me as an eccentric loner, but I plan to write a novel about my hometown one of these days. Perhaps I will include that adorable child with the red curly hair and the denim cap with the sunflower on it or that sulky-looking young woman with her arm in a cast. Perhaps she fell while she was having a fight with her boyfriend. Maybe she was trying to rescue the neighbor's cat from a tree, or maybe she has an incurable disease of the bone marrow. As you can see, I never get tired of watching people and trying to imagine what their lives are like. If they ever close the mall in my hometown, I will just have to drive until I find another one.

WRITING YOUR OWN OBSERVING ESSAY

So far, you have seen a professional writer and a fellow student at work trying to communicate an observation or experience that was significant to them. As you read the published essay and followed the writing process of another student from first to final draft, you absorbed ideas and ways of giving those ideas a form of their own. These reading and writing activities have prepared you to write your own essay focusing on an observation that is meaningful to you.

What Have You Discovered?

Before you begin your own writing task, let's review what you have learned in this chapter so far:

- Good observers use all their senses: seeing, hearing, touching, smelling, and tasting.
- When you write an observation, you cannot simply *tell* your reader what you saw; you must *show* your reader.

- Your ultimate goal in writing an observing essay is to use your words to recreate your experience for your readers.

- You should have a dominant impression you want to communicate.

- You must choose details that best express your dominant impression.

- To present your observing effectively, you need to organize your ideas.

- To help you shape your essay, you should learn as much as possible about your readers.

- Before you write a draft, you need to decide on a point of view toward your subject.

- After you write a draft, you should revise your essay for meaning and organization.

- After you revise your essay, you should edit its grammar, usage, and sentence structure.

Your Writing Topic

Choose one of the following topics for your observing essay:

1.   In "The Way to Rainy Mountain," N. Scott Momaday provides a detailed, precise, vivid observation not only of his grandmother, but also of the place she lived and of the daily rituals she performed. Choose a person whom you know or remember well, and write an essay that provides a detailed explanation of the way that person looked, the place where that person lived, and the things that person did each day.

2.   Describe for your classmates a study environment that is ideal for you. What kind of surroundings make you thrive? What should the people you live with do while you study? Where do you study best? Why?

3.   A national travel magazine is asking for honest descriptions (positive or negative) of places people have visited. They are offering $100 to the writers of the essays chosen for publication. You may decide to write about a place with a marvelous beach or about a dreadful place where you were forced to live because of circumstances beyond your control. The mood of the essay will help determine its form, so find ways to reveal your feelings about the place you choose.

4. Create your own observing topic (with the assistance of your instructor), and write an essay in response to it.

After you have selected one of these topics, you should begin your writing process in the same way Alison did. (You may find rereading her experiences helpful in giving you ideas.) This time your purpose is to write your own observing essay. If some tasks occur out of order, that adjustment is probably part of your personal writing ritual. Follow your instincts, and let them mold your own writing process, but make sure you've worked through all the stages to your final draft.

YOUR WRITING PROCESS

THINKING   Generate as many ideas on your subject as you can in as many different ways as possible: rereading, listing, freewriting, brainstorming, clustering, discussing, and questioning.

PLANNING   Begin to give your ideas shape by deciding on your approach to your topic (your content, your purpose, your audience, and your point of view). Make a list of points you want to include in your essay.

DEVELOPING   Add more details on three or four specific, focused topics that you have chosen from your list of general points.

ORGANIZING   Organize your material in a way that will be most interesting to your audience.

DRAFTING   Write a working draft of your essay in complete sentences.

REVISING   Consulting the Tips for Revising in this chapter (pp. 82–88), revise your first draft—paying special attention to developing and focusing your introduction.

EDITING   Consulting the Tips for Editing in this chapter (pp. 89–110), edit your draft for grammar and correctness—paying special attention to your sentence structure.

Turn in your revised draft to your instructor.

Some Final Thoughts

When you have completed your own essay, answer these four questions in your journal:

1. What was most difficult about this assignment?
2. What was easiest?
3. What did I learn about observing by completing this assignment?
4. What did I learn about my own writing process from this assignment—how I prepared to write, how I wrote the first draft, how I revised, and how I edited?

Writing Thesis Statements and Introductions

Checklist for Writing Thesis Statements and Introductions

✓ Does the **introduction catch the readers' attention** by using descriptions, stories, statistics, facts, definitions, or comparisons?

✓ Does the **thesis state the controlling idea** for the entire essay?

✓ Does the **thesis statement give the essay focus and direction**?

✓ Is the **thesis statement** as **complete** as it can be?

✓ Does the **thesis** appear as the **first or last sentence** in the first paragraph of the essay?

Have you ever visited a famous landmark, like the Empire State Building in New York City, that has telescopes mounted for observers? You decide you would like a closer view of the city below you. So you put your quarter in the instrument, and it begins to buzz. When you first look through the eyepiece, all you see is a blur. But when you carefully turn the knob marked "Focus," suddenly downtown Manhattan leaps into view. If it is winter, you can even see the frosty breath of scurrying pedestrians. Just as you become really intrigued with looking at things from this new perspective, the buzzing stops and the eyepiece goes dark.

Oddly enough, introductory paragraphs and thesis statements in essays work like high-powered telescopes. They offer your readers an enhanced perspective on your topic. Like tourists gazing at the streets below, readers need a way to focus on your main idea and understand your perspective at the same time. Without a clear introduction to your topic and a focused statement of purpose in your essay, your readers (like observers on the Empire State Building who have no quarters) will be in the dark about your essay's purpose.

Finding Your Focus

Your assignments throughout college are most often broad topics. To compose a good essay, you need to narrow a broad topic to an idea that you can explain within a limited number of pages. Your **thesis statement** is what provides the final limitations for your essay. Since your thesis statement presents your controlling idea for the entire essay, one good way to begin your first draft is to write a sentence that clearly states your idea and your position on your topic. Even though your thesis statement may change several times before your essay is finished, making this statement and taking a position is a good exercise for you. It will help you move from the broad subject of your assignment to your own perspective on the topic. Turning your thesis statement into a question that you will answer in the rest of your essay is also a good exercise to help you keep your focus throughout your essay.

In the title of his essay at the beginning of this chapter, "The Way to Rainy

Mountain," N. Scott Momaday suggests that he is going to talk about a path to Rainy Mountain. This is a broad topic with little to distinguish it. But Momaday uses his introduction to narrow his topic and settle on a focus in his thesis statement (boldfaced here):

> A single knoll rises out of the plain in Oklahoma, north and west of the Wichita Range. For my people, the Kiowas, it is an old landmark, and they gave it the name Rainy Mountain. The hardest weather in the world is here. Winter brings blizzards, hot tornadic winds arise in the spring, and in summer the prairie is an anvil's edge. The grass turns brittle and brown, and it cracks beneath your feet. There are green belts along the rivers and creeks, linear groves of hickory and pecan, willow, and witch hazel. At a distance in July or August the steaming foliage seems almost to writhe in fire. Great green and yellow grasshoppers are everywhere in the tall grass, popping up like corn to sting the flesh, and tortoises crawl about on the red earth, going nowhere in the plenty of time. Loneliness is an aspect of the land. All things in the plain are isolate; there is no confusion of objects in the eye, but *one* hill or *one* tree or *one* man. To look upon that landscape in the early morning, with the sun at your back, is to lose the sense of proportion. **Your imagination comes to life, and this, you think, is where Creation was begun.**

This first paragraph introduces Momaday's readers to Rainy Mountain in general terms and presents his dominant impression of this place—"where Creation was begun." Momaday's thesis appears at the end of his introductory paragraph: "Your imagination comes to life, and this, you think, is where Creation was begun." From this statement, we learn that the author will focus on various beginnings in his life.

In reviewing the assignment for her essay, Alison Winthrop decided that the topic "Crowds" would be too broad to handle in six to eight paragraphs, the average length of the essays in her composition class. Since Alison couldn't possibly cover all crowds everywhere in 500 to 700 words, she needed to find a more specific focus for her essay. She started reworking her first paragraph:

First Revision: My favorite activity is watching people in crowds. I can spend an entire day looking at how people are dressed and watching the way they interact with each other. Outdoor concerts, street fairs, and malls are some of the best places to watch people without fear of being discovered. ~~Another place that almost anyone can go to watch people is the local mall.~~ **People-watching is a bit like searching for treasures in a secondhand store. One day a small child (about six years old) caught my eye, and**

> **I ended up following him and his mother through the entire mall. The stores they stopped in and the purchases they made gave me a lot of information about their personalities.**

As she looked at her introduction again, she realized that she did not include a clear thesis that limits her subject and states her purpose. So she revised again and rewrote her thesis to define her topic more clearly:

Thesis: **I spend as much free time as possible people-watching, always looking for the most conspicuous characters, imagining what they are thinking and what their lives are like.**

As Alison studied her draft, she decided that even though her revised statement revealed her purpose, it didn't serve the other major function of a thesis statement, which is to limit her topic. As she looked back over her notes, Alison discovered that all the people she had described stood out from the rest of the crowd in some way. Finally, Alison rewrote her thesis so that it stated her purpose and focused on a specific topic:

Revised Thesis: **I spend as much free time as possible people-watching, always looking for the most conspicuous characters, imagining what they are thinking and what their lives are like. Some of my best people-watching discoveries have been couples, concertgoers, children, and teenagers on the prowl.**

After this revision, which she placed at the end of her introductory paragraph. Alison's focus was clear. Her essay would be limited to "conspicuous characters" of four types: couples, concertgoers, children, and teenagers on the prowl.

Exercise R3-1

Write an alternative thesis statement for N. Scott Momaday's "The Way to Rainy Mountain" (pp. 64–68).

Exercise R3-2

Write an alternative thesis statement for Alison's first draft (pp. 72–75).

Exercise R3-3

Read the following sentences, and decide which ones would make good thesis statements for the topic provided. Write a new thesis statement for any that you think are too broad.

1. *Pets:* For many reasons, cats make better pets for apartment dwellers than dogs do.
2. *Education:* Everyone needs a good education.
3. *Gun control:* Carefully observed gun control laws that require licensing for weapon owners will prevent many tragic deaths caused by young people who do not observe safety rules or cannot control their tempers and find guns easy to obtain.
4. *Television:* Parents are finding it harder and harder to limit the violence and smut that comes into their home via their TV sets; therefore, the new V chip that allows them to block unsuitable programs is a valuable tool for them.
5. *Television:* A strictly observed rating system for TV shows like the one used for movies will make the V chip unnecessary.

Exercise R3-4

Read the following introductory paragraph, and compose a thesis statement for it.

Solving Problems for Working Students

   As our society changes, more and more students must have part-time or full-time jobs. These students often find their stress levels rising as a result of too much to do and too little time in which to do it. Tragically, many of them give up on furthering their education when some careful thinking and scheduling could have prevented their dropping out.

Introducing Your Topic

Experienced writers know the importance of catching their audience's attention at the beginning of an essay. For example, N. Scott Momaday begins his essay (p. 64) with a detailed description of Rainy Mountain. We learn about his tribe and about the location of the mountain, its weather, its terrain, its wildlife, and its relationship to human beings.

   Another strategy that writers sometimes use to begin their essays is a brief story. In Chapter 7 of this book, Nancy Mairs begins her analyzing essay with a story:

> The other day I was thinking of writing an essay on being a cripple. I was thinking hard in one of the stalls of the women's room in my office building, as I was shoving my shirt into my jeans and tugging up my zipper. Preoccupied, I flushed, picked up my book bag, took my cane down from the hook, and unlatched the door. So many movements unbalanced me, and as I pulled the door open I fell over backward, landing fully

clothed on the toilet seat with my legs splayed in front of me: the old beetle-on-its-back routine. Saturday afternoon, the building deserted, I was free to laugh aloud as I wriggled back to my feet, my voice bouncing off the yellowish tiles from all directions. Had anyone been there with me, I'd have been still and faint and hot with chagrin. I decided that it was high time to write the essay.

Mairs catches her audience's attention by giving background information that leads naturally to her purpose for writing.

Still another strategy that works well for introducing certain topics is offering various interesting facts, statistics, or definitions to catch the readers' attention. In Chapter 8, Sara Nelson opens her persuasive essay with some interesting facts about safe sex:

Now, more than ten years into the AIDS epidemic, it seems that smart women are making foolish choices when it comes to AIDS prevention. "I always use condoms the first time with someone new," says one woman. "Sure, I keep condoms in the bedside drawer," says another, as if their mere presence is all that's required. A recent study confirms this dangerous dichotomy: *Knowing about safer sex and practicing it are all too often separate matters.* In a survey of 5,500 Canadian college students, researchers found that, despite high levels of AIDS awareness, fewer than 16 percent of the women studied said they always have their partner use condoms. Another study revealed that only one-fifth of the sexually active students at the University of Florida always use condoms during intercourse. More encouraging is a study suggesting that condom use among college students at one university increased from 12 percent in 1975 to 41 percent in 1989. Though that's a notable, heartening leap, it isn't the whole picture; a survey conducted during the 1988–1989 school year found that two in 1000 college students tested positive for HIV. A follow-up study conducted one year later showed similar results.

One other approach that helps writers get their readers' attention in the introduction is an interesting comparison or analogy. Chapter 6 includes an essay titled "The Financial Payoff of Higher Education for Women" that uses this strategy:

Nationwide, women have a median income that is 52 percent of the median income of men. Some observers believe this huge income gap is not a cause for concern. They point out that a major reason for this discrepancy is child-rearing activities. Women are much more unlikely to be steady participants in the work force and thus, not surprisingly, they have a much lower median income.

The author first compares the median income of men and women, then discusses the discrepancy and the reasons for it. This introduction focuses the audience's attention on inequities in wages between men and women and invites further exploration of the subject.

As Alison looked back over her first draft and her checklist for writing introductions, she decided that she could use a combination of these methods. The thesis statement she added is underlined in her revision.

First Draft: My favorite activity is watching people in crowds. I can spend an entire day looking at how people are dressed and watching the way they interact with each other. Outdoor concerts and street fairs are some of the best places to watch people without fear of being discovered. Another place that almost anyone can go to watch people is the local mall.

Revision: My favorite activity is watching people in crowds. I can spend an entire day looking at how people are dressed and watching the way they interact with each other. Outdoor concerts, street fairs, and malls are some of the best places to watch people without fear of being discovered. ~~Another place that almost anyone can go to watch people is the local mall.~~ **People-watching is a bit like searching for treasures in a secondhand store. One day a small child (about six years old) caught my eye, and I ended up following him and his mother through the entire mall. The stores they stopped in and the purchases they made gave me a lot of information about their**

Thesis Statement: **personalities.** <u>I spend as much free time as possible people-watching, always looking for the most conspicuous characters, imagining what they are thinking and what their lives are like.</u> Some of my best people-watching discoveries have been couples, concertgoers, children, and teenagers on the prowl.

Alison's revision is informative and very interesting. In her introduction of her topic (people-watching), she gives the readers some background information, compares people-watching to searching for treasures, and tells a brief story about one of her people-watching expeditions.

Exercise R3-5

In your opinion, what is most effective about the introductory paragraph of N. Scott Momaday's "The Way to Rainy Mountain" (p. 64)? Explain your answer.

Exercise R3-6

Rewrite Alison's introductory paragraph (p. 72) using at least one of the methods explained in this chapter.

Exercise R3-7

Using chapters from your textbooks for other classes, find examples of four different methods of introducing a topic. Photocopy and label them.

Exercise R3-8

Using a recent newspaper or magazine, find examples of four different methods of introducing topics, and share them with your classmates.

 ## COLLABORATIVE WORK

After writing a draft of your own observing essay, exchange papers with a classmate, and do the following tasks:

A. After reading the essay, do you think its purpose and focus are clearly stated in the thesis? If not, suggest revisions.

B. Make sure the thesis statement is either the first or last sentence in the introductory paragraph.

C. Decide whether the introduction to the essay effectively catches your attention. If it doesn't, suggest revisions.

D. Does the introduction leave any questions in your mind? If so, note them in the margin.

Then return the paper to its writer, and use the information in this section to revise your draft.

Sentence Structure and Sentence Combining

Checklist for Editing Sentences

✓ Does each sentence have a **complete subject** and a **complete predicate**?

✓ Does each complete subject have a **simple subject**?

✓ Does each complete predicate have a **simple predicate**?

✓ Does the writing use a variety of the following **sentence patterns**: subject-verb, subject–verb–direct object, subject–verb–indirect object–direct object, subject-verb-direct object–object complement, subject–verb–subject complement?

✓ Does the writing use a variety of **sentence structures**: simple, compound, complex, compound-complex?

In Chapter 2, you learned about words, phrases, and clauses. In this chapter you will learn how these components work together to form a **sentence**, a collection of words containing at least one independent clause. Writing essays depends on many activities, including brainstorming for ideas, choosing a thesis, organizing your thoughts, and crafting the introduction, body, and conclusion. But one thing is certain: You cannot write a paper without composing sentences. Because sentences are truly the foundation of essays, learning about sentence parts and basic patterns will help you make your prose flow smoothly and engage your readers.

Subjects

Every sentence must have a **subject,** a word or group of words that tells what the sentence is about. The subject identifies *who* or *what* exists or is performing an action. Individual nouns and pronouns serve as subjects, along with phrases and clauses composed of nouns, pronouns, and their modifiers.

The **simple subject** is the single word that answers the question *who* or *what* about the verb. Look at the first sentence of the first draft of Alison's observing essay:

Simple Subject: My favorite **activity** is watching people in crowds. (*What is? Activity is.*)

The **complete subject** is the simple subject plus all of its modifiers:

Complete Subject: **My favorite** *activity* is watching people in crowds.

89

If the simple subject has no modifiers, then the simple subject and the complete subject are one and the same, as in the second sentence of Alison's first draft:

Simple/   **I** can spend an entire day looking at how people are
Complete Subject:
dressed and watching the way they interact with each

other.

A sentence may have more than one subject. We call these subjects **compound.** Look at the third sentence in paragraph 1 of Alison's first draft. (The simple subjects are italicized.)

Compound Subjects: Outdoor *concerts* and **street** *fairs* are some of the best

places to watch people without fear of being discovered.

Of course, a sentence may have more than two subjects. These compound subjects often depend on coordinating and correlative conjunctions, as the following examples illustrate:

Compound Subjects: *Writing* **essays**, *studying* **for tests**, and *working* **at**

McDonald's take up most of Alison's time.

Alison and *Amanda* plan on going to graduate school.

Hard-to-Find Subjects

Subjects usually come before their verbs. In some instances, however, the subject may come after the verb. The subject may appear to be buried when expletives, questions, and inverted sentences are used.

In grammatical terms, an **expletive** is a word that begins a sentence and has no grammatical function. The two common expletives are *it* and *there*, which are usually followed by a form of *be* and the subject of the sentence. Look at these sentences from Alison's first draft:

Expletives: **It** would be interesting to know if they ever had a second

date.

There was another couple who fell into the first-date

category.

To find the subject, simply ask *who* or *what* about the verb. (*What is? To know is. Who was? Couple was.*) Then you can rearrange the sentences and put the subject first:

Rearranged: *To know* **if they ever had a second date** would be

interesting.

Another *couple* fell into the first-date category.

When you try to find the subject in a question, simply put the question in statement form:

Question:	What did Alison think of the latest Brad Pitt movie?
Statement:	**Alison** did think what of the latest Brad Pitt movie.
Question:	When is the next psychology test?
Statement:	**The next psychology *test*** is when.

Subjects and verbs can be inverted in a few other circumstances. To find the subject and verb for yourself, you might have to rearrange these sentences:

Inverted Sentence:	Here sat a stack of mail that held my acceptance letter.
Rearranged:	**A *stack* of mail that held my acceptance letter** sat here.
Inverted Sentence:	Under the last desk in the first row sat Alison's notebook.
Rearranged:	**Alison's *notebook*** sat under the last desk in the first row.

Exercise E3-1

List the complete subjects in paragraphs 5 and 6 of "The Way to Rainy Mountain" by N. Scott Momaday (pp. 65–66). Then underline each simple subject.

Exercise E3-2

List the complete subjects in each sentence in paragraph 3 of Alison's revised observing essay (p. 77–78). Then underline each simple subject.

Exercise E3-3

Fill in each blank with a complete subject to finish the sentence. Then underline each simple subject.

(1) _____ is the most frustrating class I have. There

are (2) _____ that try my patience. First of all,

(3) _____ gives entirely too much work. Sometimes

(4) _____ will complain, but that doesn't seem to help a bit.

And (5) _____ that he gives is usually too difficult.

(6) _____ tries to help me, but sometimes it just doesn't sink

in. (7) _____ and _____ sometimes

help, but not always. (8) _____ is pretty irritating, too.

Sometimes it's hard to understand him. I have to strain my ears or try to get

TIPS FOR EDITING

there early to get a front-row seat. (9) _____ has already

dropped the class, but I need this course before I can go on in my major.

(10) _____ suggested that I hire a tutor. I would if I could afford

one.

Exercise E3-4

Write ten sentences: two sentences with one subject each, two sentences with compound subjects, two sentences that begin with expletives, two questions, and two inverted sentences. Then circle the complete subjects and underline the simple subjects in each sentence.

Predicates

Subjects cannot function without **predicates,** words that tell what the subject is doing in the sentence. Predicates can refer to an action or a state of being. The **simple predicate** is the main verb plus any helping verbs, as the first two sentences from Alison's first draft illustrate:

> v
> **Simple Predicates:** My favorite activity **is** watching people in crowds.
>
> v   v
> I **can spend** an entire day looking at how people are
>
> dressed and watching the way they interact with each
>
> other.

The **complete predicate** is the simple predicate plus all the words that complete the predicate's meaning. These modifiers may include adjectives, adverbs, objects, and different types of phrases and clauses. Look again at the first two sentences from Alison's first draft:

> P
> **Complete Predicates:** My favorite activity **is watching people in crowds**.
>
> P
> I **can spend an entire day looking at how people are**
>
> **dressed and watching the way they interact with each**
>
> **other**.

Like subjects, predicates can also appear in **compound** form, that is, two or more predicates in the same sentence. Again, look for coordinating and correlative conjunctions, as in the following examples. (The simple predicates are italicized.)

	P	P
Compound Predicates:	Alison *got* up early this morning, *crammed* for a	

$$P$$

sociology test, and then *cleaned* the kitchen.

$$P \qquad\qquad P$$

Alison either *went* shopping or *took* a nap.

In statements that begin with expletives, you may have to look closely to identify the predicate. The best strategy is to rearrange the sentence, eliminating the expletive and placing the subject before the predicate:

Expletive: **There** are many people hoping to get off welfare.

$$P$$

Rearranged: Many people *are hoping* to get off welfare.

Identifying the predicate in a question is a much simpler task if you restate the question in sentence form:

Question: What did the manager of the store say to Alison?

$$P$$

Rearranged: The manager of the store *did say* what to Alison.

Exercise E3-5

List the complete predicates in the following sentences from N. Scott Momaday's essay "The Way to Rainy Mountain." Then underline the simple predicates.

1. A single knoll rises out of the plain in Oklahoma, north and west of the Wichita Range.
2. At a distance in July or August the steaming foliage seems almost to writhe in fire.
3. For more than a hundred years they had controlled the open range from the Smoky Hill River to the Red, from the headwaters of the Canadian to the fork of the Arkansas and Cimarron.
4. Her forbears came down from the high country in western Montana nearly three centuries ago.
5. Her long, black hair, always drawn and braided in the day, lay upon her shoulders and against her breasts like a shawl.

Exercise E3-6

Identify the complete predicates in paragraph 3 of Alison's revised essay (pp. 77–78), and then underline the simple predicates.

Exercise E3-7

Complete the following paragraph by supplying a predicate in each blank.

The debate concerning violence in television and the movies

(1) _____ . People who make movies and TV

shows (2) _____ . Then you have concerned

viewers, particularly parents. They (3) _____ .

What's the answer? Some parents (4) _____ .

But sex and violence (5) _____ . For

example, some of the biggest movie moneymakers of last year

(6) _____ . Usually some of the TV shows with

the highest ratings (7) _____ . I think people in

general are just curious. They (8) _____ . I think

people should (9) _____ . And where children

are concerned, parents should (10) _____ .

Exercise E3-8

Write sentences using the following predicates.

1. was standing at the bus stop.
2. fell on top of my mother's car
3. will be gone tomorrow
4. should have been questioned
5. counted to ten under her breath

Basic Sentence Patterns

Most sentences appear in what we call *natural order*—that is, the subject comes first, then the verb. Of course, natural order can vary, depending on what type of verb is used in the sentence. The simplest pattern is subject-verb; other variations include subject–verb–direct object, subject–verb–indirect object–direct object, subject–verb–direct object–object complement, and subject–verb–subject complement.

Subject-Verb (S-V)

The basic pattern is composed of just two words—a subject and a verb:

      S   **V**
    Alison ran.

S   V
Alison tried.

Neither of the verbs, *ran* or *tried*, has an object. When sentences appear in the subject-verb pattern, the verb is intransitive because an object does not follow the verb. (See p. 39 for more information on intransitive verbs.)

Subject–Verb–Direct Object (S-V-DO)

As you learned in Chapter 2, transitive verbs require a receiver of their action, a **direct object.** These nouns and pronouns complete the verb's meaning. Look at the following sentence from the first draft of Alison's observing essay:

                                    S   V   DO

Direct Object: The beer drinkers often bring **their own coolers**.

What do the beer drinkers bring? They bring *their own coolers*. The sentence would not make sense if Alison stopped after the verb (*The beer drinkers often bring*). Thus, the subject–transitive verb pattern requires a direct object to complete the sentence's thought.

Direct objects may also be compound. We could easily add another direct object to the previous example (The beer drinkers often bring their own *coolers* and *mugs*).

Noun phrases and noun clauses may also function as direct objects. Just look carefully at sentences, and ask the question *what* after the verb. If you can answer that question, you have found a direct object:

                              S   V

Direct Objects: Alison likes **jogging around the indoor track** more than

                              S   V

                    she likes **using the stair-stepper**.

                              S   V

Direct Object: Alison wants **to study in Europe next fall**.

                              S   V

Direct Object: Alison knew **that she had made an A on the test**.

Subject–Verb–Indirect Object–Direct Object (S-V-IO-DO)

In some sentences, the receiver of the action—the direct object—is given to someone or something. We call this secondary receiver an **indirect object,** a noun or pronoun that *indirectly* receives the action of a transitive verb. Look at this sentence from paragraph 3 of Alison's first draft:

                              S   V   IO   DO

Indirect Object: The woman asked the *man* some **questions** about his

                    interests and hobbies, but the man didn't respond.

What did the woman ask? She asked *questions* (direct object). *Of whom* did she ask questions? She asked questions *of the man;* thus, the indirect object is *man*. Notice that you can insert words like *to, of,* or *for* before the indirect object, making a prepositional phrase that tells to whom, to what, for whom, or for what something is done. Here are some verbs that often take indirect objects: *allow, ask, assign, award, bring, buy, cash, deny, do, find, get, give, leave, lend, make, pay, promise, refuse, sell, send, show, teach, tell, throw,* and *write.*

Just as they can function as direct objects, noun phrases and clauses can serve as indirect objects:

	S	V	IO
Indirect Objects:	Alison's friend Amanda	gave	*partying at local nightclubs*

DO
priority.

	S	V	IO
	Alison's mom	gave	*whoever was standing at the door* the

DO
boot!

Subject–Verb–Direct Object–Object Complement (S-V-DO-OC)

Direct objects are sometimes followed by words that rename, identify, or describe them. These words—**object complements**—are nouns, adjectives, or groups of words that complete the direct object's meaning:

	S	V	DO	OC
Object Complement:	The club president	named	**Alison**	*treasurer*.

	S	V	DO	OC
Object Complement:	Alison	considered	**Veronica**	*trustworthy*.

	S	V	DO	OC
Object Complement:	The investigation	found	the **dean**	*responsible for the*

college's debts.

Sometimes the words *to be* or *as* appear between the direct object and the object complement:

	S	V	DO	OC
Object Complement:	Alison	chose	**Andy**	to be her *date* for the holiday party.

	S	V	DO	
Object Complement:	The freshman class	elected	**Alison**	as student

OC
representative.

Subject–Verb–Subject Complement (S-V-SC)

Just as direct objects, indirect objects, and object complements follow action verbs, subject complements follow linking verbs. A **subject complement** is a noun, pronoun, or adjective that comes after a linking (or state-of-being) verb and renames, identifies, or describes the object. These words are usually nouns (or noun phrases and noun clauses) that rename the subject or adjectives that describe the subject.

Look at this sentence from paragraph 3 of Alison's first draft:

	S V SC
Subject Complement:	**He** was a *glutton*.

Here are some other examples:

	S V SC
Subject Complement:	Alison's favorite **hobby** is *fun for everyone*.

	S V SC
Subject Complement:	They can be quite *obsessive*.

	S V SC
Subject Complement:	My **destiny** is *whatever I want it to be*.

Like any other sentence parts, subject complements can be compound as well:

	S V SC SC
Compound Subject Complements:	**Andrew** was Alison's *confidant* and *mentor*.

	S V SC SC
Compound Subject Complements:	**Alison** appeared *upset* and *withdrawn* yesterday.

Exercise E3-9

Label the basic pattern of each clause of the following sentences from "The Way to Rainy Mountain."

1. For more than a hundred years they had controlled the open range from the Smoky Hill River to the Red, from the headwaters of the Canadian to the fork of the Arkansas and Cimarron.
2. From one point of view, their migration was the fruit of an old prophecy, for indeed they emerged from a sunless world.

3. Although my grandmother lived out her long life in the shadow of Rainy Mountain, the immense landscape of the continental interior lay like memory in her blood.
4. The skyline in all directions is close at hand, the high wall of the woods and deep cleavages of shade.
5. She was about seven when the last Kiowa Sun Dance was held in 1887 on the Washita River above Rainy Mountain Creek.

Exercise E3-10

Label the basic patterns of the following sentences taken from the first draft of Alison's observing essay.

1. My favorite activity is watching people in crowds.
2. Outdoor concerts and street fairs are some of the best places to watch people without fear of being discovered.
3. Their obvious enjoyment of their new skills was appreciated by dozens of people.
4. You could call him casual.
5. At the mall some of them are amazed and wide-eyed with wonder at the seasonal decorations.

Exercise E3-11

Fill in each blank with a word that will complete the sentence. Then identify each sentence's basic pattern.

When I was ten years old, my mother and father (1) _____ (intransitive verb). We all experienced great (2) _____ (noun). My (3) _____ (noun) and I saw them fighting with each other and tearing apart our lives. Of course, Mom and Dad's situation was (4) _____ (adjective) and extremely depressing. Mom would tell me a (5) _____ (noun) or two to try to get my mind off their fighting. Their arguments even made my sister (6) _____ (adjective). She would sometimes lie in bed and (7) _____ (action verb) under the covers, not moving at all for hours on end. With Dad gone, Mom dealt with her new life (8) _____ (adverbial complement). Dad (9) _____ (intransitive verb) to explain during our visits with him. We were just (10) _____ (noun), foolishly thinking Mom and Dad would always be together.

Exercise E3-12

Write sentences using the following patterns.

1. S-V-IO-DO
2. S-V-DO
3. S-V-SC (noun)
4. S-V-SC (adjective)
5. S-V-DO-OC

Sentence Combining

The basic sentence patterns (explained above) provide a model for crafting sentences with all the necessary components needed for expressing a complete thought in a single clause. Using only these basic patterns, however, will make your writing monotonous. Of course, questions and expletives will alter the subject-verb order, as you have learned. But varying your sentences—especially by moving the subject and verb to different positions—takes concentrated effort. Your writing tasks will become easier when you learn more about the four sentence structures: *simple, compound, complex,* and *compound-complex.*

Simple Sentences

Sentences can be classified according to the type and number of dependent and independent clauses they contain. A **simple sentence** contains one independent clause, that is, one subject-predicate pair. Look at these sentences from Alison's first draft:

Simple Sentences:

                               S   V   V

My favorite **activity is watching** people in crowds.

  S   V

He was a glutton.

  S   V   V

You could call him casual.

Notice that the subject and verb appear at the beginning of each simple sentence in the preceding examples. There's nothing wrong with this structure, as long as the majority of the sentences around them do not also begin with a subject and verb.

To combine short simple sentences and to move the subject and verb to different locations within a sentence, you can use these strategies:

TIPS FOR EDITING

1. Combine subjects and verbs.

Separate Sentences:	**S** **V** **Alison** decided to drop out this semester and work full time.
	S **V** Her boyfriend **Cary** decided not to go to school this semester for the same reason.
Combination:	**S** **S** **V** **Alison** and her boyfriend **Cary** decided to drop out this semester and work full time.
Separate Sentences:	**S** **V** Alison **talks** to me every day.
	S **V** She usually **gives** me a compliment too.
Combination:	**S** **V** **V** Alison **talks** to me every day and usually **gives** me a compliment.

2. Combine simple sentences using prepositional phrases.

Separate Sentences:	**S** **V** Alison plans to transfer to Utah State.
	S **V** She wants to transfer after the fall semester.
Combinations:	**S** **V** Alison plans to transfer to Utah State **after the fall semester**.
	S **V** **After the fall semester**, Alison plans to transfer to Utah State.

3. Combine simple sentences using nouns and pronouns (plus their modifiers) that rename other nouns or pronouns.

Separate Sentences:	**S** **V** Alison met Yuri at the Student Center.
	S **V** He's a lawyer.
Combination:	**S** **V** Alison met Yuri, **a lawyer**, at the Student Center.

Separate Sentences: Tennessee Williams was born in Mississippi and later moved with his family to St. Louis.

He was a Pulitzer Prize–winning playwright.

Combinations: Tennessee Williams, **a Pulitzer Prize–winning playwright**, was born in Mississippi and later moved to St. Louis.

A Pulitzer Prize-winning playwright, Tennessee Williams was born in Mississippi and later moved to St. Louis.

4. Combine simple sentences using participles and participial phrases.

Separate Sentences: Alison was fidgeting at her desk.

She was trying to remember the correct equation for the last problem on the chemistry test.

Combinations: Alison was fidgeting at her desk, **trying to remember the correct equation for the last problem on the chemistry test**.

Trying to remember the correct equation for the last problem on the chemistry test, Alison was fidgeting at her desk.

Fidgeting at her desk, Alison was trying to remember the correct equation for the last problem on the chemistry test.

Alison, **fidgeting at her desk**, was trying to remember the correct equation for the last problem on the chemistry test.

5. Combine simple sentences using absolute phrases. An **absolute phrase** is usually composed of a noun and a participle; it has no grammatical function.

	s v
Separate Sentences:	The distraught woman pleaded for her son's safe return.
	s v v
	Her voice was quavering with emotion.
	s v
Combination:	The distraught woman pleaded for her son's safe return, **her voice quavering with emotion**.
	s v
Separate Sentences:	Alison walked into the room.
	s v
	Her shoulders were slumped.
	s v v
	Her head was hanging low.
	s v
Combination:	Alison walked into the room, **shoulders slumped and head hanging low**.

Exercise E3-13

Underline the simple sentences in the first two paragraphs of "The Way to Rainy Mountain" (p. 64).

Exercise E3-14

Underline the simple sentences in Alison's first draft on p. 72–75.

Exercise E3-15

Read the following paragraphs, and combine the specified sentences using the strategy indicated.

(1) People are often procrastinators. (2) For example, my brother never pays his bills on time. (3) He just throws the bills on his desk. (4) They pile up to the ceiling. (5) Credit card companies call quite often. (6) Bill collectors constantly ask, "May I speak to Jeremy Richards?" (7) He probably inherited his procrastination. (8) Our mother is the same way. (9) Our mom is just involved in too many activities. (10) She is a very smart woman. (11) I guess you could say she's spread too thin. (12) She has two jobs and a family to care for.

(13) I read a magazine article about how to get things done. (14) It was in *Cosmopolitan*. (15) The author advised people to keep lists. (16) Prioritizing is ranking items on the list in an order of importance.

1. Combine sentences 3 and 4 using a participial phrase.
2. Combine the subjects and the verbs in sentences 5 and 6.
3. Combine sentences 9 and 10 using a noun phrase.

4. Combine sentences 13 and 14 using a prepositional phrase.
5. Combine sentences 15 and 16 using a participial phrase.

Exercise E3-16

Using the strategies discussed in this chapter, combine the simple sentences that you identified in Exercise E3-14 with other sentences in Alison's essay.

Compound Sentences

You can think of a compound sentence as two simple sentences that work together. Actually, a **compound sentence** is composed of two independent clauses, usually joined by a semicolon or a coordinating conjunction. Look at these examples from Alison's first draft:

Compound Sentences:

Independent	Independent

S   V   V   V   S   V   V
One may be dressed in a business suit; the other may be

V
wearing jeans and an old T-shirt.

Independent	Independent

S V   V   S   V
Her hair was freshly styled, and her make-up was perfect.

In compound sentences, both clauses are of equal importance and can stand alone as complete sentences. However, because the thoughts expressed in the two independent clauses are logically and closely related, writers can put these clauses together using one of these four combining strategies:

1. Use a semicolon when the clauses are similar in structure and length.

Separate Sentences:

S   S   V
Alison and her family moved seven times during her childhood.

S   V
These constant upheavals kept her from making lasting friendships.

Combination:

Independent

S   S   V
Alison and her family moved seven times during her

Independent

S   V
childhood; these constant upheavals kept her from making

lasting friendships.

2. Use a coordinating conjunction—*for, and, nor, but, or, yet, so.* Note that a comma precedes the coordinating conjunction in the combined sentence.

Separate Sentences:	$\overset{\text{S}}{\text{Alison}}$ $\overset{\text{V}}{\text{likes}}$ to observe individuals in crowds.
	$\overset{\text{S}}{\text{She}}$ $\overset{\text{V}}{\text{wrote}}$ an essay about her people-watching pastime.

Combination:	<u>────────── Independent ──────────</u> <u>── Independent ──</u> $\overset{\text{S}}{\text{Alison}}$ $\overset{\text{V}}{\text{likes}}$ to observe individuals in crowds**, and** $\overset{\text{S}}{\text{she}}$ $\overset{\text{V}}{\text{wrote}}$ wrote an essay about her people-watching pastime.

3. Use correlative conjunctions such as *either . . . or, neither . . . nor,* and *not only . . . but also.*

Separate Sentences:	$\overset{\text{S}}{\text{Alison}}$ $\overset{\text{V}}{\text{may}}$ $\overset{\text{V}}{\text{turn}}$ in her job application today.
	$\overset{\text{S}}{\text{She}}$ $\overset{\text{V}}{\text{may}}$ $\overset{\text{V}}{\text{wait}}$ until tomorrow after her last class.

Combination:	<u>────────── Independent ──────────</u> ── **Either** $\overset{\text{S}}{\text{Alison}}$ $\overset{\text{V}}{\text{will}}$ $\overset{\text{V}}{\text{turn}}$ in her job application today**, or** <u>────────── Independent ──────────</u> $\overset{\text{S}}{\text{she}}$ $\overset{\text{V}}{\text{will}}$ $\overset{\text{V}}{\text{wait}}$ until tomorrow after her last class.

4. Use conjunctive adverbs such as *however, therefore,* and *nevertheless.*

Separate Sentences:	$\overset{\text{S}}{\text{Alison}}$ $\overset{\text{V}}{\text{wasn't}}$ hungry.
	$\overset{\text{S}}{\text{She}}$ $\overset{\text{V}}{\text{was}}$ always ready to eat and $\overset{\text{V}}{\text{ordered}}$ two cheeseburgers and some fries.

Combination:	<u>── Independent ──</u> <u>── Independent ──</u> $\overset{\text{S}}{\text{Alison}}$ $\overset{\text{V}}{\text{wasn't}}$ hungry**; nevertheless,** $\overset{\text{S}}{\text{she}}$ $\overset{\text{V}}{\text{was}}$ always ready to eat and ordered two cheeseburgers and some fries.

Conjunctive adverbs in this situation are always preceded by a semicolon and followed by a comma, as the example illustrates. If the conjunctive adverb falls in the middle of an independent clause, however, set it off with commas:

Independent	Independent
S **V**	**S** **V**

Alison wasn't hungry; she was always ready to eat,

nevertheless, and ordered two cheeseburgers and some

fries.

Exercise E3-17

Underline the compound sentences in paragraph 1 of "The Way to Rainy Mountain" (p. 64).

Exercise E3-18

Underline the compound sentences in paragraphs 3 through 5 of Alison's first draft (p. 73 and 74).

Exercise E3-19

Refer to Exercise E3-15, and combine the specified sentences using the strategy indicated here.

1. Combine sentences 1 and 2 using a semicolon.
2. Combine sentences 3 and 4 using a coordinating conjunction.
3. Combine sentences 7 and 8 using a coordinating conjunction.
4. Combine sentences 10 and 11 using a conjunctive adverb.
5. Combine sentences 11 and 12 using a semicolon.

Exercise E3-20

Write six compound sentences—two using semicolons, two using coordinating conjunctions, and two using conjunctive adverbs.

Complex Sentences

Complex sentences are not necessarily more difficult to write or understand than compound sentences; however, they are sometimes more difficult to identify. **Complex sentences** are composed of both independent and dependent clauses. A complex sentence can have many dependent clauses, but it will have only one independent clause. Look at the following examples from Alison's first draft:

		Dependent	Independent
	S	**S** **V**	**V**

Complex Sentences:

The people who come for the food make a great

ceremony of getting the perfect sandwich or the most

delectable dessert.

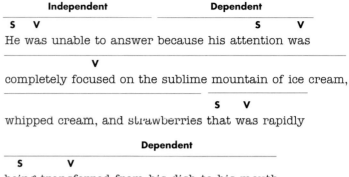

Notice that a complex sentence can begin with an independent clause or with a dependent clause. Don't be confused by the fact that complex sentences have more than one subject-verb pair. Only the subject and verb in the independent clause can stand alone as a complete thought. The subject and verb in the dependent clause cannot stand alone because they are logically dependent on the independent clause. The joining words will either be relative pronouns or subordinating conjunctions, integral components of sentence combining. Here are two strategies for combining sentences to make complex sentences:

1. Combine sentences by using a relative pronoun (*who, whom, which, that*) to make one of the independent clauses dependent.

Separate Sentences:

    S   V
Alison maintains a 4.0 average.

    S   V
She works 35 hours a week and takes six classes.

Combination:

    S   S   V   V
Alison, **who** works 35 hours a week and takes six classes,

    Independent
    V
maintains a 4.0 average.

Separate Sentences:

    S   V
Your answer was correct.

    S   V
We argued about it for nearly 20 minutes.

Combination:

    Independent   *Dependent*
    S   **S   V**
Your answer, **which** we argued about for nearly

    V
20 minutes, was correct.

2. Combine sentences using subordinating conjunctions, such as *although, because, if, since, when, whenever,* and *where.* (For a complete list of subordinating conjunctions, see p. 51.) The resulting dependent clauses are normally mobile and can appear in different places in the complex sentence.

Separate Sentences:

    S   **V**
Alison is still attending her history class.

    S **V**
She plans to drop the course after midterms.

Combinations:

Dependent

    S   **V**
Although Alison plans to drop her history course after

Independent

    S **V**   **V**
midterms, she is still attending class.

Independent   **Dependent**

 S   **V**   **V**   **S**
Alison is still attending her history class, **although** she

 V
plans to drop the course after midterms.

Separate Sentences:

      S **V** **V**
The city is asking for a property tax increase.

   S   **S**   **V**   **V**
Teachers and other school employees have not had a raise
in three years.

Combination:

Dependent

      S   **S**   **V**
Because teachers and other school employees have not

Independent

 V   **S** **V** **V**
had a raise in three years, the city is asking for a property
tax increase.

Independent

    S   **V**
The city plans to ask for a property tax increase **because**

Dependent

  S   **S**   **V**   **V**
teachers and other school employees have not had a raise
in three years.

TIPS FOR EDITING

Exercise E3-21

Put brackets around the complex sentences in paragraphs 4 through 7 of "The Way to Rainy Mountain" (pp. 65 and 66).

Exercise E3-22

Put brackets around the nine complex sentences in paragraphs 1 and 2 of Alison's revised draft, (pp. 76–77).

Exercise E3-23

Refer to Exercise E3-15 on page 102. Combine the following pairs of sentences, using relative pronouns or subordinating conjunctions to make complex sentences.

1. Sentences 3 and 4
2. Sentences 7 and 8
3. Sentences 11 and 12
4. Sentences 13 and 14
5. Sentences 15 and 16

Then add a dependent clause to the following sentences to make a complex sentence: 4, 5, 10, 13, and 15.

Sentence 3:	For example, my brother never pays his bills on time.
Complex Sentence:	For example, because my brother is very irresponsible, he never pays his bills on time.

Exercise E3-24

Add an independent or dependent clause to the following structures to make complex sentences.

1. people often say funny things
2. that the deadline had passed
3. what she understood the professor to say
4. combining sentences is rather simple and fun
5. which won the national championship

Compound-Complex Sentences

When writers combine compound and complex sentence elements, they produce compound-complex sentences. Thus, a **compound-complex sentence** consists of two or more independent clauses and one or more dependent clauses. Look at this example from paragraph 2 of Alison's first draft:

Independent	Dependent	

Compound-Complex Sentences:

              S   V   S

At one outdoor concert **that** I attended recently, a man

                   Dependent

     S   S   V   V   V

and woman **who** had obviously been taking dancing

                                Dependent

       V   S

lessons were all dressed up, **and** as soon as the music

              Independent

    V   V

started, they showed off their steps.

Notice that the clauses in compound-complex sentences can appear in a variety of orders, as long as the clauses relate to each other clearly and coherently:

                         Independent

Compound-Complex Sentences:

    S   V

Alison wanted to take an algebra class early in the morning,

        Independent   Dependent

        S   V   V   S   V

but the morning classes were all filled **when** she registered.

    Independent   Dependent   Independent

    S   V   S   V   S V

Alison wants to work **after** she graduates, **and** then she will

      Independent   Dependent

    V   S   V

apply to graduate school **since** she eventually wants to

teach on the college level.

       Dependent   Independent

      S   V   S V

Whenever Alison wants peace and quiet, she slips away

      V

and retreats to her parents' cabin deep in the woods, **but**

      Independent   Dependent

  S   V   S V

she usually stays only a day **because** she gets lonely.

As you can see, compound-complex sentences are usually longer than other structures because they include a great deal of information. As long as you make sure the clauses are logically related and punctuated correctly, readers should be able to understand the compound-complex sentences that you write.

Exercise E3-25

List the compound-complex sentences in paragraphs 6 through 8 of "The Way to Rainy Mountain" (pp. 65–66 and 66–67).

Exercise E3-26

List the compound-complex sentences in paragraphs 4 through 6 of Alison's first draft (pp. 74–75).

Exercise E3-27

Refer to Exercise E3-15 on page 102. Combine the following pairs of sentences, adding whatever words, phrases, and clauses you need to make compound-complex sentences.

1. Sentences 3 and 4
2. Sentences 5 and 6
3. Sentences 7 and 8
4. Sentences 9 and 10
5. Sentences 11 and 12

Exercise E3-28

Write five compound-complex sentences with independent and dependent clauses appearing in different orders and combinations.

 ## COLLABORATIVE WORK

After you revise your observing essay, exchange drafts with a classmate, and do the following tasks:

A. In the first two paragraphs, label the structure (simple, compound, complex, or compound-complex) of each sentence.

B. In the last paragraph, label the pattern (S-V, S-V-DO, S-V-IO-DO, S-V-DO-OC, S-V-SC) of each clause.

C. Provide suggestions for how the author can combine any sentences to vary the essay's sentence patterns and structures.

Then return the paper to its writer, and use the information in this section to edit your draft.

Explaining
Reading and Writing for a Reason

I see but one rule: to be clear.
STENDHAL

Explaining is a basic part of human life. In fact, it would probably be impossible for us to function every day if we didn't have a chance to explain ourselves: what we meant when we said something; why we were late for work or school; why we didn't do something we promised we would do; how we feel about social issues, politics, religion.

Explaining essays fall into two categories: (1) providing information about a topic or event and (2) explaining how to perform a task. In the first case, we explain to help others understand clearly and completely what we know or think and/or how we feel about certain issues or events. In the second type of explaining, we give step-by-step directions so that others can understand exactly what happened in the past or how to do something.

As you might suspect, it is often much easier to explain when you are speaking than when you are writing. When you have conversations, other people can let you know if they need more information, details, or examples. They can rely not only on your words but on the tone of your voice, the expression on your face, and the movements of your hands and body.

When you write, however, you don't have face-to-face contact with your audience. You don't have the opportunity to react to your readers, to add information, or to clarify facts. Since you often don't know who your readers are when you write, explaining yourself carefully and completely becomes essential. Your readers won't have the opportunity to ask you questions, so they will become confused and frustrated if they can't understand what you are saying. Think about how you felt the last time you tried to assemble some equipment and the directions were unclear. That's how readers often feel when reading a confusing essay.

Philip Roth, one of America's most famous and respected writers, wrote a book titled *Patrimony*. When he described the day his mother was buried, he declared, "What cemeteries prove, at least to people like me, is not that the dead are present but that they are gone." If Roth had stopped writing at that point, his readers would have probably been confused, perhaps even annoyed at his seeming coldness. However, he continued his paragraph by explaining his statement:

> At a cemetery . . . you can try talking to the dead if you feel that'll help; you can begin, as I did that morning, by saying, "Well, Ma. . . ." You can make them promises, catch them up on the news, ask for their understanding, their forgiveness, for their love—or you can take the other, the active approach, you can pull weeds, tidy the gravel, finger the letters carved in the tombstone; you can even get down and place your hands directly above their remains. . . . You can shut your eyes and remember what they were like when they were still with you. But nothing is altered by these recollections, except that the dead seem even more distant and out of reach than they did when you were driving in the car ten minutes earlier.

Philip Roth explains the reason for his feeling about cemeteries. His readers do not have to agree with him; in fact, they can have exactly the opposite feeling, but at least they understand how he feels and why he feels that way, because he gives his readers a careful and thorough explanation.

Explaining also serves as a guide to performing a process: how to get to the nearest gas station, how to bake a cake, how to study for an exam, how to write an essay. In explaining a process, clarity is the most important component. Here is a paragraph from a booklet titled *Your Guide to Jury Duty*. Notice how clearly the passage is worded:

> You must not discuss the case with your family, friends, other jurors, or any witness, attorney, or party involved in the case. You must not discuss the case even with your fellow jurors until you have heard all the evidence, the attorneys' arguments, and the charge. Doing so could lead you to form an opinion on the case before all the evidence is in. You should notify the judge if anyone persists in talking to you about the case after you have explained that you are not allowed to do so.

The explanation is clear and detailed so that prospective jurors will have no doubts whatsoever about what is expected of them.

The ability to explain through writing may be one of the most important qualities we develop in school. Through explaining, we communicate important information, and we share ideals and values. And ultimately, explaining lets us help others know, understand, and perhaps even respect our ideas and feelings.

LEARNING FROM PUBLISHED WRITERS

The following essay explains a process; in other words, it tells you how to do something. Written by William Zinsser, a college writing professor, it comes from his book *On Writing Well*, a best-seller among college students because it clearly and completely explains the process of writing. In this chapter, "Words," Zinsser explains how to use words carefully.

Before You Read

Focusing Your Attention

Before you read this explanation, take a few moments to respond to the following questions in your journal.

1. Think of a time when you had to explain how to do something to someone. Was it an easy or difficult task? Did the person understand you? Was the person able to follow your directions?

2. In the explaining essay you are about to read, the writer tells us how to use words effectively in writing. Have you ever had a problem choosing just the right words when you were writing? What did you do to solve the problem?

Expanding Your Vocabulary

Here are some words and their meanings that are important to your understanding of the essay. You might want to review them before you begin to read.

"become so **pervasive** [present everywhere]" (paragraph 1)

"you'll sound like every **hack** [someone who writes without care or concern for quality] who sits down to write" (paragraph 1)

"strong and **supple** [changeable, flexible] words" (paragraph 1)

"**endemic** [rooted in a place or people] corruption" (paragraph 3)

"writing at its most **banal** [unoriginal]" (paragraph 4)

"an **oblique** [indirect] look" (paragraph 4)

"be **finicky** [fussy, choosy] about the ones that you select" (paragraph 5)

"**cultivate** [develop and nurture] the best models" (paragraph 6)

"quite **permissive** [tolerant, not strict]" (paragraph 7)

"Learn its **etymology** [origin and development of a word]" (paragraph 7)

"small **gradations** [series of gradual changes] between words" (paragraph 7)

"such matters as rhythm and **alliteration** [using words that begin with the same consonant] are **vital** [extremely important]" (paragraph 9)

"makes the case **cogently** [convincingly and logically]" (paragraph 10)

"**cadences and sonorities** [rhythms and sounds] of the language" (paragraph 10)

"the same plodding **gait** [pace]" (paragraph 11)

William Zinsser

Words*

There's a kind of writing that might be called journalese, and it's the death of freshness in anybody's style. It's the common currency of newspaper and of magazines like *People*—a mixture of cheap words, made-up words and clichés that have become so pervasive that a writer can hardly help using them automatically. You must fight these phrases, or you'll sound like every hack who sits down to write. You'll never make your mark as a writer unless you develop a respect for words and a curiosity about their shades of meaning that is almost obsessive. The English language is rich in strong and supple words. Take the time to root around and find the ones you want.   **1**

What is "journalese"? It's a quilt of instant words patched together out of other parts of speech. Adjectives are used as nouns ("greats," "notables"). Nouns are extended into adjectives ("insightful"). Nouns are used as verbs ("to host"), or they are chopped off to form verbs ("enthuse," "emote"), or they are padded to form verbs ("beef up," "put teeth into"). This is a world where eminent people are "famed" and their associates are "staffers," where the future is always "upcoming" and someone is forever "firing off" a note. Nobody in America has merely sent a note or a memo or a telegram in years. Famed diplomat Henry Kissinger, who hosted foreign notables to beef up the morale of top State Department staffers, sat down and fired off a lot of notes. Notes that are fired off are always fired in anger and from a sitting position. What the weapon is I've never found out.   **2**

Here, for example, is an article from a famed newsmagazine that's hard to match for fatigue: **3**

> Last February, Plainclothes Patrolman Frank Serpico knocked at the door of a suspected Brooklyn heroin pusher. When the door opened a crack, Serpico shouldered his way in only to be met by a .22-cal. pistol slug crashing into his face. Somehow he survived, although there are still buzzing fragments in his head, causing dizziness and permanent deafness in his left ear. Almost as painful is the suspicion that he may well have been set up for

*William Zinsser, *On Writing Well*, 4th ed. (pp. 35–40). New York: HarperCollins, 1990.

the shooting by other policemen. For Serpico, 35, has been waging a lonely, four-year war against the routine and endemic corruption that he and others claim is rife in the New York City police department. His efforts are now sending shock waves through the ranks of New York's finest. . . . Though the impact of the commission's upcoming report has yet to be felt, Serpico has little hope that . . .

The upcoming report has yet to be felt because it is still upcoming, and, as for the "permanent deafness," it's a little early to tell. And what makes those buzzing fragments buzz? I would have thought that by now only Serpico's head would be buzzing. But apart from these lazinesses of logic, what makes the story so infinitely tired is the failure of the writer to reach for anything but the nearest cliché. "Shouldered his way," "only to be met," "crashing into his face," "waging a lonely war," "corruption that is rife," "sending shock waves," "New York's finest"—these dreary phrases constitute writing at its most banal. We know just what to expect. No surprise awaits us in the form of an unusual word, an oblique look. We are in the hands of a hack, and we know it right away. We stop reading.   4

Don't let yourself get in this position. The only way to fight it is to care deeply about words. If you find yourself writing that someone recently enjoyed a spell of illness or that a business has been enjoying a slump, stop and think how much they enjoyed it. Notice the decisions that other writers make in their choice of words and be finicky about the ones that you select from the vast supply. The race in writing is not to the swift but to the original.   5

Make a habit of reading what is being written today and what has been written before. Writing is learned by imitation. If anyone asked me how I learned to write, I'd say I learned by reading the men and women who were doing the kind of writing *I* wanted to do and trying to figure out how they did it. But cultivate the best models. Don't assume that because an article is in a newspaper or a magazine it must be good. Sloppy editing is common in American newspapers, and writers who use clichés by reflex are likely to work for editors who have seen so many clichés that they no longer even recognize them as they go limping by.   6

Also get in the habit of using dictionaries. My favorite for handy use is *Webster's New World Dictionary*, Second College Edition, though, like all word freaks, I own bigger dictionaries that will reward me in their own fashion when I'm on some more specialized search.   7

(Careful writers cling to their copy of any Webster dictionary based on the superb Second Edition, because the Third Edition is quite permissive.) If you have any doubt of what a word means, look it up. Learn its etymology and notice what curious branches its original root has put forth. See if it has any meanings you didn't know it had. Master the small gradations between words that seem to be synonyms. What's the difference between "cajole," "wheedle," "blandish," and "coax"? Get yourself a dictionary of synonyms.

And don't scorn that bulging grab bag *Roget's Thesaurus*. It's easy to regard the book as hilarious. Look up "villain," for instance, and you'll be awash in such rascality as only a lexicographer could conjure back from centuries of iniquity, obliquity, depravity, knavery, profligacy, frailty, flagrancy, infamy, immorality, corruption, wickedness, wrongdoing, backsliding, and sin. You'll find rogues and wretches, ruffians and riffraff, miscreant and malefactors, reprobates and rapscallions, hooligans and hoodlums, scamps and scapegraces, scoundrels and scalawags, jezebels and jades. You'll find adjectives to fit them all (foul and fiendish, devilish, and diabolical), and adverbs, and verbs to describe how the wrongdoers do their wrong, and cross-references leading to still other thickets of venality and vice. Still, there's no better friend to have around to nudge the memory than *Roget*. It saves you the time of rummaging in your own memory—that network of overloaded grooves—to find the word that's right on the tip of your tongue, where it doesn't do you any good. The *Thesaurus* is to the writer what a rhyming dictionary is to the songwriter—a reminder of all the choices—and you should use it with gratitude. If, having found the scalawag and the scapegrace, you want to know how they differ, *then* go to the dictionary.

Also bear in mind, when you are choosing words and stringing them together, how they sound. This may seem absurd: readers read with their eyes. But in fact they hear what they are reading—in their inner ear—far more than you realize. Therefore, such matters as rhythm and alliteration are vital to every sentence. A typical example—maybe not the best, but undeniably the nearest—is the preceding paragraph. Obviously I enjoyed making a certain arrangement of my ruffians and riffraff, my hooligans and hoodlums, and the reader enjoyed it too—far more than if I had provided a mere list. He enjoyed not only the arrangement but the effort to entertain him. He wasn't enjoying it, however, with eyes. He was enjoying it in his ear.

E. B. White makes the case cogently in *The Elements of Style* (a book that every writer should read at least once a year) when he sug-

8

9

10

gests trying to rearrange any phrase that has survived for a century or two, such as Thomas Paine's "These are the times that try men's souls":

> Times like these try men's souls.
> How trying it is to live in these times!
> These are trying times for men's souls.
> Soulwise, these are trying times.

Paine's phrase is like poetry, and the other four are like oatmeal, which is the divine mystery of the creative process. The good writer of prose must be part poet, always listening to what he writes. E. B. White continues to be my favorite stylist because I'm conscious of being with a man who cares about the cadences and sonorities of the language. I relish (in my ear) the pattern that his words make as they fall into a sentence. I try to surmise how in rewriting the sentence he reassembled it to end with a phrase that will momentarily linger or how he chose one word over another because he was after a certain emotional weight. It's the difference between, say, "serene" and "tranquil"—one so soft, the other strangely disturbing because of the unusual "n" and "q."

Such considerations of sound and rhythm should be woven through everything you write. If all your sentences move at the same plodding gait, which even you recognize as deadly but don't know how to cure, read them aloud. (I write entirely by ear and read everything aloud before letting it go out into the world.) You'll begin to hear where the trouble lies. See if you can gain variety by reversing the order of a sentence, or by substituting a word that has freshness or oddity, or by altering the length of your sentences so they don't all sound as if they came out of the same mold. An occasional short sentence can carry a tremendous punch. It stays in the reader's ear. **11**

Remember, then, that words are the only tools you've got. Learn to use them with originality and care. Value them for their strength and their precision. And remember: somebody out there is listening. **12**

 ## ? QUESTIONS FOR CRITICAL THINKING

THINKING CRITICALLY ABOUT CONTENT

1. After reading his explanation and noting the examples, what does William Zinsser mean by *journalese* and *clichés*?

2. Why do you think Zinsser gives so many examples from *Roget's Thesaurus* in paragraph 8?

THINKING CRITICALLY ABOUT PURPOSE

3. What is Zinsser's purpose in writing this essay?

4. Why do you think William Zinsser describes the work of E. B. White and quotes him in this essay?

THINKING CRITICALLY ABOUT AUDIENCE

5. What group of readers would be most interested in this essay?

6. Do you think that only good writers can benefit from this essay? Why? Explain your answer.

THINKING CRITICALLY ABOUT POINT OF VIEW

7. Describe in a complete sentence Zinsser's point of view.

8. Write a paragraph explaining whether you agree with Zinsser when he says the passage quoted in paragraph 3 is an example of bad writing.

LEARNING FROM YOUR PEERS

Explaining is an essential part of all forms of communication. It is especially important in learning, whether in school or out of school. We learn many things simply by doing them, but we learn even more by having processes explained to us. Learning how to explain a process to someone else who does not share your knowledge of the topic is a valuable skill that you will use throughout life. In response to this assignment, we are going to follow the writing process of a student named Eden Bailey.

Eden's Writing Assignment: Explaining

This is the topic Eden's instructor assigned:

All of us possess an amazing variety of skills that we take for granted: tuning up a car, shopping for the best bargains in fashion, planning and cooking a formal dinner, even pursuing childhood hobbies such as collecting stamps or baseball cards. Explain to an audience of your peers a complicated process that you have learned. Be as specific and clear as possible.

Eden goes through the process as outlined in Chapter 1: *thinking, planning, developing, organizing, drafting, revising,* and *editing.*

Thinking

Eden is a "senior citizen" in her writing class. She married during her first year of college, raised a family, and is back in school to finish her degree; she hopes to graduate at the same time as her oldest child. Eden's first reaction to this assignment is that she does not know how to do anything special. So she approaches the assignment by freewriting.

> Well, this is bound to be interesting. I sure don't know how to tune up a car. I've never collected stamps. I can cook, but a really elaborate meal at our house these days means sprinkling some almonds on the chicken salad from the Healthy Sprouts Deli. And finishing it off with a splash of bottled water.
>
> Sometimes I long for the good old days. I thought I was tied to the house back when the kids were tiny. They seemed to need food or sleep all the time, and it was just easiest to stay home until they could walk around on their own. I used to sit and sew while they napped. That sounds good about now. No cares in the world. Just the creative process unfolding before me. I made quilts for every baby and all the relatives. Not to mention wall hangings and potholders. That's it. I could write about quilts. I've still managed to get to some quilt shows and keep up my membership in my quilt guild. I guess most people wouldn't know about that.

Planning

Eden meets with her peer editing group once a week. At the next meeting, she asks them what they think about her topic. They all tell her that they know nothing about quilting, not even what questions to ask, so in the library after class Eden starts listing everything she knows about quilts.

What I know about quilts:

Different types: pieced, appliquéd, whole-cloth.

Different sizes: wall hangings, baby bed quilts, regular bed quilts.

Color combinations—wild, contemporary to traditional, subdued.

How to make one: start with the top; add the stuffing; add the backing.

Stitch through the sandwich.

Take small stitches; don't create any toe-catchers.

Quilters' idea of a dream vacation: go to big quilt shows, go to lots of quilt and fabric shops, take seminars with famous quilters. (Why does my family always want to go to the ocean, where there is no quilt shop for miles around?)

Even cowboys quilt. It's not just for little old ladies!

Developing

Eden's list gives her peer editing group a basis for asking her questions when she meets with them again. This is what they ask:

1. What is the difference between pieced, appliquéd, and whole-cloth quilts?
2. How did you learn to quilt? Did you always know how to sew?
3. Were there any other quilters in your family?
4. What is the most common size for a quilt?
5. Do most people use quilts just to sleep under?
6. What kinds of quilts do cowboys make?

Eden then answers these questions in her journal, letting her mind run freely over the details of her quilting experiences and the memories they trigger. Here are her journal entries:

1. Pieced quilts are made up of small pieces of fabric--often remnants of cloth or cut-up clothing, old pillowcases and sheets--that are laid out and sewn together in geometric designs of several colors. Whole-cloth and ap-pliquéd quilts start with large pieces of new material. Their design comes from what is added to their base fabric; an appliquéd quilt has pieces shaped in specific designs (flowers, stars, eagles) sewn to its base, and a whole-cloth quilt's design comes from the pattern of its quilting stitches.

2. When I was very young, I stayed with my grandmother during the day. To keep me busy, she taught me how to sew. Grandmother would give me scraps of material that I would cut, baste, and sew into clothes for my dolls.

As I began to sew more complicated things, I started making dolls. Eventually, I checked out books from the library about quilting. I found one about doll quilts. Grandmother and I would rummage through her scrap box and piece together pretty quilts for each of my favorite dolls.

3. I am the first quilter in my family; however, my grandmother Marian was a seamstress. She would make me pretty frilly dresses, drapes for my bedroom, and satin pillowcases for my bed, and she sewed all of her dresses for church. From my grandmother I learned how to make lasting stitches and small neat stitches, to choose fabrics for my sewing projects, and to design and lay out my quilt tops.

4. The most common quilt size is the double. A double quilt will fit on a double bed or a queen-sized bed. A dust ruffle is often used with a double quilt on a queen-sized bed.

5. Yes, most people sleep under quilts; however, quilts are also used in decorating. We often see quilts hanging from walls in country-style homes, quilted throw pillows and wall hangings, and quilted Christmas tree ornaments and table runners.

6. Cowboys made tied quilts. These were made from scraps of material cut from their old clothes, blankets, and bedding. The pieces were stitched together to form a top. This top would be attached to an old blanket and stuffed with batting. Then the cowboy would take yarn and tie the top, batting, and base together in sections. The edges would be sewn together as well. The tied quilts were not the prettiest quilts made during that time, but they were functional—they kept the cowboys warm.

Organizing

Eden does her best writing in the library, away from the telephone and the distractions of home. She usually goes to the library at least three evenings a week to read, write, or do research. She has a favorite table that is hidden in a corner, and she likes the solitude there for writing. She looks at her list of questions and her "What I Know" list and starts making notes so she can organize her essay. Then she underlines key words that identify the topic or main idea in each entry:

<u>What I like best about quilting</u>—the unique creations, completely my own.

I cannot remember <u>when I started to sew</u>. I think I always had a needle and thread in my hand. I made dolls and doll quilts when I was a child. Later, I did some for my kids. In between, I learned how to do pillows and wall hangings and table runners, all the usual stuff.

You <u>make a quilt</u> the same way you make a sandwich. Start with the top and bottom and put a batting layer in between.

Your top can be <u>appliquéd, pieced, or whole-cloth</u>. This depends on the effect you want and how good you are at any of the skills. They all demand different talents. Patience, of course, is something you need no matter what.

<u>All quilters</u> love to find out what is new in their craft. They like to go to quilting shops and read quilting magazines and get new equipment.

<u>Quilting as my profession.</u>

Eden looks at her notes and decides that, since she knows her subject so well, she is ready to start writing.

Drafting

This is Eden's draft.

Eden's Essay: First Draft

Main Idea: People make quilts for different reasons, but I use quilting to express myself.

My hobby is making quilts. I like nothing better than spending hours in my sewing room with a huge stack of books and little pieces of fabric, sketching ideas and trying them out, creating something that no one else will ever duplicate. I give my hobby a great deal of creative energy. Using quilting as a way to express myself.

I cannot remember when I started sewing, but I must have been very young. Some of my first library books. These were about making dolls. I used to try to duplicate the ones that I saw in the pictures. But I never had the right materials, so they never turned out very well. One of my favorite books. Had instructions to make some simple doll quilts. My efforts at the doll quilts were more successful than my doll-making ventures. Which frustrated me to no end. Even though my doll quilts would not have won any prizes. I was persistent. I kept trying until I developed some color sense, and I learned as much as possible about my hobby. No one in my family had ever made quilts, so I had to work on my own. To learn everything from books.

After the doll quilts, I made several small projects like potholders and placemats and tote bags. After a few years, I started developing more confidence in my design abilities, and I started making more complicated projects. I experimented with color combinations and block patterns. Learning how to sew projects very rapidly on the sewing machine. Traditional quilting was done by hand, but that is one tradition that I am willing to break. A hundred years ago, quilters probably worked by candlelight, but that did not make their quilts any better. It just ruined their eyesight at an early age.

To make a quilt, you start out with the top layer, which is where the designs appear. There are three basic methods of construction for quilts. The ones we see most often are pieced quilts. Appliquéd quilts are made by using a base fabric and sewing smaller pieces onto it. The last category of quilts is the whole-cloth quilt.

Once the quilt top is made, another piece of fabric is cut to match it, this will form the backing. Then a piece of batting or stuffing (or wadding, as the British call it) is cut to form the filling of the sandwich. This makes the quilt squeezable. The sandwich is temporarily fastened together with safety pins or long, loose stitches called basting stitches then the work of quilting begins. Quilting stitches go through all three layers and follow many different kinds of designs. Some of the pieced quilts are outlined with quilting. Appliquéd quilts are interesting and intricate. Often have quilting stitches around the designs and large areas where quilting stitches form the only design. Whole-cloth quilts follow the planned design very carefully, because there is nothing to distract the viewer's eye from the patterns formed by the stitches. Quilting stitches were traditionally done by hand, and the skill of the person doing the stitches was very obvious. The most desirable stitches are tiny puckers. In the fabric. Some expert quilters can make 20 stitches to the inch. Large, loose stitches are called toe-catchers because if people were to sleep under a quilt with loopy stitches, they might catch their toes in the loops. Machine stitching has made it possible to disguise a person's lack of talent with hand stitching, but it requires a completely different set of skills, and some people prefer to keep tradition.

Most quilters I have met would rather quilt than do anything else in their spare time. Many of them belong to one or more quilting guilds. Organizations whose members challenge each other to develop their skills and encourage and praise each other when they finish a project or try something different. For vacations, they go to national or international quilt shows. Shopping trips are not complete unless they include a stop at the fabric store. To see what is new. The best days of the month for them are the days they find new issues of the quilting magazines in their mailboxes at least an hour is required to look at each new magazine and fantasize about making a multitude of new projects. If it has been too long since a magazine arrived. A trip to a bookstore or quilt shop to check out the latest shipment of books is the next-best solution.

Every time I see a quilt, I am reminded of the sewing skills of our frugal, hardworking ancestors, most people know that women used every scrap of fabric, material usually left over from sewing projects and pieces of worn clothing. Recycling these bits into works of functional art for everyone in their families to enjoy. You may be surprised, however, to find out that some quilts were even made by cowboys on the range. When their work clothing was worn out. They salvaged the good parts of the garments and tied them together to make "tied quilts" that served as rugged bedrolls and saddle blankets.

Although quilting is my hobby, I hope someday to make it my profession. In the meantime, I am not going to quit my day job. I am going to study graphic design and accounting to make sure that I will always be able to make a living and afford to buy all the quilt books and fabric that my heart desires.

Revising

Eden feels that her first draft says what she wants it to say. Writing about this hobby that has been a part of her life since she was a child was satisfying in many ways. But she knows she still has to revise her work. Eden's instructor has asked the class to focus on different methods of developing their ideas. If the student writers can develop their ideas fully at this point in the course, they can build on this ability for the rest of the term as their writing gets more complex.

Eden reviews the Checklist for Developing an Essay at the beginning of the Tips for Revising section of this chapter. The instructor wants the students to work with whole essays, not just with isolated parts, and to concentrate on the relationship of ideas to one another. The instructor explains that these methods of development are really ways of thinking and processing information. These skills will help them, insists the instructor, in all of their classes. That's all Eden needs to hear to take these guidelines seriously; she has learned that developing her ideas is a part of everything she does.

Eden reads the Tips for Revising and does all the assigned exercises. She learns that an idea can be developed in one of seven ways and that the method of development must be suited to the idea. So Eden takes her essay apart paragraph by paragraph, checking to see whether her ideas are developed as fully as possible and in the most appropriate way for what she is trying to say. She finds problems in her essay and sets out to improve each paragraph so that her essay as a whole will be more effective.

COLLABORATIVE WORK

PEER GROUP ACTIVITY

After you read the portions of the Tips for Revising your instructor assigns, turn to Eden's first draft (pp. 122–125), and complete the following tasks in small groups:

A. Underline the topic sentence in each of Eden's body paragraphs.

B. Put brackets around any sections of the essay that are not fully developed.

C. In the margin, suggest a method for expanding the undeveloped sections you identified: definition, description, examples, classification, cause-effect, comparison-contrast, and analysis. (For definitions, see pp. 134, 135, 136, 137, 138, 139, and 139.)

Compare the brackets and underlining your group recorded with those your instructor will show you. Where do your marks differ from your instructor's? What do you need to review before writing your own essay?

CLASS ACTIVITY

As an entire class, look at the underlined portions of Eden's revised draft (pp. 127–130) to see how she changed each sentence.

A. Did you identify the **revision** problems that Eden corrected?

B. Do you think her changes are good ones? Discuss her changes.

Editing

Now that Eden's paragraphs are fully developed, she needs to do some final proofreading and editing before handing in her essay. The instructor tells the students they need to make sure they can recognize and correct fragments and run-on sentences. So Eden shifts her focus from the content of her paragraphs to specific sentence elements. She reads the Tips for Editing section in this chapter to learn that both fragments and run-ons are types of sentence errors. A fragment is a piece of a sentence punctuated as a sentence, and a run-on is a series of sentences punctuated as a single sentence. She takes the questions in the Checklist for Correcting Fragments and Run-ons one by one and makes changes so that her revised draft follows all of these requirements.

COLLABORATIVE WORK

PEER GROUP ACTIVITY

After you read the portions of the Tips for Editing your instructor assigns, turn to Eden's first draft (pp. 122–125), and do the following tasks in small groups:

A. Read each sentence in this explaining essay for completeness, and put brackets around the fragments you find.

B. Read Eden's draft again, looking for multiple sentences that are run together as one. Separate any run-on sentences with a slash.

Compare the marks your group recorded with those your instructor will show you. Where do your marks differ from your instructor's? What do you need to review before writing your own essay?

CLASS ACTIVITY

As an entire class, look at the underlined portions of Eden's revised draft (pp. 127–130) to see how she changed each sentence.

A. Did you identify the **editing** problems that Eden corrected?

B. Do you think her changes are good ones? Discuss her changes.

Eden's Revised Essay

Quilts

My hobby is making quilts. Quilts began as an ecomony measure; women used scraps from outgrown clothing or other sewing projects to provide warm covers for their families. Quilts basically consist of a top layer of pieces of fabric and a bottom layer of whole cloth with stuffing between the layers. Today, many people consider quilts an art form. I like nothing better than spending hours in my sewing room with a huge stack of books and little pieces of fabric, sketching ideas and trying them out, creating something that no one else will ever duplicate. At times like these, I feel like an artist who creates a great mural like the one on the ceiling of the Sistine Chapel. I give my hobby a great deal of creative energy/, uUsing quilting as a way to express myself.

I cannot remember when I started sewing, but I must have been very young. Some of my first library books/ ~~These~~ were about making dolls. I used to try to duplicate the ones that I saw in the pictures. But I never had the right materials, so they never turned out very well. One of my favorite books/ hHad instructions to make some simple doll quilts. My efforts at the doll quilts were more successful than my doll-making ventures/, wWhich frustrated me to no end. Even though my doll quilts would not have won any prizes/, I was persistent. I kept trying until I developed some color sense, and I learned as much as possible about my hobby. No one in my family had ever made quilts, so I had to work on my own/ tTo learn everything from books.

After the doll quilts, I made several small projects like potholders and placemats and tote bags. Once I quilted a set of placemats in flower designs for a Mother's Day gift. My mom particularly loves the one that looks like a bouquet of bright red poppies and another that looks like a huge sunflower. After a few years, I started developing more confidence in my design abilities, and I started making more complicated projects/: lap quilts, pillows, wall hangings, and a few bed quilts. I experimented with color combinations and block patterns. Learning how to sew projects very rapidly on the sewing machine/ gave me confidence. Traditional quilting was done by hand, but that is one tradition that I am willing to break. A hundred years ago, quilters probably worked by candlelight, but that did not make their quilts any better. It just ruined their eyesight at an early age.

To make a quilt, you start out with the top layer, which is where the designs appear. There are three basic methods of construction for quilts. The ones we see most often are pieced quilts/ made of small pieces of fabric sewn together, forming geometric designs of many colors. Appliquéd quilts are made by using a base fabric and sewing smaller pieces onto it/, forming flowers or animals or other more complicated designs. The last category of quilts is the whole-cloth quilt/ made by taking one large piece of fabric and stitching an elaborate design that will cover the whole surface with quilting stitches.

Once the quilt top is made, another piece of fabric is cut to match it/. T/his will form the backing. Then a piece of batting or stuffing (or wadding, as the British call it) is cut to form the filling of the sandwich. This makes the quilt squeezable. The sandwich is temporarily fastened together with safety pins or long, loose stitches called basting stitches. T/hen the work of quilting begins. Quilting stitches go through all three layers and follow many different kinds of designs. Some of the pieced quilts are outlined with quilting. Appliquéd quilts are interesting and intricate/, oØften hav∉ing quilting stitches around the designs and large areas where quilting stitches form the only design. Whole-cloth quilts follow the planned design very carefully, because there is nothing to distract the viewer's eye from the patterns formed by the stitches. They are like beautiful tapestries we often see in museums. Quilting stitches were traditionally done by hand, and the skill of the person doing the stitches was very obvious. The most desirable stitches are tiny puckers/ i/n the fabric. Some expert quilters can make 20 stitches to the inch. Large, loose stitches are called toe-catchers because if people were to sleep under a quilt with loopy stitches, they might catch their toes in the loops. Machine stitching has made it possible to disguise a person's lack of talent with hand stitching, but it requires a completely different set of skills, and some people prefer to keep tradition.

Most quilters I have met would rather quilt than do anything else in their spare time. Many of them belong to one or more quilting guilds/, oOrganizations whose members challenge each other to develop their skills and encourage and praise each other when they finish a project or try something different. For vacations, they go to national or international quilt shows. Shopping trips are not complete unless they include a stop at the fabric store/ tTo see what is new. The best days of the month for them are the days they find new issues of the quilting magazines in their mailboxes. ₐAt least an hour is required to look at each new magazine and fantasize about making a multitude of new projects. If it has been too long since a magazine arrived/, aA trip to a bookstore or quilt shop to check out the latest shipment of books is the next-best solution.

Every time I see a quilt, I am reminded of the sewing skills of our frugal, hardworking ancestors/. Mmost people know that women used every scrap of fabric, material usually left over from sewing projects and pieces of worn clothing. They worked hard to rRecyclinge these bits into works of functional art for everyone in their families to enjoy. You may be surprised, however, to find out that some quilts were even made by cowboys on the range. When their work clothing was worn out/, tThey salvaged the good parts of the garments and tied them together to make "tied quilts" that served as rugged bedrolls and saddle blankets.

Although quilting is my hobby, I hope someday to make it my profession. In the meantime, I am not going to quit my day job/, and I am planning my college career so that it will both benefit my job now and help me convert my hobby into a business later. I am going to study graphic design and accounting to make sure that I will always be able to make a living and afford to buy all the quilt books and fabric that my heart desires. In addition, the effect of taking these courses is to make me a better quilter who can run her own business when the time comes.

WRITING YOUR OWN EXPLAINING ESSAY

So far, you have seen a professional writer and a fellow student at work trying to explain an experience or process they felt was worth talking about. As you read the published essay and followed the writing process of another student from first to final draft, you absorbed ideas and ways of giving those ideas a form of their own. These reading and writing activities have prepared you to write your own essay explaining an experience or process that is meaningful to you.

What Have You Discovered?

Before you begin your own writing task, let's review what you have learned in this chapter so far:

- Explaining is a basic part of human life.

- Explaining in writing is more difficult than explaining in speech because you cannot get immediate feedback from readers about the clarity of your message.

- Explaining falls into two categories: (1) providing information about a topic or an event and (2) explaining how to perform a task.

- To present your explaining effectively, you need to organize your ideas.

- To help you shape your essay, you should learn as much as possible about your readers.

- Before you write a draft, you need to decide on a point of view toward your subject.

- After you write a draft, you should revise your essay for meaning and organization.

- After you revise your essay, you should edit its grammar, usage, and sentence structure.

Your Writing Topic

Choose one of the following topics for your explaining essay:

1. In the professional essay that you read at the beginning of this chapter, "Words," William Zinsser, explains that writers must "develop a respect for words and a curiosity about their shades of meaning that is almost obsessive." Write an essay in which you explain the importance of words to you: when you write, when you speak, when you read, when you think about important matters, and when you listen.

2. Explain an incident that made you appreciate your own life and circumstances more deeply. This event may have been something that happened to you personally, an event in the news, or segments of a novel or film that changed your perspective. Explain the incident and your response to it so that your classmates can understand its impact on your life.

3. Have you ever taken on a project or a job that required organization and specific skills? You may have decorated a room, planted a garden, or constructed a model ship or airplane. You may have worked on a job that required you to learn a special method of doing things. Write an essay in which you explain the methods and skills you learned in completing your project. (Some examples of what you *shouldn't* do might help make your point with your readers.)

4. Create your own explaining topic (with the assistance of your instructor), and write a response to it.

When you have selected one of these topics, you may begin your writing process in the same way Eden did. (You may find her experience helpful in giving you ideas.) This time your purpose is to write your own explaining essay. If some tasks occur out of order, that adjustment is probably part of your personal writing ritual. Follow your instincts, and let them mold your own writing process, but make sure you've worked through all the stages to your final draft.

YOUR WRITING PROCESS

THINKING   Generate as many ideas on your subject as you can in as many different ways as possible: rereading, listing, freewriting, brainstorming, clustering, discussing, and questioning.

PLANNING   Begin to give your ideas shape by deciding on your approach to your topic (your content, your purpose, your audience, and your point of view). Make a list of points you want to include in your essay.

DEVELOPING   Add more details on three or four specific, focused topics that you have chosen from your list of general points.

ORGANIZING   Organize your material in a way that will be most interesting to your audience.

DRAFTING   Write a working draft of your essay in complete sentences.

REVISING   Consulting the Tips for Revising in this chapter (pp. 134–142), revise your first draft—paying special attention to developing your ideas fully.

EDITING   Consulting the Tips for Editing in this chapter (pp. 143–157), edit your draft for grammar and correctness—paying special attention to avoiding sentence fragments and run-ons.

Turn in your revised draft to your instructor.

Some Final Thoughts

When you have completed your own essay, answer these four questions in your journal:

1. What was most difficult about this assignment?
2. What was easiest?
3. What did I learn about explaining by completing this assignment?
4. What did I learn about my own writing process—how I prepared to write, how I wrote the first draft, how I revised, and how I edited?

Developing an Essay

Checklist for Developing an Essay

✓ Are the writer's **ideas developed** fully and completely in each paragraph?

✓ Are the **methods of reasoning** used in the essay best for what is being said at different points in the essay: definition, description, examples, classification, cause-effect, comparison-contrast, and analysis?

A gardener begins with a controlling idea—a design for a beautiful outdoor garden. Then the gardener spends days, months, even years developing that garden. He or she may plant a hedge of roses to define the space, select one beautiful and rare plant to stand alone as a focal point, build a pool and install a fountain, or follow various other plans to develop the garden to fit the original idea.

Developing paragraphs in essays can be like developing a garden, though the task shouldn't take years the way gardens often do. Just as a garden would be bland and boring if all the beds contained the same kinds of plants or blooms of only one color, so would an essay be dull if only one type of development were used. Most writers, like most gardeners, mix a number of methods for developing an essay and its paragraphs so that the whole essay is colorful and meaningful. They usually choose from the following methods: *defining, describing, giving examples, classifying, assigning cause/effect, comparing/contrasting,* and *analyzing.*

Definition

When you explain the meaning of a term, you are **defining** it. In the professional essay in this chapter, William Zinsser defines words that writers should avoid and suggests various ways writers can find appropriate words to express their meaning. Zinsser uses many different strategies to achieve his purpose.

Early in paragraph 1 of "Words," Zinsser uses definition to familiarize his audience with a term he will be using, *journalese*:

> It's the common currency of newspapers and of magazines like *People*—a mixture of cheap words, made-up words and clichés that have become so pervasive that a writer can hardly help using them automatically.

As Eden Bailey began to revise her essay, she decided that paragraph 1 in her first draft about her quilting hobby would be better developed if she included a definition of quilting:

First Draft: My hobby is making quilts. I like nothing better than

spending hours in my sewing room with a huge stack of

books and little pieces of fabric, sketching ideas and trying them out, creating something that no one else will ever duplicate. I give my hobby a great deal of creative energy. Using quilting as a way to express myself.

Revision: My hobby is making quilts. **Quilts began as an economy measure; women used scraps from outgrown clothing or other sewing projects to provide warm covers for their families. Quilts basically consist of a top layer of pieces of fabric and a bottom layer of whole cloth with stuffing between the layers. Today, many people consider quilts an art form.** I like nothing better than spending hours in my sewing room with a huge stack of books and little pieces of fabric, sketching ideas and trying them out, creating something that no one else will ever duplicate. **At times like these, I feel like an artist who creates a great mural like the one on the ceiling of the Sistine Chapel.** I give my hobby a great deal of creative energy, using quilting as a way to express myself.

Eden defines not only *quilting,* a term that might be unfamiliar to her audience, but also her role as a quilter, comparing it to an artist. Now her audience is sure to understand her paragraph .

Description

A **description** uses words to draw a picture for your audience of a place, an object, a person or group, or a situation. It gives a fine level of detail that can make a subject come alive for the reader.

In Chapter 3, essayist N. Scott Momaday paints a vivid picture of Rainy Mountain in paragraph 1:

The hardest weather in the world is there. Winter brings blizzards, hot tornadic winds arise in the spring, and in summer the prairie is an anvil's edge. The grass turns brittle and brown, and it cracks beneath your feet. There are green belts along the rivers and creeks, linear groves of hickory and pecan, willow, and witch hazel. At a distance in July or August the steaming foliage seems almost to writhe in fire. Great green and yellow grasshoppers are everywhere in the tall grass, popping up like corn to sting the flesh, and tortoises crawl about on the red earth, going nowhere in the plenty of time.

Eden decided that she could develop her fourth paragraph by describing the three construction methods for quilts:

First Draft: To make a quilt, you start out with the top layer, which is where the designs appear. There are three basic methods of construction for quilts. The ones we see most often are pieced quilts. Appliquéd quilts are made by using a base fabric and sewing smaller pieces onto it. The last category of quilts is the whole-cloth quilt.

Revision: To make a quilt, you start out with the top layer, which is where the designs appear. There are three basic methods of construction for quilts. The ones we see most often are pieced quilts **made of small pieces of fabric sewn together, forming geometric designs of many colors.** Appliquéd quilts are made by using a base fabric and sewing smaller pieces onto it**, forming flowers or animals or other more complicated designs.** The last category of quilts is the whole-cloth quilt **made by taking one large piece of fabric and stitching an elaborate design that will cover the whole surface with quilting stitches.**

Now Eden's readers know exactly what the three kinds of quilts are and how they are made because she has described them.

Examples

If a picture is worth a thousand words, then writing an **example** is priceless. Giving an example of something you are writing about is a technique that *shows* your readers what you mean.

In paragraph 2 of "Words," William Zinsser follows his definition of *journalese* with examples of the way journalists twist words into unfamiliar forms and usage:

What is "journalese"? It's a quilt of instant words patched together out of other parts of speech. Adjectives are used as nouns ("greats," "notables"). Nouns are extended into adjectives ("insightful"). Nouns are used as verbs ("to host"), or they are chopped off to form verbs ("enthuse," "emote"), or they are padded to form verbs ("beef up," "put teeth into").

Studying her essay, Eden decided to give an example of one of her early projects so that she could show rather than tell her readers about this stage of her quilting abilities. As Eden revised paragraph 3, she included some details about a gift that especially pleased her mother.

First Draft: After the doll quilts, I made several small projects like potholders and placemats and tote bags.

Revision: After the doll quilts, I made several small projects like potholders and placemats and tote bags. **Once I quilted a set of placemats in flower designs for a Mother's Day gift. My mom particularly loves the one that looks like a bouquet of bright red poppies and another that looks like a huge sunflower.**

This addition makes Eden's paragraph much more lively and interesting to read.

Classification

Another way to develop an idea is by **classification,** grouping similar items in a paragraph. People might be classified by occupation, hobbies, regions where they live, political beliefs, and so on.

In paragraph 8 of his essay, Zinsser groups the many synonyms for the word *villain* that can be found in *Roget's Thesaurus:*

> Look up "villain," for instance, and you'll be awash in such rascality as only a lexicographer could conjure back from centuries of iniquity, obliquity, depravity, knavery, profligacy, frailty, flagrancy, infamy, immorality, corruption, wickedness, wrongdoing, backsliding, and sin.

Eden decided she could improve her essay by classifying. In paragraph 3, she added more examples after her placemat example:

First Draft: After a few years, I started developing more confidence in my design abilities, and I started making more complicated projects.

Revision: After a few years, I started developing more confidence in my design abilities, and I started making more complicated projects/: **lap quilts, pillows, wall hangings, and a few bed quilts**.

These categories help her readers more fully understand the types of quilts she made.

Cause-Effect

Explaining causes that lead to a particular effect or the effect that results from a particular cause is an important tool for writers. The papers that you will need to write for your other courses in college—history and science, for example—often draw on making **cause-effect** connections.

William Zinsser uses cause-effect reasoning in paragraph 6 of "Words" when he explains how he learned how to write:

> If anyone asked me how I learned to write, I'd say I learned by reading the men and women who were doing the kind of writing *I* wanted to do and trying to figure out how they did it. But cultivate the best models.

Eden found a place in paragraph 8 of her draft that could be improved with the use of cause-effect reasoning:

First Draft: Although quilting is my hobby, I hope someday to make it my profession. In the meantime, I am not going to quit my day job. I am going to study graphic design and accounting to make sure that I will always be able to make a living and afford to buy all the quilt books and fabric that my heart desires.

Revision: Although quilting is my hobby, I hope someday to make it my profession. In the meantime, I am not going to quit my day job/, **and I am planning my college career so that it will both benefit my job now and help me convert my hobby into a business later.** I am going to study graphic design and accounting to make sure that I will always be able to make a living and afford to buy all the quilt books and fabric that my heart desires. **In addition, the effect of**

taking these courses is to make me a better quilter who can run her own business when the time comes.

With these additions, Eden clarifies the relationship between taking certain college courses and her career goals.

Comparison-Contrast

When you point out similarities, you are using **comparison** to develop your ideas. When you emphasize differences, you are using **contrast.** To make your ideas clear about things in the same category, you should learn to use this **comparison-contrast** technique. It is another skill that will prove helpful in other courses such as literature or political science.

In the professional essay, Zinsser compares various attempts at rewriting Thomas Paine's immortal line "These are the times that try men's souls" to the original words:

> Paine's phrase is like poetry, and the other four are like oatmeal, which is the divine mystery of the creative process.

Eden decided to use comparison-contrast to make paragraph 5 of her essay more informative:

First Draft: Whole-cloth quilts follow the planned design very carefully, because there is nothing to distract the viewer's eye from the patterns formed by the stitches.

Revision: Whole-cloth quilts follow the planned design very carefully, because there is nothing to distract the viewer's eye from the patterns formed by the stitches. **They are like beautiful tapestries we often see in museums.**

With this addition, Eden helps her audience make a connection between her description of whole-cloth quilts and tapestries in museums.

Analysis

To analyze an idea, you must first break it into its basic parts. Then you need to explain the relationship between those parts. Analysis is a major component of essays on many serious topics. You might find this skill especially useful in writing for sociology, science, and psychology classes.

In paragraph 5 of the professional essay in this chapter, Zinsser analyzes how he makes word choices:

> If you find yourself writing that someone recently enjoyed a spell of ill-ness or that a business has been enjoying a slump, stop and think how much they enjoyed it. Notice the decisions that other writers make in their choice of words and be finicky about the ones that you select from the vast supply. The race in writing is not to the swift but to the original.

Eden found a weak example of analysis in paragraph 4 of her essay, so she strengthened the paragraph with more detailed information:

First Draft: To make a quilt, you start out with the top layer, which is where the designs appear. There are three basic methods of construction for quilts. The ones we see most often are pieced quilts. Appliquéd quilts are made by using a base fabric and sewing smaller pieces onto it. The last category of quilts is the whole-cloth quilt.

Revision: To make a quilt, you start out with the top layer, which is where the designs appear. There are three basic methods of construction for quilts. The ones we see most often are pieced quilts **made of small pieces of fabric sewn together, forming geometric designs of many colors.** Appliquéd quilts are made by using a base fabric and sewing smaller pieces onto it, **forming flowers or animals or other more complicated designs.** The last category of quilts is the whole-cloth quilt **made by taking one large piece of fabric and stitching an elaborate design that will cover the whole surface with quilting stitches.**

The entire paragraph is now clearer and more interesting to read.

Exercises R4-1

In William Zinsser's essay "Words" (pp. 114–117), find one example (other than the ones used in this section) of each of the methods of development you have just studied.

Exercise R4-2

Mark places in Eden's first draft (pp. 122–125), that could be developed further using at least three of the methods you have studied in this chapter. Write down the method you suggest.

Exercise R4-3

Using the methods of paragraph development that you reviewed in this chapter, supply sentences that give supporting details for each of the topic sentences below. Use each method at least once, and label each method you use.

1. Many people do not understand exactly what the mass media are.
2. Most people learn their sense of right and wrong.
3. Wages control a firm's cost of doing business.
4. My down jacket is a useful item of apparel.
5. A library is like a gold mine in many ways.
6. Rock and country are both popular types of music at my school.
7. The study methods that work for me might not be the right ones for you.
8. Every one of us has the potential for improving his or her daily life.
9. Strong paragraphs can be logically developed in several ways.
10. Who needs big business (like General Motors and McDonnell Douglas) in America?

Exercise R4-4

Complete the following paragraphs, using a combination of the strategies described in this chapter: defining, describing, giving examples, classifying, assigning cause/effect, comparing/contrasting, *and* analyzing.

1. Washing my car can be a rewarding and frustrating experience. Depending on the weather, my schedule, and my energy level, my car's outward appearance may or may not be shiny and clean.
2. Budgeting time in today's hectic world is a worthwhile task. Even with a job, classes to attend, family obligations, and social activities, an organized person can certainly achieve all of his or her goals and manage to have time for recreation and other fun activities.
3. Many people today are concerned about the ecology of the world we live in. Efforts to prevent pollution, recycle, and use safer, nontoxic materials have benefited human beings.

 ## COLLABORATIVE WORK

After writing a draft of your own explaining essay, exchange papers with a classmate, and do the following tasks:

A.   Put brackets around any sections of the essay that could be developed more fully.

B. Considering all the techniques of paragraph development that you have just studied, suggest ways to develop each paragraph further.

Then return the paper to its writer, and use the information in this section to revise your draft.

Fragments and Run-ons

Checklist for Correcting Fragments and Run-ons

✓ Is each sentence **complete**?

✓ Does each **noun phrase** that functions as a subject have a verb?

✓ Are **verb phrases** paired with subjects?

✓ Do **verbal phrases** either function as subjects and have their own verbs, or are they paired with independent clauses?

✓ Are **prepositional phrases** connected to independent clauses?

✓ Is each **dependent clause** joined to an independent clause?

✓ Does each sentence express only one **complete thought**? If not, are **run-ons** corrected?

Writers have many goals in mind when they begin putting words on paper or on the computer screen. The goal may be a passing grade, a scholarship, a job interview, or a friendly reply. Whatever the specific reason, communicating a meaningful message should be the overriding purpose of any writing activity—relating important, detailed information to readers in sentences that are structurally and grammatically sound.

Often writers fall short of their communication goals because their sentences are at fault, either providing too little or too much information for readers to take in. Sentences with too little information may simply need more details. But often these sentences are missing essential structural parts, resulting in what we call *fragments*, incomplete sentences that are difficult to understand. Similarly, sentences with too much information may simply be wordy and need minor revision. However, many of these sentences—appropriately called *run-ons*—present two or more complete thoughts without proper punctuation or transitions between them. In this section, you will learn to identify and correct sentence fragments and run-ons, a stumbling block for many writers.

Fragments

A sentence can have an unlimited number of words if they are punctuated correctly. But only two words are necessary to make a complete sentence—a subject and a verb. When either of these words is missing, the thought is incomplete, resulting in a **fragment.**

Fragments are sometimes acceptable in spoken and written language. Our everyday conversations abound in fragments, particularly when we answer questions ("Where are you going?" "Home.") or express strong emotions ("What a play!" "Incredible!"). But you should not use fragments in academic writing so that your thoughts are not misread.

If you happen to find fragments as you edit your work, correcting the incomplete sentences should be an easy process. Simply determine what sentence element is missing—a subject, a verb, or both a subject and a verb—and then supply the missing part. Sometimes you can connect the fragment to a nearby sentence by adding or deleting words. In the end, you will realize that fragments are nothing more than phrases and clauses masquerading as sentences. The subjects and verbs of each independent clause are in bold type in the examples that follow, and the fragments are underlined.

Phrase Fragments

A phrase has a subject or a verb but never both. Thus, a phrase can never stand alone as a sentence. The phrases that most often try to pass themselves off as sentences are noun phrases, verb phrases, verbal phrases, and prepositional phrases.

Noun Phrases

The first draft of Eden's explaining essay about quilting contains several fragments. Look at the following example from paragraph 2:

Fragment:	<u>Some of my first library books</u>. These were about making dolls.

It is easy to see that the first sentence is a fragment because none of the six words is a main verb. The books are not doing anything or even existing in a state of being. The noun phrase needs a main verb to be a sentence. The sentence that follows the fragment contains a verb that makes combining the two constructions a good revision choice:

Eden's Revision:	**S** **V** **Some** of my first library books./ ~~These~~ **were** about making dolls.

Of course, you can add another verb or even an entire independent clause to the noun phrase. Whatever your choice, the resulting sentence should have one main subject and one main verb:

Possible Revision:	**S** **V** **Some** of my first library books./ **kept** me occupied for hours. These were about making dolls.
Possible Revision:	**S** **V** **I** vividly **remember** s~~S~~ome of my first library books. These were about making dolls.

Verb Phrases

Obviously, a verb phrase is missing a subject. Look at this excerpt from Eden's first draft:

Fragments: One of my favorite books. Had instructions to make some

simple doll quilts.

The first fragment is a noun phrase. The second fragment is a verb phrase beginning with the verb *had*. Correcting the two fragments is a simple process of combining the two phrases and supplying the correct punctuation:

                    s   **v**
Eden's   **One** of my favorite books./ **hHad** instructions to make
Revision:
                    some simple doll quilts.

You may choose to combine the verb phrase fragment with another fragment or with a complete sentence. Or you may supply a missing subject. Look at this example from paragraph 5 of Eden's first draft:

Fragment: Appliquéd quilts are interesting and intricate. Often have

quilting stitches around the designs and large areas where

quilting stitches form the only design.

                            s   **v**   **s**
Possible   Appliquéd **quilts are** interesting and intricate. **They** o∅ften
Revision: **v**
                    have quilting stitches around the designs and large areas

where quilting stitches form the only design.

                            s   **v**
Eden's   Appliquéd **quilts are** interesting and intricate./, o∅ften
Revision:
                    hav∅ing quilting stitches around the designs and large

areas where quilting stitches form the only design.

Verbal Phrases

As you learned in Chapter 3, verbals are words that look like verbs but function as other parts of speech. There are three types of verbal phrases. **Infinitive phrases** consist of the word *to* plus a verb and other words that complete the infinitive's meaning (*to sleep late, to get off work on time*). Infinitive phrases can function as adjectives, adverbs, or nouns. **Participial phrases**, always functioning as adjectives, usually begin with a word ending in *-ing* or *-ed*. Words that refer to the participle complete the phrase (*sleeping on the couch, getting off work on time*). **Gerund phrases** begin with an *-ing* word and function as nouns (*Paying my credit card bills* is my top priority).

When infinitive phrases and participial phrases appear as fragments, you can usually correct them by joining them to nearby sentences. Look at these examples from the first two paragraphs of Eden's first draft:

Fragment:	No one in my family had ever made quilts, so I had to work on my own. <u>To learn everything from books.</u>

        S   V   V   S V

Eden's Revision:	**No one** in my family **had** ever **made** quilts, so **I had** to work on my own./ t**To** learn everything from books.

Fragment:	I give my hobby a great deal of creative energy. <u>Using quilting as a way to express myself.</u>

        S V

Eden's Revision:	**I give** my hobby a great deal of creative energy/, u**U**sing quilting as a way to express myself.

To correct gerund phrases that appear as fragments, you can usually (1) add both a subject and a verb, making the phrase the direct object, or (2) add a verb, making the phrase the subject. Look at this example from paragraph 3 of Eden's first draft:

Fragment:	<u>Learning how to sew projects very rapidly on the sewing machine.</u>

        S   V

Possible Revision:	**I** especially **liked** l**L**earning how to sew projects very rapidly on the sewing machine.

            S

Eden's Revision:	**Learning** how to sew projects very rapidly on the sewing machine./ **gave** me confidence.

                   V

Prepositional Phrases

Prepositional phrase fragments occur less frequently than the other fragments we have discussed because the preposition's function is to connect words. Of course, a prepositional phrase may begin a sentence as long as the thought is complete. The easiest way to correct a prepositional phrase fragment is to connect the phrase to the sentence it refers to.

In paragraph 5 of her first draft, Eden has written a prepositional phrase fragment:

Fragment: The most desirable stitches are tiny puckers. In the fabric.

                                                           S   V

Eden's Revision: The most desirable **stitches are** tiny puckers./ i̶In the fabric.

Eden probably added the fragment "In the fabric" in her first draft as an afterthought. But these are the kinds of errors she needs to correct in her revision. This prepositional phrase fragment can simply be added to the clause before it.

Subordinate Clause Fragments

Although phrase fragments are relatively easy to identify and correct, clause fragments pose different challenges. Writers are sometimes fooled into thinking these are complete sentences because a clause fragment is a group of words that contains a subject and verb. These fragments, however, are dependent clauses. Even though they contain subjects and verbs, dependent clauses begin with words that *subordinate* them, making the clauses dependent upon an independent clause for their meaning. Probably the best strategy for telling the difference between a dependent clause and a sentence is to review subordinating conjunctions (p. 51) and relative pronouns (p. 44), words that commonly begin dependent clauses.

Because dependent clauses rely on independent clauses for their meaning, the simplest way to correct them is to combine the two. On rare occasions, you may have to compose an independent clause to add to the dependent clause fragment. However, the sentence before or after the clause fragment will normally provide the necessary components, as these sentences from Eden's first draft illustrate:

Fragment: Even though my doll quilts would not have won any prizes. I was persistent.

Eden's Revision: Even though my doll quilts would not have won any
                            S V
prizes./, **I was** persistent.

                      S   V

Fragment: My **efforts** at the doll quilts **were** more successful than my doll-making ventures. Which frustrated me to no end.

$$ \overset{S}{} \qquad \overset{V}{} $$

Revision: My **efforts** at the doll quilts **were** more successful than

my doll-making ventures/, w~~W~~hich frustrated me to no end.

Exercise E4-1

Each of the following fragments is part of a complete sentence taken from William Zinsser's essay "Words" (pp. 114–117). First, identify the fragment as a noun phase, verb phrase, verbal phrase, prepositional phrase, or dependent clause. Then refer to the essay and copy the sentence as it originally appears. Finally, explain what the sentence needed to become complete.

Fragment: Who sits down to write. (paragraph 1)   Clause fragment.

Sentence: You must fight these phrases or you'll sound like every hack who sits down to write. (The fragment needed an independent clause to become complete.)

1. Patched together out of other parts of speech. (paragraph 2)
2. If you find yourself writing that someone recently enjoyed a spell of illness or that a business has been enjoying a slump. (paragraph 5)
3. A typical example—maybe not the best, but undeniably the nearest. (paragraph 9)
4. Always listening to what he writes. (paragraph 10)
5. Should be woven through everything you write. (paragraph 11)

Exercise E4-2

Underline the five fragments in paragraphs 6 and 7 of Eden's first draft (pp.124–125).

Exercise E4-3

Underline the fragments in the following paragraph, indicating whether they are phrase or clause fragments.

My mother is a garage sale junkie. A woman obsessed with finding bargains almost every day of the week. She scours the classifieds. Looking for estate sales, rummage sales, yard sales, moving sales—any sale within driving distance. Sometimes she gets up at 5:30 in the morning. To be first in line at a sale that sounds promising. I have to say that she is rather selective in the things she buys. Usually glassware that she collects and clothes that will fit every member of the family. She is also good about organizing the treasures that she finds. The glass items find places on the shelves in our basement. Or in boxes that are packed away in the attic. She says one day she will sell some of her things at an antique mall. The clothes go in our closets. Where they hang until we decide to wear them. She knows what we like, so we usually put her bargains to good use. I guess everyone needs a hobby. At least my mother's hobby saves our family some money. Hard-earned money at that.

Exercise E4-4

1. Correct the fragments you identified in Exercise E4-2.
2. Correct the fragments you identified in Exercise E4-3.

Run-ons

When writers sit down to work, ideas often come in a mad rush. They type or scrawl as fast as they can, trying to transform their thoughts into readable material. Sometimes those thoughts run into each other when they reach the computer screen or the notebook page, creating sentences with too many ideas that confuse and overwhelm the reader. These overloaded **run-on sentences** present two or more independent thoughts punctuated as one.

Run-ons simply don't stop where they are supposed to end. Thus, one sure sign of a run-on is incorrect punctuation, which comes in two varieties. When no punctuation separates the independent thoughts, we call the run-on a fused sentence. When the wrong punctuation mark separates the independent thoughts, a comma splice results.

Fused Sentences

Usually when two things are fused, a bonding agent, such as glue or tape, is used. In the case of a fused sentence, nothing holds the two independent thoughts together but the author's intentions. A **fused sentence** consists of two or more independent clauses run together without proper punctuation or capitalization. Look at the following example from the first draft of Eden's explaining essay.

Fused sentence: The best **days** of the month for them **are** the days they find new issues of the quilting magazines in their mailboxes / at least an **hour is required** to look at each new magazine and fantasize about making a multitude of new projects.

If you look closely and locate the subject-verb pairs, you can tell where the first complete idea ends and the second begins (marked here with a slash). Thus, the fused sentence needs punctuation that separates the independent clauses:

| **Eden's Revision:** | The best **days** of the month for them **are** the days they find new issues of the quilting magazines in their mailboxes. **A**at least an **hour is required** to look at each new magazine and fantasize about making a multitude of new projects. |

Paragraph 5 of Eden's first draft contains another fused sentence:

	S V V
Fused Sentence:	The **sandwich is** temporarily **fastened** together with safety pins or long, loose stitches called basting stitches /
	S V
	then the **work** of quilting **begins**.

Again, correcting the fused sentence is a simple process of supplying the necessary punctuation and capitalization:

| **Eden's Revision:** | The **sandwich is** temporarily **fastened** together with safety pins or long, loose stitches called basting stitches. **T**then the **work** of quilting **begins**. |

Comma Splices

Explaining the difference between a fused sentence and a comma splice is simple. Whereas no punctuation separates the independent clauses in a fused sentence, a comma by itself incorrectly separates the independent clauses in a comma splice. Because many writers overuse and misuse commas, comma splices usually occur more often than fused sentences.

Eden begins paragraph 5 of her first draft with a comma splice:

Comma Splice:	Once the quilt top is made, another **piece** of fabric **is cut**
	S V
	to match it, / **this will form** the backing.

Just as with a fused sentence, correcting a comma splice depends on identifying where the first independent clause ends and the second one begins. Isolating the subjects and verbs will help:

Eden's Revision:	Once the quilt top is made, another **piece** of fabric **is cut** to match it/. **T̸his will form** the backing.

Longer sentences with more commas may prove more challenging. Look at this example from paragraph 7 of Eden's first draft about quilting:

	S V
Comma Splice:	Every time I see a quilt, **I am reminded** of the sewing skills of our frugal, hardworking ancestors, / most
	S V
	people know that women used every scrap of fabric, material usually left over from sewing projects and pieces of worn clothing.

Even when a sentence has several commas, you can identify the independent clauses—the parts of the comma splice that can stand alone. Then revising the sentence becomes a simple proposition of providing proper punctuation and capitalization:

Eden's Revision:	Every time I see a quilt, **I am reminded** of the sewing skills of our frugal, hardworking ancestors/. **M̸m**ost **people know** that women used every scrap of fabric, material usually left over from sewing projects and pieces of worn clothing.

Other Correction Options

Breaking down fused sentences and comma splices into separate sentences is usually the simplest way to correct run-on sentence errors. All you have to do is insert periods where they are needed and provide the correct capitalization. Other correction options, however, may produce sentences that are stylistically more interesting. Whatever editing choice you make, remember that the key to eliminating fused sentences and comma splices is isolating independent clauses.

1. *Use a comma and a coordinating conjunction.* Dividing a comma splice into two separate sentences often results in choppy simple sentences that look and sound the same. For variety, insert a comma and a coordinating conjunction (*for, and, nor, but, or, yet, so*) between the two independent clauses. This editing choice will produce either a compound or compound-complex sentence.

Fused Sentence: Eden **plans** to work part-time this summer / **she will**

volunteer at the downtown food kitchen in her spare
time.

Revision: Eden **plans** to work part time this summer**, *and* she will**
volunteer at the downtown food kitchen in her spare
time.

Comma Splice: When Eden decided to major in art, her **mother was**

happy, / her **father was** disappointed because he thought
she should pursue a medical career.

Revision: When Eden decided to major in art, her **mother was**
happy, *but* her **father was** disappointed because he
though she should pursue a medical career.

2. *Use a semicolon.* When appropriate and for variety in punctuation, you can
    use a semicolon instead of a period, but note that you should not use semi-
    colons interchangeably with periods. Certain conditions must be met for a
    semicolon to be the best choice: The independent clauses should be similar
    in structure and meaning, and they should present either similar or contrast-
    ing ideas.

Fused Sentence: Eden's **teachers were** very understanding when she had to

miss class because of the flu / **all** of them **cooperated** by
giving her the assignments and letting her make up
quizzes and lab work.

Revision: Eden's **teachers were** very understanding when she had to
miss class because of the flu**;** **all** of them **cooperated** by
giving her the assignments and letting her make up
quizzes and lab work.

Comma Splice: Eden **likes** to stay up past midnight and sleep late, / her

           S   V

brother Tony **likes** to go to bed before 10 p.m. and get up before sunrise.

Revision: **Eden likes** to stay up past midnight and sleep late/**;** her **brother** Tony **likes** to go to bed before 10 p.m. and get up before sunrise.

3. *Use subordinating conjunctions and relative pronouns.* You learned in Chapter 2 that subordinating conjunctions (*because, since, although,* etc.—see p. 51) and relative pronouns (*who, whom, which, that,* etc.; see p. 46) introduce dependent clauses. By using these connecting words, you can turn one of the independent clauses in a fused sentence or comma splice into a dependent clause.

                               S   V   S

Fused Sentence: **Eden said** she didn't have anything to wear / **she** still

                       V

went to the wedding.

Revision: *Even though* **Eden said** she didn't have anything to wear**, she** still **went** to the wedding.

                     S   V

Comma Splice: **Matt went** to the driver's license bureau to buy a vanity

                                   S   V

license plate, / the **woman** who waited on him **said** the plate he wanted—BUG LVR—was already taken.

Revision: *When* **Matt went** to the driver's license bureau to buy a vanity license plate, the **woman** who waited on him **said** the plate he wanted—BUG LVR—was already taken.

                    S   V   S   V

Fused Sentence: **Eden took** a step aerobics class this semester / **this was** a good choice because she lost eight pounds and improved her cardiovascular condition.

Revision: **Eden took** a step aerobics class this semester**,** *which* ~~this~~ **was** a good choice because she lost eight pounds and improved her cardiovascular condition.

                                      S   V   S
Comma Splice: Charlie **decided** to join a fraternity, / the **one** he pledged

                      V
has over 100 members.

Revision: Charlie **decided** to join a fraternity/ *that* ~~the one he pledged~~ **has** over 100 hundred members.

4. *Use participles.* Participles, if you remember, are adjectives that are made from verbs, usually by adding *-ing* or *-ed.* Often, participles are accompanied by other words that work together to form a participial phrase. By learning how to use participles and participial phrases, you can correct sentence errors and provide more sentence variety in your essays. (For more information on using participles, see p. 53).

   Look again at some of the examples we have already discussed:

                                      S   V   S
Fused Sentence: Eden **said** she didn't have anything to wear / **she** still

                      V
went to the wedding.

Revision: *Saying* ~~Eden said~~ she didn't have anything to wear**, Eden** ~~she~~ still **went** to the wedding.

                                      S   V   S
Comma Splice: Charlie **decided** to join a fraternity, / the **one** he pledged

                      V
has over 100 members.

Revision: *Deciding* ~~Charlie decided~~ to join a fraternity, **Charlie pledged** one with ~~the one he pledged has~~ over 100 members.

5. *Eliminate any unnecessary words, or reword and shift sentence elements.* Sometimes you can accomplish two goals at once when you correct run-ons. Eliminating words that are not needed and moving words and phrases will produce a sentence that is more concise, one that communicates clearly in fewer words.

Fused Sentence: Eden **decided** to wear a pair of satin pants and a matching

                                                              S   V
blouse to the wedding / **it was** an afternoon wedding.

Revision: Eden **decided** to wear a pair of satin pants and a matching blouse to the *afternoon* wedding ~~it was an afternoon wedding.~~

Comma Splice: **s** **v**
I think I will be able to save some money every time I get a check from work, but invariably something comes along

                                 s   **v**
to take the extra money, my **car breaks** down, or I have to take the dog to the vet, or something like that.

Revision: *Every payday* **I think** I will be able to save some money, ~~every time I get a check from work~~, but invariably something comes along to take the extra money, *like my car breaking down or my dog needing a vet* ~~my car breaks down, or I have to take the dog to the vet, or something like that~~.

All these revisions communicate the important parts of their messages more directly and more concisely.

Exercise E4-5

The following run-ons are drawn from complete sentences that appear in William Zinsser's essay "Words." First indicate whether the run-on is a fused sentence or a comma splice. Then underline the independent clauses that make up each run-on sentence.

1. Last February, Plainclothes Patrolman Frank Serpico knocked at the door of a suspected Brooklyn heroin pusher when the door opened a crack, Serpico shouldered his way in only to be met by a .22-cal. pistol slug crashing into his face.
2. Writing is learned by imitation, if anyone asked me how I learned to write, I'd say that I learned by reading the men and women who were doing the kind of writing I wanted to do and trying to figure out how they did it.
3. You'll find rogues and wretches, ruffians and riffraff, miscreants and malefactors, reprobates and rapscallions, hooligans and hoodlums, scamps and scapegraces, scoundrels and scalawags, jezebels and jades, you'll find adjectives to fit them all (foul and fiendish, devilish and diabolical), and adverbs, and verbs to describe how the wrongdoers do their wrong, and cross-references leading to still other thickets of venality and vice.
4. He wasn't enjoying it, however, with his eyes, he was enjoying it in his ear.
5. The good writer of prose must be part poet, always listening to what he writes E. B. White continues across the years to be my favorite stylist because I'm so conscious of being with a man who cares about the cadences and sonorities of the language.

Exercise E4-6

The run-on sentences that follow are adapted from Eden's revised draft of "Quilts." Label each sentence fused or comma splice. Then, underline the independent clauses that make up each run-on.

1. Today, many people consider quilts, which basically consist of a top layer of pieces of fabric and a bottom layer of whole cloth sandwiched around a stuffing, an art form I like nothing better than spending hours in my sewing room with a huge stack of books and little pieces of fabric, sketching ideas and trying them out, creating something that no one else will ever duplicate.

2. To make a quilt, you start out with the top layer, which is where the designs appear, there are three basic methods of construction for quilts.

3. The ones we see most often are pieced quilts made of small pieces of fabric sewn together, forming geometric designs of many colors, appliquéd quilts are made by using a base fabric and sewing smaller pieces onto it, forming flowers or animals or other more complicated designs.

4. Quilting stitches go through all three layers and follow many different kinds of designs some of the pieced quilts are outlined with quilting.

5. Most quilters I have met would rather quilt than do anything else in their spare time many of them belong to one or more quilting guilds, organizations whose members challenge each other to develop their skills and encourage and praise each other when they finish a project or try something different.

Exercise E4-7

Edit the following paragraphs, also written by Eden, correcting run-on sentences.

Many people enjoy watching old movies. First of all, renting a classic video is cheaper than going out to the movies, often watching old films is an educational experience. It's fun looking at how the stars, fashions, and moviemaking have changed over the past decades.

You can also trace a star's career by watching many of the movies that he or she made. My favorite star from the past is Marilyn Monroe. I have watched every movie that's out on video, sometimes I will sit up into the early morning hours watching one of her films on television. Of course, Marilyn first became a star because of her glamorous, sensual beauty, which appealed to both men and women. However, I think Marilyn was an underrated actress who is being fully appreciated years after her untimely death.

Marilyn gave some great comedic and dramatic performances that make her acting career truly special. I suggest *The Seven Year Itch* or *Some Like it Hot* for comedy, for drama check out *Bus Stop*, a film performance many people think should have won her an Oscar nomination. Many people also forget that Marilyn sang and danced, quite well, I might add. *Gentlemen Prefer Blondes* and *There's No Business Like Show Business* showcase her singing and dancing talents. After watching a few Marilyn Monroe films, most fans agree that there's certainly been no star in history like her, in fact, she's more popular today than ever.

Exercise E4-8

Correct the run-on sentences in Exercises E4-5 and E4-6.

COLLABORATIVE WORK

After you revise your explaining essay, exchange papers with a classmate, and do the following tasks:

A. Put any fragments in brackets.

B. Put a slash between run-on sentences (both fused and comma splices).

Then return the paper to its writer, and use the information in this section to edit your draft.

TIPS FOR EDITING

Investigating
Reading and Writing for a Reason

Education . . . it's asking questions, all the time.
—ARNOLD WESKER

A good investigative journalist is someone who finds out all the facts and gets answers to as many questions as possible. The same definition applies to students writing investigating essays, particularly in college. In fact, most college research and term papers are based on the basic principles of investigative journalism—answering the questions *who, what, where,* and *when,* which generally lead the writer to an understanding of *why* and *how.*

Investigating means gathering as much information about a person, place, event, or topic as possible. The information needed to write an investigating essay can be gathered in several ways: from interviews with experts or witnesses; from library research; on the Internet; in visits to archives (places where books, letters, personal papers, maps, legal documents, and other records are kept); from books, newspapers, magazines, and journals; or during visits to the actual places or with the people you are writing about. As technology advances, more and more research is available by computer. Whether you need to talk to a person, visit a place, or browse through books in a library, you can do it all online. However, no matter how you gather your information, you must be certain to answer the *who, what, where,* and *when* questions. If you do a thorough and careful job of this part of the investigation, you will usually find the answers to the *why* and *how* questions in the process.

Investigating does not stop, however, when you find the answers to your questions; you must then present the information in such a way that your readers will not only understand what someone did or what happened at a particular time but also realize exactly *how* an event happened and *why* it happened. Your readers will know this not because you *told* them, but because you *showed* them with supporting evidence. Adding facts, details, examples, quotations, and anecdotes to your essays provides your readers with the material they need to understand the situation for themselves.

In her biography of Eleanor Roosevelt, the wife of President Franklin D. Roosevelt, writer Doris Kearns Goodwin wrote that Eleanor Roosevelt "shattered the ceremonial mold in which the role of the First Lady had traditionally been fashioned and reshaped it around her own skills and commitments to social reform." Here is the evidence the writer uncovered during her investigation to prove that this statement is accurate:

> She was the first wife of any President to hold press conferences, to speak before a national Party Convention, to write a syndicated column (it appeared in 135 papers six times a week), to be a radio commentator. She was able to use the office of the First Lady on behalf of the causes she believed in, rather than let it use her, and in so doing she became, in the words of the columnist Raymond Clapper, the "most influential woman of our times."

Without thorough and careful investigating, the writer would not have been able to find the information she needed to write about Eleanor Roosevelt. Kearns did not simply declare that Eleanor Roosevelt was the "most influential woman of our times"; she used her skills as a writer to *show* us—through facts, evidence, and quotations—why such a conclusion is warranted.

LEARNING FROM PUBLISHED WRITERS

The following investigating essay, "A Nation at Risk," was written in 1981 as a commission report on the quality of education in U.S. schools. It was prepared by many people, including teachers, administrators, and college presidents, under the direction of David P. Gardner, then president of the University of California. Because this report received widespread coverage in the press, everyone—from parents to politicians—began to ask questions about the quality of the U.S. educational system. Even today, more than 15 years later, the report is often cited as evidence of the need to reform our educational system; in fact, many people argue that the problems cited in the report have grown worse over time.

Before You Read

Focusing Your Attention

Before you read this investigation, take a few moments to respond to the following questions in your journal:

1. If you were asked to write an investigating essay about the quality of education being offered in a school you have attended—for example, your high school— whom would you interview, and what questions would you ask? If it has been some time since you attended high school, you could focus on the college you are currently attending.

2. In the report you are about to read, the writer claims, "Our society and its educational institutions seem to have lost sight of the basic purposes of schooling." If

you were an investigative reporter, whom would you interview to determine what the basic purposes of schooling are or should be?

Expanding Your Vocabulary

Here are some words and their meanings that are important to your understanding of the report. You might want to review them before you begin to read.

"unchallenged **preeminence** [excelling above all others] in commerce" (paragraph 1)

"**undergirds** [supports, strengthens] American prosperity" (paragraph 1)

"**squandered** [wasted, used foolishly] the gains . . . made in the wake of the **Sputnik** [the first Russian orbiting satellite] challenge" (paragraph 2)

"we have **dismantled** [taken apart, eliminated] essential support systems" (paragraph 2)

"**unilateral** [one-sided] educational **disarmament** [reduction of forces]" (paragraph 2)

"History is not kind to **idlers** [those who do nothing with their time]." (paragraph 4)

"Learning is the **indispensable** [essential] investment" (paragraph 5)

"individuals . . . will be effectively **disenfranchised** [deprived of a right]" (paragraph 6)

"the **fostering** [encouraging] of a common culture" (paragraph 6)

"a country that prides itself on **pluralism** [coexistence of many different ethnic, religious, and cultural groups within one society]" (paragraph 6)

"famous **dictum** [pronouncement, statement]" (paragraph 7)

"exercise their control with a wholesome **discretion** [prudence, self-restraint]" (paragraph 7)

"growing **chasm** [gap]" (paragraph 11)

"schools may emphasize such **rudiments** [basics] as reading and computation" (paragraph 12)

"Knowledge . . . must be **harnessed** [joined effectively] to science and technology" (paragraph 12)

"Each generation has **outstripped** [done better than] its parents" (paragraph 12)

"a **coherent continuum** [logical, ongoing sequence] of learning" (paragraph 15)

"an **incoherent** [impossible to understand], outdated patchwork quilt" (paragraph 15) "pressures that **inhibit** [prevent from fully developing] . . . achievement" (paragraph 15)

"**transcend** [rise beyond] the boundaries of our planet" (paragraph 26)

David Gardner et al.

A Nation at Risk

Our Nation is at risk. Our once unchallenged preeminence in commerce, industry, science, and technological innovation is being overtaken by competitors throughout the world. This report is concerned with only one of the many causes and dimensions of the problem, but it is the one that undergirds American prosperity, security, and civility. We report to the American people that while we can take justifiable pride in what our schools and colleges have historically accomplished and contributed to the United States and the well-being of its people, the educational foundations of our society are presently being eroded by a rising tide of mediocrity that threatens our very future as a Nation and a people. What was unimaginable a generation ago has begun to occur—others are matching and surpassing our educational attainments.

If an unfriendly foreign power had attempted to impose on America the mediocre educational performance that exists today, we might well have viewed it as an act of war. As it stands, we have allowed this to happen to ourselves. We have even squandered the gains in student achievement made in the wake of the Sputnik challenge. Moreover, we have dismantled essential support systems which helped make those gains possible. We have, in effect, been committing an act of unthinking, unilateral educational disarmament.

Our society and its educational institutions seem to have lost sight of the basic purposes of schooling, and of the high expectations and disciplined effort needed to attain them. This report, the result of 18 months of study, seeks to generate reform of our educational system in fundamental ways and to renew the Nation's commitment to schools and colleges of high quality throughout the length and breadth of our land.

The Risk

History is not kind to idlers. The time is long past when America's destiny was assured simply by an abundance of natural resources and inexhaustible human enthusiasm, and by our relative isolation from the malignant problems of older civilizations. The world is indeed one global village. We live among determined, well-educated, and strongly motivated competitors. We compete with them for international standing and markets, not only with products but also with the ideas of our laboratories and neighborhood workshops. America's position in the world may once have been reasonably secure with only a few exceptionally well-trained men and women. It is no longer.

The risk is not only that the Japanese make automobiles more effi-   5 ciently than Americans and have government subsidies for development and export. It is not just that the South Koreans recently built the world's most efficient steel mill, or that American machine tools, once the pride of the world, are being displaced by German products. It is also that these developments signify a redistribution of trained capability throughout the globe. Knowledge, learning, information, and skilled intelligence are the new raw materials of international commerce and are today spreading throughout the world as vigorously as miracle drugs, synthetic fertilizers, and blue jeans did earlier. If only to keep and improve on the slim competitive edge we still retain in world markets, we must dedicate ourselves to the reform of our educational system for the benefit of all—old and young alike, affluent and poor, majority and minority. Learning is the indispensable investment required for success in the "information age" we are entering.

Our concern, however, goes well beyond matters such as indus-   6 try and commerce. It also includes the intellectual, moral, and spiritual strengths of our people which knit together the very fabric of our society. The people of the United States need to know that individuals in our society who do not possess the levels of skill, literacy, and training essential to this new era will be effectively disenfranchised, not simply from the material rewards that accompany competent performance, but also from the chance to participate fully in our national life. A high level of shared education is essential to a free, democratic society and to the fostering of a common culture, especially in a country that prides itself on pluralism and individual freedom.

For our country to function, citizens must be able to reach some   7 common understandings on complex issues, often on short notice and on the basis of conflicting or incomplete evidence. Education helps form these common understandings, a point Thomas Jefferson made long ago in his justly famous dictum:

> I know no safe depository of the ultimate powers of the society but the people themselves; and if we think them not enlightened enough to exercise their control with a wholesome discretion, the remedy is not to take it from them but to inform their discretion.

Part of what is at risk is the promise first made on this continent: **8** All, regardless of race or class or economic status, are entitled to a fair chance and to the tools for developing their individual powers of mind and spirit to the utmost. This promise means that all children by virtue of their own efforts, competently guided, can hope to attain the mature and informed judgment needed to secure gainful employment and to manage their own lives, thereby serving not only their own interests but also the progress of society itself.

Indicators of the Risk

The educational dimensions of the risk before us have been amply **9** documented in testimony received by the Commission. For example,

- International comparisons of student achievement, completed a decade ago, reveal that on 19 academic tests American students were never first or second and, in comparison with other industrialized nations, were last seven times.

- Some 23 million American adults are functionally illiterate by the simplest tests of everyday reading, writing, and comprehension.

- About 13 percent of all 17-year-olds in the United States can be considered functionally illiterate. Functional illiteracy among minority youth may run as high as 40 percent.

- Average achievement of high school students on most standardized tests is now lower than 26 years ago when Sputnik was launched.

- Over half the population of gifted students do not match their tested ability with comparable achievement in school.

- The College Board's Scholastic Aptitude Tests (SAT) demonstrate a virtually unbroken decline from 1963 to 1980. Average verbal scores fell over 50 points and average mathematics scores dropped nearly 40 points.

- College Board achievement tests also reveal consistent declines in recent years in such subjects as physics and English.

- Both the number and proportion of students demonstrating superior achievement on the SATs (i.e., those with scores of 650 or higher) have also dramatically declined.

- There was a steady decline in science achievement scores of U.S. 17-year-olds as measured by national assessments of science in 1969, 1973, and 1977.

- Between 1975 and 1980, remedial mathematics courses in public four-year colleges increased by 72 percent and now constitute one-quarter of all mathematics courses taught in those institutions.

- Average tested achievement of students graduating from college is also lower.

- Business and military leaders complain that they are required to spend millions of dollars on costly remedial education and training programs in such basic skills as reading, writing, spelling, and computation. The Department of the Navy, for example, reported to the Commission that one-quarter of its recent recruits cannot read at the ninth grade level, the minimum needed simply to understand written safety instructions. Without remedial work they cannot even begin, much less complete, the sophisticated training essential in much of the modern military.

These deficiencies come at a time when the demand for highly **10** skilled workers in new fields is accelerating rapidly. For example:

- Computers and computer-controlled equipment are penetrating every aspect of our lives—homes, factories, and offices.

- One estimate indicates that by the turn of the century millions of jobs will involve laser technology and robotics.

- Technology is radically transforming a host of other occupations. They include health care, medical science, energy production, food processing, construction, and the building, repair, and maintenance of sophisticated scientific, educational, military, and industrial equipment.

Analysts examining these indicators of student performance and **11** the demands for new skills have made some chilling observations. Educational researcher Paul Hurd concluded at the end of a thorough national survey of student achievement that within the context of the modern scientific revolution, "We are raising a new generation of Americans that is scientifically and technologically illiterate." In a similar vein, John Slaughter, a former Director of the National Science Foundation, warned of "a growing chasm between a small scientific and technological elite and a citizenry ill-informed, indeed uninformed, on issues with a science component."

But the problem does not stop there, nor do all observers see it **12** the same way. Some worry that schools may emphasize such rudiments as reading and computation at the expense of other essential skills such as comprehension, analysis, solving problems, and drawing conclusions. Still others are concerned that an over-emphasis on technical and occupational skills will leave little time for studying the arts and humanities that so enrich daily life, help maintain civility, and develop a sense of community. Knowledge of the humanities, they maintain, must be harnessed to science and technology if the latter are to remain creative and humane, just as the humanities need to be informed by science and technology if they are to remain relevant to the human condition. Another analyst, Paul Copperman, has drawn a sobering conclusion. Until now, he has noted,

> Each generation of Americans has outstripped its parents in education, in literacy, and in economic attainment. For the first time in the history of our country, the educational skills of one generation will not surpass, will not equal, will not even approach, those of their parents.

It is important, of course, to recognize that *the average citizen* today **13** is better educated and more knowledgeable than the average citizen of a generation ago—more literate, and exposed to more mathematics, literature, and science. The positive impact of this fact on the well-being of our country and the lives of our people cannot be overstated. Nevertheless, *the average graduate* of our schools and colleges today is not as well-educated as the average graduate of 25 or 35 years ago, when a much smaller proportion of our population completed high school and college. The negative impact of this fact likewise cannot be overstated.

The Learning Society

In a world of ever-accelerating competition and change in the con- 14
ditions of the workplace, of ever-greater danger, and of ever-larger opportunities for those prepared to meet them, educational reform
should focus on the goal of creating a Learning Society. At the heart
of such a society is the commitment to a set of values and to a system
of education that affords all members the opportunity to stretch their
minds to full capacity, from early childhood through adulthood,
learning more as the world itself changes. Such a society has as a basic foundation the idea that education is important not only because
of what it contributes to one's career goals but also because of the
value it adds to the general quality of one's life. Also at the heart of
the Learning Society are educational opportunities extending far beyond the traditional institutions of learning, our schools and colleges.
They extend into homes and workplaces; into libraries, art galleries,
museums, and science centers; indeed, into every place where the individual can develop and mature in work and life. In our view, formal
schooling in youth is the essential foundation for learning throughout
one's life. But without life-long learning, one's skills will become
rapidly dated.

In contrast to the ideal of the Learning Society, however, we find 15
that for too many people education means doing the minimum work
necessary for the moment, then coasting through life on what may
have been learned in its first quarter. But this should not surprise us
because we tend to express our educational standards and expectations largely in terms of "minimum requirements." And where there
should be a coherent continuum of learning, we have none, but instead an often incoherent, outdated patchwork quilt. Many individual, sometimes heroic, examples of schools and colleges of great merit
do exist. Our findings and testimony confirm the vitality of a number
of notable schools and programs, but their very distinction stands out
against a vast mass shaped by tensions and pressures that inhibit systematic academic and vocational achievement for the majority of
students. In some metropolitan areas basic literacy has become the
goal rather than the starting point. In some colleges maintaining en-
rollments is of greater day-to-day concern than maintaining rigorous
academic standards. And the ideal of academic excellence as the primary goal of schooling seems to be fading across the board in American education.

Thus, we issue this call to all who care about America and its fu- 16
ture: to parents and students; to teachers, administrators, and school

board members; to colleges and industry; to union members and military leaders; to governors and State legislators; to the President; to members of Congress and other public officials; to members of learned and scientific societies; to the print and electronic media; to concerned citizens everywhere. America is at risk.

Recommendations

In light of the urgent need for improvement, both immediate and long term, this Commission has agreed on a set of recommendations that the American people can begin to act on now, that can be implemented over the next several years, and that promise lasting reform. The topics are familiar; there is little mystery about what we believe must be done. Many schools, districts, and States are already giving serious and constructive attention to these matters, even though their plans may differ from our recommendations in some details. **17**

We wish to note that we refer to public, private, and parochial schools and colleges alike. All are valuable national resources. Examples of actions similar to those recommended below can be found in each of them. **18**

We must emphasize that the variety of student aspirations, abilities, and preparation requires that appropriate content be available to satisfy diverse needs. Attention must be directed to both the nature of the content available and to the needs of particular learners. The most gifted students, for example, may need a curriculum enriched and accelerated beyond even the needs of other students of high ability. Similarly, educationally disadvantaged students may require special curriculum materials, smaller classes, or individual tutoring to help them master the material presented. Nevertheless, there remains a common expectation: We must demand the best effort and performance from all students, whether they are gifted or less able, affluent or disadvantaged, whether destined for college, the farm, or industry. **19**

Our recommendations are based on the beliefs that everyone can learn, that everyone is born with an *urge* to learn which can be nurtured, that a solid high school education is within the reach of virtually all, and that life-long learning will equip people with the skills required for new careers and for citizenship. **20**

Recommendation A: Content. We recommend that State and local high school graduation requirements be strengthened and that, at a minimum, all students seeking a diploma be required to lay the foundations in the Five New Basics by taking the following curricu- **21**

lum during their four years of high school: (a) four years of English:
(b) three years of mathematics; (c) three years of science; (d) three
years of social studies; and (e) one-half year of computer science. For
the college-bound, two years of foreign language in high school are
strongly recommended in addition to those taken earlier.

Recommendation B: Standards and Expectations. We recommend   **22**
that schools, colleges, and universities adopt more rigorous and mea-
surable standards, and higher expectations, for academic performance
and student conduct, and that four-year colleges and universities raise
their requirements for admission. This will help students do their best
educationally with challenging materials in an environment that supports learning and authentic accomplishment.

Recommendation C: Time. We recommend significantly more   **23**
time be devoted to learning the New Basics. This will require more
effective use of the existing school day, a longer school day, or a
lengthened school year.

Recommendation D: Teaching. This recommendation consists of   **24**
seven parts. Each is intended to improve the preparation of teachers
or to make teaching a more rewarding and respected profession. Each
of the seven stands on its own and should not be considered solely as
an implementing recommendation.

1. Persons preparing to teach should be required to meet high educational standards, to demonstrate an aptitude for teaching,
   and to demonstrate competence in an academic discipline.
   Colleges and universities offering teacher preparation programs should be judged by how well their graduates meet these
   criteria.
2. Salaries for the teaching profession should be increased and
   should be professionally competitive, market-sensitive, and
   performance-based. Salary, promotion, tenure, and retention
   decisions should be tied to an effective evaluation system that
   includes peer review so that superior teachers can be rewarded,
   average ones encouraged, and poor ones either improved or ter-
   minated.
3. School boards should adopt an 11-month contract for teachers.
   This would ensure time for curriculum and professional development, programs for students with special needs, and a more adequate level of teacher compensation.
4. School boards, administrators, and teachers should cooperate to
   develop career ladders for teachers that distinguish among the

beginning instructor, the experienced teacher, and the master teacher.

5. Substantial nonschool personnel resources should be employed to help solve the immediate problem of the shortage of mathematics and science teachers. Qualified individuals including recent graduates with mathematics and science degrees, graduate students, and industrial and retired scientists could, with appropriate preparation, immediately begin teaching in these fields. A number of our leading science centers have the capacity to begin educating and retraining teachers immediately. Other areas of critical teacher need, such as English, must also be addressed.

6. Incentives, such as grants and loans, should be made available to attract outstanding students to the teaching profession, particularly in those areas of critical shortage.

7. Master teachers should be involved in designing teacher preparation programs and in supervising teachers during their probationary years.

America Can Do It

Despite the obstacles and difficulties that inhibit the pursuit of superior educational attainment, we are confident, with history as our guide, that we can meet our goal. The American educational system has responded to previous challenges with remarkable success. In the 19th century our land-grant colleges and universities provided the research and training that developed our Nation's natural resources and the rich agricultural bounty of the American farm. From the late 1800s through mid-20th century, American schools provided the educated workforce needed to seal the success of the Industrial Revolution and to provide the margin of victory in two world wars. In the early part of this century and continuing to this very day, our schools have absorbed vast waves of immigrants and educated them and their children to productive citizenship. Similarly, the Nation's Black colleges have provided opportunity and undergraduate education to the vast majority of college-educated Black Americans.

25

More recently, our institutions of higher education have provided the scientists and skilled technicians who helped us transcend the boundaries of our planet. In the last 30 years, the schools have been a major vehicle for expanded social opportunity, and now graduate 75 percent of our young people from high school. Indeed, the proportion of Americans of college age enrolled in higher education is nearly

26

twice that of Japan and far exceeds other nations such as France, West Germany, and the Soviet Union. Moreover, when international comparisons were last made a decade ago, the top 9 percent of American students compared favorably in achievement with their peers in other countries.

In addition, many large urban areas in recent years report that average student achievement in elementary schools is improving. More and more schools are also offering advanced placement programs and programs for gifted and talented students, and more and more students are enrolling in them. **27**

We are the inheritors of a past that gives us every reason to believe that we will succeed. **28**

 ## QUESTIONS FOR CRITICAL THINKING

THINKING CRITICALLY ABOUT CONTENT

1. On the basis of your own educational experiences and your knowledge of the educational system in the United States, do you think Gardner and his colleagues present a fair and accurate assessment? Explain your answer.

2. Although the report was written in 1981, what parts are accurate and relevant today? Explain your answer.

THINKING CRITICALLY ABOUT PURPOSE

3. What do you think is the purpose of this report? Explain your answer.

4. Why do you think the report compared the achievement of American students with the achievement of students in other countries? Explain your answer.

THINKING CRITICALLY ABOUT AUDIENCE

5. What type of audience do you think would most understand and appreciate this report? Explain your answer.

6. What other groups of people would benefit from reading this report? Explain your answer.

THINKING CRITICALLY ABOUT POINT OF VIEW

7. On the basis of the tone and content of this report, do you think the authors feel optimistic or pessimistic about the future of American education? Explain your answer, and cite evidence for your answer from the report itself.

8. Write a paragraph explaining how the report would be different if students, rather than educators and educational administrators, were writing it. How would it be the same?

LEARNING FROM YOUR PEERS

The first thing most people think of when they hear the word *investigating* is detective work. Actually, satisfying your curiosity about any unfamiliar subject often requires some investigation. You may go to the library or the telephone directory in search of the answers to a particular question. When you ask friends and neighbors how to find a good used car or what restaurants have the best meals, you are investigating. From this basic sense of investigating, your goal is to construct an essay that is informative and interesting to readers. To this end, we are going to follow the writing process of a student named Albert Watson in response to an investigating essay assignment.

Albert's Writing Assignment: Investigating

This is the topic Albert's instructor assigned:

When we meet people who have unusual occupations, we often wonder what led them to pursue that line of work. Maybe you know someone who appraises real estate or installs computer systems. This writing assignment will give you an opportunity to find out about people who work in fields that you find interesting, whether or not they are related to your future profession. For this assignment, you should interview someone about his or her decision to work in a specific career and then write an essay summarizing your findings.

Albert goes through the process as outlined in Chapter 1: *thinking, planning, developing, organizing, drafting, revising,* and *editing.*

Thinking

Albert tries to think of people he knows who have unusual careers. He makes a list of his relatives, neighbors, and acquaintances from church, but he can't think of anyone he finds interesting. He calls his girlfriend, Tonja, and asks how her day is going. She tells him that her cousin is visiting and she would like them to meet each other, so Albert jumps in his car and goes to Tonja's house. "I don't feel like studying, anyway," he tells himself.

When he gets to Tonja's house, he is greeted at the door by Travis. Albert tries to conceal his surprise because Tonja had not told him that Travis was in a wheelchair. After a few minutes of small talk, Travis spontaneously begins talking about his life.

When it turns out that Travis is a drug and alcohol counselor, Albert asks him if he would mind talking about the reasons for his career choice. When Travis agrees to talk, Tonja brings Albert some paper to take notes. At the end of the evening, Albert is pleasantly surprised to discover that he has done some class preparation in spite of himself. He asks Travis for permission to call him back and ask him more questions if he needs to. Travis smiles and says that he is always happy to share his experience.

Planning

Albert looks over his notes the next day. He finds that he has most of the facts he needs to write an essay about Travis and his situation. These are his notes:

> Travis started drinking heavily in high school and became a paraplegic after he dove into an empty swimming pool at a party. He didn't quit drinking, though. In fact, he started doing drugs and wasting his life because of this tragedy. Tried to escape reality. For 10 years.
>
> But his life just kept getting worse. Finally, his mama told him to get sober or get out. His whole family was sick of him stealing and wasting his life. He was sick and tired of being sick and tired himself. Finally he went into counseling. He found a clinic that would let him stay for a month. He thought it would cool things down at home.
>
> He was surprised that he really wanted to change. Being with other people who wanted to change was real helpful.
>
> When he got out of the clinic, he studied with a tutor to take his GED. Then he applied to the community college. He was admitted and liked to study. His friends ragged on him, but he was determined to change his life.
>
> He was offered a job at the clinic as soon as he finished his associate's degree.

Developing

The next time Albert looks at his notes, he thinks something is missing. He calls Tonja (in the name of research, of course) and asks her to look over his notes. She agrees, so he goes over to her house. After she reads the notes, Tonja tells Albert that her cousin Travis is one of the most interesting people on earth, yet Albert has managed to make him sound like a world-class bore.

Albert agrees to call Travis and ask for some "quotable quotes" to make the person in his essay sound more like the "real" Travis. Albert is careful to take notes as he speaks to Travis. Here are some of the quotations that Albert thinks capture Travis's personality:

> "You might say that I 'dove' right into my career."
>
> "I was never happy with myself when I was a young teenager, so I

used to drink when I was hanging out with the older boys in my neighborhood. Back in those days, I thought it made us more attractive to the ladies. Now I know better."

"I had some help making my decision. My mama said, 'Travis, get sober or get out of my house.' Since I had no idea how I could function without all the care my mama gave me, I decided to sober up quickly."

"I had never heard of any paraplegic bank robbers."

"The problem with drinking is that it is like a roller-coaster ride. You can only go so high, and then you come crashing down. After being through so many highs and lows, I was ready for some level ground."

"There were many people who called me an inspiration. I think that's quite a reputation to live up to, and I take that as an obligation."

"My life today, along with my future, holds rewarding, challenging, and interesting opportunities. There is no way I can make my family and friends forget what a low-life scoundrel I was, but I can assure them I will never sink that low again."

Organizing

Now all that Albert has to do is take his notes and add the quotations from Travis. He also weaves in descriptions of Travis and explains Travis's family situation in more detail. Here is the order Albert decides on for the information he has:

1. Travis's immediate background
2. Hitting rock bottom
3. Self-evaluation and rehab
4. Education
5. Career and life goals

Albert begins his essay with one of Travis's remarks because Travis speaks so well for himself.

Drafting

Here is Albert's essay.

Albert's Essay: First Draft

Main Idea: Alcohol abuse was part of what made Travis a paraplegic; then he turned his life around and became a drug and alcohol counselor.

"You might say that I dove right into my career," said Travis Lawrence. He is a drug and alcohol counselor at a local rehabilitation clinic. He started drinking at the age of 15 and soon found himself a paraplegic after jumping off a diving board into the deep end of an empty swimming pool. "That ended one night of drinking," he said, but it led to many more nights and days trying to escape reality by using and abusing drugs and alcohol.

"I was never happy with myself when I was a young teenager, so I used to drink when I was hanging out with the older boys in my neighborhood," Travis explained. "Back in those days, my buddies and I was trying to make ourselves more attractive to the ladies. Now I know better."

Travis Lawrence, with help from his friends and supporters, has been sober for five years now. But he had a 10-year drinking career before he came to the decision that alcohol and drugs were making him more miserable than he already was. He had never fully adjusted to life in a wheelchair, and he realized that drinking his life away was not going to solve that problem. "Actually," he said, "I had some help making my decision. My mama said, 'Travis, get sober or get out of my house.' Don't you think this got my attention? Since I had no idea how I could function without all the care my mama gives me, I decided to sober up quickly." When someone sinks as low as he did, you have to take action.

Travis had been fighting with his sister about some missing

money, and he became enraged and pushed her down the stairs. He knew that he had given up hope of having a normal life, so he gave himself excuses for treating others in what he now sees as inexcusable ways. For example, he kept borrowing money from family members and never paid any of it back. When they stopped loaning him money, he started stealing from them. He said he was unable to go anywhere else and steal to support his habits because his getaway vehicle was too easy to identify. He said he had never heard of any paraplegic bank robbers. His mother told him that she did not want another crippled child, so he had to learn to resolve his differences with his sister without resorting to violence.

He looked at himself honestly for the first time. Everybody had been trying to get him to wise up. He saw that he was not going anywhere. He understood how important his family was and how badly he had treated them. Travis realized that his anger at his paralysis was being misdirected, and he decided to get some counseling. One of the most important things he learned was that he was responsible for his own moods and that "getting high" was almost inevitably followed by "getting low." He told me, "The problem with drinking is it is like a roller-coaster ride. You can only go so high, and then you come crashing down. After being through so many highs and lows, I was ready for some level ground." He along with his mom were able to find a clinic that let him stay for a month and learn all about the disease of alcoholism and how to overcome it. Most of the month's stay were an eye-opening experience.

After a month in the clinic, Travis decided to get his high school equivalency diploma, so he studied with a tutor until he was ready to take the test. About three-fourths of the test were easy, simple enough for Travis to pass with no problem. The day he got his certificate, he went to the local community college and applied for admission. He said that when his friends in the neighborhood found out that he was going to college, they teased him all the time and called him "school boy." They were not supportive. Everyone took their digs at him. He told me that was better than many of the things they had called him in the past, so he kept going to school and kept going to their support group meetings.

When Travis finished his associate's degree, the clinic where he first started recovering from his addictions hired him to help counsel newcomers. Not only his supervisor, Nancy Jeffries, but also his co-workers was impressed with his sense of humor and his ability to get along with others. "Imagine that," he said to me. "There were many people who called me an inspiration. I think that's quite a reputation to live up to, and I take that as an obligation." He knows that for him, he cannot drink and have a happy life. People who don't know him probably looks at him and feels sorry for him because of his mode of transportation. But they can't even guess how far down he was and how far back he's come since he started using the chair. Travis says, "My life today along with my future holds rewarding, challenging, and interesting opportunities." He works with a group of people who cares about him and wants him to succeed at his career. His family and friends have forgiven him for the bad deeds he has done. The majority of the money he stole have been paid back. He makes sure he's generous with his family and friends at holidays and birthdays. He feels everyone have been supportive. "There is no way I can make my family and friends forget what a low-life scoundrel I was, but I can assure them I will never sink that low again," says Travis. Everybody still has their opinion of him. But he hopes it's changed for the better.

Like Travis's co-workers, my friends and I was truly impressed with Travis's wit and wisdom. I am sure that the clinic supervisor made an excellent decision when they decided to hire him to help others recover from their addictions.

Revising

Albert was genuinely moved by Travis's energy and enthusiasm for his newfound career. Albert marveled at how easy and painless it was to write an essay he hadn't wanted to write in the first place. The words just came tumbling out after his interview with Travis. Albert knows that revising this essay may take more time than usual because he didn't pay much attention to the way he was making his statements; he just wanted to get his first draft on paper. His philosophy was "Write now, revise later."

Now the time has come to revise. The instructor's revision guidelines for this assignment involve focusing on methods for organizing paragraphs and essays. Albert turns to the Checklist for Organizing Paragraphs and Essays on page 185. He has learned in his writing class that, although some work with grammar and usage may be necessary, the revision process is intended to help him say exactly what he means as effectively as possible. Albert reads the Tips for Revising and completes all the exercises his instructor assigns. From his reading, he understands that he has numerous options for organizing the ideas in each paragraph and for arranging the paragraphs in the essay.

Albert returns to his essay and approaches his revision cautiously because he knows he has a lot of work to do. He knows from past experience that, when he writes fast, his ideas are not necessarily arranged as effectively as they could be. So this chapter's Tips for Revising section comes his way at an opportune time. In fact, it contains good advice for revising any essay he composes. As he rereads his draft, Albert finds several problems with ideas that aren't logically arranged, and he begins marking changes he wants to make.

 ## COLLABORATIVE WORK

PEER GROUP ACTIVITY

After you read the portions of the Tips for Revising your instructor assigns, turn to Albert's first draft (pp. 174–176), and complete the following tasks in small groups:

A. Put brackets around any sentences, paragraphs, or ideas that are not arranged as effectively as they could be.

B. In the margin, suggest a better way of organizing any material you put in brackets: general to particular, particular to general, time order, space order, or movement between extremes. (For explanations, see pp. 185–188, 188–189, 189–191, 191–192, and 192–195.)

Compare the marks your group recorded with those your instructor will show you. Where do your marks differ from your instructor's? What do you need to review before writing your own essay?

CLASS ACTIVITY

As an entire class, look at the underlined portions of Albert's revised draft (pp. 179–182) to see how he changed each sentence.

A.   Did you identify the revision problems that Albert corrected?

B.   Do you think his changes are good ones? Discuss his changes.

Editing

Now that Albert has reorganized portions of his essay, he needs to do some final proofreading and editing before handing it in. The instructor tells the students they need to understand the concept of agreement—for subjects and their verbs and for pronouns and their antecedents. So Albert shifts his focus from the order of his ideas to specific points of grammar. He reads the Tips for Editing section in this chapter to learn about both types of agreement. After he finishes the exercises his instructor assigns, he takes the questions in the Checklist for Correcting Agreement Problems one by one and makes changes so that his revised draft fulfills all these requirements.

 ## COLLABORATIVE WORK

PEER GROUP ACTIVITY

After you read the portions of the Tips for Editing your instructor assigns, turn to Albert's first draft (pp. 174–176), and complete the following tasks in small groups:

A.   Underline all the subjects and verbs that do not agree (for a definition of subject-verb agreement, see pp. 196–205).

B.   Circle any pronouns (for a definition, see p. 42) and antecedents (for a definition, see p. 42) your group finds that do not agree with one another.

Compare the marks your group recorded with those your instructor will show you. Where do your marks differ from your instructor's? What do you need to review before writing your own essay?

CLASS ACTIVITY

As an entire class, look at the underlined portions of Albert's revised draft (pp. 179–182) to see how he changed each sentence.

A.   Did you identify the **editing** problems that Albert corrected?

B.   Do you think his changes are good ones? Discuss his changes.

Albert's Revised Essay ....

An Accidental Career

"You might say that I dove right into my career," said Travis Lawrence. He is a drug and alcohol counselor at a local rehabilitation clinic. He started drinking at the age of 15 and soon found himself a paraplegic after jumping off a diving board into the deep end of an empty swimming pool. "That ended one night of drinking," he said, but it led to many more nights and days trying to escape reality by using and abusing drugs and alcohol. Finally, a combination of his mother's tough love and an honest look at his own behavior convinced Travis that he had to change his life.

Travis then told me about some mistaken ideas that had influenced him to drink. "I was never happy with myself when I was a young teenager, so I used to drink when I was hanging out with the older boys in my neighborhood," Travis explained. "Back in those days, my buddies and I ~~was~~ were trying to make ourselves more attractive to the ladies. Now I know better." Now, Travis knows about the realities of drinking, and he can help others avoid his mistakes.

Travis Lawrence, with help from his friends and supporters, has been sober for five years now. But he had a 10-year drinking career before he came to the decision that alcohol and drugs were making him more miserable than he already was. He had never fully adjusted to life in a wheelchair, and he realized that drinking his life away was not going to solve that problem. "Actually," he said, "I had some help making my decision. My mama said, 'Travis, get sober or get out of my house.' Don't you think this got my attention? Since I had no idea how I could function without all the care my mama gives me, I decided to sober up quickly." When someone sinks as low as he did, ~~you~~ he or she ~~have~~ has to take action.

~~Travis had been fighting with his sister about some missing~~ ~~money, and he became enraged and pushed her down the stairs.~~ ~~He~~ When Travis knew that he had given up hope of having a normal life, ~~so~~ he gave himself excuses for treating others in what he now sees as inexcusable ways. For example, he kept borrowing money from family members and never paid any of it back. When they stopped loaning him money, he started stealing from them. With a twisted smile, h~~H~~e said he was unable to go anywhere else and steal to support his habits because it would have been difficult to avoid police when his getaway vehicle was ~~too~~ so easy to identify. "Besides," h~~H~~e said, ~~he~~ "I had never heard of any successful paraplegic bank robbers." Finally, Travis had been fighting with his sister about some missing money, and he became enraged and pushed her down the stairs. Then, h~~H~~is mother told him that she did not want another crippled child, so he had to learn to resolve his differences with his sister without resorting to violence.

That very night h~~H~~e looked at himself honestly for the first time. For years, e~~E~~verybody had been trying to get him to wise up. Finally, h~~H~~e, too, saw that he was not going anywhere. After thinking about himself, h~~H~~e then ~~understood~~ realized how important his family was and how badly he had treated them. ~~Travis~~ He realized that his anger at his paralysis was being misdirected, and he decided to get some counseling. ~~One of the most important things~~ ~~he learned was that he was responsible for his own moods and that~~ ~~"getting high" was almost inevitably followed by "getting low." He~~ ~~told me, "The problem with drinking is it is like a roller-coaster ride.~~ ~~You can only go so high, and then you come crashing down. After~~ ~~being through so many highs and lows, I was ready for some level~~ ~~ground."~~ He along with his mom ~~were~~ was able to find a clinic that let him stay for a month and learn all about the disease of alcoholism and how to overcome it. Most of the month's stay ~~were~~

was an eye-opening experience. One of the most important things he learned was that he was responsible for his own moods and that "getting high" was almost inevitably followed by "getting low." He told me, "The problem with drinking is it is like a roller-coaster ride. You can only go so high, and then you come crashing down. After being through so many highs and lows, I was ready for some level ground."

After a month in the clinic, Travis decided to get his high school equivalency diploma, so he studied with a tutor until he was ready to take the test. About three-fourths of the test ~~were~~ was easy, simple enough for Travis to pass with no problem. The day he got his certificate, he went to the local community college and applied for admission. He said that when his friends in the neighborhood found out that he was going to college, they teased him all the time and called him "school boy." They were not supportive. Everyone took ~~their~~ his or her digs at him. He told me that was better than many of the things they had called him in the past, so he kept going to school and kept going to ~~their~~ his support group meetings.

When Travis finished his associate's degree, the clinic where he first started recovering from his addictions hired him to help counsel newcomers. Not only his supervisor, Nancy Jeffries, but also his co-workers ~~was~~ were impressed with his sense of humor and his ability to get along with others. "Imagine that," he said to me. "There were many people who called me an inspiration. I think that's quite a reputation to live up to, and I take that as an obligation." He knows that for him, he cannot drink and have a happy life. People who don't know him probably ~~looks~~ look at him and ~~feels~~ feel sorry for him because of his mode of transportation. But they can't even guess how far down he was and how far back he's come since he started using the chair. Travis says, "My life today along with my future holds rewarding, challenging, and interesting opportunities." He works with a group of people who ~~cares~~ care about him and ~~wants~~ want him to succeed at his "accidental" career. His family and friends have forgiven him for the bad deeds he has done. The majority of the money he stole ~~have~~ has been paid back. He makes sure he's generous with his family and friends at holidays and birthdays. He feels everyone ~~have~~ has been supportive. "There is no way I can make my family and friends forget what a low-life scoundrel I was, but I can assure them I will never sink that low again," says Travis. "Everybody still has ~~their~~ his or her opinion of ~~him~~ me." But he hopes it's changed for the better.

Like Travis's co-workers, my friends and I ~~was~~ were truly impressed with Travis's wit and wisdom. I am sure that the clinic supervisor made an excellent decision when ~~they~~ she decided to hire him to help others recover from their addictions.

WRITING YOUR OWN INVESTIGATING ESSAY

So far, you have seen a professional writer and a fellow student at work trying to investigate something they felt was worth writing about. As you read the published essay and followed the writing process of another student from first to final draft, you absorbed ideas and ways of giving your ideas a form of their own. These reading and writing activities have prepared you to write your own essay investigating a topic that is meaningful to you.

What Have You Discovered?

Before you begin your own writing task, let's review what you have learned in this chapter so far:

- Investigating means gathering as much information about a person, place, event, or idea as possible.

- You should answer the questions *who, what, when, where, why,* and *how* in your investigation.

- You must *show* as well as *tell* your readers the answers to these questions—furnishing concrete details and examples to support your statements.

- To present your investigation effectively, you need to organize your ideas.

- To help you shape your essay, you should learn as much as possible about your readers.

- Before you write a draft, you need to decide on a point of view toward your subject.

- After you write a draft, you should revise your essay for meaning and organization.

- After you revise your essay, you should edit its grammar, usage, and sentence structure.

Your Writing Topic

Choose one of the following topics for your investigating essay:

1. To write "A Nation at Risk," the authors investigated the condition of the educational system in the United States. Write an essay in which you investigate a school you have attended, providing precise information about such issues as the physical condition of the school, the quality of teaching there, the behavior of the students, the curriculum, the assessment process, the extracurricular activities, and the attitude of the community toward the school.

2. Interview a friend, neighbor, or relative whose life was affected by war or political problems in his or her country of origin, and write about how that person's life was changed by those events. Find out what that person thought was most difficult about the experience and what he or she is most thankful for now.

3. Interview a person who accomplished an extremely challenging task—someone who built a house with very little assistance; someone who learned to walk or read again after being disabled; someone who has completed a marathon run or another feat of physical endurance. Then write about that person's special feeling of accomplishment. How was this accomplishment different from other accomplishments? Would the person work that hard again to achieve this or a similar goal?

4. Create your own investigating topic (with the assistance of your instructor), and write a response to it.

When you have selected one of these topics, you may begin your writing process in the same way Albert did. (You may find his experience helpful in giving you ideas.) This time your purpose is to write your own investigating essay. If some tasks occur out of order, that adjustment is probably part of your personal writing ritual. Follow your instincts, and let them mold your own writing process. But make sure you've worked through all the stages to your final draft.

YOUR WRITING PROCESS

THINKING   Generate as many ideas on your subject as you can in as many different ways as possible: rereading, listing, freewriting, brainstorming, clustering, discussing, and questioning.

PLANNING   Begin to give your ideas shape by deciding on your approach to your topic (your content, your purpose, your audience, and your point of view). Make a list of points you want to include in your essay.

DEVELOPING   Add more details on three or four specific, focused topics that you have chosen from your list of general points.

ORGANIZING   Organize your material in a way that will be most interesting to your audience.

DRAFTING   Write a working draft of your essay in complete sentences.

REVISING   Consulting the Tips for Revising in this chapter (pp. 185–195), revise your first draft—paying special attention to organizing your ideas as effectively as possible.

EDITING   Consulting the Tips for Editing in this chapter (pp. 195–210), edit your draft for grammar and correctness—paying special attention to agreement.

Turn in your revised draft to your instructor.

Some Final Thoughts

When you have completed your own essay, answer these four questions in your journal:

1.   What was most difficult about this assignment?
2.   What was easiest?
3.   What did I learn about investigating by completing this assignment?
4.   What did I learn about my own writing process—how I prepared to write, how I wrote the first draft, how I revised, and how I edited?

Organizing Paragraphs and Essays

Checklist for Organizing Paragraphs and Essays

✓ Are the essay's **ideas organized** in a way that is most effective for its purpose: general to particular, particular to general, time order, space order, or movement between extremes?

✓ Are the **supporting details** in the body paragraphs organized in such a way to support the essay's overall purpose?

✓ Is a **combination** of these methods used when appropriate?

✓ Does the **method of organization** reflect the argument itself and the nature of the supporting details?

Large corporations and institutions have organizational charts that clarify the position and duties of all their employees. For example, your college or university has such a chart with a chancellor, provost, or president who is generally responsible for the whole school. As the chart descends, people who have more and more narrowly defined roles appear. At the bottom of the chart are the employees who fulfill specific minor roles in running the institution, such as custodians, security guards, and cafeteria workers.

Organizing essays and paragraphs can be like drawing up an organizational chart for a school or business. You need to consider the general purpose of your essay and how each paragraph serves that purpose, then arrange the details in a logical manner to achieve that purpose. Whereas an organizational chart uses boxes to separate responsibilities for individual members of an organization, your essay is divided into paragraphs and sentences that play specific roles in achieving the essay's general purpose.

The most common methods of organizing are from general to particular, from particular to general, by time order, by space order, or by movement between extremes. If your essay's main purpose is to describe the layout of a building, most of the details would be in *space order*, beginning with the entry point and working to the other parts of the building as if you were strolling through it. If, however, you wanted to convince a reader of the benefits of one type of building over another, you might arrange the essay so it moves *from one extreme to another*—for example, from least important detail to most important. Within this framework, you also need to organize your ideas in each paragraph. When choosing an organizational method in a paragraph, consider the purpose of the essay and the role of each paragraph in that essay. We will demonstrate each method of organization that applies to both essays and paragraphs.

General to Particular

This method of essay and paragraph development will probably be the most useful to you at this stage of your writing life. Essays and paragraphs arranged from **general to particular** usually begin with a topic sentence or general statement, then move to particular details to develop that statement. (To review methods of development, see pp. 134–141.)

The professional essay in this chapter, "A Nation at Risk," moves from general to particular. The essay begins by discussing American society and education in global terms, suggesting various reasons for the problems we face on a national level. Then, subheadings move the readers through the essay's topics and give us some insight into the writer's method of organization:

The Risk

Indicators of the Risk

The Learning Society

Recommendations

America Can Do It

The essay ends with specific examples of how the U.S. system of higher education has overcome various obstacles through the years. The conclusion—that the educational system will again succeed—is drawn from these particulars.

Paragraph 4 of the professional essay is arranged from general to particular on a smaller scale:

> History is not kind to idlers. The time is long past when America's destiny was assured simply by an abundance of natural resources and inexhaustible human enthusiasm, and by our relative isolation from the malignant problems of older civilizations. The world is indeed one global village. We live among determined, well-educated, and strongly motivated competitors. We compete with them for international standing and markets, not only with products but also with the ideas of our laboratories and neighborhood workshops. America's position in the world may once have been reasonably secure with only a few exceptionally well-trained men and women. It is no longer.

This paragraph begins with a general statement about history's treatment of idlers. Then the writers detail how America's position in the world has changed.

As Albert Watson reviewed his first draft, he decided that paragraph 4, which began with a statement about Travis's anger, would be much better if he began with a general statement of why Travis was angry and then moved to his detailed examples:

First Draft: Travis had been fighting with his sister about some missing money, and he became enraged and pushed her down the stairs. He knew that he had given up hope of having a normal life, so he gave himself excuses for treating others in what he now sees as inexcusable ways.

For example, he kept borrowing money from family members and never paid any of it back. When they stopped loaning him money, he started stealing from them. He said he was unable to go anywhere else and steal to support his habits because his getaway vehicle was too easy to identify. He said he had never heard of any paraplegic bank robbers. His mother told him that she did not want another crippled child, so he had to learn to resolve his differences with his sister without resorting to violence.

Revision: ~~Travis had been fighting with his sister about some missing money, and he became enraged and pushed her down the stairs.~~ He **When Travis** knew that he had given up hope of having a normal life, ~~so~~ he gave himself excuses for treating others in what he now sees as inexcusable ways. For example, he kept borrowing money from family members and never paid any of it back. When they stopped loaning him money, he started stealing from them. **With a twisted smile, h**~~H~~e said he was unable to go anywhere else and steal to support his habits because **it would have been difficult to avoid police when** his getaway vehicle was **too so** easy to identify. "**Besides,**" **h**~~H~~e said, "I had never heard of any **successful** paraplegic bank robbers." **Finally, Travis had been fighting with his sister about some missing money, and he became enraged and pushed her down the stairs. Then, h**~~H~~is mother told him that she did not want another crippled child, so he had to learn to resolve his differences with his sister without resorting to violence.

Paragraph 4 is now logically organized and moves from one general statement to the detailed examples that support it. This logical organization and the more fully developed ideas give Albert's audience a clear picture of Travis Lawrence's violent and self-destructive behavior.

Particular to General

When you reverse the organizational method we just discussed, you arrange your essay or paragraph from particular statements to a general one that either expresses the controlling idea or sums up the importance of the details. If you think one of your topics might be difficult for your audience to understand or agree with, you might choose this method.

If the order of the paragraphs in "A Nation at Risk" were reversed, the essay would move from **particular to general**. In this case, the essay would begin by giving us specific reasons to believe that the American educational system will pull out of its slump. Then it would reverse the topics themselves:

America Can Do It

Recommendations

The Learning Society

Indicators of the Risk

The Risk

This organization would create a much more negative message at the end, leaving the readers with a general sense of hopelessness in American society and education.

Paragraph 5 of "A Nation at Risk" follows this method of organization, moving from particular concerns, such as Japan's more efficient auto industry, to a general statement that sums up the importance of education for Americans if we are to survive in a new world order:

> The risk is not only that the Japanese make automobiles more efficiently than Americans and have government subsidies for development and export. It is not just that the South Koreans recently built the world's most efficient steel mill, or that American machine tools, once the pride of the world, are being displaced by German products. It is also that these developments signify a redistribution of trained capability throughout the globe. Knowledge, learning, information, and skilled intelligence are the new raw materials of international commerce and are today spreading throughout the world as vigorously as miracle drugs, synthetic fertilizers, and blue jeans did earlier. If only to keep and improve on the slim competitive edge we still retain in world markets, we must dedicate ourselves to the reform of our educational system for the benefit of all—old and young alike, affluent and poor, majority and minority. Learning is the indispensable investment required for success in the "information age" we are entering.

A particular-to-general organization in an introductory paragraph often provides a "hook" to catch the readers' interest. As Albert inspected his investigating essay, he decided that his first paragraph, which began with a specific detail, should end with a more informative general statement:

First Draft: "You might say that I dove right into my career," said Travis Lawrence. He is a drug and alcohol counselor at a local rehabilitation clinic. He started drinking at the age of 15 and soon found himself a paraplegic after jumping off a diving board into the deep end of an empty swimming pool. "That ended one night of drinking," he said, but it led to many more nights and days trying to escape reality by using and abusing drugs and alcohol.

Revision: "You might say that I dove right into my career," said Travis Lawrence. He is a drug and alcohol counselor at a local rehabilitation clinic. He started drinking at the age of 15 and soon found himself a paraplegic after jumping off a diving board into the deep end of an empty swimming pool. "That ended one night of drinking," he said, but it led to many more nights and days trying to escape reality by using and abusing drugs and alcohol. **Finally, a combination of his mother's tough love and an honest look at his own behavior convinced Travis that he had to change his life.**

Now, Albert's paragraph is clearer and more forceful since it moves from particulars about Travis's experience to the general topic that Albert is investigating in his essay—*how* Travis was able to change.

Time Order

Time order (also called chronological order) is a third way to organize essays and paragraphs. You probably made use of this method in your recalling essay, which told of a past experience. You may have used this strategy in your explaining essay if you described a process. In essays and paragraphs organized chronologically, words that express time sequences signal for your reader the order in which events occurred or should take place.

The student essay in this chapter is organized according to time. Although Albert begins his essay by introducing Travis's career choice, Albert soon goes back to the beginning and tells the story of Travis's life since his disability in chronological order.

On the paragraph level, the following excerpt from "A Nation at Risk" introduces a powerful conclusion to the essay with some information in chronological order about American history:

> Despite the obstacles and difficulties that inhibit the pursuit of superior educational attainment, we are confident, with history as our guide, that we can meet our goal. The American educational system has responded to previous challenges with remarkable success. In the 19th century our land-grant colleges and universities provided the research and training that developed our Nation's natural resources and the rich agricultural bounty of the American farm. From the late 1800s through mid-20th century, American schools provided the educated workforce needed to seal the success of the Industrial Revolution and to provide the margin of victory in two world wars. In the early part of this century and continuing to this very day, our schools have absorbed vast waves of immigrants and educated them and their children to productive citizenship. Similarly, the Nation's Black colleges have provided opportunity and undergraduate education to the vast majority of college-educated Black Americans.

Following the time order of this paragraph makes us realize the importance of education in American history.

Albert noticed that in discussing Travis's soul-searching (paragraph 5), he had not indicated the order in which thoughts came to the young man, so he added words to place events in time order:

First Draft: He looked at himself honestly for the first time. Everybody had been trying to get him to wise up. He saw that he was not going anywhere. He understood how important his family was and how badly he had treated them. Travis realized that his anger at his paralysis was being misdirected, and he decided to get some counseling.

Revision: **That very night h**H̶e looked at himself honestly for the first time. **For years, e**E̶verybody had been trying to get him to wise up. **Finally, h**H̶e, **too,** saw that he was not going anywhere. **After thinking about himself, h**H̶e **then** realized how important his family was and how badly he had treated them. He realized that his anger at his paralysis was being misdirected, and he decided to get some counseling.

Space Order

Organizing details in essays and paragraphs in **space order**—according to their relationship to each other in space—helps you describe the layout of your campus from its front gate to its exit or the arrangement of a beautiful garden. In Chapter 3, N. Scott Momaday's description of Rainy Mountain is spatial. Integrated with memories of his grandmother, this essay moves around the landscape with such signals as "the skyline in all directions," "descending eastward," and "at the top of a ridge." As the essay progresses, Momaday works his way around the landscape connected with Rainy Mountain.

On a smaller scale, a section of Lynda Barry's essay in Chapter 2, "The Sanctuary of School," is a good example of space order:

> He let me push his wheeled garbage can between the different portables as he unlocked each room. He let me turn on the lights and raise the window shades and I saw my school slowly come to life. I saw Mrs. Holman, our school secretary, walk into the office without her orange lipstick on yet. She waved.
>
> I saw the fifth-grade teacher, Mr. Cunningham, walking under the breezeway eating a hard roll. He waved.
>
> And I saw my teacher, Mrs. Claire LeSane, walking toward us in a red coat and calling my name in a very happy and surprised way, and suddenly my throat got tight and my eyes stung and I ran toward her crying. It was something that surprised both of us.

This description gives the readers a good sense of the writer's morning as she moves with the janitor from room to room in the school.

In the following paragraph from Albert's journal, he describes the room at home where he writes:

> My can of Pepsi sits on the same kitchen table where I do most of my writing. On my left is the oven clock that I have to avoid eye contact with if I want to keep my ideas flowing. Straight ahead of where I am sitting at the table is a wall with some pictures on it of various family events; these are great to stare at when I need new ideas or inspiration for whatever I am writing. The pictures bring back lots of memories for me to draw from. To my right is the door to the living room and the rest

of the house. I do my best writing when I can hear but not talk to people in the house. Behind me is the refrigerator where I go for snacks when I am having serious writer's blocks. I don't know why, but I always walk to the refrigerator when I am really stuck on a paper. Then I'm always convinced some junk food will get me through the temporary crisis.

From this spatial description of Albert's kitchen, we can actually imagine where he writes and what he does to get his ideas flowing.

Movement Between Extremes

Another method of organizing ideas is **movement between extremes**. You might explain how to choose a pet by elaborating on the most important qualities then considering the least important. For example, an apartment dweller's most important consideration would be the size of the pet and its need for exercise. A dalmatian, for instance, needs a minimum of four acres of running room while a Lhasa apso is quite content in a 10-by-12-foot room. Least important to an apartment dweller would be a dog's watchdog qualities or its ability to herd sheep. To accomplish another purpose, you might reverse this order and begin with the least important quality; this method is good in persuasive writing, because you end with your most important idea.

Albert's essay would be equally effective if it were organized from one extreme to another. Instead of discussing Travis's life chronologically since his disability, Albert could have discussed events in Travis's life from most difficult to least difficult or from least significant to most significant. In the first case, Albert might have started with Travis's inability to cope with being a paraplegic and then moved to his difficulty with alcoholism, his treatment of his family, his determination to turn his life around, his return to school, and his success at his job. Organizing his essay from least to most significant would probably mean that Albert would begin with Travis's general unhappiness in life and end with his influences on other people's lives through his current job, covering other topics in the middle of the essay according to his personal judgment of their significance in Travis's life.

In paragraph 13 of "A Nation at Risk," the writers move from the positive to the negative in a discussion of knowledge in our society today:

It is important, of course, to recognize that *the average citizen* today is better educated and more knowledgeable than the average citizen of a generation ago—more literate, and exposed to more mathematics, literature, and science. The positive impact of this fact on the well-being of our country and the lives of our people cannot be overstated. Nevertheless, *the average graduate* of our schools and colleges today is not as well-educated as the average graduate of 25 or 35 years ago, when a much smaller proportion of our population completed high school and college. The negative impact of this fact likewise cannot be overstated.

As Albert reviewed his essay, he decided that paragraph 5 would work better if the most important point were at the end of the paragraph. He had already added some chronological markers to the beginning of the paragraph. Now he was looking at the flow of the paragraph as a whole.

First Draft:

He looked at himself honestly for the first time. Everybody had been trying to get him to wise up. He saw that he was not going anywhere. He understood how important his family was and how badly he had treated them. Travis realized that his anger at his paralysis was being misdirected, and he decided to get some counseling. One of the most important things he learned was that he was responsible for his own moods and that "getting high" was almost inevitably followed by "getting low." He told me, "The problem with drinking is it is like a roller-coaster ride. You can only go so high, and then you come crashing down. After being through so many highs and lows, I was ready for some level ground." He along with his mom were able to find a clinic that let him stay for a month and learn all about the disease of alcoholism and how to overcome it. Most of the month's stay were an eye-opening experience.

After Albert learned about organizing from one extreme to another, he could see that paragraph 5 would work best if the sentences moved logically from Travis's being at his all-time low to getting his life back together. The two sentences that represent the lowest point in Travis's life are currently at the beginning of this paragraph. Travis's new approach to life is captured in "one of the most important things he learned" at the clinic, which, along with his quotation about this important discovery, is currently buried in the middle of the paragraph. Albert moved these sentences to the end to complete his revisions on this paragraph.

Revision:

That very night h He looked at himself honestly for the first time. **For years, e**Everybody had been trying to get him to wise up. **Finally, h~~He~~, too,** saw that he was not going anywhere. **After thinking about himself, h~~He~~ then** realized how important his family was and how badly he had treated them. He realized that his anger at his paralysis was being misdirected, and he decided to get some counseling. ~~One of the most important things he learned was that he was responsible for his own moods and that "getting high" was almost inevitably followed by "getting low." He told me, "The problem with drinking is it is like a roller coaster ride. You can only go so high, and then you come crashing down. After being through so many highs and lows, I was ready for some level ground."~~ He along with his mom was able to find a clinic that let him stay for a month and learn all about the disease of alcoholism and how to overcome it. Most of the month's stay was an eye-opening experience. **One of the most important things he learned was that he was responsible for his own moods and that "getting high" was almost inevitably followed by "getting low." He told me, "The problem with drinking is it is like a roller-coaster ride. You can only go so high, and then you come crashing down. After being through so many highs and lows, I was ready for some level ground."**

These changes make the paragraph's meaning clearer and easier to follow.

Exercise R5-1

Identify the method of development in paragraph 9 of "A Nation at Risk" (pp. 163–164).

Exercise R5-2

Identify the method of development Albert used in paragraph 6 of his revised investigating essay (p. 181).

Exercise R5-3

Make up a topic sentence that introduces the following details in a paragraph. Then arrange the details in logical order and write a paragraph.

Generating ideas
Sticking to one topic
Writing a working thesis
Finding details or examples

Exercise R5-4

List the best method of development for paragraphs on the following topics.

1. How to make a pineapple upside-down cake.
2. We should clean up our environment before it is too late.
3. What I will wear to class tomorrow.
4. Today, scientists question the age of our universe.
5. Some people put their time to good use.

 ## COLLABORATIVE WORK

After writing a draft of your own investigating essay, exchange papers with a class-mate, and do the following tasks:

A. Read the entire essay, and decide whether the organizational plan presents the thesis and supporting ideas in the best possible way. Make suggestions for changes if you think using another order would improve the essay.

B. Look at each paragraph, and put an X next to any paragraphs that could be improved through another method of organization. Then write your suggested method next to the X.

Then return the paper to its writer, and use the information in this section to revise your draft.

Agreement

Checklist for Correcting Agreement Problems

✓ Do **singular subjects** agree with **singular verbs**?
✓ Do **plural subjects** agree with **plural verbs**?
✓ Do **pronouns** and **antecedents** agree in **number, person,** and **gender**?
✓ Do **pronouns with no antecedents** refer to themselves?
✓ Do you **avoid sexist references** with indefinite pronouns?

By now you have realized that writing an essay can be an involved process. Besides coming up with an idea, you have to state your thesis in an introduction that is informative and interesting. Then you must develop your topic with well-organized body paragraphs and end with a conclusion that neatly wraps everything up.

In addition to making sure that all the elements in your essay "agree" and connect, you should pay close attention to agreement in the sentences within your paragraphs. Two areas that often cause problems are agreement between subjects and their verbs and agreement between pronouns and their antecedents. In this section, you will learn to master special problems in agreement so you can make your writing clear and coherent.

Subject-Verb Agreement

To express a complete thought, every sentence must have a subject and verb. But to use subjects and verbs correctly, you must do more than just supply sentences with words that fit a model. Subjects and verbs must agree in **number**: singular subjects require singular verbs, and plural subjects require plural verbs. The following chart shows how the forms of the verb *to be*, which is irregular, change between singular and plural.

Singular	Plural
I am.	We are.
He, she, it is.	They are.
I, he, she, it was.	We, they were.
He, she, it has been.	They have been.

Look at these sentences from the first draft of Albert's investigating essay, which illustrate subject-verb agreement:

Singular:	**S V** **He is** a drug and alcohol counselor at a local rehabilitation clinic.
Plural:	**S V** **They were** not supportive.

196

Hard-to-Find Subjects

The first step in making sure that subjects and verbs agree is to identify the subject. Next, you must determine whether the subject is singular or plural. This is usually not difficult, but sometimes locating the subject can be tricky, as the following examples show:

1. *Separated subjects and verbs.*   Sometimes words or phrases come between the subject and verb, making the subject difficult to pinpoint. Just remember that the simple subject must agree with the simple verb, no matter what words come between them. Look at this sentence from Albert's first draft. The subjects and verbs are in bold print.

Separated Subjects and Verbs:

                    S
Travis Lawrence, with help from his friends and

            V
supporters, **has been** sober for five years now.

To locate the subject and verb, you can begin by eliminating any phrases. Eliminating the three prepositional phrases from the previous example leaves a simple sentence with a subject and a verb:

            S   **V**
Travis Lawrence, has been sober.

In some instances, locating the verb first may work best. For example, suppose the previous sentence read, "Travis Lawrence, a quiet man with many friends and supporters, has been sober for five years now." The verb is relatively simple to locate—*has been. Who* has been? *Travis Lawrence,* not *man,* which is part of the phrase that renames Travis Lawrence.

2. *Compound subjects.*   Sometimes we overlook subjects, especially when a sentence has more than one. Logically, more than one subject is a plural subject. These compound subjects are usually joined by *and,* as this sentence from Albert's first draft illustrates:

Compound Subjects:

                S   **S**   **V**   **V**
His **family** *and* **friends have forgiven** him for the bad

deeds he has done.

Other key words besides *and* may suggest another subject: *along with, as well as, like, including, together with, with.* But these words begin phrases that do not change the original subject's number:

Single Subject:

                S   **V**
"My **life** today [along with my future] **holds** rewarding,

challenging, and interesting opportunities."

When compound subjects are joined by *either . . . or, neither . . . nor, not only . . . but also,* and *whether . . . or,* the verb agrees with the subject closest to it:

**Compound
Subjects:**

Either Albert's **mom** or his best **friends are** going with him to the courthouse.

Either Albert's best **friends** or his **mom is** going with him to the courthouse.

Not only my **letter** from Frank but also my **bills were** lost in the mail.

Not only my **bills** but also my **letter** from Frank **was** lost in the mail.

3. *Inversions.*   Normally, the subject comes before the verb: *He sleeps. We eat. They go home.* We call this the *natural order* of sentences. In some instances, however, the verb may come before the subject, an *inversion* of the basic subject-verb order.

    The most common type of inversion is the **question.** Just put the question in statement form, and the sentence will appear in natural order. Look at this example from Albert's first draft:

Question: **Don't you think** this got my attention?

Rearranged: **You do** not **think** this got my attention.

When statements appear in inverted order, they are often introduced by **expletives,** words such as *there* or *it* that serve as sentence starters. *There* never serves as a subject. When an expletive begins the sentence, you will find the subject following the verb, as this sentence from Albert's first draft illustrates:

Expletive: "There **were** many **people** who called me an inspiration."

Remember that *it* always takes a singular verb:

Expletive: **It is** an inspiring story that gets attention.

It is days since I've had any rest.

An entire phrase may begin a sentence, causing an inversion. Simply re-arrange the sentence in natural order to find the subject and verb:

Inverted:	On top of the counter **sit** Albert's **keys**, right where he left them.

(V above **sit**, S above **keys**)

Rearranged:	Albert's **keys sit** on top of the counter, right where he left them.

(S above **keys**, V above **sit**)

Inverted:	Beside the front door **lies** our canine **pal** Buster.

(V above **lies**, S above **pal**)

Rearranged:	Our canine **pal** Buster **lies** beside the front door.

(S above **pal**, V above **lies**)

Exercise E5-1

Underline the simple subjects once and the simple verbs twice in the following sentences from "A Nation at Risk," and label them as singular or plural.

1. Our society and its educational institutions seem to have lost sight of the basic purposes of schooling, and of the high expectations and disciplined effort needed to attain them.
2. This report, the result of 18 months of study, seeks to generate reform of our educational system in fundamental ways and to renew the Nation's commitment to schools and colleges of high quality throughout the length and breadth of our land.
3. Our concern, however, goes well beyond matters such as industry and commerce.
4. International comparisons of student achievement, completed a decade ago, reveal that on 19 academic tests American students were never first or second and, in comparison with other industrialized nations, were last seven times.
5. The positive impact of this fact on the well-being of our country and the lives of our people cannot be overstated.

Exercise E5-2

Correct the subject-verb agreement problems in the following sentences from Albert's first draft.

1. Back in those days, my buddies and I was trying to make ourselves more attractive to the ladies.
2. He along with his mom were able to find a clinic that let him stay for a month and learn all about the disease of alcoholism and how to overcome it.
3. Not only his supervisor, Nancy Jeffries, but also his co-workers was impressed with his sense of humor and his ability to get along with others.

4. People who don't know him probably looks at him and feels sorry for him because of his mode of transportation.

5. Like Travis's co-workers, my friends and I was truly impressed with Travis's wit and wisdom.

Exercise E5-3

Choose the correct verb in parentheses to complete each sentence in the following paragraph.

One of my favorite places to hang out (1) (*is, are*) a little coffeehouse located on a downtown side street. People from all walks of life (2) (*find, finds*) their way to the Café Olé. As you can tell by its name, the cafe along with the employees (3) (*sport, sports*) a Spanish theme. The waitresses and hostesses (4) (*wear, wears*) bright, full skirts and flowers in their hair. Meanwhile, the only male employee I've ever seen always (5) (*wear, wears*) a toreador outfit, as if he were ready to step into the bullfighting ring. They always (6) (*play, plays*) soft guitar music to help give the atmosphere an authentic feeling. Whenever I go to the Café Olé, there (7) (*is, are*) always interesting people to watch and talk to. Either my friends or I usually (8) (*make, makes*) at least one more friend with each trip. It (9) (*has, have*) been several days since I've been to the café. But buried underneath my pile of responsibilities (10) (*is, are*) plans to go there soon.

Exercise E5-4

Write complete sentences using the following words and phrases as subjects and is, are, was, *or* were *as the main verb or as helping verbs.*

1. Mom, Dad, and my brothers
2. either Mom, Dad, or my brothers
3. running
4. traveling with my parents
5. Jackie along with Brian and Mike

Confusing Subjects

In some instances, making subjects and verbs agree can be difficult because the subject's number is vague or hard to determine. The following rules will help you solve any agreement problems between subjects and verbs:

1. *Collective nouns.*   Words such as *audience, army, family,* and *team* are **collective nouns**. Collective nouns are often tricky subjects because they may be singular or plural. When a collective noun represents a group as a single unit, the noun

is singular. When a collective noun represents the individual members of a group, however, the noun is plural:

                                   S   V

Singular: The **team practices** every day at 4 p.m.

                                   S   V

Plural: The **team receive** their physical examinations tomorrow morning.

Other common collective nouns include *army, band, chorus, class, committee, crew, crowd, faculty, flock, gang, herd, jury, majority, minority, navy, orchestra, quartet, senate, trio,* and *troop.*

2. *Singular nouns with plural forms.* Some nouns end in *-s* but have a singular meaning: *measles, molasses, mumps, news.* These nouns take singular verbs:

                                   S   V

Singular: **Mumps is** a childhood illness that causes swelling below the ears.

Still other nouns end in *-s* and refer to only one item, but require a plural verb. Examples include *eyeglasses, pants, pajamas, pliers,* and *scissors.*

                                   S   V

Plural: The **scissors are** in the bottom drawer where I put them.

Nouns ending in *-ics* (*aerobics, athletics, ceramics, civics, economics, ethics, mathematics, physics, politics, statistics*) are singular when they refer to a branch of knowledge or a field of study and plural when they indicate characteristics or the practical application of knowledge:

                                   S   V

Singular: **Statistics is** one of Anthony's most difficult courses.

                                   S   V

Plural: **Statistics are** provided throughout the article, mainly in charts.

3. *Amounts, measurements, and mathematical processes.* Amounts and measurements that appear to be plural usually require a singular verb:

                                   S   V

Singular: **Five miles is** too far to run.

 S   V   V
One-third cup of milk **is needed** for the recipe.

              S   V   V
About **20 percent** of the land **was sold.**

If a fraction or percentage refers to individual items or members, a plural verb is required:

Plural:
                      S   V
                      One-fourth of the applicants **have** graduated from college.

                      S   V   V
                      Twenty percent of the items **were damaged.**

Note that when the phrases *a number of* and *a percentage of* are used as part of the subject, a plural verb is needed. However, when the phrases *the number of* and *the percentage of* function as part of the subject, a singular verb is required.

Plural:
                          S   V   V
                          A number of people are standing outside waiting for the
                          doors to open.

                            S   V   V
                            A percentage of the respondents have indicated they
                            would like to participate in future surveys.

Singular:
                          S   V   V
                          The number of people standing outside **is growing.**

                            S
                            The percentage of people who responded to the survey
                          V
                          was low.

For mathematical processes, either a singular or plural verb is acceptable for addition and multiplication, even though singular verbs are used more often. But references to subtraction and division require singular verbs.

Addition:
                  S   V   S   V
                  Two plus two **is** four.   or   Two plus two **are** four.

Multiplication:
                  S   V   S   V
                  Two times two **is** also four.   or   Two times two **are**
                                                          also four.

Subtraction:
                  S   V
                  Four minus two **is** two.

Division:
                  S   V
                  Four divided by two **is** two.

TIPS FOR EDITING

4. *Titles.*   Titles of literary works, musical compositions, and other works of art are always singular, even when the words are plural in form:

Singular:

          S   V
The Beans of Egypt, Maine **is** a novel by Carolyn Chute.

          S   V
The Days of Our Lives **is** my mother's favorite soap opera.

       S   V
Compositions **is** an album by Anita Baker.

Pronouns as Subjects

Normally, pronouns do not cause problems in agreement when they serve as subjects. Certain pronouns are singular (*he, she, it, this, that*), and other pronouns are plural (*we, they, these, those*). However, two categories of pronouns can prove troublesome: indefinite pronouns and relative pronouns.

Indefinite Pronouns

Certain **indefinite pronouns** used as subjects are always singular: *another, anybody, anything, each, either, everybody, everyone, everything, neither, no one, nobody, nothing, one, somebody, someone,* and *something.* If you remember that pronouns ending in *-body, -one,* and *-thing* are singular, you will have little trouble recalling this rule. Look at these sentences from Albert's revised draft, which illustrate agreement between indefinite pronouns and verbs:

Singular:

          S   V   V
Everybody had been trying to get him to wise up.

          S   V
One of the most important things he learned **was** that he was responsible for his own moods and that "getting high" was almost inevitably followed by "getting low."

A few indefinite pronouns are always plural: *both, few, many, others,* and *several.*

Plural:

          S   V   V
Both have signed up to run for student government president.

          S   V   V
Several were damaged in shipping.

Other indefinite pronouns can be either singular or plural, depending on the antecedent (the word to which the pronoun refers). These include *all*, *any*, *more*, *most*, *none*, and *some*.

Singular:	**S V V V** *Some* of the pie **has been eaten.**
Plural:	**S V V V** *Some* of the pie slices **have been eaten.**

Relative Pronouns

As you learned in Chapter 2, **relative pronouns** introduce dependent clauses in sentences and often serve as the subjects of those clauses. These words include *that*, *which*, *what*, *whatever*, *who*, and *whoever*. They always take a verb that agrees in number with the pronoun's antecedent:

Singular:	**S V** Albert sits beside a man **who sleeps** in class every day.
Plural:	The professor worked his way through the piles of papers **S V V** **that were stacked** upon his desk.

Exercise E5-5

Choose the form of the verb in parentheses that will correctly complete each sentence adapted from "A Nation at Risk."

1. Over half the population of gifted students (*do, does*) not match their tested ability with comparable achievement in school.
2. Both the number and proportion of students demonstrating superior achievement on the SATs (i.e., those with scores of 650 or higher) (*has, have*) also dramatically declined.
3. Some (*worry, worries*) that schools may emphasize such rudiments as reading and computation at the expense of other essential skills such as comprehension, analysis, solving problems, and drawing conclusions.
4. Thus, we issue this call to all who (*care, cares*) about America and its future.
5. In light of the urgent need for improvement, both immediate and long term, this Commission (*has, have*) agreed on a set of recommendations that the American people can begin to act on now, that can be implemented over the next several years, and that promise lasting reform.

Exercise E5-6

Correct the agreement errors in the following sentences from the first draft of Albert's investigating essay (pp. 174–176).

1. Most of the month's stay were an eye-opening experience.
2. About three-fourths of the test were easy, simple enough for Travis to pass with no problem.

3. He works with a group of people who cares about him and wants him to succeed at his career.
4. The majority of the money he stole have been paid back.
5. He feels everyone have been supportive.

Exercise E5-7

Complete the sentences in the following paragraph by choosing the verb that agrees with each subject.

Last month two friends and I went to Chicago for a taping of Jerry Springer's talk show. Most of the ride over (1) (*was, were*) uneventful. We did stop at McDonald's on the way to get a snack. My friend Jenna's fries (2) (*was, were*) cold, so that was our excitement. Kathy was quiet because she was engrossed in a romance novel, her favorite reading material. *Forbidden Secrets* (3) (*was, were*) the name of the book, a paperback she had picked up at WalMart. Anyway, we finally got into the city and found a parking garage near the NBC building. Twelve dollars (4) (*was, were*) too much to pay, so we drove three blocks away and parked for six dollars. Walking as fast as we could, we entered the building and made our way to wait in line for the show. The number of people in line (5) (*was, were*) about a hundred. The prospective audience (6) (*was, were*) a mixture of all kinds of people. About 80 percent of the people who (7) (*was, were*) waiting (8) (*was, were*) under thirty, I'd guess. Probably just over half of the audience (9) (*was, were*) composed of women. A number of people (10) (*was, were*) shouting as they waited for the seating to begin.

Exercise E5-8

Write sentences using the following nouns and pronouns as subjects and is, are, was, *or* were *as either main verbs or helping verbs.*

1. politics
2. one-fifth
3. news
4. whoever
5. none

Pronoun-Antecedent Agreement

As you learned in Chapter 2, most pronouns refer to an easily identifiable word appearing in the same sentence or in a previous sentence. This word, the pronoun's **antecedent,** must agree with the pronoun in three ways: number, person, and gender.

Number

Just as subjects and verbs must agree in number, pronouns and antecedents must also match in **number**. This means that singular pronouns refer to singular an-

T I P S   F O R   E D I T I N G

tecedents, and plural pronouns refer to plural antecedents. Usually agreement within sentences causes few problems, as this sentence from Albert's revised draft illustrates:

Antecedent

Singular: Now, **Travis** knows about the realities of drinking, and **he**

can help others avoid his mistakes.

Travis is singular, one person. Therefore, a singular pronoun—*he*—is needed.

Pronoun-antecedent agreement is often this simple. However, there are three situations that merit close attention:

1. *Compound antecedents.*   When two or more antecedents are joined by *and*, a plural pronoun is needed:

    Plural: **Albert** and **Roderick** spent **their** entire paychecks during one weekend trip to Minneapolis.

                        The **winner** and the **losers** took **their** time walking off the stage.

    When compound antecedents are joined by *either . . . or, neither . . . nor, not only . . . but also,* or *whether . . . or,* the pronoun agrees with the noun or pronoun that is nearest to it.

    Plural: Either the **manager** or the hourly **workers** will have to check **their** time cards.

    Singular: Either the team **members** or the **coach** has to show **her** identification card.

2. *Collective noun antecedents.*   As explained earlier in this chapter, **collective nouns** refer either to a single unit or group or to individual members of the group. When a collective noun represents a group that functions as a single unit, a singular pronoun is needed. But when a collective noun focuses on the actions of individual members, a plural pronoun is required.

    Singular: The **audience** gave **its** approval to the singer by loudly clapping and cheering.

    Plural: The **audience** took **their** seats when the speaker waved her hands.

3. *Indefinite pronoun antecedents.*   As just discussed, some indefinite pronouns are always singular:

another	everyone	somebody
anybody	everything	someone

anyone	neither	something
anything	nobody	whatever
each	no one	whichever
either	nothing	whoever
everybody	one	

When a singular indefinite pronoun serves as an antecedent, the pronoun it refers to should also be singular:

Singular: **Neither** of Albert's friends won a blue ribbon for **his** artwork at the fair.

Something left **its** tracks in the flower beds in our backyard.

The indefinite pronouns *both, few, others,* and *several* are always plural. So when they are used as antecedents for a pronoun, the pronoun should also be plural:

Plural: **Few** promised that **they** would show up at 6:30 in the morning.

Several of the runners said that **they** would pull out of the race if it took place at night.

Some indefinite pronouns may be either singular or plural: *all, any, more, most, some.* If the pronoun represents something that cannot be counted, a singular antecedent is required. If the pronoun represents something that can be counted, a plural antecedent is needed.

Singular: **Some** of our success is credited to our grandfather because he nurtured **it** with emotional and monetary support.

Plural: **Some** of Albert's classmates typed **their** notes while reviewing for the test.

Person

Person refers to the person speaking: first person (*I, we*), second person (*you*), and third person (*he, she, it, they*). Usually, agreement in person poses few problems because logic guides our choices. However, writers often change from a first person or third person pronoun to a second person pronoun within the same sentence. Look at this sentence from Albert's first draft:

Shift: When **someone** sinks as low as he did, **you** have to take

action.

Revisions: When **someone** sinks as low as he did, **he or she** has to take action.

Anyone who sinks as low as he did has to take action.

Nouns that serve as antecedents are considered third person. Sometimes the pronouns they refer to will not agree in person, as the following example illustrates:

Shift: If **drivers** hit the brake too hard, **you** may find **yourself** skidding into a 360-degree turn.

Revision: If **drivers** hit the brake too hard, **they** may find **themselves** skidding into a 360-degree turn.

Gender

Pronouns may be **masculine, feminine,** or **neuter** (referring to neither males or females). The third person singular pronouns are the only pronouns that indicate gender: *he, him, his, she, her, hers.* All other personal pronouns—*I, me, my, mine, we, us, our, ours, you, your, yours, they, them, their, it, its*—are neuter.

Making pronouns agree in gender is usually a simple task, as the following sentences from Albert's first draft illustrate:

Examples: **Travis** had been fighting with **his sister** about some missing money, and **he** became enraged and pushed **her** down the stairs.

For example, he kept borrowing **money** from family members and never paid any of **it** back.

Problems sometimes arise, however, when an antecedent is not clearly masculine, feminine, or neuter. For example, indefinite pronouns such as *everyone, somebody,* or *each* do not specify gender. The generally accepted practice is to use *he or she* or *him or her* to refer to these words so that you avoid sexist references.

Singular: Everyone can learn how to use a computer if *he or she* tries.

Somebody left *his or her* book in the classroom yesterday.

If you find the use of *his or her* awkward, you can reword the sentence, replace the personal pronoun with an article, or make the antecedent plural.

Reworded: **Everyone** who tries can learn how to use a computer.

TIPS FOR EDITING

Article:	**Somebody** left **a** book in the classroom yesterday.
Plural:	**People** can learn how to use a computer if **they** try.

Exercise E5-9

Choose the correct pronouns in parentheses to complete each of the following sentences adapted from the essay "A Nation at Risk."

1. Our society and (*its, their*) educational institutions seem to have lost sight of the basic purposes of schooling, and of the high expectations and disciplined effort needed to attain (*it, them*).
2. This promise means that all children by virtue of (*its, their*) own efforts, competently guided, can hope to attain the mature and informed judgment needed to secure gainful employment and to manage their own lives.
3. The Department of the Navy, for example, reported to the Commission that one-quarter of (*its, their*) recent recruits cannot read at the ninth grade level, the minimum needed simply to understand written safety instructions.
4. Knowledge of the humanities, (*it, they*) maintain, must be harnessed to science and technology if the latter are to remain creative and humane, just as the humanities need to be informed by science and technology if (*it, they*) are to remain relevant to the human condition.
5. In the early part of this century and continuing to this very day, our schools have absorbed vast waves of immigrants and educated (*him or her, them*) and (*his or her, their*) children to productive citizenship.

Exercise E5-10

Correct the errors in pronoun-antecedent agreement in the following sentences from the first draft of Albert's investigating essay.

1. His mother told him that she did not want another crippled child, so he had to learn to resolve his differences with his sister without resorting to violence.
2. Everyone took their digs at him.
3. He told me that was better than many of the things they had called him in the past, so he kept going to school and kept going to their support group meetings.
4. Everybody still has their opinion of me.
5. I am sure that the clinic supervisor made an excellent decision when they decided to hire him to help others recover from their addictions.

Exercise E5-11

Choose the correct pronoun in parentheses to complete the sentences in the following paragraphs.

I recently served on a committee to review acts for our sorority's annual talent contest, which raises money for muscular dystrophy. Any student on campus could give it (1) (*his or her, their*) best shot in three minutes. After all, we were giving $300 in prize money to the contestants who performed (2) (*his or her, their*) act the best, according to a panel of judges. We decided beforehand to choose twenty acts who would try (3) (*his or her, their*) hand at the big money.

The committee held (4) (*its, their*) auditions on a Thursday night. Over fifty acts showed up. One of our favorites was a trio of male dancers. Each of them had (5) (*his, their*) own solo part in the routine. None of the guys looked like (6) (*he, they*) missed a beat. We also liked a couple of rappers. Both of them looked like (7) (*he, they*) had stepped off MTV. Most of the people who tried out were singers who brought (8) (*his or her, their*) own accompanists. A couple of them thought (9) (*he or she, they*) were really good, and they had cocky attitudes that turned some of us off. When the committee cast (10) (*its, their*) ballots, the singers with attitude still made the final cut because they were obviously talented.

Exercise E5-12

Write sentences using the following words and phrases as antecedents.

> **Example:** somebody
>
> **Sentence:** Somebody left his or her key in the door.

1. army
2. employees and managers
3. neither the boys nor their father
4. each
5. few

COLLABORATIVE WORK

After you revise your investigating essay, exchange papers with a classmate, and do the following tasks:

A. Circle any subjects and verbs that do not agree in number.

B. Underline any pronouns that do not agree with their antecedents in number, person, or gender.

Then return the paper to its writer, and use the information in this section to edit your draft.

Restating
Reading and Writing for a Reason

Word carpentry is like any other kind of carpentry: you must join your sentences smoothly.
—ANATOLE FRANCE

Although much of what we write is inspired by our own ideas, experiences, thoughts, attitudes, and responses to events and circumstances, another type of writing, called restating, is a skill we are often required to use—in college, in graduate school, and in our careers. **Restating** is just a fancy way of saying, "Put it in your own words." You restate all the time in conversation when you describe a movie you saw, a book you read, or a conversation you had. In these descriptions, you usually do not use the exact words you heard in the original version. Instead, you *paraphrase* (put in your own words) for your listener, using your own words to capture the original content and meaning of your source.

Restating in writing is much like restating in speaking. You take the information provided by some other source—a textbook, a lecture, a graph, an illustration, a map, a movie, a meeting—and explain the material in your own words so that your readers can understand it as completely as if they had read, seen, or heard the original source.

Think of the last time you took an essay examination in school. When you wrote your essay responses, you were restating the information you read in your textbook or heard in a class discussion or lecture. If you were asked in a history class, for example, to describe the way that President Franklin D. Roosevelt decided to aid England during World War II through lend-lease agreements, your instructor would not expect you to remember the words exactly as you had read them in your textbook or heard them in a lecture. In fact, if you did, you would either be praised for having a photographic memory or be accused of plagiarism! (*Plagiarism* is copying words or ideas from the original source without giving credit to that writer.) Rather, you would be expected to restate the information so that your instructor would know you understood the assigned course material. In the same way, if your supervisor at work asked you to prepare a report, you would be expected to restate information you gathered from reading reports, attending meetings, and interpreting statistics.

The primary goal in restating is to be able to use your own words to express the content, purpose, and meaning of the original source. You should concentrate on explaining the main ideas of the material and on showing how the details support the main ideas. If you want to use any of the exact wording from the source, you must put words, phrases, or sentences from the original in quotation marks. (See pp. 320–321 for rules about using quotation marks.) The use of quotation marks should be reserved for special expressions that you cannot reword effectively. Otherwise, your restatement should capture the essence of the original without using its phrasing at all. Restating helps you accomplish several important goals: You are able to see the relationships among ideas; you develop a better understanding of the material; and you can show the reader that you understand the material.

LEARNING FROM PUBLISHED WRITERS

In the following excerpt from a college textbook titled *Psychology and Industry Today*, the authors describe acceptable and unacceptable employment practices. After the passage is an essay that restates the content of the excerpt. Notice how the writer of the restating essay begins with the main idea of the passage and then summarizes the evidence and information furnished in support of the main idea. The writer also summarizes the material contained in the preemployment questionnaire in the excerpt.

Before You Read

Focusing Your Attention

Before you read this excerpt and restatement, take a few moments to respond to the following questions in your journal:

1. Make a list of the occasions, both in and out of school, when you have found restating what you have heard or read to be useful or necessary.

2. In the passage you are about to read, the writers describe laws that have been put into effect to prevent unfair hiring practices in the United States. In light of your own experiences or the experiences of friends or relatives, do you think such laws are needed?

Expanding Your Vocabulary

Here are some words and their meanings that are important to your understanding of the chapter excerpt. You might want to review them before you begin to read.

"**rendered** [made] even more challenging" (paragraph 1)

"It has been **alleged** [claimed]" (paragraph 1)

"to **discharge** [to fire, to let go] any individual" (paragraph 2)

"an **adverse** [negative] impact" (paragraph 3)

"**markedly** [noticeably] worse" (paragraph 3)

"this **constitutes** [equals, means] adverse impact" (paragraph 3)

"educational **deprivation** [lacking or denied advantages]" (paragraph 5)

"**predominantly** [mostly] black high schools and colleges" (paragraph 6)

"all **selection devices** [tests and procedures used in hiring]" (paragraph 7)

"techniques are **validated** [proved fair and effective]" (paragraph 7)

"convicted of **embezzlement** [stealing]" (paragraph 11)

"**detrimental** [damaging] to their careers" (paragraph 12)

"**impetus** [desire, incentive] to hire and promote members of minority groups" (paragraph 13)

"preferential treatment, **albeit** [although] of a negative kind" (paragraph 15)

"must not be unnecessarily **restrained** [held back]" (paragraph 17)

Duane P. Schultz and Sidney Ellen Schultz

The Challenge of Fair Employment*

Successful selection [of employees] has been rendered even more   **1**
challenging in recent years by the requirements of the Equal Employment Opportunity Commission (EEOC). All job applicants, regardless of race, religion, sex, or national origin, must be given equal
opportunities for employment. This problem has special relevance for
members of minority groups. It has been alleged that some of the selection procedures used by employing organizations discriminate
against educationally and culturally deprived individuals. Not only is
such discrimination unethical and immoral, but it is also illegal. The
Civil Rights Act of 1964 and the enforced guidelines of the EEOC
(established in 1972) have declared it against the law to discriminate
against job applicants.

Title VII, Section 703, of the Civil Rights Act states, "It shall be   **2**
an unlawful employment practice for an employer to fail or refuse to

*Duane P. Schultz and Sidney Ellen Schultz, *Psychology and Industry* (pp. 87–90). New York: Macmillan, 1990.

hire or to discharge any individual, or otherwise to discriminate against any individual with respect to his compensation, terms, conditions, or privileges of employment, because of such individual's race, color, religion, sex, or national origin." The EEOC is empowered to bring legal action against any organization employing 15 or more persons that violates the provisions of Title VII.

Employment practices that have an *adverse impact* on any of the groups protected by Title VII are prohibited by law. When any minority group applying to an organization is treated markedly worse than the majority group then that minority group is said to be the target of adverse impact in the selection process. Any selection rate for a minority group that is less than 80% of the selection rate for the majority group is evidence of adverse impact. For example, say a company had 100 job applicants (50 whites and 50 blacks) and hired 50 persons (40 whites and 10 blacks). In this case, 80% of the white applicants were hired but only 20% of the black applicants. Thus, the selection rate for blacks was one fourth of that for whites; this constitutes adverse impact. A company can be legally challenged for maintaining such a vastly different rejection rate for minority and majority groups.   3

As a result, employing organizations must try to ensure that all persons have equal access to job and training opportunities. Because of this legislation and increased social awareness, personnel departments have had to examine their screening procedures to ensure that a job applicant is not discriminated against because he or she is black, Hispanic, physically handicapped, or over a certain age, and, thus, may have had less opportunity to develop job and personal skills.   4

Suppose, for example, that a personnel department has established specific levels of arithmetic ability and verbal skill plus a high school diploma as requirements for a particular job. These requirements may disqualify certain minority-group members who may not have been able to complete high school for reasons having nothing to do with their mental ability. Similarly, some psychological tests may place a minority-group member at a disadvantage because he or she may have experienced cultural and educational deprivation.   5

To further equalize employment possibilities of minority groups, employers have been actively seeking minority job applicants. Recruiters are sent to predominantly black high schools and colleges, for example, instead of waiting for interested individuals to come to the personnel office.   6

The law requiring equal opportunity of employment has placed   7 specific limitations on virtually all selection devices. Every method of selection should minimize adverse impact and be clearly related to performance on the job. The burden of proof rests on the employing organization. Personnel psychologists have put forth a great deal of effort to ensure that selection techniques are job related and that measures of job performance (against which selection techniques are validated) are as objective as possible. . . . Interviews and application blanks are particularly affected. Psychologists and personnel departments are highly sensitive to what can and cannot be asked of a job applicant. Questions that might discriminate against minority-group members or women can result in lawsuits. Also, what is considered discriminatory varies among states, depending on the wording of each state's human rights laws.

To give you some idea of the kinds of questions that can no longer be asked of job applicants, consider the pre-employment questionnaire [on page 216].   **8**

Only three of these 19 inquiries, numbers 6, 10, and 12, are considered to be lawful questions to ask a job applicant. A prospective employer can ask applicants if they are citizens of the United States (according to Title VII, they *must* ask this question), about their knowledge of foreign languages, and details of prior work experience. It is unlawful, at least in some states, to ask any of the other questions.   **9**

Let us examine some of these items to learn why they could be considered discriminatory. Items 2, 3, 4, and 5 could easily identify the national origin, race, creed, or color of an applicant, as could items 7, 8, 13, 14, 15, and 16. Also, much of the information asked in these items has no bearing on the applicant's ability to perform the job for which he or she is being considered. Therefore, in addition to being possibly discriminatory, these questions serve no useful purpose in predicting the applicant's potential for success on the job.   **10**

It is considered unlawful to ask applicants if they have ever been arrested; minority-group members are much more likely to be arrested on suspicion, owing to the possible prejudices of arresting officers, and this should not be held against them. It *is* lawful, however, to ask applicants if they have ever been *convicted* of crimes. This could be relevant to job performance, for example, in the case of a person convicted of embezzlement who is applying for a job in a bank.   **11**

In addition to the discriminatory nature of some questions, there is the issue of personal privacy. Some authorities have suggested that job applicants leave blank any item on an application form that they consider to be irrelevant to the job for which they are applying, or to be an   **12**

Pre-employment Questionnaire

Pre-employment inquiry	Lawful	Unlawful
1. Asking applicants if they have ever worked under another name.		✓
2. Asking applicants to name their birthplace.		✓
3. Asking for the birthplace of applicants' parents, spouse, or other close relatives.		✓
4. Asking applicants to submit proof of age by supplying birth certificate or baptismal record.		✓
5. Asking applicants for religious affiliation, name of church, parish, or religious holidays observed.		✓
6. Asking applicants if they are citizens of the United States.	✓	
7. Asking applicants if they are naturalized citizens.		✓
8. Asking applicants for the date their citizenship was acquired.		✓
9. Asking applicants if they have ever been arrested for any crime, and to indicate when and where.		✓
10. Asking applicants to indicate what foreign languages they can read, write, or speak fluently.	✓	
11. Asking applicants how they acquired the ability to read, write, or speak a foreign language.		✓
12. Asking applicants about their past work experience.	✓	
13. Requesting applicants to provide names of three relatives other than parents, spouse, or minor-age dependent children.		✓
14. Asking male applicants for their wives' maiden names.		✓
15. Asking applicants for their mothers' maiden names.		✓
16. Asking for the full names of the applicants' brothers and sisters.		✓
17. Asking applicants for a list of names of all clubs, societies, and lodges to which they belong.		✓
18. Asking applicants to include photographs with their applications for employment.		✓
19. Asking applicants to supply addresses of relatives such as cousins, uncles, aunts, nephews, nieces, or grandparents who can be contacted for references.		✓

Adapted from "Human Rights Laws and Pre-Employment Inquiries" by R.L. Minter, 1972, *Personnel Journal, 51,* p. 432.

unfair invasion of their privacy. Such behavior may be detrimental to their careers, however. In one study, managers viewed those applicants who did not answer application blank questions dealing with criminal convictions as being less suitable for employment than those who reported having no criminal convictions. The researchers noted that "a potential employer views a nonresponse to an application blank item as an attempt to conceal facts that would reflect poorly on an applicant."

The impetus to hire and promote members of minority groups has sometimes resulted in discrimination against members of the majority group. For example, a company may be so intent on raising the number of women in its plant to meet federal guidelines that it denies job or promotion opportunities to men.   **13**

This phenomenon, known as *reverse discrimination*, has occurred frequently as organizations have tried to implement EEOC rulings. It has also occurred in graduate and professional schools, where white applicants have been denied admission in favor of minority-group applicants whose test scores or college boards may not have been as high as those of the white applicants.   **14**

The question of reverse discrimination is complex and controversial. The intent of Title VII was to prevent preferential treatment for *any* group. Yet, when any applicant, otherwise qualified, is denied educational or job opportunities because institutions must by law have more persons of a certain sex or ethnic background, those persons are also receiving preferential treatment, albeit of a negative kind.   **15**

The issue reached the U.S. Supreme Court in 1979, which ruled in favor of a company's racial quota for admission to a training program. A white employee who had been denied admission to the program sued the company, claiming that he had been discriminated against because of his race. He lost the case.   **16**

More recent Supreme Court decisions have sometimes upheld charges of reverse discrimination. These rulings have noted that the rights of majority groups must not be unnecessarily restrained in order to help minorities, and that minorities should not be hired or promoted simply on the basis of percentages or some other quota system. Rather, the Supreme Court ruled that only fully qualified minority employees should be hired or promoted.   **17**

Restatement of "The Challenge of Fair Employment"

In recent years, because of the requirements of the Equal Employment Opportunity Commission (EEOC), companies have had to be sure that their hiring practices guarantee that all applicants are considered equally and fairly for jobs no matter what their race, religion, sex, or nationality. The Civil Rights Act of 1964 and the rules set by the

EEOC declare it illegal to discriminate against applicants. The EEOC has the power to sue any organization with over 15 employees if discrimination in hiring practices is suspected. These rules are particularly important to members of minority groups whose lack of educational and cultural opportunities put them at a disadvantage to majority groups.

Hiring practices that have an adverse impact on any particular group can be judged based on the number of applicants from particular groups compared with the number hired from that particular group; this is known as the "selection rate." If a company is found to hire a higher percentage from one group of applicants than another, the company can be legally challenged by the EEOC. Because of these laws, employers must be certain that their hiring practices are not discriminatory. They must examine the types of tests they administer, and they must seek out minority applicants rather than wait for them to come to the employment office.

Even more important, the questions that employers ask applicants must be chosen carefully. Questions may be asked to determine how well an employee will perform on the job but not to determine the national origin, race, creed, or color of the applicant. If the answer to a question asked during the employment interview does not relate to the applicant's ability to do the job for which he or she is applying, then the question could be considered discriminatory and unlawful. For example, while it is unlawful to ask an applicant whether he or she has ever been arrested, it is lawful to ask an applicant whether he or she has been convicted of a crime because this could reflect on the applicant's ability to do the job.

In addition, the personal privacy of the applicant must be protected, and applicants are permitted to leave certain questions blank if they think the answer is not relevant. This is not a perfect solution, however, because researchers have discovered that the blanks are often interpreted by potential employers as an admission of guilt or as an attempt to hide information.

The EEOC rules are intended to equalize employment opportunities for all groups, but sometimes this has resulted in "reverse discrimination": Members of the majority group do not get jobs or places in college because these openings were given to members of minority groups in order to make up for past inequalities. This is a complex and controversial problem, and many lawsuits have resulted that were taken all the way to the Supreme Court. In 1979, the U.S. Supreme Court found that a company had a right to reject a white applicant in order to satisfy its racial quota, but more recently, the Supreme Court has upheld findings of reverse discrimination and has ordered the job or place to go to the white applicant, stating that "only fully qualified minority employees should be hired or promoted."

QUESTIONS FOR CRITICAL THINKING

THINKING CRITICALLY ABOUT CONTENT

1. In your opinion, did the writer of the restating essay identify and correctly restate the main idea of the essay? Explain your answer.

2. In your opinion, did the writer identify and accurately restate the essential supporting details of the essay? Explain your answer.

THINKING CRITICALLY ABOUT PURPOSE

3. What do you think is the purpose of the original chapter excerpt?

4. Is the restating essay less effective because it simply restates the content of the questionnaire rather than giving readers the opportunity to see each question for themselves? Explain your answer.

THINKING CRITICALLY ABOUT AUDIENCE

5. What readers do you think would benefit most from the information in this essay?

6. Which version of the material had more impact on you, the original chapter excerpt or the restating essay? Explain your answer.

THINKING CRITICALLY ABOUT POINT OF VIEW

7. Write a paragraph explaining how you would react to the information contained in the original excerpt if you were applying for a job.

8. Write a paragraph explaining how you would react to the information contained in the original excerpt if you were an employer.

INTERPRETING GRAPHICS

Another type of restating involves summarizing information presented in graphic form. The term *graphic* refers to illustrations of any sort, such as drawings, maps, charts, or graphs. Much of the material that you will read in college, and later in your professional career, will contain such *visuals* (a synonym for *graphics*), and your ability to interpret these visuals will enhance your understanding of the information. If you look in any newspaper or magazine, you will notice that many of the articles include graphics containing statistics, percentages, costs—information that is much easier to present in chart or graph form than in words. Facts presented in graphic form are often more dramatic than words because sudden or sharp changes in percentages, numbers, or amounts are obvious in the visuals.

The following graphic was published in a book titled *Two Nations*, by Andrew Hacker, which describes the different employment experiences of black and white

Americans in the contemporary United States. This graph illustrates African-American representation within various occupations from 1960 to 1990. Notice how much useful information can be contained in a small space when it is presented graphically. (You might consider whether the changes reflected in this graph have anything to do with the actions of the Equal Employment Opportunity Commission as described in the excerpt you have just read.) Following the graph is a restating essay that summarizes the graph's information.

Before You Read

Focusing Your Attention

Before you study this graph and restatement, take a few moments to respond to the following questions in your journal:

1. Think of the last time you referred to a graph or a chart. Were you able to understand all the information contained in it? Was the graphic a more effective method of presenting the information than written form? Explain your answer.

2. The chart you are about to view illustrates the increases and decreases in the number of African Americans employed in various occupations from 1960 to 1990. Try to predict which occupations will be filled by African Americans in far greater numbers because of the Equal Employment Opportunity Commission rules.

BLACK REPRESENTATION WITHIN OCCUPATIONS
1960 to 1990

Representation More than Doubled

	1960	1990
Telephone operators	2.6%	19.7%
Aircraft mechanics	4.6%	9.8%
Firefighters	2.5%	11.5%
Accountants & Auditors	1.6%	7.4%
Secretaries	2.0%	7.6%
Retail salespersons	2.4%	9.5%
Electricians	2.2%	6.2%
Lawyers	1.3%	3.2%

Smaller Increases

	1960	1990
Painters	7.7%	9.5%
Librarians	5.1%	5.5%
Automobile mechanics	7.4%	8.7%
College teachers	4.4%	4.5%

BLACK REPRESENTATION WITHIN OCCUPATIONS
1960 to 1990 (*CONTINUED*)

Decreases

Domestic servants	54.3%	24.7%
Chefs and cooks	24.9%	18.3%
Hairdressers	12.7%	9.2%
Structural metal workers	5.0%	3.7%
Physicians	4.4%	3.0%

from *Two Nations* by Andrew Hacker, 1992 p. 113, Charles Schribner's
Sons, Macmillan Publishing Co., 866 Third Avenue, NY NY 10022

Restatement of "Black Representation Within Occupations"

In the 30-year period from 1960 to 1990 in the United States, the number of blacks in some occupations more than doubled; in other jobs the black representation increased slightly; and in still others the number of blacks decreased.

The largest increases (more than double) came in the following fields: telephone operators (from 2.6% to 19.7%), aircraft mechanics (from 4.6% to 9.8%), firefighters (from 2.5% to 11.5%), accountants and auditors (from 1.6% to 7.4%), secretaries (from 2.0% to 7.6%), retail salespersons (from 2.4% to 9.5%), electricians (from 2.2% to 6.2%), and lawyers (from 1.3% to 3.2%).

Smaller increases came in the following fields: painters (from 7.7% to 9.5%), librarians (from 5.1% to 5.5%), automobile mechanics (from 7.4% to 8.7%), and college teachers (from 4.4% to 4.5%).

Decreases occurred in the following fields: domestic servants (from 54.3% to 24.7%), chefs and cooks (from 24.9% to 18.3%), hairdressers (from 12.7% to 9.2%), structural metal workers (from 5.0% to 3.7%), and physicians (from 4.4% to 3.0%).

Perhaps large decreases occurred in the lower-paying jobs (domestic servants, chefs, cooks, hairdressers, and metal workers) because of the new opportunities for African Americans in the other two categories. This does not, however, account for the decrease in the number of African-American physicians.

QUESTIONS FOR CRITICAL THINKING

THINKING CRITICALLY ABOUT CONTENT

1. Do you think the writer captured the full meaning and purpose of the graph in the restating essay? Explain your answer.

2. Do you think the writer included enough details in restating the graph? Explain your answer.

THINKING CRITICALLY ABOUT PURPOSE

3. What do you think is the main purpose of the graph?

4. In your opinion, which format is more effective, the graph or the restating essay? Explain your answer.

THINKING CRITICALLY ABOUT AUDIENCE

5. What readers do you think would find the graph and the restating essay most interesting? Explain your answer.

6. As a student, how could you make use of the information provided in the graph and the restating essay? Explain your answer.

THINKING CRITICALLY ABOUT POINT OF VIEW

7. Although graphs and charts are supposed to be objective statements that provide facts and statistics without commentary or opinion, could this graph be interpreted differently by people with differing points of view? Explain your answer.

8. Reread the last paragraph of the restating essay, which is an interpretation of the information presented in the graph. Write a paragraph in response to the interpretation.

LEARNING FROM YOUR PEERS

The writing assignments in this chapter are slightly different from the other writing tasks you have completed so far. Instead of drawing on your own experiences to write an essay, you must restate information presented by someone else. By restating another writer's thoughts in your own words, you will find out whether you completely understand those ideas. This technique will help you whenever you have to summarize someone else's thoughts or findings. It will also benefit you in taking short-answer and essay tests. To see the process of restating in action, we are going to follow the procedure of a student named Antwan Jones as he works through two restating assignments.

Antwan's Writing Assignment: Restating Information from a Professional Essay

This is the first part of the topic Antwan's instructor assigned:

Restate the following article about the financial rewards of higher education for women. The purpose of this assignment is to make sure you understand what the author is saying. Because this restatement is part of a larger research project, it is very important to complete this assignment accurately and thoroughly.

The second part of Antwan's assignment, designed to demonstrate his ability to understand and restate the information contained in a graph, is on page 228.

The Financial Payoff of Higher Education for Women*

Nationwide, women have a median income that is 52 percent of the median income of men. Some observers believe this huge income gap is not a cause for concern. They point out that a major reason for this discrepancy is child-rearing activities. Women are much more unlikely to be steady participants in the work force and thus, not surprisingly, they have a much lower median income. **1**

However, this shortsighted explanation accounts for only a small part of gender-based income inequality. Even when we compare men and women who hold year-round, full-time jobs, we find that women have a median income that is only 71 percent of the median income of men. **2**

The Education Payoff

How does education affect the gender income gap? In order to compare similar groups of employed people, we will examine government statistics that include only year-round, full-time workers. Thus we eliminate the large group of women who do not work or who work only part-time. **3**

Women full-time workers who have completed high school but have not gone on to college had a median income of $18,761, or 71.6 percent of the median income of men with only a high school diploma. By gaining a college degree, women improve their median income by 56.9 percent, to $29,436, over women with only a high school diploma. Men who complete college improve their median income by 56.2 percent compared to men who have only completed high school. Thus the educational payoff of a college degree is slightly higher for women than it is for men. Keep in mind that women with a college degree still have a median income that is on **4**

*From *The Monthly Forum on Women in Higher Education* (Dec. 1995), p. 5.

average more than $10,000 less than men with similar educational attainment.

Master's Degrees

For those who have earned master's degrees, women who work full-time have a median income of $35,993, or 72 percent of the median income of men with a master's degree. Here again, a master's degree results in a slightly higher income premium for women than men when compared to members of their gender with only a bachelor's degree. However, men with a master's degree have a median income that is $14,000 larger than women with a master's degree. Women with a master's degree have a median income that is less than the median income of men with only a bachelor's degree.

The largest discrepancy in the gender income gap is for full-time workers with professional degrees. Women professionals have a median income of $45,588, only 59 percent of the median income of men professionals, which stood at $76,321. This large gap can be explained in part by the tendency of women professionals to gravitate toward specialties that are not as financially lucrative as the professions favored by men. Glass ceiling barriers for women in many professional firms and the interruption of professional practice during early child-rearing years also factor into the huge income gap at this educational level.

Women with Doctorates

Women with doctorates fare better vis-à-vis men than women at other educational levels. In 1993 women doctorates had a median income of $45,776, or 79 percent of the median income of men with doctorates.

In sum, it appears that the economic payoff of higher education is slightly higher for women than it is for men except for those who graduate from professional school. However, despite the economic advantages of higher education for women, advanced degrees do very little to close the overall gender income gap. At all educational levels, women who work full-time still earn far less than men.

Antwan goes through the process as outlined in Chapter 1: *thinking, planning, developing, organizing, drafting, revising,* and *editing.*

Thinking

Antwan reads through the article quickly and decides to check unfamiliar words in the dictionary. He looks up the following words in his CD-ROM *American Heritage Dictionary* and copies their definitions in his writing journal:

median: Statistics. Relating to or constituting the middle value in a distribution. The middle value in a distribution, above and below which lie an equal number of values.

discrepancy: divergence or disagreement, as between facts or claims; difference.

lucrative: producing wealth; profitable.

glass ceiling: This expression was not in Antwan's dictionary.

After looking up these words, Antwan reads the article more slowly and takes notes on his reading. He reminds himself to ask his instructor what the term *glass ceiling* means.

Planning

Antwan's task is to restate the information in this essay as accurately and concisely as possible. He does not want to leave out any facts. He also wants to make sure he does not draw any incorrect conclusions, so he takes careful notes.

As he takes notes, Antwan tries to make the material as clear to himself as possible. Sometimes he has to look back at his list of definitions to make sure that he is interpreting the material correctly. Antwan has never taken a statistics class and is not sure what the term *median* means even after looking it up in the dictionary, so he calls a friend who is a psychology major and asks for an explanation. When the friend tells him that it means "the exact middle of a list of numbers," Antwan thinks that he now has a better understanding of the term.

Then he finishes his notes and checks them to make sure that he has not left anything out. He remembers that he has not found out the meaning of *glass ceiling* and makes another note to ask his instructor.

Developing

In class the next day, Antwan finds out that *glass ceiling* is a term that means "invisible barrier." His instructor explains that the article refers to the fact that women make up only about 5 percent of upper management in U.S. businesses. Some women are promoted to fairly high positions in certain companies, but then their promotions seem to stop, and 95 percent of the most responsible and highest-paying positions go to men.

Looking at the article again, Antwan does not think that he can draw many conclusions from it, but he notices one comment in particular. "Keep in mind that women with a college degree still have a median income that is on average more than $10,000 less than men with similar educational attainment." Antwan sees that the article includes some interpretation as well as facts.

Organizing

Antwan looks over his notes and checks them against the excerpt. He wants to make sure he understands each statement so that he can restate it in the order the original writer presents it. He is satisfied that he understands all the word meanings and the statistical comparisons. He looks at his notes and decides he is ready to restate the article.

Drafting

Here is Antwan's restatement of the article "The Financial Payoff of Higher Education for Women."

Antwan's Essay: First Draft
Restating Information from an Essay ....

Main Idea: There is still inequality in men's and women's wages at all educational levels, but the more education, the less inequality.

All over the United States, women in the middle of the income range earn only $52 for every $100 earned by men in the same range. Some people say this is not a critical problem because women take many years out of their income-earning years to raise children. Therefore, they say it is not surprising that women should earn less than men.

Women rearing children may explain part of the inequality, but child care does not explain why women who hold year-round, full-time jobs earn only $71 for every $100 earned by men in the same income group (the median). The following statistics (from the U.S. Bureau of the Census) are based only on year-round, full-time workers, so women who work seasonal jobs or earn no income are not included.

The annual median income of women who completed high school was $18,761. This amounted to only $71.60 for every $100 earned by similar males. Women with college degrees improved their income in relation to women with high school diplomas. They earned 56.9 percent more than the female high school graduates, so their median income was $29,436. Men who earn college degrees improve their wages in relation to male high school graduates by a similar percentage (56.2%), but since they earn more than women high school graduates, this means that their income is still more than $10,000 above the median income of women college graduates.

For those full-time workers with master's degrees, there is still a large difference between male and female workers. Women earn $72 for every similarly educated male's $100. For women, this means a median income of $35,993, but the median income of men with master's degrees is $14,000 more. Women with a master's degree actually earn less than men with a bachelor's degree.

The biggest gap between groups actually occurs among recipients of professional degrees. Women professionals have a median income of $45,588, or only $59 for every $100 earned by men with similar educations. The median income of men with professional degrees is $76,321. Part of the reason for this discrepancy is that women and men specialize in different areas. Women may also bump into a "glass ceiling," meaning that they will not be promoted above a certain level, due to discrimination. The problem of interrupting careers to raise children also affects women, even at this level.

Women with doctorates are better off compared to men than women with other degrees. In 1993, the median income for women in this group was $45,776, or $79 for every $100 earned by men with doctorates.

In conclusion, if you compare median dollars earned at various educational levels, it still pays to become better educated. It is clear that men still earn more than women at all educational levels.

Antwan's Writing Assignment: Restating Information from a Graph

This is the second part of the topic Antwan's instructor assigned:

Restate in your own words the information contained in the following graph, "Women Have Made Tremendous Progress in Medical School Education." Do not worry about the length of your restating essay; just be as thorough and as informative as possible so that your reader will know you have interpreted and understood all the information in the graph.

Antwan goes through the entire writing process again to restate this graph.

Thinking

As Antwan begins this part of the restating assignment, he notices that there are five separate graphs with the headings "Applicants," "Accepted Applicants," "New Entrants," "Total Enrollment," and "Graduates." Antwan looks at each graph and thinks about its meaning. He looks at the years for each graph and notices that all are for the years 1989 through 1995. The title of the graph tells us this information is about women only.

Planning

Antwan looks at the graphs and lists the conclusions he can draw from the visual information:

Graph 1: Applicants

1. In 1989, slightly more than 10,000 women applied to medical school.

2. By 1995, that number had almost doubled, to 20,000.

Graph 2: Accepted applicants

1. In 1989, about 6,400 women applicants were accepted to medical school.

2. In 1995, about 7,500 women applicants were accepted to medical school.

Graph 3: New entrants

1. Of those women accepted to medical school in 1989, 6,000 began medical studies.

2. Of those women accepted to medical school in 1995, about 7,000 began medical studies.

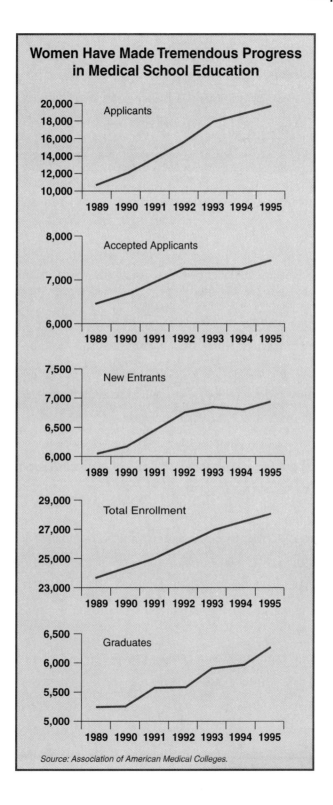

Women Have Made Tremendous Progress in Medical School Education

Source: Association of American Medical Colleges.

Graph 4: Total enrollment

1. In 1989, there were slightly more than 23,000 women enrolled in medical school.

2. By 1995, that number had risen to over 28,000.

Graph 5: Graduates

1. In 1989, about 5,200 women graduated from American medical schools.

2. In 1995, the number of women graduates had risen to about 6,200.

Developing

Antwan looks at the statements he has listed. He wants to draw some conclusions on the basis of these graphs. He lists the following conclusions:

Graphs 1 and 2:

The percentage of women applicants who were admitted to medical school in 1989 was 6,400 / 10,000 = 64%.

In 1995, there were 20,000 applicants, and about 7,500 were admitted. This is about 37.5% of the applicants.

Conclusion: Even though there were many more applicants, medical schools only accepted about 15% more women. Competition for the spots available is getting tougher.

Graph 2:

About 1,000 more women were admitted to medical school in 1995 than in 1989.

Conclusion: It looks like the number of women accepted to medical school is rising, although it hit a plateau from 1992 to 1994.

Graph 3:

The total number of women who entered medical school went up from 6,000 in 1989 to 7,000 in 1995.

Conclusion: Unless there were more spaces created for new students, the percentage of women in medical schools must be increasing.

Conclusion: The number of women who entered medical school in

1989–1995 is very close to the number of female applicants in those same years.

Graph 4:

The total number of women enrolled in medical school increased from 23,000 in 1989 to slightly over 28,000 in 1995.

Conclusion: Since 1989, women's enrollment in medical school has increased about 20%.

Conclusion: There is not enough information in this set of graphs to conclude what percentage of medical school graduates are women.

Graph 5:

The number of women graduates rose from about 5,000 to slightly over 6,000 over the six-year period 1989–1995.

Conclusion: The number of women who have graduated from medical school has risen about 20% over this period.

Organizing

Antwan is beginning to understand why words are necessary to understand graphs. He knows that at first glance these graphs look fairly simple, but explaining the information in words is a challenging task. He also realizes that the graphs may not contain all the information he needs to be absolutely sure of his conclusions. He decides that before he accepts the accuracy of these numbers, he will check another source.

Antwan looks over his restatements and decides he is ready to begin his draft. He knows that he can revise later if new information contradicts his conclusions.

Drafting

Here is Antwan's draft.

Antwan's Essay: First Draft
Restating Information from a Graph ....

Main Idea: There have been increases in the number of women in medical school.

The number of women applicants to medical school almost doubled from 1989 to 1995. While there were only about 10,000 women applicants in 1989, there were almost 20,000 in 1995.

Although the number of women applicants admitted to medical school rose from about 6,500 to about 7,500 from 1989 to 1995, the percentage of women applicants who were accepted to medical school actually dropped from 64 percent to 37.5 percent over this time period.

The total number of women who actually entered medical school increased from 6,000 in 1989 to 7,000 in 1995, which is roughly equivalent to the number of women accepted into medical school during those same years.

Since 1989, the total number of women enrolled in medical school has went from 23,000 to slightly over 28,000 in 1995. This represents a 20 percent rise.

The total number of women medical school graduates rose from slightly over 5,000 in 1989 to about 6,200 in 1995--another 20 percent increase.

This profile of women in medical school shows that there were increases in all categories over this six-year period. There were more women who applied to medical school, an increase in the number of women admitted, increased entrants, and more women who attended and graduated from medical school in 1995 than there were in 1989.

Revising

Antwan has written his restatement drafts as clearly and accurately as he can. He believes he has captured the essence of the article and the graph. But now he needs to review what he has written and smooth it out so that it is as effective as possible. The focus of the revision this time, the instructor tells the class, is on writing coherent essays. As class members get stronger in their writing, they are able to move to such complex issues in their revisions as clear pronouns, well-chosen transitions, effective repetition, and parallelism.

Antwan reviews the Checklist for Writing Coherent Essays at the beginning of the Tips for Revising section of this chapter. Even though many of these items deal with grammar and usage, the real issue is the role they play in holding sentences and paragraphs together and in emphasizing important ideas. Each piece of information in this section will move Antwan closer to a revised draft that is unified, efficient, and focused.

Antwan reads the Tips for Revising and does the assigned exercises. Returning to his draft, he works through the checklist carefully, first locating problems with coherence and then putting into practice some of the strategies he learned in this section. As he finds problems, he tries to resolve them in his revised draft.

COLLABORATIVE WORK

PEER GROUP ACTIVITY

After you read the portions of the Tips for Revising your instructor assigns, turn to Antwan's first drafts (pp. 226–227 and 232), and complete the following tasks in small groups:

A.   Circle all pronouns (for a definition, see p. 42) in both essays, and put an X through any nouns that would work better as pronouns.

B.   Underline all transitions (for a definition, see p. 241) in both essays, and put a caret (^) where you think the writer should add a transition.

C.   Double-underline any words or phrases that are repeated within a single paragraph. Put a diagonal line through those repetitions that are not effective.

D.   Put brackets around any items in a series that are not parallel in form (for a definition, see p. 245).

Compare the marks your group made with those your instructor will show you. Where do your marks differ from your instructor's? What do you need to review before writing your own essay?

CLASS ACTIVITY

As an entire class, look at the underlined portions of Antwan's revised drafts (pp. 235–236 and 236–237) to see how he changed some of his sentences.

A.   Did you identify the **revision** problems that Antwan corrected?

B.   Do you think his changes are good ones? Discuss his changes.

Editing

Now that the sentences say what Antwan wants them to say, he needs to complete his proofreading and editing before handing in his essay. The instructor asks the class to notice specific words in our language that use their forms to alter their meanings. Noticing these fine details of language at this point in the term, the instructor explains, helps everyone see how even a letter or a single punctuation mark can change a word's meaning and role in its sentence. So Antwan reads the Tips for Editing section in this chapter to learn about the forms of verbs, nouns, pronouns, and modifiers. Returning to his drafts, he takes the questions in the Checklist for Editing Verb Forms, Noun Forms, Pronoun Forms, and Modifiers one by one and makes changes so that his revised draft fulfills all these requirements.

 COLLABORATIVE WORK

PEER GROUP ACTIVITY

After you read the portions of the Tips for Editing your instructor assigns, turn to Antwan's first draft (pp. 226–227 and 232), and complete the following tasks in small groups:

A.   Underline all the verbs (for a definition, see p. 39).

B.   Circle all the nouns and pronouns (for definitions, see pp. 41 and 42).

C.   Draw squares around all the adjectives and adverbs (for definitions, see pp. 45 and 47).

D.   Put an X through any incorrect forms of the words you have identified on these drafts.

Compare your group's marks with those your instructor will show you. Where do your marks differ from your instructor's? What do you need to review before writing your own essay?

CLASS ACTIVITY

As an entire class, look at the underlined portions of Antwan's revised drafts (pp. 235–236 and 236–237) to see how he changed each sentence.

A.   Did you identify the **editing** problems that Antwan corrected?

B.   Do you think his changes are good ones? Discuss his changes.

Antwan's Revised Essay
Restating Information from an Essay ....

Women in Higher Education

All over the United States, women in the middle of the income range earn only $52 for every $100 earned by men in the ~~same~~ median range. <u>Median income means half of the people in the group earn more than this amount and half earn less; it is the exact middle.</u> Some people say this is not a critical problem because women take many years out of their income-earning years to raise children. Therefore, they say it is not surprising that women should earn less than men.

~~Women rearing children~~ <u>This</u> may explain part of the inequality, but ~~child care~~ <u>it</u> does not explain why women who hold year-round, full-time jobs earn only $71 for every $100 earned by men in the same income group (the median). The following statistics (from the U.S. Bureau of the Census) are based only on year-round, full-time workers, so women who work seasonal jobs or earn no income are not included.

The annual median income of women who completed high school was $18,761. This amounted to only $71.60 for every $100 earned by ~~similar males~~ <u>the male high school graduates</u>. Women with college degrees improved their income in relation to women with high school diplomas/; ~~They~~ <u>women with college degrees</u> earned 56.9 percent more than the female high school graduates, so their median income was $29,436. Men who earn college degrees improve their ~~wages~~ <u>median income</u> in relation to male high school graduates by a similar percentage (56.2%), but since ~~they~~ <u>the male high school graduates</u> earn more than women high school graduates, this means that ~~their~~ <u>the median</u> income <u>of male college graduates</u> is still more than $10,000 above the median income of women college graduates.

For those full-time workers with master's degrees, there is still a large difference between male and female workers. Women earn $72 for every similarly educated male's $100. For women, this means a median income of $35,993, but the median income of men with master's degrees is $14,000 more. Women with a master's degree actually earn less than men with a bachelor's degree.

The biggest gap between groups actually occurs among recipients of professional degrees. For example, wWomen professionals have a median income of $45,588, or only $59 for every $100 earned by men with similar educations/, whereas tThe median income of men with professional degrees is $76,321. Although pPart of the reason for this discrepancy is that women and men specialize in different areas/, wWomen may also bump into a "glass ceiling," meaning that they will not be promoted above a certain level, due to discrimination. The problem of interrupting careers to raise children also affects women, even at this level.

Women with doctorates are better off compared to men than women with other degrees. In 1993, the median income for women in this group was $45,776, or $79 for every $100 earned by men with doctorates.

In conclusion, if you compare median dollars earned at various educational levels, it still pays to become better educated. It is clear that men still earn more than women at all educational levels.

Antwan's Revised Essay
Restating Information from a Graph ....

Women in Medical School

The number of women applicants to medical school almost doubled from 1989 to 1995. While there were only about 10,000 women applicants in 1989, there were almost 20,000 in 1995.

Although the number of women applicants admitted to medical school rose from about 6,500 to about 7,500 from 1989 to 1995, the percentage of women applicants who were accepted to medical school actually dropped from 64 percent to 37.5 percent over this time period.

The total number of women who actually entered medical school increased from 6,000 in 1989 to 7,000 in 1995, which is roughly equivalent to the number of women accepted into medical school during those same years.

Since 1989, the total number of women enrolled in medical school has ~~went~~ <u>gone</u> from 23,000 to slightly over 28,000 in 1995. This represents a 20 percent rise.

The total number of women medical school graduates rose from slightly over 5,000 in 1989 to about 6,200 in 1995--another 20 percent increase.

This profile of women in medical school shows that there were increases in all categories over this six-year period. There were more women who applied to medical school, ~~an increase in the number of women~~ <u>more women who were</u> admitted, ~~increased entrants~~ <u>more women who entered</u>, and more women who attended and graduated from medical school in 1989 than there were in 1995.

WRITING YOUR OWN RESTATING ESSAY

So far, you have seen a professional writer and a fellow student at work trying to restate an idea or body of information as accurately as possible. They have worked with both essays and graphics and have demonstrated that they understand the original sources. As you read the professional essay and followed the writing process of another student from first to final draft, you absorbed ideas and ways of giving those ideas a form of their own. These reading and writing activities have prepared you to write your own restatements.

What Have You Discovered?

Before you begin your own writing task, let's review what you have learned in this chapter so far:

- When you restate, you put information from another source (for example, a textbook, a lecture, a graph, an illustration, or a map) into your own words.

- When you restate, you can show your reader you are able to comprehend and analyze the assigned material.

- You should concentrate on explaining the main ideas of the material and then on showing how the details support those ideas.

- To present your restatement effectively, you need to organize your ideas.

- To help you shape your essay, you should learn as much as possible about your readers.

- Before you write a draft, you need to understand the original author's point of view toward your subject.

- After you write a draft, you should revise your essay for meaning and organization.

- After you revise your essay, you should edit its grammar, usage, and sentence structure.

Your Writing Topic

Choose one of the following topics for your restating essay:

1.   Find a short editorial or comic strip in a newspaper or newsmagazine, and restate it. Include a photocopy of the original, and highlight the section you chose to restate.

2.   Find a scientific or technical article that interests you, and interpret one of its accompanying graphs or charts. Include a photocopy of the original, and highlight the section you chose to restate.

3.   Find a difficult section of a textbook for a course you are now taking, and restate it clearly. Include a photocopy of the original, and highlight the section you chose to restate.

4.   Create your own restating essay topic (with the assistance of your instructor). Include a photocopy of the material you have chosen, and highlight the section you chose to restate.

When you have selected one of these topics, you may begin your writing process in the same way Antwan did. (You may find his experience helpful in giving you ideas for writing your own restating essay.) If some tasks occur out of order, that adjustment is probably part of your personal writing ritual. Follow your instincts and let them mold your writing process, but make sure you've worked through all the stages to your final draft.

YOUR WRITING PROCESS

THINKING   Paraphrase the original source in as many different ways as possible.

PLANNING   Make sure you understand the order of the original material and know as much as you can about the author's approach to the topic.

DEVELOPING   Decide which topics you will develop most fully in your restatement.

ORGANIZING   Organize your material so that it follows the original as closely as possible.

DRAFTING   Write a working draft of your essay in complete sentences.

REVISING   Consulting the Tips for Revising in this chapter (pp. 240–247), revise your first draft—paying special attention to ways of writing coherent essays.

EDITING   Consulting the Tips for Editing in this chapter (pp. 248–272), edit your draft for grammar and correctness—paying special attention to verbs, nouns, pronouns, and modifiers.

Turn in your revised draft to your instructor.

Some Final Thoughts

When you have completed your own essay, answer these four questions in your journal:

1.   What was most difficult about this assignment?
2.   What was easiest?
3.   What did I learn about restating by completing this assignment?
4.   What did I learn about my own writing process from this assignment—how I prepared to write, how I wrote the first draft, how I revised, and how I edited?

Writing Coherent Essays

Checklist for Writing Coherent Essays

✓ Are **pronoun references** clear and functional?
✓ Are **transition words, phrases,** and **clauses** used effectively?
✓ Are **key words** repeated wisely?
✓ Is **parallelism** used appropriately?

When computer engineers set up a new system, they must first plan a logical configuration. A big part of their planning involves finding a way to connect all the components in the system so that they work together. For your readers to follow your thoughts in an essay, you need to make logical connections between your paragraphs and between the sentences within your paragraphs in much the same way a computer engineer connects the parts in a new computer system.

Coherence in writing means achieving a consistent relationship among parts. **Cohesive devices** show the logical relationships between the various parts of an essay as well as between sentences and paragraphs. Cohesive devices include pronoun references, transitional words and expressions, repetition, and parallelism.

Pronoun Reference

Many writers link sentences in a paragraph with **pronoun references**—that is, by using a pronoun to refer to a noun in a preceding sentence. Using pronouns that refer to nouns or other pronouns in previous sentences or paragraphs is a way of providing road signals to your readers. For example, the introductory paragraph in "The Financial Payoff of Higher Education for Women" uses pronouns to link ideas:

> Nationwide, women have a median income **that** is 52 percent of the median income of men. Some observers believe **this** high income gap is not a cause for concern. **They** point out **that** the major reason for **this** discrepancy is child-rearing activities. Women are much more unlikely to be steady participants in the work force and thus, not surprisingly, **they** have a much lower median income.

The pronouns in this passage serve two purposes: (1) They link the ideas in the paragraph, and (2) they prevent needless repetition of nouns. Notice that the noun each pronoun replaces is absolutely clear.

As Antwan Jones looked back over his essay restating the professional article, he decided that using pronouns would connect his first and second paragraphs better:

First Draft: Some people say this is not a critical problem because

women take many years out of their income-earning years

to raise children. Therefore, they say it is not surprising that women should earn less than men.

Women rearing children may explain part of the inequality, but child care does not explain why women who hold year-round, full-time jobs earn only $71 for every $100 earned by men in the same income group (the median). The following statistics (from the U.S. Bureau of the Census) are based only on year-round, full-time workers, so women who work seasonal jobs or earn no income are not included.

Revision: Some people say this is not a critical problem because women take many years out of their income-earning years to raise children. Therefore, they say it is not surprising that women should earn less than men.

~~Women rearing children~~ **This** may explain part of the inequality, but ~~child care~~ **it** does not explain why women who hold year-round, full-time jobs earn only $71 for every $100 earned by men in the same income group (the median). The following statistics (from the U.S. Bureau of the Census) are based only on year-round, full-time workers, so women who work seasonal jobs or earn no income are not included.

Not only do the pronouns make the second paragraph smoother, but each pronoun refers to a previous idea and links the ideas in the paragraphs together.

Transitions

Words, phrases, and clauses that guide readers through ideas are often called **transitions.** Specific transition words, phrases, and clauses establish time, space or distance, contrasts, examples, additions, order, and conclusions. Here are some examples of these transitions that will be useful in your writing:

Time: now, then, meanwhile, before, afterward
Space: nearby, farther, on the other side, above, below, down

Cause-effect:	because, due to, whereas, since, thus, therefore
Contrast:	although, despite this, however, on the other hand
Example:	in fact, for example, for instance
Addition:	also, besides, furthermore, in addition
Conclusion:	finally, lastly, since, thus, therefore

Transitions help your reader fit the pieces of your essay together in the way you intended because they establish logical relationships between your ideas. In the concluding paragraph of "The Financial Payoff of Higher Education for Women," the phrase *in sum* signals the conclusion will follow, and *however* lets the reader know that two ideas will be contrasted. The phrase *At all educational levels* stresses the main point of the paragraph and brings the paragraph to a conclusion:

> **In sum,** it appears that the economic payoff of higher education is slightly higher for women than it is for men except for those who graduated from professional school. **However,** despite the economic advantages of higher education for women, advanced degrees do very little to close the overall gender income gap. **At all educational levels,** women who work full-time still earn far less than men.

Antwan continued revising his restatement of an essay for coherence, he decided that adding more transitional words, phrases, and clauses would clarify and establish relationships for his audience in paragraph 5:

| **First Draft:** | The biggest gap between groups actually occurs among recipients of professional degrees. Women professionals have a median income of $45,588, or only $59 for every $100 earned by men with similar educations. The median income of men with professional degrees is $76,321. Part of the reason for this discrepancy is that women and men specialize in different areas. Women may also bump into a "glass ceiling," meaning that they will not be promoted above a certain level, due to discrimination. The problem of interrupting careers to raise children also affects women, even at this level. |
| **Revision:** | The biggest gap between groups actually occurs among recipients of professional degrees. **For example,** |

T I P S   F O R   R E V I S I N G

wW̶omen professionals have a median income of
$45,588, or only $59 for every $100 earned by men
with similar educations̶/, **whereas t**T̶he median income
of men with professional degrees is $76,321. **Although**
pP̶art of the reason for this discrepancy is that women
and men specialize in different areas̶/, **w**W̶omen may
also bump into a "glass ceiling," meaning that they will
not be promoted above a certain level, due to
discrimination. The problem of interrupting careers to
raise children also affects women, even at this level.

The transitions in Antwan's revised paragraph supply the logical information readers
need in order to understand how his ideas are related.

Repetition

The repetition of key words is another strategy that holds a paragraph together and
contributes to the coherence of an entire essay. This device not only lends coherence to your writing but also emphasizes important ideas. Look at this example from
paragraph 3 of the restating essay on "The Challenge of Fair Employment" (p. 218).
(The repeated words are in bold type.)

> Even more important, the **questions** that employers ask applicants
> must be chosen carefully. **Questions** may be asked to **determine** how well
> an employee will perform on the job but not to **determine** the national
> origin, race, creed, or color of the applicant. If the answer to a **question**
> asked during the employment interview does not relate to the **applicant's**
> **ability to do the job** for which he or she is applying, then the **question**
> could be considered discriminatory and **unlawful.** For example, while it
> is **unlawful to ask an applicant whether he or she** has ever been arrested, it is **lawful to ask an applicant whether he or she** has been convicted of a crime because this could reflect on **the applicant's ability to**
> **do the job.**

These boldfaced words bind the various ideas in this paragraph together and make it
a coherent statement. If repetition is used in moderation, as in this example, it emphasizes main ideas and stresses important details. But if it is overused, it loses its effect and becomes confusing.

As Antwan looked back over the first draft of his essay restating the article, he saw that he could show the relationship between his ideas in paragraph 3 and emphasize the inequities in women's and men's salaries by repeating key words:

First Draft: The annual median income of women who completed high school was $18,761. This amounted to only $71.60 for every $100 earned by similar males. Women with college degrees improved their income in relation to women with high school diplomas. They earned 56.9 percent more than the female high school graduates, so their median income was $29,436. Men who earn college degrees improve their wages in relation to male high school graduates by a similar percentage (56.2%), but since they earn more than women high school graduates, this means that their income is still more than $10,000 above the median income of women college graduates.

Revision: The annual **median income** of women who completed high school was $18,761. This amounted to only $71.60 for every $100 earned by ~~similar males~~ **the male high school graduates**. **Women with college degrees** improved their income in relation to women with high school diplomas/; ~~They~~ **women with college degrees** earned 56.9 percent more than the female high school graduates, so their **median income** was $29,436. Men who earn college degrees improve their ~~wages~~ **median income** in relation to **male high school graduates** by a similar percentage (56.2%), but since ~~they~~ **the male high school graduates** earn more than women **high school graduates**, this means that ~~their~~ the **median income** of male **college graduates** is still more than $10,000 above the median income of women **college graduates**.

These selective repetitions not only strengthen Antwan's paper, but they also make his references clear while emphasizing the fact that women's salaries even among the well educated do not compare to men's earnings.

Parallelism

Writers often put certain words and phrases in parallel form to show their relationship to one another. These words and phrases are **parallel** when they fall into the same grammatical pattern. The professional statement of a graph (see p. 221) offers an excellent example of how well parallelism works to make an essay coherent.

> The largest increases (more than double) came in the following fields: telephone operators (from 2.6% to 19.7%), aircraft mechanics (from 4.6% to 9.8%), firefighters (from 2.5% to 11.5%), accountants and auditors (from 1.6% to 7.4%), secretaries (from 2.0% to 7.6%), retail salespersons (from 2.4% to 9.5%), electricians (from 2.2% to 6.2%) and lawyers (from 1.3% to 3.2%).

Each item in this list consists of a noun phrase and a parenthetical statement in the same form (*from X% to Y%.*) This format not only lays out the information clearly but also establishes an interesting rhythm in the prose that builds up the readers' expectations for the next item in the series.

After reading the explanation of parallelism, Antwan realized this device would tighten up paragraph 4 of his restatement of the graph:

First Draft: This profile of women in medical school shows that there were in increases all categories over this six-year period. There were <u>more women who</u> applied to medical school, <u>an increase in</u> the number of women admitted, <u>increased</u> entrants, and <u>more women who</u> attended and graduated from medical school in 1989 than there were in 1995.

Revision: This profile of women in medical school shows that there were increases in all categories over this six-year period. There were **more women who** applied to medical school, ~~an increase in the number of women~~ **more women who** were admitted, ~~increased entrants~~ **more women who** entered, and **more women who** attended and graduated from medical school in 1989 than there were in 1995.

The changes Antwan made improve both the context and the style of his paragraph.

Exercise R6-1

In paragraphs 4 and 5 of "The Challenge of Fair Employment," underline and label the pronouns, transitions, repetitions, and parallel structures that connect and emphasize ideas.

Exercise R6-2

Read paragraph 2 of Antwan's first-draft essay restating a professional article (p. 226), and suggest some cohesive devices that might improve it.

Exercise R6-3

By adding pronouns, transitions, repetitions, and parallelism, rewrite the following sentences adapted from "The Challenge of Fair Employment" to make them coherent.

1. When any minority group is treated markedly worse than the majority group, it is said to be the target of adverse impact in the selection process.
2. Employing organizations must try to ensure that all people have equal access to jobs and to the fact that they are trained.
3. What if a personnel department established math skills, using words well, and the desire to learn as the requirements for a particular job?
4. Employers are actively seeking minority applicants. Recruiters are sent in to increase it.
5. More recent Supreme Court decisions have sometimes upheld charges of reverse discrimination. These say that the rights of majority groups must not be unnecessarily restrained in order to help minorities, and that they should not be hired or promoted simply on the basis of a quota system.

Exercise R6-4

Rewrite the following paragraph, using pronouns, transitions, repetition, and parallelism to make the sentences coherent. You might combine some of the sentences.

Many people have good reasons for earning a college degree. One good reason is a better life. Another good reason is to gain respect. Another reason for women we have just discovered is to earn more money, avoiding, perhaps, the "glass ceiling," and get equal with men.

 COLLABORATIVE WORK

After writing a draft of your own restating essay, exchange papers with a classmate, and do the following tasks:

A. Mark with a caret (∧) places where you feel cohesive devices are needed, either within a sentence or paragraph or between sentences and paragraphs.

B. In the margin beside each mark you made, suggest a method or specific words, phrases, or clauses that the writer might use to make the sentence or paragraph more coherent.

Then return the paper to its writer, and use the information in this section to revise your draft.

Verb Forms, Noun Forms, Pronoun Forms, and Modifiers

Checklist for Editing Verb Forms, Noun Forms, Pronoun Forms, and Modifiers

✓ Are **verbs** in their correct forms?
✓ Are **nouns** used correctly according to case?
✓ Are **pronouns** in their proper cases?
✓ Are **adjectives** located near the words they modify?
✓ Are **comparative adjective forms** used correctly?
✓ Are **adverbs** located near the words they modify?
✓ Are **comparative adverb forms** used correctly?

In English, verbs, nouns, pronouns, and modifiers (adjectives and adverbs) change form to serve different purposes in their sentences. Verbs change form to show *tense*, *voice*, and *mood*; nouns and pronouns show *case* (subjective, objective, and possessive) by changing form; and modifiers indicate *comparisons* through their forms. Even the slightest change in a letter or the addition of an apostrophe to a word sends a different message to the reader. The more you understand about these words and their various forms, the more precise your communication will be.

Verb Forms

In Chapter 2, you learned that the verb is probably the most important word in a sentence. Think about it. Without a verb, a sentence would show neither action nor existence. Since verbs are such integral, influential parts of sentences, learning as much as you can about them is essential to your writing. After you study their principal parts, tenses, voice, and mood, you will be able to increase the effectiveness of these important words in your sentences.

Principal Parts

Each verb in our language has four principal parts—*present*, *present participle*, *past*, and *past participle*. The six verb tenses are formed from these principal parts. Two of the main verbs used in paragraph 1 of Antwan's restating essay on page 226 are *earn* and *say*. The following chart explains their principal parts:

Present	Present Participle	Past	Past Participle
Base form: infinitive minus *to*.	Add *-ing*; cannot serve as a main verb; requires a helper or auxiliary verb.	Describes action that occurred in the past.	Describes action that occurred in the past; requires a helping verb.
earn	is earning	earned	(had) earned
say	is saying	said	(had) said

Notice that the past and past participles for the two verbs are formed differently. *Earn* is a **regular verb,** meaning that its past and past participle forms are made by adding *-d* or *-ed* to the base form. (For some verbs, the final consonant is doubled before the *-d* or *-ed* ending is added: *bat, batted; can, canned; slap, slapped.*)

Say is an **irregular verb,** meaning that its past and past participle forms are not formed by adding *-d* or *-ed*. Instead, the approximately 250 irregular verbs vary widely in their past and past participle forms, producing spellings that are best committed to memory. Or you can refer to the following list, which provides the principal parts of the most widely used irregular verbs. Since all verbs form the present participle the same way (by adding *-ing*), only the present, past, and past participle forms are furnished here.

Irregular Verbs

Present	Past	Past Participle
be	was, were	been
bear	bore	borne
beat	beat	beaten
become	became	become
begin	began	begun
bend	bent	bent
bet	bet, betted	bet, betted
bite	bit	bitten, bit
bleed	bled	bled
blow	blew	blown
break	broke	broken
bring	brought	brought
build	built	built
burst	burst	burst
buy	bought	bought
catch	caught	caught
choose	chose	chosen
come	came	come

Present	Past	Past Participle
cost	cost	cost
cut	cut	cut
deal	dealt	dealt
dig	dug	dug
dive	dived, dove	dived
do	did	done
draw	drew	drawn
dream	dreamed, dreamt	dreamed, dreamt
drink	drank	drunk
drive	drove	driven
eat	ate	eaten
fall	fell	fallen
feed	fed	fed
fight	fought	fought
find	found	found
fly	flew	flown
forget	forgot	forgotten
freeze	froze	frozen
get	got	got, gotten
give	gave	given
go	went	gone
grow	grew	grown
hang (suspend)	hung	hung
have	had	had
hear	heard	heard
hide	hid	hidden
hit	hit	hit
hold	held	held
hurt	hurt	hurt
keep	kept	kept
know	knew	known
lay (to place)	laid	laid
lead	led	led
leave	left	left
lend	lent	lent
lie (to recline)	lay	lain
lose	lost	lost
make	made	made
mean	meant	meant
meet	met	met
pay	paid	paid
prove	proved	proved, proven
put	put	put
quit	quit	quit

Present	Past	Past Participle
read	read	read
ride	rode	ridden
ring	rang	rung
rise	rose	risen
run	ran	run
say	said	said
see	saw	seen
seek	sought	sought
sell	sold	sold
send	sent	sent
set	set	set
sew	sewed	sewn, sewed
shake	shook	shaken
shine	shone, shined	shone, shined
shoot	shot	shot
show	showed	shown, showed
shrink	shrank	shrunk
shut	shut	shut
sing	sang	sung
sink	sank	sunk
sit	sat	sat
sleep	slept	slept
slide	slid	slid
speak	spoke	spoken
spend	spent	spent
spread	spread	spread
spring	sprang	sprung
stand	stood	stood
steal	stole	stolen
stick	stuck	stuck
sting	stung	stung
stink	stank	stunk
strike	struck	struck
string	strung	strung
strive	strove, strived	striven, strived
swear	swore	sworn
sweep	swept	swept
swim	swam	swum
swing	swung	swung
take	took	taken
teach	taught	taught
tear	tore	torn
tell	told	told
think	thought	thought

TIPS FOR EDITING

Present	Past	Past Participle
throw	threw	thrown
upset	upset	upset
wake	woke, waked	woken, waked
wear	wore	worn
wed	wedded, wed	wedded, wed
weep	wept	wept
win	won	won
wring	wrung	wrung
write	wrote	written

Exercise E6-1

Choose five regular and five irregular verbs from the professional restating essay for "The Challenge of Fair Employment" (pp. 217–218). Then make a chart of each verb's principal parts (see p. 248).

Exercise E6-2

Complete the following chart, supplying the principal parts for these five verbs found in the first draft of Antwan's restatement of an essay (pp. 226–227).

Present	Present Participle	Past	Past Participle
occurs	_____	_____	_____
_____	paying	_____	_____
specialize	_____	_____	_____
_____	_____	improved	_____
_____	meant	_____	_____

Exercise E6-3

Fill in each blank with the correct principal part of the verb in parentheses to complete the sentences in the following paragraph.

Usually I (1) _____ (*get*, present) junk mail or nothing at all when I reach inside our mailbox. But a few weeks ago, I (2) _____ (*receive*, past) a surprise—a letter requesting my presence at the county courthouse for jury duty. I had (3) _____ (*know*, past participle) only one other person who had served on a jury, my dad. He (4) _____ (*say*, past) it was rather uneventful. Of course, he was (5) _____ (*sit*, present participle)

on a jury for a simple burglary case. Anyway, I had been

(6) _____ (*teach*, past participle) in civics class that serving on a

jury was part of our civic duty. Plus, I (7) _____ (*think*, past) it

would be interesting. The day before I was to report to the courthouse, I was

(8) _____ (*talk*, present participle) to my boss at work

and reminded him that I had jury duty the next day. I had

(9) _____ (*tell*, past participle) him two weeks before, but I guess

he hadn't remembered. He (10) _____ (*fly*, past) into a rage,

saying that it was a bad time for me to be off, that I should have reminded him. But

there was nothing he could do because when you're called for jury duty, you have to

go.

TIPS FOR EDITING

Exercise E6-4

Write sentences using the following verbs.

1. determine (present participle)
2. drink (past participle)
3. exasperate (past)
4. acknowledge (present)
5. swim (past participle)

Time and Tense

Tense refers to the time of the verb's action or state of being. Verbs in the English language have six tenses—three *simple* or *basic* tenses and three *perfect* tenses.

Simple Tenses

The three simple or basic tenses are present, past, and future. **Present tense** expresses action that occurs now, in the immediate or present time. For most verbs, the present tense is formed from the base form, or present principal part, of the verb. For example, in the sentence "I jog every day," the verb *jog* is in the present tense, which is also its base form. Note that you may have to add an *-s* or *-es* to the verb, depending on the subject of the sentence: Antwan *jogs* every day. (For more information on agreement between subjects and verbs, see p. 196.)

Antwan uses several present tense verbs in the first draft of his restatement of an article. Look at the second sentence of his introduction shown on p. 254.

Present: Some people **say** this **is** not a critical problem because

women **take** many years out of their income-earning years

to raise children.

This sentence refers to some immediate responses to the problem raised in the essay.

The **past tense,** indicating action that has already been completed, is also one of the verb's principal parts:

Past: Antwan **raked** the lawn. Then he **showered** and **took** a nap.

The verbs *raked* and *showered* are regular verbs that form the past tense by adding *-d* or *-ed*, while *took* is the past tense of the irregular verb *take*.

The **future tense** refers to action that has not yet been completed. To form the future tense, simply add *will* to the base form of the verb:

Future: Antwan **will jog** today.

Antwan **will rake** the lawn.

The future tense is also used to indicate conditions that occur and persist in time:

Future: After a while, the new mattress **will become** softer.

Perfect Tenses

The word *perfect* in describing tenses refers to the time when the action will be completed. Each of the three perfect tenses uses a form of the verb *to have* plus a past participle to indicate when the action or condition was or will be "perfected."

The **present perfect tense** refers to actions or conditions that began in the past and continue in the present or will be completed in the present. Add *have* or *has* to the past participle to form the present perfect tense:

Present Perfect: Antwan and his friends **have gone** out the last three nights in a row.

Present Perfect: Antwan **has decided** to take five classes next semester.

Past perfect tense verbs are used to indicate that one past action or condition happened before another action or condition. Simply add *had* to the past participle to form the past perfect tense:

Past Perfect: By summer's end, Antwan **had saved** over $2,000.

Past Perfect: Antwan **had completed** his paper when the teacher called time.

The **future perfect tense** expresses an action or condition that will begin and end at some time in the future. To form the future perfect tense, add *will have* to the past participle:

Future Perfect:	Antwan **will have made** over $100 in tips by the day's end.
Future Perfect:	Next month Antwan's aunt and uncle **will have been** married for ten years.

Exercise E6-5

Choose five different verbs from the professional restating essay of "The Challenge of Fair Employment" (pp. 217–218), and write each verb's simple and perfect tense forms.

Exercise E6-6

Choose three sentences from the first draft of Antwan's restatement of an essay (pp. 226–227), and rewrite each sentence five times, supplying a different verb tense for each sentence.

> **Example:** The annual median income of women who completed high school **was** $18,761. (past)
>
> The annual median income of women who completed high school **is** $18,761. (present)
>
> The annual median income of women who completed high school **will be** $18,761. (future)
>
> The annual median income of women who completed high school **has been** $18,761. (present perfect)
>
> The annual median income of women who completed high school **had been** $18,761. (past perfect)
>
> The annual median income of women who completed high school **will have been** $18,761. (future perfect)

Exercise E6-7

Fill in each blank with the correct tense of the verb indicated in parentheses.

I (1) _____ (*collect*, present perfect) many things in my lifetime. When I (2) _____ (*be*, past) in elementary school, I (3) _____ (*like*, past) marbles. I (4) _____ (*keep*, past) them in big fruit jars. I (5) _____ (*think*, present) they are stored away in the basement. My mother probably (6) _____ (*sell*, future) them in a garage sale someday, which (7) _____ (*be*, present) fine with me.

After I started junior high school, I (8) _____ (*become*, past) interested in stamps. My seventh grade social studies teacher (9) _____ (*bring*, past perfect) his collection to school one day. That (10) _____ (*kindle*, past) my interest, I'm sure. For a while, I (11) _____ (*spend*, past) every extra dime on stamps and began trading with my friends and going to stamp shows in our town. If I (12) _____ (*keep*, past perfect) buying and trading stamps, I'm sure I would have filled several books with my treasures.

Now I collect matchbooks. One matchbook that I saved on a trip to Disney World (13) _____ (*grow*, present perfect) into a sizable collection of over 500 pieces. By next year the number (14) _____ (*rise*, future perfect) to over 1000, I'm sure. People (15) _____ (*know*, present) about my hobby and bring me matchbooks from all over the world.

Exercise E6-8

Write a sentence for each of the following verb forms.

1. had requested
2. will demand
3. balanced
4. frustrate
5. has delivered

Emphatic Form

The emphatic is a special verb form that is used only in the present and past tenses. To form the **present emphatic,** add the verb *do* or *does* to the present stem. For **past emphatic,** add *did* to the past tense. The emphatic is commonly used in three instances:

1. *For emphasis.*

   Present Emphatic: Antwan **does like** his job.

   Past Emphatic: Antwan **did send** his payment in on time.

2. *For a negative sentence.*

Present Emphatic: We **do** not **plan** on sending troops to Honduras.

Past Emphatic: The governor **did** not **pardon** the inmate.

3. *For a question.*

Present Emphatic: **Do** you **remember** what he said?

Past Emphatic: **Did** Richard Nixon **precede** Lyndon Johnson as president?

Progressive Form

The **progressive form** indicates the continuity of an action or condition. Each of the six tenses has a progressive form that indicates an action or condition persisting over time. The progressive forms are made by adding the appropriate helping verb to the present participle (the *-ing* form), as the following examples demonstrate:

1. *Present progressive* expresses continuing action or condition.

Present: Antwan **is collecting** baseball cards as a hobby.

Present: They **are deliberating** for a long time.

2. *Past progressive* indicates continuous actions or conditions that began and ended sometime in the past.

Past: We **were talking** outside the door when we heard the alarm.

Past: Alex **was being** obnoxious because his former girlfriend showed up.

3. *Future progressive* explains action that will be happening at a future time.

Future: Chad **will be joining** the air force when he completes his degree.

Future: Antwan **will be studying** for his finals.

4. *Present perfect progressive* expresses past action continuing into the present.

Present Perfect: For years my mother **has been telling** my dad to quit smoking.

Present Perfect: The Supreme Court justices **have been hearing** the case for three days.

5. *Past perfect progressive* indicates past action that continues from an unspecified time to a specific time.

Past Perfect:	Antwan **had been expecting** good news when he got the mail.
Past Perfect:	Claire **had been sleeping** soundly when her alarm rang.

6. *Future perfect progressive* expresses some future action that will be completed before another action will be finished.

Future Perfect:	By the time the doors open, **I will have been standing** here for three hours.
Future Perfect:	By the time I graduate, **I will have been going** to college for four years.

Exercise E6-9

Choose five verbs from "The Challenge of Fair Employment" (pp. 213–217), and write the emphatic and progressive forms for each of the verbs.

Exercise E6-10

Write sentences using the emphatic and progressive forms of the verbs for the examples you chose in Exercise E6-6 from Antwan's restatement on pp. 226–227.

Example:	Women with college degrees **did improve** their income in relation to women with high school diplomas. (past)
	Women with college degrees **do improve** their income in relation to women with high school diplomas. (present)
	Women with college degrees **will be improving** their income in relation to women with high school diplomas. (future)
	Women with college degrees **have been improving** their income in relation to women with high school diplomas. (present perfect)
	Women with college degrees **had been improving** their income in relation to women with high school diplomas. (past perfect)
	Women with college degrees **will have been improving** their income in relation to women with high school diplomas. (future perfect)

TIPS FOR EDITING

Exercise E6-11

Fill in each blank with the correct verb form indicated in parentheses.

I (1) _____ (*give*, present progressive) my studies as much time as I can find. But my parents (2) _____ (*believe*, present emphatic—negative) me. I admit that during the first part of the semester I was slacking off. But I (3) _____ (*work*, past progressive) not one but two part-time jobs. They forget that. At least I (4) _____ (*try*, past emphatic) to do something constructive with my time. However, I (5) _____ (*spend*, past progressive) too much time making money and not enough time keeping up with my course work.

I (6) _____ (*waste*, present emphatic) time sometimes. I admit that. But I like to study during the day and save my nights for myself. So while Mom and Dad (7) _____ (*work*, present progressive), I (8) _____ (*keep*, present progressive) my nose to the grindstone. They will see the results of my hard work when I receive my final grades in about six weeks. Then Mom and Dad (9) _____ (*eat*, future progressive) their words. They also (10) _____ (*pay*, future progressive) me some money because they bet me $50 that I wouldn't make a B average.

Exercise E6-12

Write sentences using the following verb forms.

1. recognize (present emphatic)
2. predict (past emphatic)
3. save (present progressive)
4. calculate (past progressive)
5. publicize (future progressive)

Voice

Besides possessing principal parts and expressing time, verbs also have a characteristic called **voice.** When the subject performs the action of the verb (I *see* her), the verb is in the **active voice.** Look at these sentences from the first draft of Antwan's first restating essay:

Active Voice: All over the United States, women in the middle of the income range **earn** only $52 for every $100 earned by men in the same range.

Some people **say** this is not a critical problem because women take many years out of their income-earning years to raise children.

In the first example, the subject *women* is the performer of the action—women are the ones who *earn*. In the second example, *people*, the sentence's subject, is the doer, actively carrying out the action of the verb *say*.

On some occasions the subject will receive the action of the verb (She *was seen* by me). When this occurs, the verb is in the **passive voice:**

Passive Voice: Antwan's girlfriend **is given** a great deal of attention by his family.

Antwan **was elected** chairperson by the committee.

In the first example, the subject, *girlfriend*, receives the action of the verb—the girlfriend *is given* attention. In the second example, the subject, *Antwan*, passively receives the action of the committee.

Passive verbs always consist of a form of *be* (*is, was*) plus a past participle form of a verb (*given, elected*). The tense of the *be* verb will determine the tense of the passive verb.

Mood

Verbs can state an action or a condition in different forms of expression we call **moods.** In the English language, writers can choose from three moods to help relate their feelings and attitudes about their subjects: indicative, imperative, and subjunctive.

The **indicative mood** is the most widely used mood because it allows writers to state facts and pose questions:

Indicative: Antwan **pays** his own tuition each semester.

Does Antwan **plan** to apply for a scholarship?

The **imperative mood** lets the writer make requests and give orders, commands, and directions:

Imperative: **Close** the door, please.

Complete the top half of the application and **leave** the bottom part blank.

Go past three stop signs and **take** the first right.

Note that the subject for each of the imperative examples is the understood *you:*

(*You*) **close** the door, please.

(*You*) **complete** the top half of the application and (*you*) **leave** the bottom part blank.

(*You*) **go** past three stop signs and (*you*) **take** the first right.

The understood *you* may refer to either a single individual or to a group of people.

The **subjunctive mood** is not used very often in everyday English. However, knowing how to use this mood correctly is important in writing. Writers use the subjunctive to express conditions and ideas contrary to fact. Look for clauses that begin with *if*, *as if*, or *as though.*

Subjunctive: *If* Antwan **were** more serious about his job, he might get more hours at work.

Antwan looks *as if* he **were** upset.

I rattled on and on *as though* I **were** racing a clock.

In the first example, the subjunctive mood of the verb tells us that Antwan is not receiving more hours of work time because his attitude has not changed. In the second and third examples, the subjunctive forms of the verbs express present, ongoing conditions. Note that the subjunctive in each of these examples requires the verb *were*.

The subjunctive is also used to express wishes, demands, requests, or propositions:

Subjunctive: I wish *that* I **were** available.

Antwan's employer requires *that* every employee **buy** a uniform.

They request *that* Antwan **be** on time.

The group agrees *that* the motion **be** passed.

The helping verbs *could*, *should*, and *would* can also be used to express the subjunctive mood:

Subjunctive: *If* Antwan **could type** faster, he would save time working on his papers.

Antwan **should have rested** longer, but he got up and cleaned his room.

I would have bought another pair of shoes *if* I **had known** they **were** so comfortable.

Just remember always to use *have* or the contraction *-'ve* rather than *of* when using helping verbs in subjunctive constructions. *Could of, should of,* and *would of* are non-standard spellings of *could've* (or *could have*), *should've* (or *should have*), and *would've* (or *would have*).

Exercise E6-13

Underline the main verb(s) in each of these sentences from the restating essay for "The Challenge of Fair Employment," and label them as either active or passive.

1. The Civil Rights Act of 1964 and the rules set by the EEOC declare it illegal to discriminate against applicants.
2. The EEOC has the power to sue any organization with over 15 employees if discrimination in hiring practices is suspected.
3. If a company is found to hire a higher percentage from one group of applicants than another, the company can be legally challenged by the EEOC.
4. Even more important, the questions that employers ask applicants must be chosen carefully.
5. The U. S. Supreme Court found that a company had a right to reject a white applicant in order to satisfy its racial quota, but more recently, the Supreme Court has upheld findings of reverse discrimination and has ordered the job or place to go to the white applicant, stating that "only fully qualified minority employees should be hired or promoted."

Exercise E6-14

Label the mood of each main verb in the following paragraph.

(1) If people were nicer to each other, we would have far fewer problems. (2) I think that most people are so wrapped up in their own lives that they become immune to other people's feelings. (3) Think about it. (4) When was the last time you performed an unprovoked act of kindness for someone? (5) Honestly, I try to do at least one good deed a day. (6) All it takes is a little effort. (7) Try it. (8) You might be surprised at the results.

Exercise E6-15

Complete each sentence by adding the proper form and mood of the verb indicated in parentheses.

1. If Tasha knew what she wanted to do with her life, she

   _____ (helping verb + *to be*, subjunctive)

   more focused and responsible.

2. They _____ (*to decide*, indicative, present

perfect tense) to sell their house and rent an apartment.

3. First, _____ (*to mix*, imperative) the butter

and eggs together before adding the powdered sugar.

4. When J. D. wants something, he _____ (*to

go*, indicative, present tense) after it.

5. The city asks that every citizen, _____ (*to be

aware*, subjunctive) of the new leash law.

Exercise E6-16

Write two sentences for each of the following verbs, using the active voice in one and the passive voice in the other.

Example: to play

The DJ played records for three hours without stopping. (active)

The records were played for three hours without stopping. (passive)

1. to choose
2. to throw
3. to avoid
4. to pack
5. to dictate

Nouns and Pronouns

Whereas verbs have tenses and moods, nouns and pronouns have **cases,** forms that indicate the role of a noun or pronoun in its sentence. The subjective, objective, and possessive cases of nouns are relatively easy to distinguish. Pronouns, however, pose challenges that require closer attention.

Noun Forms

A noun in the **subjective case** can serve as a subject, a predicate noun, or an appositive; a noun in the **objective case** can serve as a direct object, an indirect object, an object of a preposition, or an object complement. Nouns in the subjective and objective cases show no difference in form. The difference lies in how these nouns function in their sentences. Look at the following sentences from Antwan's first draft restatement of an essay, which illustrate the subjective and objective cases of nouns:

$$\overset{\text{subj}}{}\qquad\overset{\text{obj}}{}$$

The annual median **income** of **women** who completed

$$\overset{\text{obj}}{}$$

high school was $18,761.

$$\overset{\text{subj}}{}\qquad\overset{\text{obj}}{}\qquad\overset{\text{obj}}{}$$

Women with college **degrees** improved their **income** in

$$\overset{\text{obj}}{}\qquad\overset{\text{obj}}{}$$

relation to **women** with high school **diplomas**.

To form the **possessive case,** nouns depend on an apostrophe to show ownership. Most nouns add an *-s* (*Antwan's, women's*), and some nouns ending in *-s* (particularly plural nouns) simply add an apostrophe (*hobbies', materials'*). (For more on apostrophes, see pp. 323–326).

Possessive: **Antwan's** girlfriend is my best friend.

Many people wish they had **Antwan's** summer job.

Pronoun Forms

Like nouns, pronouns have subjective, objective, and possessive cases. Unlike nouns, however, pronouns can change form in each of their three cases. The *personal* and *interrogative* pronouns usually cause the most confusion. Use the following charts for handy reference.

Personal Pronouns

	Subjective	Objective	Possessive
Singular	I, you, he, she, it	me, you, him, her, it	my, mine, your, yours, his, her, hers, its
Plural	we, you, they	us, you, them	our, ours, your, yours, their, theirs

Interrogative Pronouns (singular or plural)

Subjective	Objective	Possessive
who, whoever	whom, whomever	whose

Some pronouns, like *which*, *this*, *that*, *these*, and *those*, do not change form at all when they change case. The reflexive pronouns (*myself*, *yourself*, *themselves*) have only one form and are used in only the objective case. Still other pronouns form the possessive like most nouns, relying on an *-s*: *someone's*, *everybody's*, *no one's*.

Personal Pronouns

Using pronouns in different cases can be confusing. The following rules and examples will help you use personal pronouns correctly:

1. *Use the subjective case when a pronoun serves as a subject, a subject complement, or an appositive, even when the pronoun is part of a compound element.*

    Subject: My brother and **she** graduated from Auburn High School last year.

    Antwan is more responsible than **I**. (Note that *I* is the subject of the dependent clause whose verb *am* is understood—*than I am.*)

    Subject Complement: This is **she**.
    The winners are Racquel, Veronica, and **he**.

    Appositive: The two people standing in the corner, Robert and **she**, are both veterinarians.

    When a pronoun is used with a noun to form an appositive, the pronoun should be in the same case as the noun or pronoun it refers to:

    Appositive: The manager told us—Antwan and **me**—to clean the oven.

    We employees would like a raise.

2. *Use the objective case when the pronoun is used as a direct object, an indirect object, or an object of a preposition.*

    Direct Object: We sent **her** to the convention as our representative.

    Indirect Object: The school sent **him** a letter of congratulations after he made the dean's list.

    Object of a Preposition: Antwan gave his place in line to **her**.

3. *Use the possessive case to show ownership.*

    Possessive: **His** Saturn is the same color as **her** Jeep.

    His watching television until 3 a.m. gets on our nerves.

TIPS FOR EDITING

Interrogative and Relative Pronouns

The pronouns *who, whom, whoever,* and *whomever* pose special problems, not only because they can serve as both relative and interrogative pronouns but also because they change form to indicate case. *Who* and *whoever* are used in the subjective case as subjects and subject complements, while *whom* and *whomever* are used in the objective case as direct objects and objects of prepositions:

Subject:	**Who** is calling on line 1?
	Whoever would think of putting those shoes with that dress?
Subject Complement:	The caller was **who?**
Direct Object:	**Whom** did they choose as their convention delegate?
Object of a Preposition:	**Whom** did they give the tickets to?

In the last two examples, both of which require *whom,* the question can be reworded as a statement to make choosing the correct case easier:

> They did choose **whom** as our convention delegate.
>
> They did give the tickets to **whom.**

Often, determining the correct case is a confusing task because *who/whom* and *whoever/whomever* are used in a variety of ways within their own clauses. Basically, you must isolate the dependent clause and determine whether it requires a subjective or objective case pronoun:

Subjective:	Antwan wonders [**who** sent him the anonymous letter].
	[**Who** plans to drop out of the race] is anyone's guess.
	The winner will be [**whoever** gets the most correct answers within the allotted time].
	[**Whoever** left the door open] should close it.
Objective:	We will give the tickets to [**whomever** you decide].
	The reporter is trying to find out [**whom** the police charged].
	[**Whomever** you voted for] is bound to win.

Notice that in the objective case examples, the subjects and objects are inverted. To determine the correct case, rearrange the clause in natural order with the subject and verb coming first (you decide *whomever*; the police charged *whom*; you voted for *whomever*).

Sometimes parenthetical expressions such as *I think, people say, you know,* or *experts agree* appear within a dependent clause. When trying to determine the pronoun's case, omit these unnecessary words, which do not affect the structure of the rest of the sentence:

subj

Selena was a talented singer, **who,** ~~I think,~~ **would**

have reached the pinnacle of success if she had lived.

obj   **subj**

Selena is a singer **whom,** ~~I feel,~~ **everyone should**

respect because she accomplished so much in such a

short time.

Writers have few problems with the correct usage of the pronoun *whose,* which shows possession. Just remember that *whose* differs from the contraction *who's,* which stands for *who is:*

Antwan doesn't know **whose** keys are in backseat of his car.

Every day we wonder **who's** going to show up late for class.

Exercise E6-17

List each noun in paragraph 7 of "The Challenge of Fair Employment" (pp. 214–215), and identify its case.

Exercise E6-18

List each pronoun in paragraphs 5 through 7 of the revised draft of Antwan's first restating essay (p. 236), and identify its case.

Exercise E6-19

Fill in each blank in the following sentences with the appropriate noun or pronoun named in parentheses.

With four (1) _____ (noun, objective) living under one

roof, you can image that the phone rings all the time. Seriously,

(2) _____ (pronoun, possessive) phones are always in use.

By the way, there are six of (3) _____ (pronoun, objective)

scattered throughout the (4) _____ (noun, objective). The

phone in (5) _____ (proper noun, possessive) bedroom is

probably the busiest because (6) _____ (pronoun, subjective)

is the person (7) _____ (pronoun, subjective) gets the most

calls. Sometimes my other roommates and (8) _____ (pronoun,

subjective) have to ask (9) _____ (pronoun, objective) for

phone time for ourselves. (10) _____ (noun, subjective)

usually don't call after midnight because we have to get some sleep. Plus,

(11) _____ (pronoun, possessive) phones need some rest, too.

Exercise E6-20

Write two sentences for each of the following pronouns.

1. who
2. whom
3. whose
4. whoever
5. whomever

Modifiers

To *modify* means to change something. In English, **modifiers** change words by making them more specific, giving additional details that enlarge and enhance a word's meaning. The most common modifiers are adjectives and adverbs. These modifiers can appear as single words or as groups of words in both *positive* and *comparative* forms.

Adjective and Adverb Comparative Forms

Adjectives describe nouns and pronouns, while adverbs describe verbs, adjectives, and other adverbs. Sometimes adjectives and adverbs are used to indicate comparisons. Both of these modifiers have three forms:

Positive — the basic form of the adjective or adverb when it is not being used to compare anything

Comparative — the form used to compare two things

Superlative — the form used to compare three or more things

Adjectives and adverbs form the comparative and superlative degrees in one of three ways. The most common method is to add *-er* for the comparative and *-est* for the superlative. Most one- and two-syllable words use these standard endings, shown in the following chart.

Positive	Comparative	Superlative
white (adj)	whiter	whitest
quick (adv)	quicker	quickest
dirty (adj)	dirtier	dirtiest
happy (adj)	happier	happiest

The second way of forming the comparative is to add *more* or *most* before the adjective or adverb. Writers should use *more* and *most* with all three-syllable modifiers, as the following sentence shows:

Superlative: Of the new employees, Antwan is the **most responsible.**

More and *most* are also used when *-er* and *-est* would sound strange with one- and two-syllable words.

Positive	Comparative	Superlative
just (adj)	more just	most just
often (adv)	more often	most often
daring (adj)	more daring	most daring
spacious (adj)	more spacious	most spacious
neatly (adv)	more neatly	most neatly
beautiful (adj)	more beautiful	most beautiful
dependable (adj)	more dependable	most dependable
relentlessly (adv)	more relentlessly	most relentlessly

You can also use *less* and *least*, the opposite of *more* and *most*, to form comparisons. Simply place *less* or *least* before the positive adjective or adverb form.

Positive	Comparative	Superlative
happy (adj)	less happy	least happy
often (adv)	less often	least often
dependable (adj)	less dependable	least dependable

Some adjectives and adverbs do not form the comparative and superlative in either of the first two ways. We call these modifiers *irregular* because they change their spellings to form their comparatives. Here is a list of the most common modifiers and their irregular forms.

Irregular Modifiers

Positive	Comparative	Superlative
bad (adj)	worse	worst
badly (adv)	worse	worst
good (adj)	better	best
ill (adj)	worse	worst
little (adv)	less	least
many (adj)	more	most
much (adj or adv)	more	most
well (adv)	better	best

Avoid double comparisons with any modifiers. Never use the *-er* and *-est* endings with *more* and *most*.

Incorrect:	Antwan's friend Dave is **more stronger** than he is.
Correct:	Antwan's friend Dave is **stronger** than he is.
Incorrect:	I feel **more worse** today than I did yesterday.
Correct:	I feel **worse** today than I did yesterday.

Finally, note that some adjectives and adverbs cannot be logically compared. We call these modifiers **absolute.** For example, if something is *final*, it cannot be *more final*. Either it's final or it's not. Other absolute modifiers include the following:

Absolute Modifiers

complete/completely	horizontal	opposite
dead	identical	round
empty	impossible/impossibly	square
endless/endlessly	invisible/invisibly	unanimous/unanimously
equal/equally	parallel	unique/uniquely
eternal/eternally	perfect/perfectly	universal/universally
fatal/fatally	pregnant	vertical
favorite		

All of these words have only a positive form.

Exercise E6-21

Identify the form of the italicized adjectives and adverbs in the following sentences from the professional restatement of "The Challenge of Fair Employment." Then supply each word's other forms.

1. In recent years, because of the requirements of the Equal Employment Opportunity Commission (EEOC), companies have had to be sure that their

hiring practices guarantee that all applicants are considered *equally* and *fairly* for jobs no matter what their race, religion, or sex or what country they were born in.

2. If a company is found to hire a *higher* percentage from one group of applicants than another, the company can be legally challenged by the EEOC.

3. Even more important, the question that employers ask applicants must be chosen *carefully*.

4. This is not a *perfect* solution, however, because researchers have discovered that the blanks are *often* interpreted by potential employers as an admission of guilt or as an attempt to hide information.

5. This is a *complex* and controversial problem, and many lawsuits have resulted that were taken all the way to the Supreme Court.

Exercise E6-22

Label the form of each of the adjectives and adverbs italicized in the following sentences that appear in the first draft of Antwan's first restatement. Then supply the other forms for each word.

1. Some people say this is not a *critical* problem because women take many years out of their income-earning years to raise children.

2. For those full-time workers with master's degrees, there is still a *large* difference between male and female workers.

3. The *biggest* gap between groups actually occurs among recipients of professional degrees.

4. Part of the reason for this discrepancy is that women and men specialize in *different* areas.

5. Women with doctorates are *better* off compared to men than women with other degrees.

Exercise E6-23

Complete the following sentences by supplying the correct form of the adjective or adverb indicated in parentheses.

When it comes to preparing for an exam, I'm not sure if one method is

(1) _____ (*good*, comparative) than another. What works for

one person may not work for someone else. But people have many study options

to choose from. One of the (2) _____ (*popular*, superlative)

things to do is to review notes that you took in class. This often proves

(3) _____ (*productive*, superlative) when you have little

time and want to concentrate on the important points. Usually, the

(4) _____ (*good*, superlative) teachers cover the

(5) _____ (*critical*, superlative) information during their

lectures. The (6) _____ (*bad*, superlative) teacher I ever had

lectured for hours on end, but when it came test time, the questions seemed to come

out of left field. It was (7) _____ (*frustrating*, superlative), to

say the least. A (8) _____ (*expensive*, comparative)

alternative would be to hire a tutor. This might work for some of the

(9) _____ (*technical*, comparative) subjects, such as math and

chemistry. But you had better have money in your pocket because tutors don't

come (10) _____ (*cheap*, positive).

Exercise E6-24

Write sentences using the following modifiers.

1. most agreeable
2. more thoroughly
3. farther
4. heavily
5. least

 ## COLLABORATIVE WORK

After you revise your restating essay, exchange papers with a classmate, and do the
following tasks:

A. Circle any verbs that are not in their correct form or tense.

B. Circle any nouns or pronouns that are not in the correct case.

C. Underline any adjective or adverb forms that are incorrect.

Then return the paper to its author, and use the information in this section to edit
your draft.

CHAPTER SEVEN

Analyzing
Reading and Writing for a Reason

In order to understand complex issues and situations and events, we need to analyze them from multiple perspectives; every position or every viewpoint ought to have reasons to support it; and the quality of the conclusion is dependent on the quality of the reasoning that went before it.

—JOHN CHAFFEE

Analyzing is what we do to make sense of ideas, theories, feelings, behavior, even of life itself. We analyze all the time; it's what makes us human. Analyzing enables us to have a deeper and richer understanding of what is happening to us and around us in the world. As humans, we don't simply let our feelings or first impressions guide our actions; rather we consider and evaluate many factors so that we can reach conclusions that are logical and useful.

Every time you are asked what you think about something—a political debate, a book you have read, a movie you have seen, the performance of your favorite baseball or basketball team—you engage in the process of analysis. You consider the topic from different perspectives; you evaluate the information you have; and you consider the quality of each alternative solution *before* you decide how you feel or what you think. In much the same way, when you write an analyzing essay, your purpose is to give your readers a thorough understanding of the topic you are writing about. You will present information that provides your audience with a far more complete picture than they had before. Analyzing involves more than giving an opinion, more than persuading your readers, more than offering a solution to a problem, though you often do all of these things when you analyze. What your analysis gives your reader (and you) is a deeper understanding of the topic.

In an essay titled "A Woman's Work," published in *Harper's* magazine in 1993, Louise Erdrich, who had just given birth to a baby girl, wondered why so little was written about being a mother of a new infant and why, although writing is her occupation, she had no time to write. After thinking carefully about the situation, she wrote the following analysis:

One reason there is not a great deal written about what it is like to be the mother of a new infant is that there is rarely a moment to think of anything else besides the infant's needs. Endless time with a small baby is spent asking, *What do you want?* . . . I do what she "tells" me to do—feed, burp, change, amuse, distract, hold, look at, help to sleep, reassure—without consciously choosing to do it. I take her instructions without translating her meaning into words but simply bypassing straight to action. Until I've satisfied her need, my brain is a white blur. I lose track of what I've been doing, where I've been, who I am.

This process of analysis helped Louise Erdrich understand why she could not write about the birth of her new baby—or do much of anything else, for that matter.

LEARNING FROM PUBLISHED WRITERS

In the essay that follows, the writer has considered her topic carefully and thoughtfully so that her readers can have a fuller understanding of the topic than they had before. "On Being a Cripple" analyzes what it is like to be handicapped. It was written by Nancy Mairs, a teacher of writing and English who has had several books of short fiction and essays published. The essay first appeared in her collection *Plaintext*, published in 1992.

Before You Read

Focusing Your Attention

Before you read this analysis, take a few moments to respond to the following questions in your journal:

1. Think of the last time you were particularly successful at something; analyze the actions you took and the procedures you followed in order to achieve that success.

2. In the essay you are about to read, Nancy Mairs analyzes the way that her handicap affects every aspect of her life. What has the greatest impact on your life: your family, your friends, or your job? Analyze the effect one of these groups has on your life.

Expanding Your Vocabulary

Here are some words and their meanings that are important to your understanding of the essay. You might want to review them before you begin to read.

"hot with **chagrin** [a feeling of embarrassment and/or annoyance]" (paragraph 1)

"the matter of **semantics** [the way a word is used]" (paragraph 2) "**wince** [shrink in pain] at the word" (paragraph 2)

"I **swagger** [walk with excessive self-confidence]" (paragraph 2)

"any **incapacity** [inability to do something]" (paragraph 3)

"the recently coined **euphemism** [a mild word or phrase substituted for a more offensive one]" (paragraph 3)

"the **dictates** [rules] of language" (paragraph 3)

"George Orwell's thesis" (paragraph 4) [Orwell was a British writer (1903–1950) who often wrote about language and the way it should be used]

"the **degeneration** [deterioration, destruction] of the language" (paragraph 4)

"this **calamitous** [disastrous] disease" (paragraph 4)

"I consulted a **neurologist** [a doctor who specializes in the nervous system]" (paragraph 6)

"**disseminated** [distributed] in space and time" (paragraph 6)

"a **chronic** [ongoing] **degenerative** [causing deterioration] disease . . . in which the **myelin** [fatty material around nerve fibers] that **sheathes** [surrounds, protects] the nerves is somehow eaten away" (paragraph 7)

"My world has . . . been **circumscribed** [restricted] by my losses" (paragraph 8)

"I begin to sound like **Pollyanna** [a children's literature character who is always happy, cheerful, and smiling]" (paragraph 9)

"I spend a lot of time *in extremis* [Latin term meaning in distress or serious circumstances]" (paragraph 9)

"The **offspring** [child] of a **puritanical tradition** [belief in hard work and rigid morality] of exceptional **venerability** [age and distinction]" (paragraph 9)

"my **predilections** [tendencies toward] were already . . . **sedentary** [inactive], and bookish" (paragraph 10)

"we imagine our **counterparts** [those who are like us] in **Leningrad** [now St. Petersburg, a major city in Russia]" (paragraph 11)

"its **bleak component** [unpleasant element]" (paragraph 12)

"**ingress and egress**" [entrance and exit] (paragraph 12)

"I am **immobilized** [made unable to move] by **acute** [sharp] attacks of depression, which may or may not be **physiologically** [physically] related to MS but are certainly its logical **concomitant** [side effect]." (paragraph 12)

"My students, with one **anonymous** [no name given] exception . . . have been **unperturbed** [not disturbed] by my disability" (paragraph 14) "**tacking down the aisle** . . . **like a Cape Cod dinghy in a stiff breeze** [moving from side to side as a sailboat moves against the wind]" (paragraph 15)

"the **corroboration** [confirmation of the truth]" (paragraph 17)

"**deviates** [behaves differently] from the norm" (paragraph 18)

"no **recriminations** [accusations]" (paragraph 18)

"I make **vichyssoise** [French potato soup]" (paragraph 19)

"violent **self-loathing** [hatred of oneself]" (paragraph 20)

"a **charismatic** [one who claims special powers]" (paragraph 20)

"moral **disapprobation** [disapproval]" (paragraph 20)

"**imperfection** . . . still **defies** [goes against] the ideal" (paragraph 20)

"I carried this sense of **self-alienation** [uncomfortable with oneself] with me into adulthood, where it **regenerated** [came back to life] in response to the **depredations** [destruction] of MS" (paragraph 21)

"I feel **ludicrous** [ridiculous], even **loathsome** [repulsive to look at]." (paragraph 21)

"The burning **egocentricity** [concern only for oneself] of adolescence" (paragraph 22)

"outlined by **Elizabeth Kübler-Ross** [a death researcher who maintains that grieving for a loved one occurs in five distinct stages]" (paragraph 24)

"she is **incontinent** [unable to control her bladder]" (paragraph 25)

"I thought about having MS almost **incessantly** [continually]" (paragraph 26)

"some connection between **largesse** [generosity in spirit or gift giving] and laughter" (paragraph 27)

"an **exacerbation** [worsening]" (paragraph 28)

"life is something other than a **quantitative phenomenon** [measurable event]" (paragraph 30)

"an **autoimmune reaction** [a response by the nervous system against one of its own parts]" (paragraph 30)

"no matter how **bizarre** [strange]" (paragraph 30)

"Doctors are . . . the new **shamans** [tribal healers]" (paragraph 31)

"disease in its **intransigence** [refusal to cooperate]" (paragraph 31)

"I **incarnate** [represent] the limitation of their powers." (paragraph 31)

"I do not **deprecate** [devalue, downplay] such knowledge" (paragraph 32)

Nancy Mairs

On Being a Cripple*

The other day I was thinking of writing an essay on being a cripple. I was thinking hard in one of the stalls of the women's room in my office building, as I was shoving my shirt into my jeans and tugging up my zipper. Preoccupied, I flushed, picked up my book bag, took my cane down from the hook, and unlatched the door. So many movements unbalanced me, and as I pulled the door open, I fell over backward, landing fully clothed on the toilet seat with my legs splayed in front of me: the old beetle-on-its-back routine. Saturday afternoon, the building deserted, I was free to laugh aloud as I wriggled back to my feet, my voice bouncing off the yellowish tiles from all directions. Had anyone been there with me, I'd have been still and faint and hot with chagrin. I decided that it was high time to write the essay. **1**

First, the matter of semantics. I am a cripple. I choose this word to name me. I choose from among several possibilities, the most common of which are "handicapped" and "disabled." I made the choice a number of years ago, without thinking, unaware of my motives for doing so. Even now, I'm not sure what those motives are, but I recognize that they are complex and not entirely flattering. People—crippled or not—wince at the word "cripple," as they do not at "handicapped" or "disabled." Perhaps I want them to wince. I want them to see me as a tough customer, one to whom the fates/gods/viruses have not been kind, but who can face the brutal truth of her existence squarely. As a cripple, I swagger. **2**

But, to be fair to myself, a certain amount of honesty underlies my choice. "Cripple" seems to me a clean word, straightforward and precise. It has an honorable history, having made its first appearance in the Lindisfarne Gospel in the tenth century. As a lover of words, I like the accuracy with which it describes my condition: I have lost the full use of my limbs. "Disabled," by contrast, suggests any incapacity, physical or mental. And I certainly don't like "handicapped," which implies that I have deliberately been put at a disadvantage, by whom I can't imagine (my God is not a Handicapper General), in order to equalize chances in the great race of life. These words seem to **3**

*From *Plaintext* (Tucson: University of Arizona Press, 1992), pp. 9–20.

me to be moving away from my condition, to be widening the gap between word and reality. Most remote is the recently coined euphemism "differently abled," which partakes of the same semantic hopefulness that transformed countries from "undeveloped" to "underdeveloped," then to "less developed," and finally to "developing" nations. People have continued to starve in those countries during the shift. Some realities do not obey the dictates of language.

Mine is one of them. Whatever you call me, I remain crippled. But I don't care what you call me, so long as it isn't "differently abled," which strikes me as pure verbal garbage designed, by its ability to describe anyone, to describe no one. I subscribe to George Orwell's thesis that "the slovenliness of our language makes it easier for us to have foolish thoughts." And I refuse to participate in the degeneration of the language to the extent that I deny that I have lost anything in the course of this calamitous disease; I refuse to pretend that the only differences between you and me are the various ordinary ones that distinguish any one person from another. But call me "disabled" or "handicapped" if you like. I have long since grown accustomed to them, and if they are vague, at least they hint at the truth. Moreover, I use them myself. Society is no readier to accept crippledness than to accept death, war, sex, sweat, or wrinkles. I would never refer to another person as a cripple. It is the word I use to name only myself.   **4**

I haven't always been crippled, a fact for which I am soundly grateful. To be whole of limb is, I know from experience, infinitely more pleasant and useful than to be crippled; and if that knowledge leaves me open to bitterness at my loss, the physical soundness I once enjoyed (though I did not enjoy it half enough) is well worth the occasional stab of regret. Though never any good at sports, I was a normally active child and young adult. I climbed trees, played hopscotch, jumped rope, skated, swam, rode my bicycle, sailed. I despised team sports, spending some of the wretchedest afternoons of my life, sweaty and humiliated, behind a field-hockey stick and under a basketball hoop. I tramped alone for miles along the bridle paths that webbed the woods behind the house I grew up in. I swayed through countless dim hours in the arms of one man or another under the scattered shot of light from mirrored balls, and gyrated through countless more as Tab Hunter and Johnny Mathis gave way to the Rolling Stones, Creedance Clearwater Revival, Cream. I walked down the aisle. I pushed baby carriages, changed tires in the rain, marched for peace.   **5**

When I was 28, I started to trip and drop things. What at first **6** seemed my natural clumsiness soon became too pronounced to shrug off. I consulted a neurologist, who told me that I had a brain tumor. A battery of tests, increasingly disagreeable, revealed no tumor. About a year and a half later, I developed a blurred spot in one eye. I had, at last, the episodes "disseminated in space and time" requisite for a diagnosis: multiple sclerosis. I have never been sorry for the doctor's initial misdiagnosis, however. For almost a week, until the negative results of the tests were in, I thought that I was going to die right away. Every day for the past nearly 10 years, then, has been a kind of gift. I accept all gifts.

Multiple sclerosis is a chronic degenerative disease of the central **7** nervous system, in which the myelin that sheathes the nerves is somehow eaten away and scar tissue forms in its place, interrupting the nerves' signals. During its course, which is unpredictable and uncontrollable, one may lose vision; hearing; speech; the ability to walk; control of bladder and/or bowels; strength in any or all extremities; sensitivity to touch, vibration, and/or pain; potency; coordination of movements—the list of possibilities is lengthy and, yes, horrifying. One may also lose one's sense of humor. That's the easiest to lose and the hardest to survive without.

In the past 10 years, I have sustained some of these losses. Characteristic of MS are sudden attacks, called exacerbations, followed by **8** remissions, and these I have not had. Instead, my disease has been slowly progressive. My left leg is now so weak that I walk with the aid of a brace and a cane; and for distances I use an Amigo, a variation on the electric wheelchair that looks rather like an electrified kiddie car. I no longer have much use of my left hand. Now my right side is weakening as well. I still have the blurred spot in my right eye. Overall, though, I've been lucky so far. My world has, of necessity, been circumscribed by my losses, but the terrain left me has been ample enough for me to continue many of the activities that absorb me: writing, teaching, raising children and cats and plants and snakes, reading, speaking publicly about MS and depression, even playing bridge with people patient and honorable enough to let me scatter cards every which way without sneaking a peak.

Lest I begin to sound like Pollyanna, however, let me say that I **9** don't like having MS. I hate it. My life holds realities—harsh ones, some of them—that no right-minded human being ought to accept without grumbling. One of them is fatigue. I know of no one with MS who does not complain of bone-weariness; in a disease that presents an astonishing variety of symptoms, fatigue seems to be a common factor. I wake up in the morning feeling the way most people do at the end of a bad day, and I take it from there. As a result, I spend a lot of time *in extremis* and, impatient with limitation, I tend to ignore my fatigue until my body breaks down in some way and forces rest. Then I miss picnics, dinner parties, poetry readings, the brief visits of old friends from out of town. The offspring of a puritanical tradition of exceptional venerability, I cannot view these lapses without shame. My life often seems a series of small failures to do as I ought.

I lead, on the whole, an ordinary life, probably rather like the one I   **10** would have led had I not had MS. I am lucky that my predilections were already solitary, sedentary, and bookish—unlike the world-famous French cellist I have read about or the young woman I talked with one long afternoon who wanted only to be a jockey. I had just begun graduate school when I found out something was wrong with me, and I have remained, interminably, a graduate student. Perhaps I would not have if I'd thought I had the stamina to return to a full-time job as a technical editor; but I've enjoyed my studies.

In addition to studying, I teach writing courses. I also teach med-   **11** ical students how to give neurological examinations. I pick up freelance editing jobs here and there. I have raised a foster son and sent him into the world, where he has made me two grandbabies, and I am still escorting my daughter and son through adolescence. I go to Mass every Saturday. I am a superb, if messy, cook. I am also an enthusiastic laundress, capable of sorting a hamper full of clothes into five subtly differentiated piles, but a terrible housekeeper. I can do italic writing and, in an emergency, bathe an oil-soaked cat. I play a fiendish game of Scrabble. When I have the time and the money, I like to sit on my front steps with my husband, drinking Amaretto and smoking a cigar, as we imagine our counterparts in Leningrad and make sure that the sun gets down once more behind the sharp childish scrawl of the Tucson Mountains.

This lively plenty has its bleak complement, of course, in all the   **12** things I can no longer do. I will never run again, except in dreams, and one day I may have to write that I will never walk again. I like to go camping, but I can't follow George and the children along the trails that wander out of a campsite through the desert or into the mountains. In fact, even on the level I've learned never to check the weather or try to hold a coherent conversation: I need all my attention for my wayward feet. Of late, I have begun to catch myself wondering how people can propel themselves without canes. With only one usable hand, I have to select my clothing with care not so much for style as for ease of ingress and egress, and even so, dressing can be laborious. I can no longer do fine stitchery, pick up babies, play the piano, braid my hair. I am immobilized by acute attacks of depression, which may or may not be physiologically related to MS but are certainly its logical concomitant.

These two elements, the plenty and the privation, are never pure, **13** nor are the delight and wretchedness that accompany them. Almost every pickle that I get into as a result of my weakness and clumsiness—and I get into plenty—is funny as well as maddening and sometimes painful. I recall one May afternoon when a friend and I were going out for a drink after finishing up at school. As we were climbing into opposite sides of my car, chatting, I tripped and fell, flat and hard, onto the asphalt parking lot, my abrupt departure interrupting him in mid-sentence. "Where'd you go?" he called as he came around the back of the car to find me hauling myself up by the door frame. "Are you all right?" Yes, I told him, I was fine, just a bit rattly, and we drove off to find a shady patio and some beer. When I got home an hour or so later, my daughter greeted me with "What have you done to yourself?" I looked down. One elbow of my white turtleneck with the green froggies, one knee of my white trousers, one white kneesock were blood-soaked. We peeled off the clothes and inspected the damage, which was nasty enough but not alarming. That part wasn't funny: The abrasions took a long time to heal, and one got a little infected. Even so, when I think of my friend talking earnestly, suddenly, to the hot thin air while I dropped from his view as though through a trap door, I find the image as silly as something from a Marx Brothers movie.

I may find it easier than other cripples to amuse myself because I **14** live propped by the acceptance and the assistance and, sometimes, the amusement of those around me. Grocery clerks tear my checks out of my checkbook for me, and sales clerks find chairs to put into dressing rooms when I want to try on clothes. The people I work with make sure I teach at times when I am least likely to be fatigued, in places I can get to, with the materials I need. My students, with one anonymous exception (in an end-of-the-semester evaluation), have been unperturbed by my disability. Some even like it. One was immensely cheered by the information that I paint my own fingernails; she decided, she told me, that if I could go to such trouble over fine details, she could keep on writing essays. I suppose I became some sort of bright-fingered muse. She wrote good essays, too.

The most important struts in the framework of my existence, of course, are my husband and children. Dismayingly few marriages survive the MS test, and why should they? Most 22- and 19-year-olds, like George and me, can vow in clear conscience, after a childhood of chicken pox and summer colds, to keep one another in sickness and health so long as they both shall live. Not many are equipped for catastrophe: the dismay, the depression, the extra work, the boredom that a degenerative disease can insinuate into a relationship. And our society, with its emphasis on fun and its association of fun with physical performance, offers little encouragement for a whole spouse to stay with a crippled partner. Children experience similar stresses when faced with a crippled parent, and they are more helpless, since parents and children can't usually get divorced. They hate, of course, to be different from their peers, and the child whose mother is tacking down the aisle of a school auditorium packed with proud parents like a Cape Cod dinghy in a stiff breeze jolly well stands out in a crowd. Deprived of legal divorce, the child can at least deny the mother's disability, even her existence, forgetting to tell her about recitals and PTA meetings, refusing to accompany her to stores or church or the movies, never inviting friends to the house. Many do.   **15**

But I've been limping along for 10 years now, and so far George and the children are still at my left elbow, holding tight. Anne and Matthew vacuum floors and dust furniture and haul trash and rake up dog droppings and button my cuffs and bake lasagna and Toll House cookies with just enough grumbling so I know that they don't have brain fever. And far from hiding me, they're forever dragging me by racks of fancy clothes or through teeming school corridors, or welcoming gaggles of friends while I'm wandering through the house in Anne's filmy pink babydoll pajamas. George generally calls before he brings someone home, but he does just as many dumb thankless chores as the children. And they all yell at me, laugh at some of my jokes, write me funny letters when we're apart—in short, treat me as an ordinary human being for whom they have some use. I think they like me. Unless they're faking. . . .   **16**

Faking. There's the rub. Tugging at the fringes of my consciousness always is the terror that people are kind to me only because I'm a cripple. My mother almost shattered me once, with that instinct mothers have—blind, I think, in this case, but unerring nonetheless—for striking blows along the fault lines of their children's hearts, by telling me, in an attack on my selfishness, "We all have to make allowances for you, of course, because of the way you are." From the   **17** distance of a couple of years, I have to admit that I haven't any idea just what she meant, and I'm not sure that she knew either. She was awfully angry. But at the time, as the words thudded home, I felt my worst fear, suddenly realized. I could bear being called selfish: I am. But I couldn't bear the corroboration that those around me were doing in fact what I'd always suspected them of doing, professing fondness while silently putting up with me because of the way I am. A cripple. I've been a little cracked ever since.

Along with this fear that people are secretly accepting shoddy goods comes a relentless pressure to please—to prove myself worth the burdens I impose, I guess, or to build a substantial account of goodwill against which I may write drafts in times of need. Part of the pressure arises from social expectations. In our society, anyone who deviates from the norm had better find some way to compensate. Like fat people, who are expected to be jolly, cripples must bear their lot meekly and cheerfully. A grumpy cripple isn't playing by the rules. And much of the pressure is self-generated. Early on I vowed that, if I had to have MS, by God I was going to do it well. This is a class act, ladies and gentlemen. No tears, no recriminations, no faint-heartedness.

One way and another, then, I wind up feeling like Tiny Tim, peering over the edge of the table at the Christmas goose, waving my crutch, piping down God's blessing on us all. Only sometimes I don't want to play Tiny Tim. I'd rather be Caliban, a most scurvy monster. Fortunately, at home no one much cares whether I'm a good cripple or a bad cripple as long as I make vichyssoise with fair regularity. One evening several years ago, Anne was reading at the dining-room table while I cooked dinner. As I opened a can of tomatoes, the can slipped in my left hand and juice spattered me and the counter with bloody spots. Fatigued and infuriated, I bellowed, "I'm so sick of being crippled!" Anne glanced at me over the top of her book. "There now," she said, "do you feel better?" "Yes," I said, "yes, I do." She went back to her reading. I felt better. That's about all the attention my scurviness ever gets.

Because I hate being crippled, I sometimes hate myself for being a cripple. Over the years I have come to expect—even accept—attacks of violent self-loathing. Luckily, in general our society no longer connects deformity and disease directly with evil (though a charismatic once told me that I have MS because a devil is in me) and so I'm allowed to move largely at will, even among small children. But I'm not sure that this revision of attitude has been par-

18

19

20

ticularly helpful. Physical imperfection, even freed of moral disapprobation, still defies and violates the ideal, especially for women, whose confinement in their bodies as objects of desire is far from over. Each age, of course, has its ideal, and I doubt that ours is any better or worse than any other. Today's ideal woman, who lives on the glossy pages of dozens of magazines, seems to be between the ages of 18 and 25; her hair has body, her teeth flash white, her breath smells minty, her underarms are dry; she has a career but is still a fabulous cook, especially of meals that take less than 20 minutes to prepare; she does not ordinarily appear to have a husband or children; she is trim and deeply tanned; she jogs, swims, plays tennis, rides a bicycle, sails, but does not bowl; she travels widely, even to out-of-the-way places like Finland and Samoa, always in the company of the ideal man, who possesses a nearly identical set of characteristics. There are a few exceptions. Though usually white and often blonde, she may be black, Hispanic, Asian, or Native American, so long as she is unusually sleek. She may be old, provided she is selling a laxative or is Lauren Bacall. If she is selling a detergent, she may be married and have a flock of strikingly messy children. But she is never a cripple.

Like many women I know, I have always had an uneasy relationship with my body. I was not a popular child, largely, I think now, because I was peculiar: intelligent, intense, moody, shy, given to unexpected actions and inexplicable notions and emotions. But as I entered adolescence, I believed myself unpopular because I was homely: my breasts too flat, my mouth too wide, my hips too narrow, my clothing never quite right in fit or style. I was not, in fact, particularly ugly, old photographs inform me, though I was well off the ideal; but I carried this sense of self-alienation with me into adulthood, where it regenerated in response to the depredations of MS. Even with my brace I walk with a limp so pronounced that, seeing myself on the videotape of a television program on the disabled, I couldn't believe that anything but an inchworm could make progress humping along like that. My shoulders droop and my pelvis thrusts forward as I try to balance myself upright, throwing my frame into a bony S. As a result of contractures, one shoulder is higher than the other and I carry one arm bent in front of me, the fingers curled into a claw. My left arm and leg have wasted into pipe-stems, and I try always to keep them covered. When I think about how my body must look to others, especially to men, to whom I have been trained to display myself, I feel ludicrous, even loathsome. **21**

At my age, however, I don't spend much time thinking about my **22** appearance. The burning egocentricity of adolescence, which assures one that all the world is looking all the time, has passed, thank God, and I'm generally too caught up in what I'm doing to step back, as I used to, and watch myself as though upon a stage. I'm also too old to believe in the accuracy of self-image. I know that I'm not a hideous crone, that in fact, when I'm rested, well dressed, and well made up, I look fine. The self-loathing I feel is neither physically nor intellectually substantial. What I hate is not me but a disease.

I am not a disease.   **23**

And a disease is not—at least not singlehandedly—going to de-   **24**
termine who I am, though at first it seemed to be going to. Adjusting to a chronic incurable illness, I have moved through a process similar to that outlined by Elizabeth Kübler-Ross in *On Death and Dying*. The major difference—and it is far more significant than most people recognize—is that I can't be sure of the outcome, as the terminally ill cancer patient can. Research studies indicate that, with proper medical care, I may achieve a "normal" life span. And in our society, with its vision of death as the ultimate evil, worse even than decrepitude, the response to such news is, "Oh well, at least you're not going to *die*." Are there worse things than dying? I think that there may be.

I think of two women I know, both with MS, both enough older   **25**
than I to have served me as models. One took to her bed several years ago and has been there ever since. Although she can sit in a high-backed wheelchair, because she is incontinent she refuses to go out at all, even though incontinence pants, which are readily available at any pharmacy, could protect her from embarrassment. Instead, she stays at home and insists that her husband, a small quiet man, a retired civil servant, stay there with her except for a quick weekly foray to the supermarket. The other woman, whose illness was diagnosed when she was 18, a nursing student engaged to a young doctor, finished her training, married her doctor, accompanied him to Germany when he was in the service, bore three sons and a daughter, now grown and gone. When she can, she travels with her husband; she plays bridge, embroiders, swims regularly; she works, like me, as a symptomatic-patient instructor of medical students in neurology. Guess which woman I hope to be.

At the beginning, I thought about having MS almost incessantly.   **26**
And because of the unpredictable course of the disease, my thoughts were always terrified. Each night I'd get into bed wondering whether I'd get out again the next morning, whether I'd be able to see, to

speak, to hold a pen between my fingers. Knowing that the day might come when I'd be physically incapable of killing myself, I thought perhaps I ought to do so right away, while I still had the strength. Gradually I came to understand that the Nancy who might one day lie inert under a bedsheet, arms and legs paralyzed, unable to feed or bathe herself, unable to reach out for a gun, a bottle of pills, was not the Nancy I was at present, and that I could not presume to make decisions for that future Nancy, who might well not want in the least to die. Now the only provision I've made for the future Nancy is that when the time comes—and it is likely to come in the form of pneumonia, friend to the weak and the old—I am not to be treated with machines and medications. If she is unable to communicate by then, I hope she will be satisfied with these terms.

Thinking all the time about having MS grew tiresome and intrusive, especially in the large and tragic mode in which I was accustomed to considering my plight. Months and even years went by without catastrophe (at least without one related to MS), and really I was awfully busy, what with George and children and snakes and students and poems, and I hadn't the time, let alone the inclination, to devote myself to being a disease. Too, the richer my life became, the funnier it seemed, as though there were some connection between largesse and laughter, and so my tragic stance began to waver until, even with the aid of a brace and a cane, I couldn't hold it for very long at a time.   **27**

After several years I was satisfied with my adjustment. I had suffered my grief and fury and terror, I thought, but now I was at ease with my lot. Then one summer day I set out with George and the children across the desert for a vacation in California. Part way to Yuma I became aware that my right leg felt funny. "I think I've had an exacerbation," I told George. "What shall we do?" he asked. "I think we'd better get the hell to California," I said, "because I don't know whether I'll ever make it again." So we went to San Diego and then to Orange, up the Pacific Coast Highway to Santa Cruz, across to Yosemite, down to Sequoia and Joshua Tree, and so back over the desert to home. It was a fine two-week trip, filled with friends and fair weather, and I wouldn't have missed it for the world, although I did in fact make it back to California two years later. Nor would there have been any point in missing it, since in MS, once the symptoms have appeared, the neurological damage has been done, and there's no way to predict or prevent that damage.   **28**

The incident spoiled my self-satisfaction, however. It renewed my   **29** grief and fury and terror, and I learned that one never finishes adjusting to MS. I don't know now why I thought one would. One does not, after all, finish adjusting to life, and MS is simply a fact of my life—not my favorite fact, of course—but as ordinary as my nose and my tropical fish and my yellow Mazda station wagon. It may at any time get worse, but no amount of worry or anticipation can prepare me for a new loss. My life is a lesson in losses. I learn one at a time.

And I had best be patient in the learning, since I'll have to do it **30** like it or not. As any rock fan knows, you can't always get what you want. Particularly when you have MS. You can't, for example, get cured. In recent years researchers and the organizations that fund research have started to pay MS some attention even though it isn't fatal; perhaps they have begun to see that life is something other than a quantitative phenomenon, that one may be very much alive for a very long time in a life that isn't worth living. The researchers have made some progress toward understanding the mechanism of the disease: It may well be an autoimmune reaction triggered by a slow-acting virus. But they are nowhere near its prevention, control, or cure. And most of us want to be cured. Some, unable to accept incurability, grasp at one treatment after another, no matter how bizarre: megavitamin therapy, gluten-free diet, injections of cobra venom, hypothermal suits, lymphocytopharesis, hyperbaric chambers. Many treatments are probably harmless enough, but none are curative.

The absence of a cure often makes MS patients bitter toward their **31** doctors. Doctors are, after all, the priests of modern society, the new shamans, whose business is to heal, and many an MS patient roves from one to another, searching for the "good" doctor who will make him well. Doctors too think of themselves as healers, and for this reason many have trouble dealing with MS patients, whose disease in its intransigence defeats their aims and mocks their skills. Too few doctors, it is true, treat their patients as whole human beings, but the reverse is also true. I have always tried to be gentle with my doctors, who often have more at stake in terms of ego than I do. I may be frustrated, maddened, depressed by the incurability of my disease, but I am not diminished by it, and they are. When I push myself up from my seat in the waiting room and stumble toward them, I incarnate the limitation of their powers. The least I can do is refuse to press on their tenderest spots.

This gentleness is part of the reason that I'm not sorry to be a crip- **32** ple. I didn't have it before. Perhaps I'd have developed it anyway— how could I know such a thing?—and I wish I had more of it, but I'm glad of what I have. It has opened and enriched my life enormously, this sense that my frailty and need must be mirrored in others, that in searching for and shaping a stable core in a life wrenched by change and loss, change and loss, I must recognize the same process, under individual conditions, in the lives around me. I do not deprecate such knowledge, however I've come by it.

All the same, if a cure were found, would I take it? In a minute. I   **33** may be a cripple, but I'm only occasionally a loony and never a saint. Anyway, in my brand of theology God doesn't give bonus points for a limp. I'd take a cure; I just don't need one. A friend who also has MS startled me once by asking, "Do you ever say to yourself, 'Why me, Lord?'" "No, Michael, I don't," I told him, "because whenever I try, the only response I can think of is 'Why not?'" If I could make a cosmic deal, who would I put in my place? What in my life would I give up in exchange for sound limbs and a thrilling rush of energy? No one. Nothing. I might as well do the job myself. Now that I'm getting the hang of it.

 # QUESTIONS FOR CRITICAL THINKING

THINKING CRITICALLY ABOUT CONTENT

1. Why do you think the writer describes her day-to-day life in such great detail?

2. Does Nancy Mairs explain her disease in a way that makes it possible for all readers to understand it? Find examples in the essay of these explanations.

THINKING CRITICALLY ABOUT PURPOSE

3. What do you think Nancy Mairs's purpose is in this essay?

4. What emotions do you think Nancy Mairs is trying to evoke in her readers as she analyzes her disease?

THINKING CRITICALLY ABOUT AUDIENCE

5. Do you think that all people with disabilities would agree with the writer's attitude about her illness? Explain your answer.

6. Do you think that this essay is interesting only to people with disabilities, or can other groups of people benefit from reading it? Who are they?

THINKING CRITICALLY ABOUT POINT OF VIEW

7. Describe in a complete sentence this writer's point of view.

8. Write a paragraph analyzing the way that Nancy Mairs's husband and children

might describe her disease, showing the ways in which their description would differ from hers and the ways it would be the same.

LEARNING FROM YOUR PEERS

Analysis helps us understand why something happened and the effects of that event on our lives. In the process of writing an analytical essay, we should make these connections very clear, both for ourselves and for our readers. Learning to write analytically is a skill that will be useful in many areas of life. In other college classes, you may be asked to analyze a scientific process, a political or historical event, or a piece of literature. The skills you use to write essays of this type are basically the same: You take the event apart, and you put it together again in a way that makes sense to you. Watching an analysis take shape is an extremely informative experience. To help you learn how to approach writing assignments that require analysis, we are going to follow the writing process of a student named Jefferson Wright.

Jefferson's Writing Assignment: Analyzing

This is the topic Jefferson's instructor assigned:

Some events in our lives are confusing to us when they are happening, and it takes us months or even years to fully understand their impact on us. As we look back at these events, we see how they helped us become the people we are today. Confronting obstacles, facing conflicts, or working through disheartening problems often helps us become stronger and more confident; at the very least, these situations increase our self-knowledge. Think of an event in your life that changed you in an important way, and write an essay analyzing that change.

Jefferson goes through the process as outlined in Chapter 1: *thinking, planning, developing, organizing, drafting, revising,* and *editing.*

Thinking

Jefferson is a basketball player who hopes to be in the NBA some day. When he gets this assignment, Jefferson thinks immediately of the times he has spent training, practicing, and recovering from injuries. This is what he writes in his journal:

It seems I am always getting stronger. Working out in the weight

room will do that. Of course, that's exactly the point. I complain about

practice and arranging classes and homework around the basketball schedule, but actually that stuff works out pretty well as long as I follow a routine.

I've had a lot of self-discipline in sports because physical activity has always been pretty easy for me. Much easier than reading, for example. Of course I could go into that whole experience. All the strange schools and flash cards and wondering if I would ever understand what people wanted me to learn.

Jefferson decides that he will discuss his ideas with the athletic department's tutor to see what she thinks about his possible topics.

Planning

The next afternoon, Jefferson shows his journal to his tutor. She asks him questions about how he finally learned to read and what happened. He tells her that he went to several schools before he learned to read. His tutor knows that Jefferson is dyslexic, but she does not know the complicated story of how he learned to deal with his handicap. She tells him to jot down the main events of his experiences with reading as he remembers them.

Jefferson does all his writing on a computer. Because spelling is so difficult for him, he saves time by entering all his notes and ideas into his word-processing files and checking his spelling later with a spelling checker. He thinks about his process of learning to read, then starts listing the memories in chronological order. This is Jefferson's list:

1. After attending kindergarten and first grade in my neighborhood school, I went to a private residential school. I did not understand why I was being sent away from home.

2. Once I got there, I felt like I was in prison. We spent so much time reading aloud, I memorized every book they stuck in front of me. I liked the teachers--I just couldn't learn to read.

3. I stayed in that school until I was in fifth grade. When my parents came to visit me, they figured out that I still could not read.

4. They sent me to another school that had "structure." Too much, if you ask me.

5. Things kept getting worse.

6. Then my dad was transferred overseas, and my mom and sisters

taught me to read at home. There weren't any English-speaking schools, so it worked out great. For me, anyway.

7. When I finally came back to the States, I was ready for high school.

8. My computer and tape recorder helped me a lot.

Developing

The next day Jefferson meets with his peer editing group. He goes through his list and tells them what it was like for him to learn to read. They are all surprised and ask him questions about what happened and why it took him so long to learn to read. Jefferson tells them that there is no satisfactory explanation for why it takes some people so long to recognize the symbols that others easily perceive as letters and words. He tells them that he was about 12 or 13 years old before he realized that certain words are always spelled the same way. He says that some words still do not appear the same to him from one day to the next, but he can often guess their meaning with the help of the context or a dictionary. Sometimes he has to ask his roommate or tutor how to spell certain words.

The other students in Jefferson's group encourage him to develop this topic further. They tell him to put in all the details he can remember about the different schools he went to. They tell him to write about the gruesome details of his least favorite boarding school as well as about the encouragement he received from his parents and sisters.

Jefferson goes home and spends time remembering specifics about each school that he attended. He goes back to his original list on the computer and adds these details. This is what Jefferson's list looks like now:

1. After attending kindergarten and first grade in my neighborhood school, I went to a private residential school. I did not understand why I was being sent away from home. I didn't really understand what reading was, and I did not like being away from my family.

2. Once I got there, I felt like I was in prison. We spent so much time reading aloud, I memorized every book they stuck in front of me. I liked the teachers--I just couldn't learn to read. They were really nice and we practiced all the time. I never got to go home for summer vacation though.

3. I stayed in that school until I was in fifth grade. When my parents came to visit me, they figured out that I still could not read. My parents were really upset and took me home with them that day.

4. They sent me to another school that had "structure." Too much, if you ask me. We had to run all the time because they had this theory that the reason we couldn't read was that our large muscles weren't coordinated enough. They used running as a punishment. If you got to class late or got out of bed late, you had to run laps in the gym. I called home and cried on the phone so much that the school tried to cut off my telephone privileges.

5. Things kept getting worse. To say the least.

6. Then my dad was transferred overseas, and my mom and sisters taught me to read at home. There weren't any English-speaking schools, so it worked out great. For me, anyway. It sounds easy when I say it this way, but we actually had to spend hours every day with flash cards and stories. Somehow, everything worked, though, and I finally understood what reading was.

7. When I came back to the States, I was ready for high school. And, thanks to that school that had us running laps all the time, I had developed some athletic ability. I got to play basketball in high school, which was great.

8. My computer and tape recorder helped me a lot. I also had one of those electronic spellers before I got a computer. That was really great because I could find words a lot faster than when I was trying to use a regular dictionary.

Organizing

Jefferson is used to arranging his thoughts in chronological order with the help of his computer, so he has already done most of the organizational work. He just needs to fill in additional details and add transitions as he changes his notes into essay form.

First, he takes his list and copies it into another file on his computer. Then he removes the numbers from the list and shows the results to his tutor. She tells him that she thinks his organization is easy to follow and he is ready to draft his essay, but he needs to analyze in more depth his process of learning how to read.

The more Jefferson thinks about the process he went through to learn how to read and write, the better he understands how he finally succeeded. He attributes most of his verbal skills to two things that helped: (1) the patience of his mother and sisters and (2) technology. As he writes and rewrites, he realizes that after he learned the basics of reading from his family members, he was able to continue to develop his writing skills because of the technology he had access to: Computers with spelling checkers and grammar checkers gave him confidence and abilities that he had lacked.

Drafting

Jefferson now knows where his paper is headed, and he has made important discoveries about his learning disability. He feels like he is ready to write. Here is Jefferson's draft.

Jefferson's Essay: First Draft

Main Idea: Learning to read was exceptionally difficult for me.

Learning to read was the most difficult ordeal that I have ever experienced. My parents discovered when I was very young that I had a problem I was dyslexic. But the schools that I attended in the 80s simply couldnt help me learn to read. I was always very bright and interested in schoolwork. Nevertheless no matter how hard I tried I could not perceive the patterns in words especially if the type of print changed. If the words were written in someone's handwriting, I was completely lost. What was I supposed to do? It took several years of trial and error, however, before these problems became clear to me, my teachers, and my parents.

For a few years in elementary school, I attended The Silmon Learning Center, a well-known residential school that specializes in teaching students with learning disabilities. I stayed at that school twelve months of the year because my parents wanted me to learn to read before it was too late. The teachers were very kind and helpful but I always ended up memorizing the books we read because we spent so much time going over them. However whenever anything unfamiliar was given to me I had to start all over again. They thought I could read the books pages, and I thought I could read them too. My brain just did not recognize words and phrases, even though my eyes had seen them repeatedly. I especially had trouble with words that had ds and bs in them.

During the Parents Day visit at that school, when I was in the 5th grade, my parents realized that I still did not know how to read. Of course they had a talk with the teachers and the headmaster Mister Smithers. They all decided that I should go to a school that had more "structure."

I was sent to another Residential School that emphasized physical exercise as a preliminary to Reading. The teachers at downybrook day school did not believe that we could learn to read until all our large muscles were fully coordinated. Therefore for every half hour that we spent in the classroom working at our desks we had to run around in the gym or on the playground for a half hour. What a drag! By the end of a month. I was so exhausted that I did not even want to get out of bed, in the morning. Surprise! If we were late for breakfast we had to go run around the track for fifteen min. before breakfast. My friend doug was always late and always running. It didnt take me long at that school to become extremely discouraged. I called home so much that the school wanted to restrict my telephone privileges. I asked my parents why they couldn't bring me home. "How would you feel mom if you were separated from your family?" I asked her. Luckily, my Father was transferred overseas at that time to the Far East. His position with Trans World Airlines allowed the family to go with him. I thought I understood what it must feel like to be out on parole after a long prison sentence. Can you imagine how I felt?

We lived in a country that did not have any schools where English was the language of instruction. For two years, my mother and older sisters spent hours every day helping me work on my reading. They used flash cards. There were about three hundred flash

cards. They never got mad at me if it I didnt recognize a short easy
phrase and they never made me run around if I didnt feel like it. At
the end of two years I was starting to feel a little confidence in my
ability to recognize the most common Eng. words and phrases. Was I
ever ready to go home!

Luckily, my U.S. school allowed me to carry a tape recorder, and
a portable computer with me to all my classes. It helped me I believe
because writing was especially difficult for me. It takes me about 6 or
7 times as long as most people to write a short paper. Don't think I'm
exaggerating. I have the ideas in my head however it is not always
clear to me if they are written correctly. The computer helps me with
those problems, making my life much easier and simpler.

In the past two or three years, I have learned more about
reading and writing than I had in all my previous years of school,
especially from Miss Grayson, my senior English teacher. She
encouraged me and was very patient. I had always wanted to read
and write, but these were not the skills that came easily to me. I am
glad that I was able to persist and reach my goals. I am also grateful
for all those who had faith in me and helped my learn persistence.
Without them, I might still be trying to figure out the alphabet.

Revising

In writing his first draft, Jefferson feels he has learned many new things about himself and his lifelong struggle with dyslexia. In fact, he believes that writing this essay
has moved him a step further in learning to live positively with his disability. Now it
is time to revise his work. The instructor wants students to concentrate their revision process this time on levels of generality or movement from general to particular
throughout their essays.

Jefferson reviews the Checklist for Varying Levels of Generality at the beginning
of the Tips for Revising section of this chapter. He reads the Tips for Revising and
does the exercises his instructor assigns.

Jefferson begins to revise with a great deal of hesitation, not feeling very confident about the items on the checklist. But after he works with his draft for a while,
he starts to see how all the guidelines are related and how they work together to im-

prove the essay as a whole. When he applies these criteria to his first draft, he discovers many problems that he sets out to remedy one by one.

COLLABORATIVE WORK

PEER GROUP ACTIVITY

After you read the portions of the Tips for Revising your instructor assigns, turn to Jefferson's first draft (pp. 293–295), and complete the following tasks in small groups:

A. Underline the essay's thesis statement (for a definition, see p. 31), and cross out any sentences in the introduction that are too specific.

B. Put parentheses around any topic sentences that your group believes are not directly related to the thesis.

C. Put a check mark to the left of any paragraphs your group thinks need more details.

Compare the marks your group made to those your instructor will show you. Where do your marks differ from your instructor's? What do you need to review before writing your own essay?

CLASS ACTIVITY

As an entire class, look at the underlined portions of Jefferson's revised draft (pp. 297–300) to see how he changed each sentence.

A. Did you identify the **revision** problems that Jefferson corrected?

B. Do you think his changes are good ones? Discuss his changes.

Editing

Now that his sentences say what Jefferson wants them to say, he needs to do some final proofreading and editing before handing in his essay. The instructor tells the class how the rules of punctuation and mechanics help make communication as precise as possible. So Jefferson shifts his focus from the content of his essay to the mechanics. He reads the Tips for Editing section in this chapter to learn about the rules of punctuation and mechanics. After he finishes the assigned exercises, he takes the questions in the Checklist for Editing Punctuation and Mechanics one by one and makes changes so that his revised draft fulfills all these requirements.

COLLABORATIVE WORK

PEER GROUP ACTIVITY

After you read the portions of the Tips for Revising your instructor assigns, turn to Jefferson's first draft (pp. 293–295), and complete the following tasks in small groups:

A. Circle any errors in end punctuation—periods, question marks, and exclamation points (for explanations, see pp. 311–313).

B. Circle any errors in internal punctuation—commas, semicolons, colons, quotation marks, italics, apostrophes, hyphens, dashes, parentheses, brackets, slashes, and ellipses (for explanations, see pp. 313–332).

C. Circle any capitalization errors that you find (for explanations, see pp. 333–337).

D. Circle any abbreviation errors that you find (for explanations, see pp. 337–341).

E. Circle any errors you find in writing numbers (for explanations, see pp. 341–343).

Compare the circles your group made with those your instructor will show you. Where do your circles differ from your instructor's? What do you need to review before writing your own essay?

CLASS ACTIVITY

As an entire class, look at the underlined portions of Jefferson's revised draft (pp. 297–300) to see how he changed each sentence.

A. Did you identify the **editing** problems that Jefferson corrected?

B. Do you think his changes are good ones? Discuss his changes.

Jefferson's Revised Essay

Learning to Read

Learning to read was the most difficult ordeal that I have ever experienced. My parents discovered when I was very young that I had a problem: I was dyslexic. But the schools that I attended in the '80s simply couldn't help me learn to read. I was always very bright and interested in schoolwork/, but ~~Nevertheless~~ no matter how hard I tried, I could not perceive the patterns in words--especially if the type of print changed. If the words were written in someone's handwriting, I was completely lost. ~~What was I supposed to do?~~ It took several years of trial and error, however, before these problems became clear to me, my teachers, and my parents. <u>Then, several more years were needed before I learned to solve my problems.</u>

For a few years in elementary school, I attended t<u>T</u>he Silmon Learning Center, a well-known residential school that specializes in teaching students with learning disabilities. I stayed at that school ~~twelve~~ <u>12</u> months of the year because my parents wanted me to learn to read before it was too late. The teachers were very kind and helpful, but I always ended up memorizing the books we read because we spent so much time going over them. However, whenever anything unfamiliar was given to me, I had to start all over again. They thought I could read the books' pages, and I thought I could read them too. My brain just did not recognize words and phrases, even though my eyes had seen them repeatedly. I especially had trouble with words that had d's and b's in them.

During the Parents' Day visit at that school, when I was in the ~~5th~~ <u>fifth</u> grade, my parents realized that I still did not know how to read. Of course they had a talk with the teachers and the headmaster, ~~Mister~~ <u>Mr.</u> Smithers. They all decided that I should go to a school that had more "structure."

I was sent to another r<u>R</u>esidential s<u>S</u>chool that emphasized physical exercise as a preliminary to r<u>R</u>eading. The teachers at D<u>d</u>ownybrook D<u>d</u>ay S<u>s</u>chool did not believe that we could learn to read until all our large muscles were fully coordinated. Therefore, for every half hour that we spent in the classroom working at our desks, we had to run around in the gym or on the playground for a

half hour. What a drag! By the end of a month/, I was so exhausted

that I did not even want to get out of bed/ in the morning. Surprise!

If we were late for breakfast, we had to go run around the track for

~~fifteen~~ ~~min~~ 15 minutes. ~~before breakfast.~~ My friend D̶d̶oug was

always late and always running. It didn't take me long at that school

to become extremely discouraged. I called home so much that the

school wanted to restrict my telephone privileges. I asked my

parents why they couldn't bring me home. "How would you feel,

M̶m̶om, if you were separated from your family?" I ~~asked her~~ would

ask. Luckily, my f̶F̶ather was transferred overseas ~~at that time~~ to the

Far East at that time. His position with ~~Trans World Airlines~~ TWA

allowed the family to go with him. I thought I understood what it

must feel like to be out on parole after a long prison sentence. Can

you imagine how I felt?

We lived in South Korea, a country that did not have any

schools where English was the language of instruction./, so f̶F̶or two

years, my mother and older sisters spent hours every day helping

me work on my reading. They used flash cards printed with the

same type of print as most books; they had short, simple phrases on

them instead of individual words. There were about ~~three hundred~~

300 flash cards, so I could not memorize them, especially because

they were presented to me at random. They never got mad at me if

I didn't recognize a short, easy phrase, and they never made me

run around if I didn't feel like it. At the end of two years, I was

starting to feel a little confidence in my ability to recognize the most

common ~~Eng.~~ English words and phrases. Boy, w̶W̶as I ever ready to

go home!

Then we came back to the United States, specifically

Pennsylvania, and I was ready to start high school. My high school

experiences gave me the strength and skills to attend college. I learned to read well and write effectively in high school. Then I was able to bring these new skills with me to college. Luckily, my U.S. school allowed me to carry a tape recorder/ and a portable computer with me to all my classes. It helped me, I believe, because writing was especially difficult for me. It takes me about ~~6 or 7~~ six or seven times as long as most people to write a short paper. Don't think I'm exaggerating. I have the ideas in my head; however, it is not always clear to me if they are written correctly. The computer helps me with those problems, making my life much easier and simpler.

In the past two or three years, I have learned more about reading and writing than I had in all my previous years of school, especially from Miss Grayson, my senior English teacher. She encouraged me and was very patient. I had always wanted to read and write, but these were not the skills that came easily to me. I am glad that I was able to persist and reach my goals. I am also grateful for all those who had faith in me and helped ~~my~~ me learn persistence. Without them, I might still be trying to figure out the alphabet.

Without positive high school experiences, I would never have had the courage to attend college. I am grateful that I learned to read and write well in high school. With the help of my computer, I could write essays that earned good marks. In addition, I could handle essay questions on tests and exams and keep laboratory logs in my science courses.

WRITING YOUR OWN ANALYZING ESSAY

So far, you have seen a professional writer and a fellow student at work trying to analyze an idea, impression, experience, or item of information as accurately as possible. As you read the published essay and followed the writing process of another student from first to final draft, you absorbed ideas and ways of giving those ideas a form of their own. These reading and writing activities have prepared you to write your own analysis of a topic that is meaningful to you.

What Have You Discovered?

Before you begin your own writing task, let's review what you have learned in this chapter so far:

- Analyzing is making sense of ideas, theories, feelings, behavior, even of life itself.

- Your purpose in an analyzing essay is to give your readers a thorough understanding of the topic you are writing about.

- You must support your analysis with relevant details and examples.

- To present your analysis effectively, you need to organize your ideas.

- To help you shape your essay, you should learn as much as possible about your readers.

- Before you write a draft, you need to decide on a point of view toward your subject.

- After you write a draft, you should revise your essay for meaning and organization.

- After you revise your essay, you should edit its grammar, usage, and sentence structure.

Your Writing Topic

Choose one of the following topics for your analyzing essay:

1. In this chapter's professional essay, "On Being a Cripple," Nancy Mairs analyzes the effect her illness has had on every aspect of her life. Choose a defining factor or event in your life (the death of someone close to you, a move from one place to another, a change of school, a marriage, a divorce, the birth of a child, an award, a punishment) and write an essay in which you analyze the effect, temporary or permanent, that the event or incident has had on you.

2. Write about an unexpected change that occurred earlier in your life, and analyze the effects of that change on your life today.

3. Write an essay that analyzes a current social problem—homelessness, drugs, environmental concerns—including the reasons for its existence.

4. Create your own analyzing essay topic (with the assistance of your instructor), and write a response to it.

After you have chosen one of these topics, you may begin the writing process in the same way Jefferson did. (You may find rereading Jefferson's experience helpful.) This time your purpose is to write your own analyzing essay. If some tasks occur out of order, that adjustment is probably part of your personal writing ritual. Follow your instincts, and let them mold your own writing process. But make sure you've worked through all the stages to your final draft.

YOUR WRITING PROCESS

THINKING   Generate as many ideas on your subject as you can in as many different ways as possible: rereading, listing, freewriting, brainstorming, clustering, discussing, and questioning.

PLANNING   Begin to give your ideas shape by deciding on your approach to your topic (your content, your purpose, your audience, and your point of view). Make a list of points you want to include in your essay.

DEVELOPING   Add more details on three or four specific, focused topics that you have chosen from your list of general points.

ORGANIZING   Organize your material in a way that will be most interesting to your audience.

DRAFTING   Write a working draft of your essay in complete sentences.

REVISING   Consulting the Tips for Revising in this chapter (pp. 303–309), revise your first draft—paying special attention to your levels of generality.

EDITING   Consulting the Tips for Editing in this chapter (pp. 310–344), edit your draft for grammar and correctness—paying special attention to punctuation and mechanics.

Turn in your revised draft to your instructor.

Some Final Thoughts

When you have completed your own essay, answer these four questions in your journal:

1.   What was most difficult about this assignment?
2.   What was easiest?
3.   What did I learn about analyzing by completing this assignment?
4.   What did I learn about my own writing process—how I prepared to write, how I wrote the first draft, how I revised, and how I edited?

Varying Levels of Generality

Checklist for Varying Levels of Generality

✓ Does the introduction introduce the **subject** of the essay?
✓ Does the essay have enough **main ideas** that develop the subject?
✓ Does each **body paragraph** contain both main ideas and details?
✓ Does a **full range of details** develop each main idea?
✓ Are the **details** as **vivid and specific** as possible?

Scientists have devised an intricate but accurate system for identifying all the plants and animals that our planet supports. The most general category in this system is the *kingdom*; we belong to the animal kingdom, as do mice. The most specific categories are *genus* and *species*. Only at this level can humans and mice be distinguished. The mouse in the closet belongs to the species *Mus musculus*; we belong to the species *Homo sapiens*.

Likewise, plants are broadly classified in the same general groupings, with families being the largest category, followed by genus and species. This may seem a great deal of trouble for naming plants, but it can be important in distinguishing the specific properties of different species. A gardener who bought *Verbenaceae clerodendrum foetidum* instead of *Verbenaceae clerodendrum trichotomum* would have a very unpleasant surprise because of its bad smell. He or she would have to uproot the *foetidum* (from the Latin word for "foul smelling"), replace it with its sweet-smelling relative *trichotomum,* and read plant labels more carefully in the future. Just as careful gardeners must pay attention to levels of general groupings and specific types of plants, writers need to pay attention to the general and specific in writing.

General Topics for Essays

A good essay contains both general statements and specific details, and, in fact, the writer constantly moves back and forth between the general and specific throughout the essay. The introduction is where you must not only capture your readers' interest but also lay out the boundaries of your essay's general subject. This paragraph should simply introduce your topic on a general level and not go into very much detail. When Nancy Mairs begins her essay "On Being a Cripple," she devotes her first paragraph to introducing her **general topic** — that is, her decision to write the essay on being a cripple. As we read, we learn that the essay is intended to encourage others to accept their lot in life, no matter what it is.

> The other day I was thinking of writing an essay on being a cripple. I was thinking hard in one of the stalls of the women's room in my office building, as I was shoving my shirt into my jeans and tugging up my zip-

303

per. Preoccupied, I flushed, picked up my book bag, took my cane down from the hook, and unlatched the door. So many movements unbalanced me, and as I pulled the door open I fell over backward, landing fully clothed on the toilet seat with my legs splayed in front of me: the old beetle-on-its-back routine. Saturday afternoon, the building deserted, I was free to laugh aloud as I wriggled back to my feet, my voice bouncing off the yellowish tiles from all directions. Had anyone been there with me, I'd have been still and faint and hot with chagrin. I decided that it was high time to write the essay.

As Jefferson Wright began to revise his first draft, he decided that, like Mairs, he needed to state his general topic—namely, how he solved his problem—in his first paragraph rather than simply describe the specific details of his problem:

First Draft: Learning to read was the most difficult ordeal that I have ever experienced. My parents discovered when I was very young that I had a problem I was dyslexic. But the schools that I attended in the 80s simply couldnt help me learn to read. I was always very bright and interested in schoolwork. Nevertheless no matter how hard I tried I could not perceive the patterns in words especially if the type of print changed. If the words were written in someone's handwriting, I was completely lost. What was I supposed to do? It took several years of trial and error, however, before these problems became clear to me, my teachers, and my parents.

Revision: Learning to read was the most difficult ordeal that I have ever experienced. My parents discovered when I was very young that I had a problem: I was dyslexic. But the schools that I attended in the '80s simply couldn't help me learn to read. I was always very bright and interested in schoolwork, but ~~Nevertheless~~ no matter how hard I tried, I could not perceive the patterns in words--especially if the type of print changed. If the words were written in someone's handwriting, I was completely lost. ~~What was I supposed to do?~~ It took several years of trial and error, however, before these problems became clear to me, my

teachers, and my parents. **Then, several more years were**

needed before I learned to solve my problems.

The revised introduction keeps the discussion on a general level and ends with a much more focused thesis sentence than Jefferson's first draft.

Main Ideas for the Body Paragraphs

After you have established the general topic for the entire essay, you need to generate enough main ideas for the body of your essay. **Main ideas** are the major points to be developed in the body paragraphs of an essay. These main ideas are expressed in topic sentences. In professional essays such as Mairs's, writers may take several paragraphs to develop each of their main ideas. For example, Mairs first explains in paragraphs 1 through 4 why she chooses to be called a "cripple." Then she moves to her next main idea, a definition of her disease and its effects on her life, in paragraphs 5 through 9. Finally, she moves to her final topic, the pleasure she still finds in life and her family's support and love.

As Jefferson worked on his revision, he realized that he had overlooked an important topic that should have been included in his essay—how his high school experience gave him the courage to attend college. He added the following sentences to the beginning of paragraph 6 of his revised essay.

Revision: **Then we came back to the United States, specifically**

Pennsylvania, and I was ready to start high school. My

high school experiences gave me the strength and skills to

attend college. I learned to read well and write effectively

in high school. Then I was able to bring these new skills

with me to college.

Jefferson added a new main idea to his essay (his experience in high school), but he knew he still had to fill in the paragraph with some details.

Specific Details

Essays that fully develop a general topic have a balance of supporting ideas (such as topic sentences) and specific, vivid details that explain those ideas. In fact, body paragraphs should move freely from general to specific and back to general again. An excellent example of this movement is in paragraph 5 of "On Being a Cripple":

I haven't always been crippled, a fact for which I am soundly grateful.
To be whole of limb is, I know from experience, infinitely more pleasant

TIPS FOR REVISING

and useful than to be crippled; and if that knowledge leaves me open to bitterness at my loss, the physical soundness I once enjoyed (though I did not enjoy it half enough) is well worth the occasional stab of regret. Though never any good at sports, I was a normally active child and young adult. I climbed trees, played hopscotch, jumped rope, skated, swam, rode my bicycle, sailed. I despised team sports, spending some of the wretchedest afternoons of my life, sweaty and humiliated, behind a field-hockey stick and under a basketball hoop. I tramped alone for miles along the bridle paths that webbed the woods behind the house I grew up in. I swayed through countless dim hours in the arms of one man or another under the scattered shot of light from mirrored balls, and gyrated through countless more as Tab Hunter and Johnny Mathis gave way to the Rolling Stones, Creedence Clearwater Revival, Cream. I walked down the aisle. I pushed baby carriages, changed tires in the rain, marched for peace.

Notice how this paragraph begins with a fairly general idea ("I haven't always been crippled") and gets down to the specific activities she did as a child ("I climbed trees, played hopscotch, jumped rope, skated, swam, rode my bicycle, sailed") before moving to the general again ("I despised team sports") and back to the specific ("as Tab Hunter and Johnny Mathis gave way to the Rolling Stones, Creedence Clearwater Revival, Cream"). This paragraph presents a good balance of main ideas and details and serves as a model for any body paragraph.

As Jefferson worked on his revision, he added details to paragraph 5 so that his audience would have a clear picture of how his mother and sisters helped him overcome his dyslexia:

First Draft: We lived in a country that did not have any schools where English was the language of instruction. For two years, my mother and older sisters spent hours every day helping me work on my reading. They used flash cards. There were about three hundred flash cards. They never got mad at me if I didnt recognize a short easy phrase and they never made me run around if I didnt feel like it. At the end of two years I was starting to feel a little confidence in my ability to recognize the most common Eng. words and phrases. Was I ever ready to go home!

Revision: We lived in **South Korea,** a country that did not have any schools where English was the language of instruction, so for two years, my mother and older sisters spent hours every day helping me work on my reading. They used flash cards **printed with the same type of print as most books; they had short, simple phrases on them instead of individual words.** There were about ~~three hundred~~ **300** flash cards, **so I could not memorize them, especially because they were presented to me at random.** They never got mad at me if I didn't recognize a short, easy phrase, and they never made me run around if I didn't feel like it. At the end of two years, I was starting to feel a little confidence in my ability to recognize the most common English words and phrases. Boy, was I ever ready to go home!

Now we can actually picture how Jefferson's mother and sisters helped him learn to read.

Jefferson also realized he now had to fill out his new paragraph 6 on his high school experience with interesting, relevant details. He made a few lists and did a little freewriting to get his ideas flowing on this topic. He soon noticed that his freewriting included many of the details in the first part of his next paragraph. So he took the information he needed from his next paragraph to develop his new paragraph and used the rest of his old paragraph 6 to form a new paragraph 7:

Revision: **Then we came back to the United States, specifically Pennsylvania, and I was ready to start high school. My high school experiences gave me the strength and skills to attend college. I learned to read well and write effectively in high school. Then I was able to bring these new skills with me to college.** Luckily, my U.S. school allowed me to carry a tape recorder and a portable computer with me to all my classes. It helped me, I believe, because writing was especially difficult for me. It takes me about six or seven times as long as most people to write a short paper. Don't think I'm exaggerating. I have the ideas in my head; however, it is not always clear to me if they

are written correctly. The computer helps me with those
problems, making my life much easier and simpler.

Now Jefferson's new paragraph has the details it needs to take the reader from general to particular on the topic of his high school experiences.

Finally, Jefferson realized that his essay didn't tie together all his main ideas and details at the end. So he added a final paragraph to his essay.

Revision: **Without positive high school experiences, I would never have had the courage to attend college. I am grateful that I learned to read and write well in high school. With the help of my computer, I could write essays that earned good marks. In addition, I could handle essay questions on tests and exams and keep laboratory logs in my science courses.**

Jefferson's essay is now complete, moving back and forth from general to particular in the essay as a whole and an individual paragraphs.

Exercise R7-1

State the main idea and list the specific supporting details for paragraph 9 in Nancy Mairs's essay (pp. 279–280).

Exercise R7-2

Paragraph 3 in Jefferson's first draft (p. 294) would benefit from more specific details. List some possibilities.

Exercise R7-3

Read the following sentences and decide whether they are main ideas or details.

1. Honesty is almost always the best policy.
2. A whale, for example, is one species of mammal.
3. Judo and karate are both Asian martial arts.
4. Almost all the states that have established lotteries, among them Florida and Louisiana, have found that overall funding for education has dropped.
5. Two of my many assignments were to write a paper for political science and to begin research for my biology project.

Exercise R7-4

Read and complete the following main idea. Then add sentences with details that will fully develop it.

The most difficult subject for me in college has been _____ .

COLLABORATIVE WORK

After writing a draft of your own analyzing essay, exchange papers with a classmate, and do the following tasks.

A. Check to see whether the introduction contains mostly general (rather than specific) ideas and whether it ends with a thesis statement. Cross out any sentences that are too specific, and put an X at the end of the paragraph if it is missing a thesis.

B. Check each body paragraph to make sure its topic sentence is directly related to the thesis statement. Put brackets around any questionable topic sentences.

C. Make sure each topic sentence is developed with vivid, interesting details. Put a check mark in the left margin next to paragraphs that would benefit from a few more details.

Then return the paper to its writer, and use the information in this section to revise your draft.

TIPS FOR REVISING

Punctuation and Mechanics

Checklist for Editing Punctuation and Mechanics

✓ Does each sentence use correct **end punctuation** (a period, a question mark, or an exclamation point)?

✓ Are **commas** used correctly?

✓ Are **semicolons** used correctly?

✓ Are **colons** used correctly?

✓ Are **quotation marks** used correctly?

✓ Are the correct words, phrases, and titles **underlined** or **italicized**?

✓ Are **apostrophes** used correctly?

✓ Are **hyphens** used correctly?

✓ Are **dashes** used correctly?

✓ Are **parentheses** and **brackets** used correctly?

✓ Are **slashes** and **ellipses** used correctly?

✓ Is **capitalization** used correctly?

✓ Are **abbreviations** used correctly?

✓ Are **numbers** appropriately spelled or written in figures?

If the English language had no punctuation and mechanics, readers would have trouble making any sense out of writing. Words, sentences, and paragraphs would run together in one seemingly endless stream of babble, producing confusing, almost indecipherable prose.

Punctuation and mechanics are the signposts we need to communicate our messages as precisely as possible. Without signals, such as periods, commas, capital letters, and quotation marks, readers would have to interpret a string of words for themselves. Look at these lines from Nancy Mairs's essay "On Being a Cripple" with the signposts omitted:

> all the same if a cure were found would I take it in a minute

> I may be a cripple but i'm only occasionally a loony and never a saint

These sentences from Mairs's last paragraph are difficult to understand without signals telling us how to read them.

Punctuation

Writers communicate most effectively when they use punctuation marks according to rules that govern them. Some of these punctuation marks signal where sentences begin and end; other marks indicate pauses that help readers see how words, phrases, and clauses relate to one another; and still other punctuation marks are used to emphasize certain grammatical units. Correctly punctuated writing communicates clearly and accurately.

End Marks

One of the primary purposes of punctuation is to indicate where sentences begin and end. Three marks of punctuation signal the completion of a statement: the period, the question mark, and the exclamation point.

Period

Even though it is just a dot on a page, a period signals the reader to come to a complete stop. Periods are used at the end of three types of sentences: (1) **declarative sentences**, statements that state a simple fact or proposition; (2) **imperative sentences**, statements that give commands or directions; and (3) **indirect questions**, statements that include a request or question that is not stated directly. Look at these examples from Jefferson's first draft:

Statement:	Learning to read was the most difficult ordeal I have ever experienced.
Command:	Don't think I'm exaggerating.
Indirect Question:	I asked my parents why they couldn't bring me home.

As discussed on page 337, periods are also used with abbreviations (St., a.m., Dr.), decimals (1.2 million, 0.09 percent), and money figures ($5.60, $100.50).

Question Mark

Writers should use a question mark after a **direct question**, an independent clause that asks for an answer. Note these examples, the first of which comes from Jefferson's first draft:

Questions:	What was I supposed to do?
	Who left the refrigerator door open?
	When did you pay the electricity bill?
	Why was Jefferson late for work?
	How many pieces of pizza did Beano eat?

Question marks are also used in less common situations:

1. *Use a question mark with a direct question located within a direct quotation, a statement, or another question.*

    Questions: "What are we going to do?" she asked as tears rolled down her face.

    "How long has this been going on?" is the question we want answered.

    When did Jefferson ask, "Where is my check?"

2. *Use a question mark in parentheses if a date, fact, or figure is uncertain.*

    Uncertainty: Sophocles (496?–406 B.C.) was a great dramatist.

Exclamation Point

When writers want to express strong feeling or emotion, they use exclamation points after words, phrases, sentences, and commands—even in direct quotations.

Pow!

Man alive!

You can't be serious!

"Hold it down!" the teacher yelled at the boisterous students.

When you want to express mild emotion, a comma is sufficient in such structures:

Well, I can tell you stayed up all night.

Yes, we did do what you told us to do.

Exercise E7-1

Explain the end punctuation marks in all the sentences in paragraph 19 of "On Being a Cripple" (pp. 279–280).

Exercise E7-2

Explain the end punctuation marks for all the sentences in paragraph 4 of Jefferson's revised essay (pp. 298–299).

Exercise E7-3

Supply correct end punctuation for the sentences in the following paragraph.

(1) Read this paragraph carefully (2) Are you reading closely (3) If you are not, then you need to follow directions more closely (4) Research indicates that people

often read too fast, making retention a problem (5) You might ask what you can do to improve your retention skills (6) Stop (7) Before you begin reading, identify your reading purpose (8) Also, if there are questions at the end of the reading selection, look at them first (9) Don't you think that knowing the important points to look for will help you locate them as you read (10) Follow these tips and your retention should improve

Exercise E7-4

Write two sentences using each type of end punctuation mark—period, question mark, and exclamation point.

Commas

Whereas periods indicate complete stops in sentences, commas call for pauses; they act like yield signs or speed markers that tell readers to slow down. Since commas are used within sentences to indicate pauses, they are naturally the most common punctuation marks. The following general rules of comma usage will help you communicate more confidently and accurately:

1. *Use commas between words, phrases, and clauses in a series of three or more items.*

Words:	Jefferson bought **detergent, bread, and frozen yogurt** at the grocery store.
Phrases:	Jefferson **studies history, talks on the phone, and watches television** all at the same time.
Clauses:	**After you apologize, after you ask for forgiveness, and after you get down on your hands and knees,** I may take you back.

2. *Use commas to set off introductory words, phrases, and clauses.* Look at these examples from Jefferson's revised essay:

Words:	**Therefore,** for every half hour that we spent in the classroom working at our desks, we had to run around in the gym or on the playground for a half hour.
Phrases:	**At the end of two years,** I was starting to feel a little confidence in my ability to recognize the most common English words and phrases.
Clauses:	**If the words were written in someone's handwriting,** I was completely lost.

3. *Use commas to set off parenthetical expressions.*   Some introductory words and phrases can appear within sentences, interrupting the flow of the sentence. We call these elements **parenthetical expressions**, extra sentence elements that are not needed to understand the main clause. Look at these examples from Jefferson's revised draft:

Parenthetical Expressions:	"How would you feel, **Mom,** if you were separated from your family?" I would ask.
	It took several years of trial and error, **however,** before these problems became clear to me, my teachers, and my parents.
	It helped me, **I believe,** because writing was especially difficult for me.

4. *Use a comma before a coordinating conjunction* (for, and, nor, but, or, yet, so) *that joins two independent clauses.*   Look at this sentence from Jefferson's revised essay:

Coordinating Conjunction:	They never got mad at me if I didn't recognize a short, easy phrase, **and** they never made me run around if I didn't feel like it.

5. *Use commas to separate coordinate adjectives not joined by the conjunction* and, *as in this example from Jefferson's revised draft:*

Coordinate Adjectives:	They had **short, simple** phrases on them instead of individual words.

   One reliable test for commas in this location is to insert the word *and* between the two adjectives. If the sentence makes sense, you can replace *and* with a comma:

They had short **and** simple phrases on them instead of individual words.

If the sentence sounds strange when you insert *and* between the adjectives, do not use a comma.

Correct:	Jefferson keeps a miniature black poodle as a pet.
Incorrect:	Jefferson keeps a miniature **and** black poodle as a pet.

6. *Use commas to set off nonessential sentence elements.*   Some phrases and clauses that appear within sentences give additional information or clarify

details. Sometimes these phrases or clauses are not necessarily needed for the sentence to make sense; they are expendable or nonessential. Phrases and clauses that can be eliminated from the sentence are set off by commas; they are **nonessential** (or **nonrestrictive**). But phrases and clauses that are necessary in completing the sentence's meaning are **essential** (or **restrictive**) and are not set off by commas. Where phrases and dependent clauses are concerned, usually you can remove what lies between the commas (or before or after the comma, in some cases) without damaging the sentence's main message. Look at the following examples from Jefferson's writing:

Essential:	My friend **Doug** was always late and always running.
Nonessential:	For a few years in elementary school, I attended the Silmon Learning Center, **a well-known residential school that specializes in teaching students with learning disabilities.**
Essential:	They used flash cards **printed with the same type of print as most books.**
Nonessential:	The computer helps me with those problems, **making my life much easier and simpler.**

7. *Use commas for direct quotations to separate the speaker's exact words from the rest of the sentence.*

Quotations:	"I want to major in electrical engineering," Jefferson said.
	When he opened his eyes, he said, "I think I'll go back to sleep."

8. *Use commas to separate the digits in a number.*

Numbers:	The total enrollment for 1995 was **24,053**.

Exceptions to the rule include years (1997), page numbers (p. 1456), and serial numbers (584937098).

9. *Use commas to separate the parts of a geographical location.*   Notice that the name of a state is set off by two commas.

Places:	**Dubuque, Iowa,** is located west of the Mississippi River, and **Memphis, Tennessee,** is located east of the river.

TIPS FOR EDITING

10. *Use commas to separate the parts of an address.*

> **Address:**   My stepdad's address is **2105 Croydon Ave., Loves Park, IL 61111.**

11. *Use a comma to separate the parts of a full date.*

> **Date:**   Jefferson's parents bought their house on **July 14, 1983,** and have lived there ever since.

12. *Use a comma to set off a title that appears after a name.*

> **Title:**   One of the job applicants listed his name as **James M. Stockwell, Ph.D.**

Exercise E7-5

Explain the use of each comma in the first paragraph of "On Being a Cripple" (p. 277).

Exercise E7-6

Correct the comma errors in the following sentences from Jefferson's first draft. You may add commas where they are needed or remove unnecessary commas.

1. Nevertheless no matter how hard I tried I could not perceive the patterns in words especially if the type of print changed.
2. The teachers were very kind and helpful but I always ended up memorizing the books we read, because we spent so much time going over them.
3. However whenever anything unfamiliar was given to me I had to start all over again.
4. By the end of a month I was so exhausted that I did not even want to get out of bed, in the morning.
5. They never got mad at me if I didn't recognize a short easy phrase and they never made me run around if I didn't feel like it.

Exercise E7-7

Punctuate the following paragraph, adding commas wherever necessary.

Taking a class at college algebra to be exact was not my idea of summer fun. However I went back home after the spring semester to live with my parents and I also wanted to work at my old job since I knew the routine and most of the people I would be working with. My mom who is always thinking of things to keep me busy suggested that I take a class at the local community college. Thinking how this would cut into my free time I initially balked at the idea. But she said she would pay my tuition buy my books and give me $100 to boot. How could I refuse? I guess she was really desperate to get me out of the house and back into the classroom. Anyway I signed up for algebra a class I had been putting off at the university. Whenever I tried taking algebra in the past I always ended up dropping it. This time however was a different story. I not only made it through the class but I made a B an accomplishment I thought I could never achieve.

Exercise E7-8

Write a short dialogue between two speakers, making sure you use commas correctly.

Semicolon

Inexperienced writers often want to use semicolons interchangeably with commas and periods. When it comes to pausing in a sentence, however, a semicolon lies somewhere between a comma and a period. The guiding rule in using semicolons is to remember that they usually connect equal sentence elements. The following examples provide clear illustrations that will make semicolon usage less confusing:

1. *Use a semicolon to connect independent clauses that are closely related in thought and equal in structure.*

    Independent Clauses: Charles Dickens is my favorite author; I have read *A Tale of Two Cities* at least five times.

    In our house the kitchen table is a drop-off point for books, packages, mail, you name it; the living room couch is for eating so we can watch the news.

    Note that in the preceding examples the independent clauses concern the same subject, and they are mirror images in structure. Do not use semicolons if the independent clauses are unrelated or if the clauses are not similar in structure.

    Incorrect: We had to clean the apartment twice and make some minor repairs before our landlord refunded our deposit; he lives in another city.

    Correct: We had to clean the apartment twice and make some minor repairs before our landlord refunded our deposit; we also had to clean out our storage area and return our keys.

2. *Use semicolons with conjunctive adverbs and certain transitional phrases to join independent clauses.*   Commonly used conjunctive adverbs are *accordingly, indeed, otherwise, consequently, meanwhile, rather, furthermore, moreover, still, hence, nevertheless, therefore, however, nonetheless,* and *thus.* Some commonly used transitional phrases include *at any rate, on the one hand, for example, on the other hand,* and *in fact.*

    With Transitions: Jefferson had saved over $2,000 to help pay his tuition this fall; **however,** he had to withdraw $500 to repair his car.

TIPS FOR EDITING

> While many cities in America are experiencing an up-surge in crime, New York City is enjoying lower crime rates; **in fact,** in 1996 the murder rate was the lowest in over 20 years.

3. *Use semicolons to separate phrases and clauses that contain commas.*

Between Phrases and Clauses: Ursula's wild outfit consisted of a big, black, furry hat; a floral silk shirt in shades of pink, purple, blue, and green; and tall, clunky, massive platform shoes made of red and black metallic leather.

Some of Jodie Foster's movies are *Taxi Driver,* in which she co-starred with Robert DeNiro; *The Accused,* which won her an Oscar; and *Silence of the Lambs,* a thriller that brought her a second Academy Award.

Colon

Like a semicolon, a **colon** indicates a strong pause in a sentence, not a complete stop. A colon signals that something more is coming: a list, an explanation, a dialogue, or subtitles. Following are some examples:

1. *Use a colon to introduce a list.*

   Jefferson had to buy several things for his dorm room: a rug, a wastebasket, a broom, a comforter, and a fan.

2. *Use a colon to join two complete sentences when the second sentence summarizes or explains the first.*

   Roger Maris set a professional baseball record in 1961: No one else has come close to hitting 61 home runs in a season.

   The sentence after the colon can begin with either a capital or a lower-case letter.

3. *Use a colon to direct attention to a quotation or to introduce dialogue or a lengthy quotation.*

   We grew tired of hearing Tiger repeat his favorite saying: "If I'm lying, I'm dying."

   In Kate Chopin's novel *The Awakening,* the sea beckons the main character Edna Pontellier: "The water of the Gulf stretched out before her, gleaming with the million lights of the sun."

4. *Use colons in the following instances where lists or introductions are not involved.*

Time:	12:30 a.m. 7:15 p.m.
Biblical References:	Proverbs 24:12 (separating the chapter and verse numbers)
Bibliographic Entries:	Upper Saddle River, NJ: Prentice Hall, 1998 12 Oct. 1955: 134–40
Business Letter Salutations:	Dear Mr. Jones:
Ratios:	The probability is 4 : 1 that we will win.
Subtitles:	*Mosaics: Focusing on Essays*

Exercise E7-9

Explain the reasons for the semicolons and colons in the following sentences from Nancy Mairs's essay "On Being a Cripple" (pp. 277–288).

1. So many movements unbalanced me, and as I pulled the door open I fell over backward, landing fully clothed on the toilet seat with my legs splayed in front of me: the old beetle-on-its-back routine.
2. And I refuse to participate in the degeneration of the language to the extent that I deny that I have lost anything in the course of this calamitous disease; I refuse to pretend that the only differences between you and me are the various ordinary ones that distinguish any one person from another.
3. I have long since grown accustomed to them; and if they are vague, at least they hint at the truth.
4. My left leg is now so weak that I walk with the aid of a brace and a cane; and for distances I use an Amigo, a variation on the electric wheelchair that looks rather like an electrified kiddie car.
5. My world has, of necessity, been circumscribed by my losses, but the terrain left me has been ample enough for me to continue many of the activities that absorb me: writing, teaching, raising children and cats and plants and snakes, reading, speaking publicly about MS and depression, even playing bridge with people patient and honorable enough to let me scatter cards every which way without sneaking a peek.

Exercise E7-10

The following sentences adapted from Jefferson's essay are incorrectly punctuated. Supply semicolons and colons where needed.

1. My parents discovered when I was very young that I had a problem I was dyslexic.
2. They used flash cards printed with the same type as most books they had short, simple phrases on them instead of individual words.
3. I had the ideas in my head however it is not always clear to me if they are written correctly.

Exercise E7-11

Supply semicolons and colons in the following paragraphs where needed.

Last semester my friend Doug and I decided to take a trip to Florida during spring break. Most of my friends were headed to Daytona Beach or Fort Lauderdale however, we decided to go to Pensacola since we didn't think it would be as crowded.

A few days before we were going to leave we started assembling everything we would need for our beach vacation suntan lotion, four bottles to be exact, beach chairs, a large plastic ice chest, a boom box, a couple of striped umbrellas, and huge beach towels. Of course, we had some clothes and our snacks for the ride down. We planned to leave at 530 in the morning, so we didn't want to be rummaging around in the dark trying to make last-minute adjustments. My mom, who is a travel agent, had made our reservations at a beachside inn she had stayed there a couple of years before and said it was nice. Plus, it was reasonably priced, well within our budget.

Exercise E7-12

Write five sentences, three with semicolons and two with colons.

Quotation Marks

Quotation marks always appear in pairs; they can be double (" ") or single (' '). They draw attention to what is located between them, serving as indicators of importance. Quotation marks are most often used to indicate a speaker's or writer's exact words:

"I hope I get a good grade on my essay," Jefferson said.

Jefferson said, "If I don't get a good grade, I will be very disappointed."

In his essay about how he learned to read, Jefferson says that he was "always very bright and interested in schoolwork."

Note that some punctuation marks are placed inside the quotation marks in these examples. Other punctuation marks, however, fall outside the final quotation mark:

Question Mark:	Did you say, "I will not go to the party"?
Exclamation Point:	Don't say "ain't"!
Semicolon:	When she took the witness stand, the defendant's wife said, "I know nothing"; then she slumped over and began crying.
Colon:	Several things made the wedding reception the "event of the year": excellent food, beautiful people, and a great band.

When you restate or paraphrase a speaker's or writer's words, no quotation marks are needed:

Restatements:	Jefferson hopes to make a good grade on his essay.
	In his essay about learning how to read, Jefferson says that he always liked school and did well, except when it came to reading.

Single quotation marks surround a quotation within another quotation:

Single Quotation Marks:	"Why did she write 'elliptical' on my paper?" Jefferson asked.
	"I think Amanda's exact words to Tom are 'Go to the moon—you selfish dreamer,'" the teacher said.

Besides indicating dialogue and a writer's exact words, quotations are used in other instances:

1. *Use quotation marks to indicate the titles of short literary, musical, and media works:* poems, songs, book chapters, short stories, speeches, radio and TV episodes, reference books, and articles in magazines, journals, and newspapers. Longer works are underlined or italicized.

Short Works:	Alanis Morissette's song "Hand in My Pocket" appears on her *Jagged Little Pill* album.
	For my American literature class, I wrote a paper about the Robert Frost poem "Mending Wall."

2. *Use quotation marks to focus attention on a word used as a word.*

Emphasis:	Do you know what the word "dowager" means?

Underlining/Italics

Just as quotation marks highlight short phrases and titles, italicizing and underlining isolate elements, drawing the reader's attention to them. When words are written in italics, they appear in a slanted script form: *This sentence is italicized.*

Most book publishers use italics, and most up-to-date computers have an italics function. If you cannot indicate italics on your computer, word processor, or typewriter, you can underline the highlighted word.

Following are specific instances where italics or underlining should be used:

1. *Italicize/underline to set off certain titles:*

Books:	*Encyclopedia Britannica*

Plays:	*Romeo and Juliet*
Long poems:	*Evangeline*
Magazines and journals:	*Vogue, Journal of Accountancy*
Pamphlets:	*Reducing Heart Attack Risk*
Movies:	*Jurassic Park*
TV Shows:	*60 Minutes*
Radio shows:	*The Green Hornet*
Operas:	*Madame Butterfly*
Albums:	*Smells Like Teen Spirit*
Paintings:	*Blue Boy*
Sculptures:	*The Thinker*
Art exhibits:	*A Renoir Retrospective*
Trains:	*The City of New Orleans*
Ships:	*Queen Elizabeth*
Aircraft:	*Spirit of St. Louis*
Spacecraft:	*Apollo 13*

2.   *Italicize/underline scientific names, foreign words, and foreign phrases that are not commonly used by English speakers and writers.*

The scientific name for dogs is **Canis familiaris.**

In **A Streetcar Named Desire**, a Mexican woman appears several times saying, "**Flores para los muertos**," which means "Flowers for the dead."

3.   *When you want to emphasize a word, letter, or number, or when such items refer to themselves, you can use italics or quotation marks.*

If you plan to be empathetic, you need to learn how to **listen**.

How many **s**'s are in Mississippi?

Jefferson's social security number has four **3**'s.

Exercise E7-13

Explain the usage of quotation marks and italics in the following sentences from "On Being a Cripple."

1.   "Cripple" seems to me a clean word, straightforward and precise.

2. I subscribe to George Orwell's thesis that "the slovenliness of our language makes it easier for us to have foolish thoughts."

3. As a result, I spend a lot of time *in extremis* and, impatient with limitation, I tend to ignore my fatigue until my body breaks down in some way and forces rest.

4. When I got home an hour or so later, my daughter greeted me with "What have you done to yourself?"

5. I have moved through a process similar to that outlined by Elizabeth Kübler-Ross in *On Death and Dying*.

Exercise E7-14

Edit the following paragraphs, adding quotation marks and italics where needed.

When I have a couple of hours to kill, I love to hang out at Media World, a huge store that has every book, video, and CD you can imagine. My mom asks me Why do you spend so much time there. Why don't you just go to the library. To me the library is boring. There's always something happening at Media World.

Usually I just skim through books, but sometimes I settle down and read. In fact, I read The Bridges of Madison County curled up in one of Media World's easy chairs. Sometimes I flip through magazines like Glamour and Elle, and sometimes I'll buy them if there's a good article I want to keep. For example, Take It Off, Keep It Off, an article in last month's Cosmopolitan, helped me drop five pounds.

Sometimes I look at CDs. You can even listen to the most popular ones. Personally, I like classic pop and rock, like Carole King's Tapestry, my all-time favorite. It has great songs—Natural Woman and Smackwater Jack, to name a couple.

If I get bored with books or music, I go to the video section. Personally, I like old tearjerker movies like Madame X and Imitation of Life, two Lana Turner classics. I also enjoy the classic TV videos like I Love Lucy. If I buy anything, it's usually a video because I like to watch movies again and again.

I guess you could say when it comes to Media World, the word boredom certainly doesn't come to mind. See you there!

Exercise E7-15

Write a short dialogue between two speakers, at least eight to ten sentences. Be sure to use punctuation marks correctly and indent when speakers change.

Apostrophe

An apostrophe looks like a single quotation mark, but its function is quite different. Whereas quotation marks highlight words, an apostrophe indicates ownership, plural, or the omission of letters in a contraction.

The rules of possession can be confusing and difficult to remember because of the many exceptions and special cases. Refer to the following guidelines to make apostrophe usage a less difficult task:

1. *Use an apostrophe and an -s with singular nouns and indefinite pronouns to show ownership.*

   the student's book, the cat's collar, the door's knob, the fish's gills, the bus's tires, the boss's schedule, the class's project, Jefferson's essay, Russ's car, anyone's money, nobody's pop, someone's magazine, Mr. Williams's check.

2. *Add just an apostrophe for plural nouns ending in -s. For plural nouns that do not end in -s, add an apostrophe and an s.*

   the students' papers, the cats' collars, the fishes' gills, the buses' tires, the bosses' schedules, the classes' projects, the children's paintings, the women's dresses

3. *If two or more nouns share ownership, add an apostrophe or an –s' to the last noun. If both nouns individually show ownership, add an apostrophe and an –s to both nouns.*

   Shared: Tracy and Diana's apartment is on Church Street.

   My aunt and uncle's car is a 1966 Cadillac.

   Individual: Tracy's and Diana's parents both live in Milwaukee.

   My aunt's and uncle's bowling averages lead their leagues.

4. *When compound nouns show ownership, place the apostrophe and -s after the last word.*

   father-in-law's golf clubs, someone else's mail

5. *Use an apostrophe and an -s with certain adjectives that refer to time or amounts.*

   yesterday's headlines, the day's ending, the year's inflation rate

6. *Use an apostrophe to indicate the plural of a letter, number, sign, abbreviation, or a word discussed as a word.*

   There are two r's and two s's in the word *embarrassment*.

   The computer kept printing 8's and #'s at the top of every page.

   Jefferson's essay had too many *etc.*'s.

The man's speech contained too many *consequently*'s and *nevertheless*'s.

The apostrophe may be omitted in cases where it appears to indicate plurality and not ownership.

CD-ROMs   MIAs

Also note that where dates are concerned, the apostrophe is optional, unless part of the date has been left out.

Optional: The 1960's was a turbulent decade.

The 1960s saw three great American leaders assassinated.

Required: Dresses from the '30s featured side zippers and padded shoulders.

7. Use an apostrophe in a contraction to indicate that letters have been omitted.

Contractions: doesn't, can't, she'd, would've, it's

Exercise E7-16

Explain the use of each apostrophe in the following sentences from "On Being a Cripple."

1. And I certainly don't like "handicapped," which implies that I have deliberately been put at a disadvantage, by whom I can't imagine (my God is not a Handicapper General), in order to equalize chances in the great race of life.
2. I subscribe to George Orwell's thesis that "the slovenliness of our language makes it easier for us to have foolish thoughts."
3. Multiple sclerosis is a chronic degenerative disease of the central nervous system, in which the myelin that sheathes the nerves is somewhat eaten away and scar tissue forms in the its place, interrupting the nerves' signals.
4. Perhaps I would not have if I'd thought I had the stamina to return to a full-time job as a technical editor; but I've enjoyed my studies.
5. And far from hiding me, they're forever dragging me by racks of fancy clothes or through teeming school corridors, or welcoming gaggles of friends while I'm wandering through the house in Anne's filmy pink babydoll pajamas.

Exercise E7-17

Add apostrophes in the following sentences from Jefferson's first draft.

1. But the schools that I attended in the 80s simply couldnt help me learn to read.
2. They thought I could read the books pages, and I thought I could read them, too.
3. I especially had trouble with words that had ds and bs in them.

TIPS FOR EDITING

4. During the Parents Day visit at that school, when I was in the 5th grade, my parents realized that I still didnt know how to read.
5. It didnt take me long at that school to become extremely discouraged.

Exercise E7-18

Edit the following paragraph, adding apostrophes where needed.

Do you play the lottery? I dont because Im saving my money for next semesters tuition. But my grandmother plays anything she can get her hands on. When shes not going to bingo somewhere, shes picking numbers or scratching cards. Her favorite number is 3, so anything with 3s is a winner to her. In fact, she did win $1,200 earlier this year in Little Lotto. Last week she won $250 in the instant lottery by finding four $s when she scratched her card. But how much has she spent over the years? Even she admits that shes probably pretty deep in the hole.

Exercise E7-19

Write sentences using the following words and phrases.

1. century's
2. Larry's and William's
3. Larry and William's
4. it's
5. and's

Hyphen

Hyphens perform dual functions. They can either separate parts of words or join words to form compounds. If you ever took a typing course, you learned about dividing words at the end of a line. Words are separated between syllables, the guiding rule. Of course, two syllable words should not be divided, and you should never isolate a one-letter syllable.

Incorrect: Jefferson told his mother that after lunch he was go—ing to buy new tires for his car.

Life magazine had some sad pictures of several peo—ple killed in the avalanche in France.

Since computers help us avoid dividing words, we usually don't have to worry about such problems. Consult a dictionary if you do have questions about where a break falls in a word.

Using hyphens to make compound words can be confusing because some compounds are divided with punctuation and others are not. The best advice is try to commit troublesome words to memory or to rely on a dictionary. Following is a list for quick reference.

Hyphenated Compounds:	father-in-law, walkie-talkie, daughter-in-law, water-skier, run-of-the-mill, great-grandfather, stick-in-the-mud, poet-songwriter, four-year-old, bull's-eye, Clinton-Gore
Unhyphenated Compounds:	schoolteacher, school board, schoolchildren, cab driver, hope chest, horsehair, lunch break, bedroll

Hyphens are also used in the following instances:

1. *Use a hyphen to connect the prefixes* all-, anti-, ex-, great-, *and* self- *and the suffix* -elect *to other words.*

   all-time, ex-husband, great-grandson, self-reliant, president-elect

2. *Use a hyphen to join two or more words that function together as an adjective. Do not use hyphens if the compound adjective does not come before a noun.*

   We bought a late-eighteenth-century painting at the auction.

   At the auction we bought a painting dating from the late eighteenth century.

   I would agree that Jefferson is a well-dressed young man.

   When Jefferson attended the wedding, he was well dressed.

3. *Do not use hyphens with adverbs ending in* -ly.

   The neatly arranged shelf was thrown into disarray when the baby bumped up against it.

   Paula's hastily planned vacation was still a success.

4. *Use a hyphen to join a capital letter to a noun or a participle.*

   A-bomb, U-turn, S-shaped

5. *Use hyphens to avoid confusion in meaning or pronunciation.*

   My mother plans on re-covering our dining room chairs.

   Jefferson gets along well with his co-workers.

6. *Use hyphens when giving scores, indicating life spans, and spelling fractions.*

Scores:	The Tigers won the championship over the Hurricanes 9-8.
Dates:	Emily Dickinson (1830-1886) is generally regarded as one of America's outstanding poets.
Fractions:	Approximately one-fourth of the students have not completed their research project.

Dash

A dash is twice as long as a hyphen. In fact, to indicate a dash you should type two hyphens (--). Unlike a hyphen, a dash interrupts the flow of a sentence, indicating a pause stronger than a comma.

A dash focuses attention on the words that are separated from the rest of the sentence. Used singly, a dash will highlight a word or phrase at the end of the sentence:

> When I was in the hospital, all I could think of was my favorite food—shrimp.

> Jefferson plans on buying a new car this fall—that is, if he can sell his old one.

Phrases or clauses inserted into the middle of a sentence are punctuated by two dashes:

> Our choice for dinner—the oldest Italian restaurant in town—was closed because of a broken water main.

> Tennessee Williams's play *Cat on a Hot Tin Roof*—set in the South on a plantation—was made into a movie starring Paul Newman and Elizabeth Taylor.

In the preceding examples, the phrases set off by dashes contain no internal punctuation. Therefore, commas could have been used in place of the dashes if the author did not want to emphasize the inserted information. But when the additional phrases and clauses contain internal punctuation, dashes are needed for clarity. Usually these insertions are explanations, summaries, or parenthetical expressions that could be omitted.

> The characteristics of a good employee—maturity, energy, honesty, and punctuality—are sometimes hard to find in potential workers.

> Jefferson's grandparents—they live in Georgia near Savannah—are coming for a visit next month.

Another common use of dashes is to indicate interruptions in dialogue, stops and starts that communicate halting speech:

"Why are you—wait, calm down—we can work things out—now, don't cry," Kevin told Melinda as he tried to smooth things out on the phone.

Parentheses

Parentheses ( ) and dashes serve similar separating functions. However, parentheses always work in pairs to enclose explanatory or supplementary material. While they are not such abrupt interrupters as dashes, parentheses provide an additional choice in relaying extra information.

When you use parentheses, add punctuation as needed, as in the following examples:

Senator Carol Moseley-Braun (D-Ill.) was first elected in 1992.

We had a guest speaker in class, the local president of the National Rifle Association (NRA).

In Jefferson's short story that he wrote for his creative writing class, the main characters get married in the end. (Actually, they get married before the ending, but the story implies that trouble lies ahead.)

Note that if a complete sentence is in parentheses, the period goes *inside* the parentheses.

Special uses of parentheses include the following:

1. *Use parentheses to indicate a person's life span.*

    Dates: Margaret Sanger (1883–1966) was an American nurse who advocated birth control and founded the organization that came to be known as the Planned Parenthood Federation.

2. *Use parentheses to mark numbers and letters when indicating items in a series.*

    Series: My boss gave me three things to do my first day alone at the office: (1) answer correspondence, (2) file receipts, and (3) post late payments on accounts.

3. *Use parentheses with quotations from secondary sources to indicate reference information.*

    References: According to Marcus Cunliffe, "there is still a question as to whether there is an American language" (11).

Jim is "a lone wolf who wants to belong," but he is handicapped by his social ineptness (Weales 40).

Brackets

Like parentheses, brackets work in pairs [ ] and contain inserted information. However, brackets are used far less frequently than parentheses and only in special cases:

1. *Use brackets to add clarifying information within a direct quotation.*

   Additions: "We [the school board] plan to iron out the budget and present it at our next regularly scheduled meeting," the superintendent said.

   "I think that she [Janet] is the most promising student in our acting class," the professor said.

2. *Indicate errors in quoted material by placing the word* sic (*Latin for "thus" or "so"*) *within brackets.*

   Errors: The coach wrote "Don't loose [sic] any more games!" on the blackboard.

   Billy Bonds writes in his autobiography that he "never new [sic] real love" until he met his wife.

3. *Use brackets to add words or minor changes to quoted material in order to clarify information or make the quotation fit grammatically within the remainder of the sentence.*

   Changes: Of my performance, the reviewer said that "in the second act [I need] stronger voice projection."

Slash

A slash is sometimes called a diagonal because it is a slanted line (/). The rarely used slash functions as a separator in these cases:

1. *Use a slash, preceded and followed by a space, to separate lines of poetry quoted within a sentence.*

   Poetry: Throughout "The Love Song of J. Alfred Prufrock," the speaker offers the refrain "In the room the women come and go / Talking of Michelangelo."

2. *Use a slash (with no spaces) to indicate alternative choices between words and expressions.*

Alternatives: Use comparison/contrast to write your essay.

I signed up for step aerobics for a pass/fail grade.

3. *Use a slash to separate the day, month, and year in dates and to separate the numerator and denominator in a fraction.*

Dates: The birth date on the tombstone read 12/25/25.

Fractions: Jefferson's chest measures 42 inches while his waist is 32 1/2 inches.

Ellipsis

An ellipsis consists of three periods with spaces (. . .) and shows the omission of words or a pause.

1. *An ellipsis is most often used to indicate that material was omitted from a quotation.*

If an ellipsis appears in the middle of a sentence, leave a space before and after each period when typing:

Omission: "By attending college . . . I was able to fulfill a lifelong dream," the author recalls.

If the ellipsis occurs at the end of a sentence, the ellipsis is placed after the period:

Omission: The article said that "Rudy Galindo almost gave up on skating. . . . After losing his coach and his brother to AIDS, he was drained."

2. *An ellipsis is used to show that a line or more of poetry is missing when you quote four or more lines from a work. The ellipsis should extend the entire length of the line:*

Omission: But sometimes everything I write
with the threadbare art of my eye
seems a snapshot,

. . . .

lurid, rapid, garish, grouped,
heightened from life,
yet paralyzed by fact.

3. *An ellipsis may also be used to indicate a pause. Just remember to add a space before and after the ellipsis:*

Pause: Either you come home early **. . .** or I won't be here when you get back.

Exercise E7-20

Explain the use of each hyphen, dash, parentheses, and slash in the following sentences from "On Being a Cripple."

1. I want them to see me as a tough customer, one to whom the fates/gods/viruses have not been kind, but who can face the brutal truth of her existence squarely.
2. My life holds realities—harsh ones, some of them—that no right-minded human being ought to accept without grumbling.
3. I am lucky that my predilections were already solitary, sedentary, and bookish— unlike the world-famous French cellist I have read about, or the young woman I talked with one long afternoon who wanted only to be a jockey.
4. My students, with one anonymous exception (in an end-of-the-semester evaluation), have been unperturbed by my disability.
5. During its course, which is unpredictable and uncontrollable, one may lose vision; hearing; speech; the ability to walk; control of bladder and/or bowels; strength in any or all extremities; sensitivity to touch, vibration, and/or pain; potency; coordination of movements—the list of possibilities is lengthy and, yes, horrifying.

Exercise E7-21

Add hyphens, dashes, parentheses, ellipses, slashes, and brackets to punctuate the following paragraph correctly.

When I went to college, I decided to go through fraternity rush a good decision that has changed my life. After all, I was a seventeen year old freshman at a huge university 1,000 miles away from home. And I knew no one. You might wonder why I went to a university so far away, but I received a full tuition scholarship. Before the actual events started, I attended a seminar where each of the fraternity presidents and housemothers talked about his her organization. Then rush a flurry of parties, special events, dances, receptions, and more parties began. I admit that I was really tired when I went to classes because I stayed up so late visiting the different frats. But after the week was over I had decided I wanted to join either Theta Xi 42 members or SAE Sigma Alpha Epsilon over 100 members. I thought the two fraternities would give me a good choice between a smaller group and a larger organization. In the end, I received bids to both. My choice was Theta Xi by the way, my grandfather was a Theta Xi, too.

Exercise E7-22

Write one sentence using each of the following punctuation marks correctly: hyphen, dash, parentheses, ellipsis, slash, and brackets.

Mechanics

Mechanic is a word that calls to mind a person tinkering with a car or something else mechanical, trying to find out how the machine works—or doesn't work. A mechanic analyzing the technical aspects of a machine often follows guidelines and makes changes to ensure that a particular piece of equipment works correctly and efficiently. The word *mechanics* also refers to language guidelines for writers that make communication clear, coherent, and as concise as possible. Mechanics includes the rules governing the use of capitalization, abbreviation, and numbers, conventions that you should follow to make your writing technically sound.

Capitalization

When words are capitalized in a sentence, they demand special attention. The capital letter may signify the beginning of a new sentence, or it may designate a specific person, place, or thing. Studying the following capitalization rules for sentences and proper nouns will help you emphasize the correct words in your sentences for maximum effect.

Sentence Capitalization

1. *Always capitalize the first word in each sentence and question, as Jefferson does in his explaining essay.*

    Learning to read was the most difficult ordeal I have ever experienced.

    What was I supposed to do?

2. *Capitalize the first word in interjections and commands that are written for effect.*

    Hey! What are you doing?

    Get out of here!

3. *Capitalize the first word in a quotation if it is a complete sentence or question.*

    "**T**he championship game is Sunday," Jefferson said.

    "**W**hat time do you want to leave?" Rob asked.

    Mae West said, "**B**etween two evils, I always pick the one I never tried before."

4. *Capitalize O and I (a pronoun) wherever they appear in a sentence.*

    The first line reads "Be still, **O** my heart."

    I had to withdraw $100 from my savings account so that **I** could pay for my books.

Capitalization of Proper Nouns

Common nouns (*car, beach, university*) are general classifications of persons, places, things, or ideas and are not capitalized. Proper nouns are specific people, locations, or things and are capitalized, as the following examples illustrate:

1. *Capitalize all proper nouns—names of specific people, places, and things.*

People:	Jefferson, Michael Jackson
Places:	Italy, Coney Island, Chicago, Muscle Beach
Deities:	God, Buddha, Allah
Ideas:	New Criticism

    These rules also apply to the following references:

Specific buildings:	World Trade Center, Superdome
Businesses:	Sparkle Cleaners, Sears
Corporations:	General Motors, Hanes
Organizations and associations:	Salvation Army, Young Democrats
Institutions:	Riverview Nursing Home, St. Michael's Hospital, Purdue University
Teams:	Atlanta Falcons, Minnesota Twins
Geographical locations:	Mississippi River, Lincoln County, Pacific Coast Highway, Lockwood Avenue
Special events:	Final Four, Academy Awards
Brand names:	Chrysler LeBaron, Mellow Yellow
Religions:	Baptist, Islam
Languages:	Japanese, Dutch
Nationalities:	Chinese, Colombian

2. *Capitalize titles (and their abbreviations) used with the names of people.*

    Miss Abigail Box; **Mr.** Terrence Mathews; **Dr.** Grant Williams; President Clinton; Sergeant Arnold

3. *Capitalize words referring to relatives—mother, father, grandmother, grandfather, aunt, uncle—when used with a proper name or as a substitute for a name. Do not capitalize these words if a possessive pronoun (my, his, her, our, their) comes before them.*

My father is younger than Uncle Frank.

I know that Mother is upset because my aunt refuses to come home for Christmas.

4. *Capitalize the adjective forms of proper nouns.*

American, Shakespearean, English, Buddhist, Martian

5. *Capitalize the first and last words in titles and all other words except articles* (a, an, the), *short prepositions* (of, to, at, etc.), *and conjunctions* (for, and, etc.)*:*

Books:	*The Last of the Mohicans*
Newspapers:	*The New York Times*
Magazines:	*Sports Illustrated*
Short stories:	"A Rose for Emily"
Poems:	"The Passing of Arthur"
Plays:	*Love Is the Doctor*
Songs:	"Hand in My Pocket"
Albums and CDs:	"*The Woman in Me*"
Movies:	*A Place in the Sun*
Television shows:	*Party of Five*
Radio Programs:	*Kasey Kasem's Top 40 Countdown*
Articles:	"Ten Steps to Success"
Works of art:	the *Mona Lisa*
Computer programs:	*Windows, The Writer's Toolkit*

6. *Capitalize days of the week* (Saturday), *months* (May), *and special holidays* (Labor Day).

7. *Capitalize the names of historical events* (Custer's Last Stand), *time periods or eras* (the Renaissance), *and documents* (the Declaration of Independence).

8. *Capitalize sections of the country but not words that indicate directions.*

When you drive east from Colorado, you will find yourself in the Midwest in 12 hours.

9. *Capitalize specific course titles.*

The teacher for **P**sychology 201 is listed in the schedule book, but I have no ideas who my **s**ociology instructor will be.

Exercise E7-23

Explain why the italicized words in the following sentences from "On Being a Cripple" are capitalized or lowercased.

1. And I certainly don't like "*handicapped*," which implies that I have deliberately been put at a disadvantage, by whom I can't imagine (my *God* is not a *Handicapper General*), in order to equalize chances in the great race of life.
2. I subscribe to *George Orwell's* thesis that "*the* slovenliness of our language makes it easier for us to have foolish thoughts."
3. I swayed through countless dim hours in the arms of one man or another under the scattered shot of light from mirrored balls, and gyrated through countless more as *Tab Hunter* and *Johnny Mathis* gave way to the *Rolling Stones, Creedence Clearwater Revival, Cream.*
4. Lest I begin to sound like *Pollyanna*, however, let me say that I don't like having MS.
5. I like to sit on my front steps with my husband, drinking *Amaretto* and smoking a cigar, as we imagine our counterparts in *Leningrad* and make sure the sun gets down once more behind the sharp childish scrawl of the *Tucson Mountains.*

Exercise E7-24

Find the capitalization errors in paragraph 4 of Jefferson's first draft (p. 294), and correct them.

Exercise E7-25

Correct the 15 capitalization errors in the following paragraph, and explain each correction.

Whenever my family goes on a vacation, my parents spend weeks, even months, planning the excursion. After we all voice our opinions about where we'd like to go, my Mother and father make the final decision. Then mom maps out the route we'll take, and Dad makes the hotel reservations and other necessary arrangements. Last year we drove from our home in Southern Missouri to las Vegas. Since we'd never been through the rocky mountains, we took a Northern route through Colorado, a little out of the way but worth it. Our trusty dodge van chugged up the steep Mountains just fine. We even stopped and visited with Jim Perkins, a retired army Sergeant who served with my dad in the Vietnam Conflict. After two and a half days of driving, we pulled into Vegas and were immediately dazzled by the strip, the long stretch of brightly colored Casinos and hotels. We had a reservation at the hacienda, an older economy hotel that was our base for four days of fun.

Exercise E7-26

Write a sentence using a specific noun for each of the following categories.

1. a movie
2. a city and state
3. a model of car or truck
4. a singing group
5. a class you have taken

Abbreviations and Initialisms

Many years ago, before typewriters and computers made writing a faster process, people wrote in longhand. To save time and space, writers of English began developing abbreviations, shortened forms of words that are generally accepted by the educated public. Over the years, abbreviations have taken on increasing importance as our society has become more concerned with brevity and efficiency in all areas.

To use abbreviations effectively, you need to know the basic guidelines that govern their use. Abbreviations are used most often with titles, locations, and government and business references.

Titles

1. *Always abbreviate titles before proper names.*

   Mr. George Jenkins, **Mrs.** Linda Kobler, **Ms.** Penny Miley, **Dr.** Tywan Jackson, **Rev.** William Baxter

2. *Abbreviate titles after proper nouns, including academic degrees.*

   James A. Woods, **Sr.**; Thad V. Hall, **Jr.**; **B.A.** (bachelor of arts); **B.S.** (bachelor of sciences); **M.A.** (master of arts); **M.S.** (master of science); **M.B.A.** (master of business administration); **M.F.A.** (master of fine arts); **Ed.D.** (doctor of education); **Ph.D.** (doctor of philosophy); **R.N.** (registered nurse); **M.D.** (doctor of medicine); **D.D.S.** (doctor of dental science); **D.M.V.** (doctor of veterinary medicine); **LL.D.** (doctor of laws). Remember to avoid redundancies such as **Dr.** Candace Carroll, **D.D.S.**

3. *Abbreviate religious, military, and governmental titles when used with an entire proper name. When used with a last name only, spell out the title.*

   Rev. John Grayson will be the speaker tonight.

   Reverend Grayson will speak tonight.

Locations

1. *Abbreviate certain places commonly known by their abbreviations, such as D.C. and U.S. Remember to abbreviate U.S. only when used as an adjective.*

    Countries: The **U.S.** flag is flying at half-mast today.

                           Sang's family has been in the **United States** for five years.

2. *Abbreviate the names of states and countries in addresses; otherwise, spell them out.*

    States: The business is located at 1014 Harrison, Seattle, **WA** 98119.

                           Jefferson wants to move to Seattle, **Washington**.

    Refer to the following list of U.S. Postal Service abbreviations for the fifty states:

AL	Alabama	MO	Missouri
AK	Alaska	NB	Nebraska
AZ	Arizona	NV	Nevada
AR	Arkansas	NH	New Hampshire
CA	California	NJ	New Jersey
CO	Colorado	NM	New Mexico
CT	Connecticut	NY	New York
DE	Delaware	NC	North Carolina
FL	Florida	ND	North Dakota
GA	Georgia	OH	Ohio
HI	Hawaii	OK	Oklahoma
ID	Idaho	OR	Oregon
IL	Illinois	PA	Pennsylvania
IN	Indiana	RI	Rhode Island
IA	Iowa	SC	South Carolina
KS	Kansas	SD	South Dakota
KY	Kentucky	TN	Tennessee
LA	Louisiana	TX	Texas
ME	Maine	UT	Utah
MD	Maryland	VT	Vermont
MA	Massachusetts	VA	Virginia
MI	Michigan	WA	Washington
MN	Minnesota	WV	West Virginia
MS	Mississippi	WI	Wisconsin
MT	Montana	WY	Wyoming

3. *Abbreviate certain locations when used in specific addresses only.*

    Addresses: Jefferson's grandfather lives at 212 Spring **St.**

                           Jefferson's grandfather lives on Spring **Street**.

Government and Business References

1. *Abbreviate the names of certain government agencies and organizations.*

    CIA (Central Intelligence Agency); **FCC** (Federal Communications Commission); **FDIC** (Federal Deposit Insurance Corporation); **GOP** (Grand Old Party, the Republican Party); **IRS** (Internal Revenue Service; **NATO** (North Atlantic Treaty Organization); **OAS** (Organization of American States); **UN** (United Nations)

2. *Abbreviate certain business firms and labor organizations.*

    ABC (American Broadcasting Corporation); **CBS** (Capitol Broadcasting Corporation); **HBO** (Home Box Office); **GM** (General Motors); **NBC** (National Broadcasting Corporation); **TWA** (Trans World Airlines); **UAW** (United Auto Workers)

3. *Abbreviate parts of business names.*

    Bros. (Brothers), **Co.** (Company), **Corp.** (Corporation), **Inc.** (Incorporated), and **Ltd.** (Limited)

Other Common Abbreviations

1. *Use a.m. and p.m. with numbers to denote specific times of day.*

    The plane leaves at 10:10 **a.m.**, not 10:10 **p.m.**

2. *Use B.C. (before Christ) or B.C.E. (before current era) to denote time before Christ, and use A.D. (anno domini) or C.E. (current era) to denote years after Christ's birth.*

    425 **B.C.**, 425 **B.C.E.**; 2000 **A.D.**, 2000 **C.E.**

3. *Use **F** (degrees Fahrenheit), **C** (degrees Celsius), **mph** (miles per hour), **km** (kilometers), **rpm** (revolutions per minute), and **mg** (milligrams) with numbers.*

    85° **F**, 400 **rpm**, 30 **km**, 100 **mph**

4. *Use the symbols ° (degrees), % (percent), and $ (dollars) when referring to specific quantities or statistics except in the body of essays where the words* degrees *and* percent *should be spelled out.*

    70°, 70%, $70

    70 **degrees**, 70 **percent**, and $70 in essays.

In Chapter 6, both the professional and student restatement essays illustrate the use of percent in sentences (spelled out) and as statistics in parentheses (with the symbol %).

5. *Abbreviate certain Latin terms in documentation notes.*

    c. (*circa*, meaning "about"); **e.g.** (*exempli gratia*, meaning "for example"); **et al.** (*et alii*, meaning "and others"); **etc.** (*et cetera*, meaning "and so forth"); and **vs.** (*versus*, meaning "against").

Exercise E7-27

Correct the abbreviation errors in the following sentences, which appear in their correct forms in Nancy Mairs's essay "On Being a Cripple."

1. Sat. afternoon, the bldg. deserted, I was free to laugh aloud as I wriggled back to my feet, my voice bouncing off the yellowish tiles from all directions.
2. I lead, on the whole, an ordinary life, prob. rather like the one I would have led had I not had MS.
3. Deprived of legal divorce, the child can at least deny the mother's disability, even her existence, forgetting to tell her about recitals and PTA mtgs., refusing to accompany her to stores or church or the movies, never inviting frnds. to the house.
4. Though usually white and often blnd., she may be black, Hisp., Asian, or Native Am., so long as she is unusually sleek.
5. Then one summer day I set out with Geo. and the children across the desert for a vacation in Calif.

Exercise E7-28

Correct the abbreviation errors in the following sentences adapted from the first draft of Jefferson's analyzing essay.

1. They had a talk with the teachers and the headmaster, Mister Smithers.
2. If we were late for breakfast, we had to go run around the track for at least fifteen min. before breakfast.
3. His position with Trans World Airlines allowed the whole family to accompany him.
4. At the end of two years I was starting to feel a little confidence in my ability to recognize the most common Eng. words and phrases.
5. Then we came back to the U.S., specifically Penn.

Exercise E7-29

Correct the abbreviation errors in the following paragraph.

   Last week in my psych. class we had a guest speaker, Dr. Andrew Spruel, M.D. He began private practice 30 yrs. ago (1969 anno domini) in Calif. after serving as a sergeant in the United States army for a decade. He also served as a consultant for The Wellness Corporation, a business that specializes in helping people overcome addictions. He says he is successful about 60% of the time. Doctor Spruel spoke about why people have addictive personalities. He explained that often we think of drugs and alcohol when we think of addictions. But people can become dependent on many things (food, sex, shopping, et cetera). He was extremely interesting and helpful, and he told us to come by and visit his personal library at his office on Lincoln Blvd. if we needed sources for additional research.

Exercise E7-30

Write sentences using the following abbreviations.

1. CIA
2. ABC
3. mph
4. Col.
5. Sen.

Numbers

The main problem when using numbers is determining whether to spell out the number or use numerals. You will notice some variation among grammar textbooks in guidelines for number usage. As the following rules illustrate, however, the trend leans toward using numerals:

1. *In most cases, spell out numbers from one to nine and use numerals for numbers composed of two or more digits.*

   Jefferson has had **two** speeding tickets in the last **three** months.

   Tamara has earned **64** credits so far, not quite half of the **130** credits she needs for her degree.

2. *Always spell out a number that begins a sentence, rearranging the sentence or adding words if necessary.*

   Seventy-seven people were evacuated from their homes because of a gas leak.

   Over **100,000** people have moved to the suburbs in the last five years.

3. *Spell out numerical references that are used as adjectives indicating order.*

   I was the **twelfth** person in line at the ticket counter.

4. *Use numerals in the following cases:*

Dates:	Jefferson was born on January **31, 1976**.
Addresses:	My aunt's address is Rt. **1**, Box **22**, Mangham, LA **71259**.
Telephone numbers:	Our new number is **815-877-1420**.
Time:	The luncheon starts at **11:30** a.m.
Fractions:	The recipe calls for **1/3** cup sugar.
Decimals:	Last year's city population increased **1.3** percent.
Measurements:	The building is **40** feet long and **26** feet wide.
Money:	Jefferson's paycheck was **$112.36** last week.
Identification numbers:	My social security number is **438-82-9421**.
Statistics:	Last semester **11,356** full-time students were enrolled in classes.

5. *For very large numbers, use a combination of numerals and words.*

The city received a **2.2-million-dollar** federal grant for street improvements.

Exercise E7-31

Explain why the numbers are either spelled out or written in numerals in the following sentences from "On Being a Cripple."

1. It has a honorable history, having made its first appearance in Lindisfarne Gospel in the tenth century.
2. About a year and half later I developed a blurred spot in one eye.
3. Every day for the past nearly 10 years, then, has been a kind of gift.
4. I am also an enthusiastic launderess, capable of sorting a hamper full of clothes into five subtly differentiated piles, but a terrible housekeeper.
5. It was a fine two-week trip, filled with friends and fair weather, and I wouldn't have missed it for the world, though I did in fact make it back to California two years later.

Exercise E7-32

Correct any mistakes in number usage in the following sentences adapted from Jefferson's first draft.

1. I stayed at that school twelve months of the year because my parents wanted me to learn to read before it was too late.

2. During the Parents Day visit at the school, when I was in the 5th grade, my parents realized that I still did not know how to read.
3. If we were late for breakfast, we had to go run around the track for at least fifteen minutes before breakfast.
4. There were about three hundred flash cards, so I could not memorize them, especially because they were presented to me at random.
5. It takes me about 6 or 7 times as long as most people to write a short paper.

Exercise E7-33

Fill in each blank with a number that will complete the sentence.

Last weekend (1) _____ friends and I went to Monroe

for the Garth Brooks concert. We had ordered our tickets about

(2) _____ months in advance, paying

(3) _____ for each ticket, which we didn't think was too

expensive. Since we live about (4) _____ miles away from

Monroe, we had to allow at least an hour for driving. We all met at my house and

piled into my friend Chad's van, and we made it to the Civic Center with

(5) _____ minutes to spare. As we walked up to the doors, we

saw about (6) _____ people outside asking other people if they

had any tickets to sell. When we got inside, we walked around the concession area

and checked out the T-shirts and programs that featured Garth and his band. Chad

paid (7) $ _____ for a jacket and the rest of us bought four

T-shirts for (8) $ _____ apiece. We knew the Civic Center

could seat about (9) _____ people, and every seat was filled.

Garth took the stage right on time, at (10) _____ p.m., for the

best concert I've ever seen.

Exercise E7-34

Write sentences using the following numbers.

1. 20,000
2. eight
3. 1/4
4. $4.5 million
5. 99

COLLABORATIVE WORK

After you revise your analyzing essay, exchange papers with a classmate, and do the following tasks:

A.   Read the essay carefully, and circle any punctuation errors you find.

B.   Read the essay again, and circle any errors in mechanics (capitalization, abbreviations, and numbers).

Then return the paper to its writer, and use the information in this section to edit your draft.

CHAPTER EIGHT

Persuading
Reading and Writing for a Reason

Those who do not know their opponent's arguments do not completely understand their own.

—DAVID BENDER

Persuading is one of our most important forms of communication because it helps us get what we want in life. When you write an essay for a college application, you are trying to persuade the admissions office to accept you. When you go through a job interview, you want to convince an employer to hire you. On the flip side, others try to persuade you to do things all the time: Politicians make speeches trying to persuade you to vote for them; your friends try to persuade you to go to a movie when you know you should do your homework; toy companies try to persuade you to run to your local toy store and buy their products.

Some of the most important decisions ever made in the United States have been the result of persuasive arguments in the Supreme Court: the death penalty, abortion, desegregation, immigrants' rights, children's rights. Every Supreme Court decision is based on the ability of lawyers to persuade a majority of the Supreme Court Justices of the truth and logic of a certain position. They do this by presenting a carefully and thoroughly researched argument that represents their evidence on a specific issue.

In writing a persuading essay, you must present an argument of your own. First, you should choose a topic you feel strongly about. Then you should gather as much evidence and information as possible and use it to convince your readers to agree with your point of view. Presenting an argument is not as easy as it sounds, however, because your readers will often feel just as strongly about the opposite side of the issue. As a result, your evidence must be accurate, logical, and convincing. **Evidence** is probably the most important factor in writing a persuading essay. Without solid evidence, your essays will be nothing more than opinion; with it, your essays will be logical and convincing arguments that help your readers not only understand your position, but perhaps agree with it. Your ability to persuade through writing gives you the potential to change things for the better, to right wrongs, and to help others.

The following example of persuasion concerns the scores that students receive on the Scholastic Aptitude Test (SAT), which is generally thought to measure a student's intelligence and ability. But in this excerpt from his book *Two Nations*, Andrew Hacker, a political science professor at Queens College in New York, presents evidence to the contrary, arguing that the test does *not* measure intelligence or aptitude:

> The Scholastic Aptitude Test has become the closest thing we have to a national IQ test. So it is best that we be clear about what this three-hour examination measures. Clearly, it does not gauge [measure] "intelligence" or "aptitude" in a broad sense. At best, it rates a narrow range of academic-oriented skills. Some have argued that, as much as anything, scores simply reflect how adept [skillful] people are at taking that kind of test. . . . The sponsors of the SAT have known for many years that their test fails to identify how people will do in later life. A follow-up of Yale University graduates revealed that "no significant relation could be found between original scores and . . . honors and standing [ranking] within their occupations." A similar study concluded that "no consistent relationships exist between Scholastic Aptitude Test scores in college students, and their actual accomplishments in social leadership, the arts, sciences, music, writing, and speech and drama."

Notice that Hacker does not simply make a claim; he supports the claim logically so that his readers can understand his viewpoint and either agree with it or at least give serious consideration to it. This is how a good piece of persuasion should work, offering conclusions based on clear evidence.

LEARNING FROM PUBLISHED WRITERS

The following essay, by Dr. Martin Luther King, Jr., is one of the most famous persuading essays ever written by an American. Composed as a letter, it was written in response to another letter. In April 1963, King demonstrated in Birmingham, Alabama, for an end to racism, despite the fact that a court injunction had been issued prohibiting him and his followers from holding the demonstration. As a result of his actions, King was arrested and placed in a Birmingham jail. On the same day, eight white clergymen from Birmingham published a letter in the *Birmingham News* trying to persuade King that he should have obeyed the court order, that he should have been more patient in seeking equal treatment for African Americans, and that he should stop demonstrating and work "peacefully for a better Birmingham." King composed the first draft of his letter responding to the clergymen while he was still in his jail cell; he wrote on scraps of paper and in the margins of newspapers. The revised version of his letter is printed here.

Before You Read

Focusing Your Attention

Before you read this essay, take a few moments to answer the following questions in your journal:

1. Think of protests and demonstrations that you have either participated in, witnessed for yourself, seen on television, or read about. What emotions did the demonstrators exhibit? Did you admire and respect the demonstrators? Explain your answer.

2. Martin Luther King, Jr., once said, "If a man hasn't discovered something he would die for, he isn't fit to live." Which causes or beliefs would you be willing to die for or sacrifice a great deal for?

Expanding Your Vocabulary

Here are some words and their meanings that are important to your understanding of the essay. You might want to review them before you begin to read.

"**affiliated** [connected, related] organizations" (paragraph 2)

"the **Macedonian** call for aid [St. Paul helped the people of Macedonia]" (paragraph 3)

"I am **cognizant** of [aware of] the **interrelatedness** [connection] of all communities" (paragraph 4)

"network of **mutuality** [interests in common]" (paragraph 4)

"You **deplore** [strongly disapprove of] the demonstrations" (paragraph 5)

"does not **grapple** with [deal with] underlying causes" (paragraph 5)

"There can be no **gainsaying** [denying] the fact" (paragraph 6)

"agreed to a **moratorium** [temporary halt]" (paragraph 7)

"**Socrates** [ancient Greek philosopher recognized for his wisdom]" (paragraph 10)

"the **bondage** [imprisonment] of myths and half-truths" (paragraph 10)

"the **unfettered realm** [place or condition of freedom]" (paragraph 10)

"bring the **millennium** [period of great happiness or peace] to Birmingham" (paragraph 12)

"**Lamentably** [sadly], it is an historical fact" (paragraph 12)

"**Reinhold Niebuhr** [twentieth-century theologian and philosopher]" (paragraph 12)

"you have to **concoct** [make up] an answer" (paragraph 14)

"Since we so **diligently** [earnestly] urge people to obey the Supreme Court's decision . . . it may seem rather **paradoxical** [confusing, contradictory] for us to consciously break laws" (paragraph 15)

"**Conversely** [on the other hand], one has a moral responsibility to disobey unjust laws." (paragraph 15)

"**Paul Tillich** [twentieth-century theologian and philosopher]" (paragraph 16)

"**existential** [philosophical term meaning based on experience] expression" (paragraph 16)

"Sometimes a law is just **on its face** [in the way it was written] and unjust in its **application** [the way it is applied]" (paragraph 19)

"the **rabid** [mad, consumed with rage] segregationist" (paragraph 20)

"the refusal of **Shadrach**, **Meshach and Abednego** to obey the laws of **Nebuchadnezzar** [in the Old Testament, these three men were unjustly cast into a furnace by King Nebuchadnezzar, but they came out miraculously unharmed]" (paragraph 21)

"they **precipitate** [cause, bring on] violence" (paragraph 25)

"they made him [Socrates] drink **hemlock** [poison drawn from the hemlock tree]" (paragraph 25)

"wheels of **inevitability** [what is guaranteed to happen]" (paragraph 26)

"a force of **complacency** [acceptance of things as they are]" (paragraph 27)

"who have absolutely **repudiated** [rejected] Christianity, and who have concluded that the white man is an **incorrigible** [unable to change] 'devil'" (paragraph 27)

"we need **emulate** [imitate]" (paragraph 28)

"The **yearning** [desire] for freedom eventually **manifests** [shows] itself" (paragraph 30)

"caught up by the *Zeitgeist* [spirit of the times]" (paragraph 30)

"the need for . . . **antidotes** [cures for poison]" (paragraph 32)

"I must honestly **reiterate** [repeat]" (paragraph 34)

"I was suddenly **catapulted** [thrown unexpectedly] into the leadership" (paragraph 35)

"behind the **anesthetizing** [suffocating, sleep-inducing] security" (paragraph 35)

"**admonish** [warn] their worshipers to **comply** with [obey] . . . the law" (paragraph 37)

"mouth **pious irrelevancies and sanctimonious trivialities** [words that sound devout or moral]" (paragraph 37)

"the lips of **Governor Barnett** [governor of Mississippi] dripped with words of **interposition** [interfering] and **nullification** [cancellation]" (paragraph 38)

"when **Governor Wallace** [governor of Alabama] gave a **clarion call** [battle cry] for defiance and hatred" (paragraph 38) "the **laxity** [neglectfulness] of the church" (paragraph 39)

"brought an end to such ancient evils as **infanticide** [killing of babies] and **gladiatorial contests** [ancient Roman spectacle of men fighting to the death]" (paragraph 40)

"lose its **authenticity** [genuineness], **forfeit** [give up] the loyalty of millions" (paragraph 42)

"the true *ekklesia* [Greek word meaning "church"]" (paragraph 43)

"**embodied** [given form] in our echoing demands" (paragraph 44)

"warmly **commended** [praised] the Birmingham police force" (paragraph 45)

"**T. S. Eliot** [highly regarded poet, 1888–1965]" (paragraph 46)

"great **provocation** [stirring up of anger and resentment]" (paragraph 47)

"responded with **ungrammatical profundity** [Although the speaker, Rosa Parks, made a grammatical error, her words were important and full of meaning.]" (paragraph 47)

Martin Luther King, Jr.

Letter from Birmingham Jail*

April 16, 1963

My Dear Fellow Clergymen:

1   While confined here in the Birmingham city jail, I came across your recent statement calling my present activities "unwise and untimely." Seldom do I pause to answer criticism of my work and ideas. If I sought to answer all the criticisms that cross my desk, my secretaries would have little time for anything other than such correspondence in the course of the day, and I would have no time for constructive work. But since I feel that you are men of genuine good will and that your criticisms are sincerely set forth, I want to try to answer your statement in what I hope will be patient and reasonable terms.

2   I think I should indicate why I am here in Birmingham, since you have been influenced by the view which argues against "outsiders coming in." I have the honor of serving as president of the Southern Christian Leadership Conference, an organization operating in every

*Martin Luther King, Jr., "Letter from Birmingham Jail" from *Why We Can't Wait*. Reprinted with the permission of Writers House, Inc.

southern state, with headquarters in Atlanta, Georgia. We have some eighty-five affiliated organizations across the South, and one of them is the Alabama Christian Movement for Human Rights. Frequently we share staff, educational, and financial resources with our affiliates. Several months ago the affiliate here in Birmingham asked us to be on call to engage in a nonviolent direct-action program if such were deemed necessary. We readily consented, and when the hour came we lived up to our promise. So I, along with several members of my staff, am here because I was invited here. I am here because I have organizational ties here.

But more basically, I am in Birmingham because injustice is here. 3 Just as the prophets of the eighth century B.C. left their villages and carried their "thus saith the Lord" far beyond the boundaries of their home towns, and just as the Apostle Paul left his village of Tarsus and carried the gospel of Jesus Christ to the far corners of the Greco-Roman world, so am I compelled to carry the gospel of freedom beyond my own home town. Like Paul, I must constantly respond to the Macedonian call for aid.

Moreover, I am cognizant of the interrelatedness of all communities and states. I cannot sit idly by in Atlanta and not be concerned about what happens in Birmingham. Injustice anywhere is a threat to justice everywhere. We are caught in an inescapable network of mutuality, tied in a single garment of destiny. Whatever affects one directly, affects all indirectly. Never again can we afford to live with the narrow, provincial "outside agitator" idea. Anyone who lives inside the United States can never be considered an outsider anywhere within its bounds.

You deplore the demonstrations taking place in Birmingham. But 5 your statement, I am sorry to say, fails to express a similar concern for the conditions that brought about the demonstrations. I am sure that none of you would want to rest content with the superficial kind of social analysis that deals merely with effects and does not grapple with underlying causes. It is unfortunate that demonstrations are taking place in Birmingham, but it is even more unfortunate that the city's white power structure left the Negro community with no alternative.

In any nonviolent campaign there are four basic steps: collection 6 of the facts to determine whether injustices exist; negotiation; self-purification; and direct action. We have gone through all these steps in Birmingham. There can be no gainsaying the fact that racial injustice engulfs this community. Birmingham is probably the most thoroughly segregated city in the United States. Its ugly record of brutality is widely known. Negroes have experienced grossly unjust treatment in the courts. There have been more unsolved bombings of Negro homes and churches in Birmingham than in any other city in the nation. These are the hard, brutal facts of the case. On the basis of these conditions, Negro leaders sought to negotiate with the city fathers. But the latter consistently refused to engage in good-faith negotiation.

Then, last September, came the opportunity to talk with leaders of Birmingham's economic community. In the course of the negotiations, certain promises were made by the merchants—for example, to remove the stores' humiliating racial signs. On the basis of these promises, the Reverend Fred Shuttlesworth and the leaders of the Alabama Christian Movement for Human Rights agreed to a moratorium on all demonstrations. As the weeks and months went by, we realized that we were the victims of a broken promise. A few signs, briefly removed, returned; the others remained.   **7**

As in so many past experiences, our hopes had been blasted, and the shadow of deep disappointment settled upon us. We had no alternative except to prepare for direct action, whereby we would present our very bodies as a means of laying our case before the conscience of the local and the national community. Mindful of the difficulties involved, we decided to undertake a process of self-purification. We began a series of workshops on nonviolence, and we repeatedly asked ourselves: "Are you able to accept blows without retaliating?" "Are you able to endure the ordeal of jail?" We decided to schedule our direct-action program for the Easter season, realizing that except for Christmas, this is the main shopping period of the year. Knowing that a strong economic-withdrawal-program would be the by-product of direct action, we felt that this would be the best time to bring pressure to bear on the merchants for the needed change.   **8**

Then it occurred to us that Birmingham's mayoral election was coming up in March, and we speedily decided to postpone action until after election day. When we discovered that the Commissioner of Public Safety, Eugene "Bull" Connor, had piled up enough votes to be in the run-off, we decided again to postpone action until the day after the run-off so that the demonstrations could not be used to cloud the issues. Like many others, we waited to see Mr. Connor defeated, and to this end we endured postponement after postponement. Having aided in this community need, we felt that our direct action program could be delayed no longer.   **9**

You may well ask: "Why direct action? Why sit-ins, marches, and so forth? Isn't negotiation a better path?" You are quite right in calling for negotiation. Indeed, this is the very purpose of direct action. Nonviolent direct action seeks to create such a crisis and foster such a tension that a community which has constantly refused to negotiate is forced to confront the issue. It seeks so to dramatize the issue that it can no longer be ignored. My citing the creation of tension as part of the work of the nonviolent-resister may sound rather shocking. But I must confess that I am not afraid of the word "tension." I have earnestly opposed violent tension, but there is a type of constructive, nonviolent tension which is necessary for growth. Just as Socrates felt that it was necessary to create a tension in the mind so that individuals could rise from the bondage of myths and half-truths to the unfettered realm of creative analysis and objective appraisal, so must we see the need for nonviolent gadflies to create the kind of tension in society that will help men rise from the dark depths of prejudice and racism to the majestic heights of understanding and brotherhood.

10

The purpose of our direct-action program is to create a situation so crisis-packed that it will inevitably open the door to negotiation. I therefore concur with you in your call for negotiation. Too long has our beloved Southland been bogged down in a tragic effort to live in monologue rather than dialogue.

11

One of the basic points in your statements is that the action that I and my associates have taken in Birmingham is untimely. Some have asked: "Why didn't you give the new city administration time to act?" The only answer that I can give to this query is that the new Birmingham administration must be prodded about as much as the outgoing one, before it will act. We are sadly mistaken if we feel that the election of Albert Boutwell as mayor will bring the millennium to Birmingham. While Mr. Boutwell is a much more gentle person than Mr. Connor, they are both segregationists, dedicated to maintenance of the status quo. I have hope that Mr. Boutwell will be reasonable enough to see the futility of massive resistance to desegregation. But he will not see this without pressure from devotees of civil rights. My friends, I must say to you that we have not made a single gain in civil rights without determined legal and nonviolent pressure. Lamentably, it is an historical fact that privileged groups seldom give up their privileges voluntarily. Individuals may see the moral light and voluntarily give up their unjust posture; but, as Reinhold Niebuhr has reminded us, groups tend to be more immoral than individuals.

12

We know through painful experience that freedom is never voluntarily given by the oppressor; it must be demanded by the oppressed. Frankly, I have yet to engage in a direct-action campaign that was "well timed" in the view of those who have not suffered unduly from the disease of segregation. For years now I have heard the word "Wait!" It rings in the ear of every Negro with piercing familiarity. This "Wait" has almost always meant "Never." We must come to see, with one of our distinguished jurists, that "justice too long delayed is justice denied." **13**

We have waited for more than 340 years for our constitutional and God-given rights. The nations of Asia and Africa are moving with jetlike speed toward gaining political independence, but we still creep at horse-and-buggy pace toward gaining a cup of coffee at a lunch counter. Perhaps it is easy for those who have never felt the stinging darts of segregation to say, "Wait." But when you have seen vicious mobs lynch your mothers and fathers at will and drown your sisters and brothers at whim; when you have seen hate-filled policemen curse, kick, and even kill your black brothers and sisters; when you see the vast majority of your twenty million Negro brothers smothering in an airtight cage of poverty in the midst of an affluent society; when you suddenly find your tongue twisted and your speech stammering as you seek to explain to your six-year-old daughter why she can't go to the public amusement park that has just been advertised on television, and see tears welling up in her eyes when she is told that Funtown is closed to colored children, and see ominous clouds of inferiority beginning to form in her little mental sky, and see her beginning to distort her personality by developing an unconscious bitterness toward white people; when you have to concoct an answer for a five-year-old son who is asking: "Daddy, why do white people treat colored people so mean?"; when you take a cross-country drive and find it necessary to sleep night after night in the uncomfortable corners of your automobile because no motel will accept you; when you are humiliated day in and day out by nagging signs reading "white" and "colored"; when your first name becomes "nigger," your middle name becomes "boy" (however old you are) and your last name becomes "John," and your wife and mother are never given the respected title "Mrs."; when you are harried by day and haunted by night by the fact that you are a Negro, living constantly at tiptoe stance, never quite knowing what to expect next, and are plagued with inner fears and outer resentments; when you are forever fighting a degenerating sense of "nobodiness"—then you will understand why we find it difficult to wait. There comes a time when the cup of en- **14** durance runs over, and men are no longer willing to be plunged into the abyss of despair. I hope, sirs, you can understand our legitimate and unavoidable impatience.

You express a great deal of anxiety over our willingness to break laws. This is certainly a legitimate concern. Since we so diligently urge people to obey the Supreme Court's decision of 1954 outlawing segregation in the public schools, at first glance it may seem rather paradoxical for us consciously to break laws. One may well ask: "How can you advocate breaking some laws and obeying others?" The answer lies in the fact that there are two types of laws: just and unjust. I would be the first to advocate obeying just laws. One has not only a legal but a moral responsibility to obey just laws. Conversely, one has a moral responsibility to disobey unjust laws. I would agree with St. Augustine that "an unjust law is no law at all."

Now, what is the difference between the two? How does one determine whether a law is just or unjust? A just law is a man-made code that squares with the moral law or the law of God. An unjust law is a code that is out of harmony with the moral law. To put it in the terms of St. Thomas Aquinas: An unjust law is a human law that is not rooted in eternal law and natural law. Any law that uplifts human personality is just. Any law that degrades human personality is unjust. All segregation statutes are unjust because segregation distorts the soul and damages the personality. It gives the segregator a false sense of superiority and the segregated a false sense of inferiority. Segregation, to use the terminology of the Jewish philosopher Martin Buber, substitutes an "I–it" relationship for an "I–thou" relationship and ends up relegating persons to the status of things. Hence segregation is not only politically, economically and sociologically unsound, it is morally wrong and sinful. Paul Tillich has said that sin is separation. Is not segregation an existential expression of man's tragic separation, his awful estrangement, his terrible sinfulness? Thus it is that I can urge men to obey the 1954 decision of the Supreme Court, for it is morally right; and I can urge them to disobey segregation ordinances, for they are morally wrong.

Let us consider a more concrete example of just and unjust laws. An unjust law is a code that a numerical or power majority group compels a minority group to obey but does not make a binding on itself. This is *difference* made legal. By the same token, a just law is a code that a majority compels a minority to follow and that it is willing to follow itself. This is *sameness* made legal.

Let me give another explanation. A law is unjust if it is inflicted on   **18**
a minority that, as a result of being denied the right to vote, had no
part in enacting or devising the law. Who can say that the legislature of
Alabama which set up that state's segregation laws was democratically
elected? Throughout Alabama all sorts of devious methods are used to
prevent Negroes from becoming registered voters, and there are some
counties in which, even though Negroes constitute a majority of the
population, not a single Negro is registered. Can any law enacted under
such circumstances be considered democratically structured?

Sometimes a law is just on its face and unjust in its application. For   **19**
instance, I have been arrested on a charge of parading without a permit. Now, there is nothing wrong in having an ordinance which requires a permit for a parade. But such an ordinance becomes unjust
when it is used to maintain segregation and to deny citizens the First-
Amendment privilege of peaceful assembly and protest.

I hope you are able to see the distinction I am trying to point out.   **20**
In no sense do I advocate evading or defying the law, as would the rabid segregationist. That would lead to anarchy. One who breaks an
unjust law must do so openly, lovingly, and with a willingness to accept the penalty. I submit that an individual who breaks a law that
conscience tells him is unjust, and who willingly accepts the penalty
of imprisonment in order to arouse the conscience of the community
over its injustice, is in reality expressing the highest respect for law.

Of course, there is nothing new about this kind of civil disobedi-   **21**
ence. It was evidenced sublimely in the refusal of Shadrach, Meshach,
and Abednego to obey the laws of Nebuchadnezzar, on the ground that
a higher moral law was at stake. It was practiced superbly by the early
Christians, who were willing to face hungry lions and the excruciating
pain of chopping blocks rather than submit to certain unjust laws of
the Roman Empire. To a degree, academic freedom is a reality today
because Socrates practiced civil disobedience. In our own nation, the
Boston Tea Party represented a massive act of civil disobedience.

We should never forget that everything Adolf Hitler did in Ger-   **22**
man was "legal" and everything the Hungarian freedom fighters did
in Hungary was "illegal." It was "illegal" to aid and comfort a Jew in
Hitler's Germany. Even so, I am sure that, had I lived in Germany at
the time, I would have aided and comforted my Jewish brothers. If today I lived in a Communist country where certain principles dear to
the Christian faith are suppressed, I would openly advocate disobey-
ing that country's antireligious laws.

I must make two honest confessions to you, my Christian and Jewish brothers. First, I must confess that over the past few years I have been gravely disappointed with the white moderate. I have almost reached the regrettable conclusion that the Negro's great stumbling block in his stride toward freedom is not the White Citizen's Counciler or the Ku Klux Klanner, but the white moderate, who is more devoted to "order" than to justice; who prefers a negative peace which is the absence of tension to a positive peace which is the presence of justice; who constantly says: "I agree with you in the goal you seek, but I cannot agree with your methods of direct action:" who paternalistically believes he can set the timetable for another man's freedom; who lives by a mythical concept of time and who constantly advises the Negro to wait for a "more convenient season." Shallow understanding from people of good will is more frustrating than absolute misunderstanding from people of ill will. Lukewarm acceptance is much more bewildering than outright rejection.

23

I had hoped that the white moderate would understand that law and order exist for the purpose of establishing justice and that when they fail in this purpose they become the dangerously structured dams that block the flow of social progress. I had hoped that the white moderate would understand that the present tension in the South is a necessary phase of the transition from an obnoxious negative peace, in which the Negro passively accepted his unjust plight, to a substantive and positive peace, in which all men will respect the dignity and worth of human personality. Actually, we who engage in nonviolent direct action are not the creators of tension. We merely bring to the surface the hidden tension that is already alive. We bring it out in the open, where it can be seen and dealt with. Like a boil that can never be cured so long as it is covered up but must be opened with all its ugliness to the natural medicines of air and light, injustice must be exposed, with all the tension its exposure creates, to the light of human conscience and the air of national opinion before it can be cured.

24

In your statement you assert that our actions, even though peaceful, must be condemned because they precipitate violence. But is this a logical assertion? Isn't this like condemning a robbed man because his possession of money precipitated the evil act of robbery? Isn't this like condemning Socrates because his unswerving commitment to truth and his philosophical inquiries precipitated the act by the misguided populace in which they made him drink hemlock? Isn't this like condemning Jesus because his unique God-consciousness and never-ceasing devotion to God's will precipitated the

25

evil act of crucifixion? We must come to see that, as the federal courts have consistently affirmed, it is wrong to urge an individual to cease his efforts to gain his basic constitutional rights because the quest may precipitate violence. Society must protect the robbed and punish the robber.

I had also hoped that the white moderate would reject the myth   **26** concerning time in relation to the struggle for freedom. I have just received a letter from a white brother in Texas. He writes: "All Christians know that the colored people will receive equal rights eventually, but it is possible that you are in too great a religious hurry. It has taken Christianity almost two thousand years to accomplish what it has. The teachings of Christ take time to come to earth." Such an attitude stems from a tragic misconception of time, from the strangely irrational notion that there is something in the very flow of time that will inevitably cure all ills. Actually, time itself is neutral; it can be used either destructively or constructively. More and more I feel that the people of ill will have used time much more effectively than have the people of good will. We will have to repent in this generation not merely for the hateful words and actions of the bad people but for the appalling silence of the good people. Human progress never rolls in on wheels of inevitability; it comes through the tireless efforts of men willing to be co-workers with God, and without this hard work, time itself becomes an ally of the forces of social stagnation. We must use time creatively, in the knowledge that time is always ripe to do right. Now is the time to make real the promise of democracy and transform our pending national elegy into a creative psalm of brotherhood. Now is the time to lift our national policy from the quicksand of racial injustice to the solid rock of human dignity.

You speak of our activity in Birmingham as extreme. At first I was   **27** rather disappointed that fellow clergymen would see my nonviolent efforts as those of an extremist. I began thinking about the fact that I stand in the middle of two opposing forces in the Negro community. One is a force of complacency, made up in part of Negroes who, as a result of long years of oppression, are so drained of self-respect and a sense of "somebodiness" that they have adjusted to segregation; and in part of a few middle-class Negroes who, because of a degree of academic and economic security and because in some ways they profit by segregation, have become insensitive to the problems of the masses. The other force is one of bitterness and hatred, and it comes perilously close to advocating violence. It is expressed in the various black nationalist groups that are springing up across the nation, the largest and best-known being Elijah Muhammad's Muslim movement. Nourished by the Negro's frustration over the continued existence of racial discrimination, this movement is made up of people who have lost faith in America, who have absolutely repudiated Christianity, and who have concluded that the white man is an incorrigible "devil."

28   I have tried to stand between these two forces, saying that we need emulate neither the "do-nothingism" of the complacent nor the hatred and despair of the black nationalist. For there is the more excellent way of love and nonviolent protest. I am grateful to God that, through the influence of the Negro church, the way of nonviolence became an integral part of our struggle.

29   If this philosophy had not emerged, by now many streets of the South would, I am convinced, be flowing with blood. And I am further convinced that if our white brothers dismiss as "rabble-rousers" and "outside agitators" those of us who employ nonviolent direct action, and if they refuse to support our nonviolent efforts, millions of Negroes will, out of frustration and despair, seek solace and security in black-nationalist ideologies—a development that would inevitably lead to a frightening racial nightmare.

30   Oppressed people cannot remain oppressed forever. The yearning for freedom eventually manifests itself, and that is what has happened to the American Negro. Something within has reminded him of his birthright of freedom, and something without has reminded him that it can be gained. Consciously or unconsciously, he has been caught up by the *Zeitgeist*, and with his black brothers of Africa and his brown and yellow brothers of Asia, South America, and the Caribbean, the United States Negro is moving with a sense of great urgency toward the promised land of racial justice. If one recognizes this vital urge that has engulfed the Negro community, one should readily understand why public demonstrations are taking place. The Negro has many pent-up resentments and frustrations, and he must release them. So let him march; let him make prayer pilgrimages to the city hall; let him go on freedom rides—and try to understand why he must do so. If his repressed emotions are not released in nonviolent ways, they will seek expression through violence; this is not a threat but a fact of history. So I have not said to my people: "Get rid of your discontent." Rather, I have tried to say that this normal and healthy discontent can be channeled into the creative outlet of nonviolent direct action. And now this approach is being termed extremist.

But though I was initially disappointed at being categorized as an   **31**
extremist, as I continued to think about the matter, I gradually
gained a measure of satisfaction from the label. Was not Jesus an extremist for love: "Love your enemies, bless them that curse you, do
good to them that hate you, and pray for them which despitefully use
you, and persecute you." Was not Amos an extremist for justice: "Let
justice roll down like waters and righteousness like an ever-flowing
stream." Was not Paul an extremist for the Christian gospel: "I bear
in my body the marks of the Lord Jesus." Was not Martin Luther an
extremist: "Here I stand; I cannot do otherwise, so help me God."
And John Bunyan: "I will stay in jail to the end of my days before I
make a butchery of my conscience." And Abraham Lincoln: "This
nation cannot survive half slave and half free." And Thomas Jefferson: "We hold these truths to be self-evident, that all men are created
equal . . ." So the question is not whether we will be extremists, but
what kind of extremists we will be. Will we be extremists for hate or
for love? Will we be extremists for the preservation of injustice or for
the extension of justice? In that dramatic scene on Calvary's hill,
three men were crucified. We must never forget that all three were
crucified for the same crime—the crime of extremism. Two were extremists for immorality, and thus fell below their environment. The
other, Jesus Christ, was an extremist for love, truth, and goodness,
and thereby rose above his environment. Perhaps the South, the nation, and the world are in dire need of creative extremists.

I had hoped that the white moderate would see this need. Perhaps I   **32**
was too optimistic; perhaps I expected too much. I suppose I should
have realized that few members of the oppressor race can understand
the deep groans and passionate yearnings of the oppressed race, and still
fewer have the vision to see that injustice must be rooted out by strong,
persistent, and determined action. I am thankful, however, that some of
our white brothers in the South have grasped the meaning of this social
revolution and committed themselves to it. They are still all too few in
quantity, but they are big in quality. Some—such as Ralph McGill, Lil-
lian Smith, Harry Golden, James McBride Dabbs, Ann Braden, and
Sarah Patton Boyle—have written about our struggle in eloquent and
prophetic terms. Others have marched with us down nameless streets of
the South. They have languished in filthy, roach-infested jails, suffering
the abuse and brutality of policemen who view them as "dirty nigger-
lovers." Unlike so many of their moderate brothers and sisters, they
have recognized the urgency of the moment and sensed the need for
powerful "action" antidotes to combat the disease of segregation.

Let me take note of my other major disappointment. I have been   **33**
so greatly disappointed with the white church and its leadership. Of
course, there are some notable exceptions. I am not unmindful of the
fact that each of you has taken some significant stands on this issue. I
commend you, Reverend Stallings, for your Christian stand on this
past Sunday, in welcoming Negroes to your worship service on a non-
segregated basis. I commend the Catholic leaders of this state for in-
tegrating Spring Hill College several years ago.

But despite these notable exceptions, I must honestly reiterate that   **34**
I have been disappointed with the church. I do not say this as one of
those negative critics who can always find something wrong with the
church. I say this as a minister of the gospel, who loves the church;
who was nurtured in its bosom; who has been sustained by its spiritual blessings and who will remain true to it as long as the cord of life
shall lengthen.

When I was suddenly catapulted into the leadership of the bus   **35**
protest in Montgomery, Alabama, a few years ago, I felt we would
be supported by the white church. I felt that the white ministers,
priests, and rabbis of the South would be among our strongest al-
lies. Instead, some have been outright opponents, refusing to understand the freedom movement and misrepresenting its leaders;
all too many others have been more cautious than courageous and
have remained silent behind the anesthetizing security of stained-
glass windows.

In spite of my shattered dreams, I came to Birmingham with the   **36**
hope that the white religious leadership of this community would see
the justice of our cause and, with deep moral concern, would serve as
the channel through which our just grievances could reach the power
structure. I had hoped that each of you would understand. But again I
have been disappointed.

I have heard numerous southern religious leaders admonish their   **37**
worshipers to comply with a desegregation decision because it is the
law, but I have longed to hear white ministers declare: "Follow this
decree because integration is morally right and because the Negro is
your brother." In the midst of blatant injustices inflicted upon the
Negro, I have watched white churchmen stand on the sideline and
mouth pious irrelevancies and sanctimonious trivialities. In the midst
of a mighty struggle to rid our nation of racial and economic injustice, I have heard many ministers say: "Those are social issues, with
which the gospel has no real concern." And I have watched many
churches commit themselves to a completely otherworldly religion

which makes a strange, un-Biblical distortion between body and soul, between the sacred and the secular.

I have traveled the length and breadth of Alabama, Mississippi and all the other southern states. On sweltering summer days and crisp autumn mornings I have looked at the South's beautiful churches with their lofty spires pointing heavenward. I have beheld the impressive outlines of her massive religious-education buildings. Over and over I have found myself asking: "What kind of people worship here? Who is their God? Where were their voices when the lips of Governor Barnett dripped with words of interposition and nullification? Where were they when Governor Wallace gave a clarion call for defiance and hatred? Where were their voices of support when bruised and weary negro men and women decided to rise from the dark dungeons of complacency to the bright hills of creative protest?" **38**

Yes, these questions are still in my mind. In deep disappointment, I have wept over the laxity of the church. But be assured that my tears have been tears of love. There can be no deep disappointment where there is not deep love. Yes, I love the church. How could I do otherwise? I am in the rather unique position of being the son, the grandson, and the great-grandson of preachers. Yes, I see the church as the body of Christ. But, oh! How we have blemished and scarred that body through social neglect and through fear of being nonconformists. **39**

There was a time when the church was very powerful—in the time when the early Christians rejoiced at being deemed worthy to suffer for what they believed. In those days the church was not merely a thermometer that recorded the ideas and principles of popular opinion; it was a thermostat that transformed the mores of society. Whenever the early Christians entered a town, the people in power became disturbed and immediately sought to convict the Christians for being "disturbers of the peace" and "outside agitators." But the Christians pressed on, in the conviction that they were "a colony of heaven," called to obey God rather than man. Small in number, they were big in commitment. They were too God-intoxicated to be "astronomically intimidated." By their effort and example they brought an end to such ancient evils as infanticide and gladiatorial contests. **40**

Things are different now. So often the contemporary church is a weak, ineffectual voice with an uncertain sound. So often it is an arch-defender of the status quo. Far from being disturbed by the presence of the church, the power structure of the average community is consoled by the church's silent—and often even vocal—sanction of things as they are. **41**

But the judgment of God is upon the church as never before. If to-   **42**
day's church does not recapture the sacrificial spirit of the early
church, it will lose its authenticity, forfeit the loyalty of millions, and
be dismissed as an irrelevant social club with no meaning for the
twentieth century. Every day I meet young people whose disappointment with the church has turned into outright disgust.

Perhaps I have once again been too optimistic. Is organized reli-   **43**
gion too inextricably bound to the status quo to save our nation and
the world? Perhaps I must turn my faith to the inner spiritual church,
the church within the church, as the true *ekklesia* and the hope of the
world. But again I am thankful to God that some noble souls from the
ranks of organized religion have broken loose from the paralyzing
chains of conformity and joined us as active partners in the struggle
for freedom. They have left their secure congregations and walked
the streets of Albany, Georgia, with us. They have gone down the
highways of the South on tortuous rides for freedom. Yes, they have
gone to jail with us. Some have been dismissed from their churches,
have lost the support of their bishops and fellow ministers. But they
have acted in the faith that right defeated is stronger than evil tri-
umphant. Their witness has been the spiritual salt that has preserved
the true meaning of the gospel in these troubled times. They have
carved a tunnel of hope through the dark mountain of disappointment.

I hope the church as a whole will meet the challenge of this deci-   **44**
sive hour. But even if the church does not come to the aid of justice,
I have no despair about the future. I have no fear about the outcome
of our struggle in Birmingham, even if our motives are at present misunderstood. We will reach the goal of freedom in Birmingham and all
over the nation, because the goal of America is freedom. Abused and
scorned though we may be, our destiny is tied up with America's destiny. Before the pilgrims landed at Plymouth, we were here. Before
the pen of Jefferson etched the majestic words of the Declaration of
Independence across the pages of history, we were here. For more
than two centuries, our forebears labored in this country without
wages; they made cotton king; they built the homes of their masters
while suffering gross injustice and shameful humiliation—and yet
out of a bottomless vitality they continued to thrive and develop. If
the inexpressible cruelties of slavery could not stop us, the opposition
we now face will surely fail. We will win our freedom because the sacred heritage of our nation and the eternal will of God are embodied
in our echoing demands.

Before closing I feel impelled to mention one other point in your **45**
statement that has troubled me profoundly. We warmly commended
the Birmingham police force for keeping "order" and "preventing violence." I doubt that you would have so warmly commended the police force if you had seen its dogs sinking their teeth into unarmed,
nonviolent Negroes. I doubt that you would so quickly commend the
policemen if you were to observe their ugly and inhumane treatment
of Negroes here in the city jail; if you were to watch them push and
curse old Negro women and young Negro girls; if you were to see
them slap and kick old Negro men and young boys; if you were to observe them, as they did on two occasions, refuse to give us food because we wanted to sing our grace together. I cannot join you in your
praise of the Birmingham Police Department.

It is true that the police have exercised a degree of discipline in **46**
handling the demonstrators. In this sense they have conducted themselves rather "nonviolently" in public. But for what purpose? To preserve the evil system of segregation. Over the past few years I have
consistently preached that nonviolence demands that the means we
use must be as pure as the ends we seek. I have tried to make clear
that it is wrong to use immoral means to attain moral ends. But now
I must affirm that it is just as wrong, or perhaps even more so, to use
moral means to preserve immoral ends. Perhaps Mr. Connor and his
policemen have been rather nonviolent in public, as was Chief
Pritchett in Albany, Georgia, but they have used the moral means of
nonviolence to maintain the immoral end of racial injustice. As T. S.
Eliot has said, "The last temptation is the greatest treason: To do the
right deed for the wrong reason."

I wish you had commended the Negro sit-inners and demonstrators **47**
of Birmingham for their sublime courage, their willingness to suffer,
and their amazing discipline in the midst of great provocation. One day
the South will recognize its real heroes. They will be the James Mered-
iths, with the noble sense of purpose that enables them to face jeering
and hostile mobs, and with the agonizing loneliness that characterizes
the life of the pioneer. They will be old, oppressed, battered Negro
women, symbolized in a seventy-two-year-old woman in Montgomery,
Alabama, who rose up with a sense of dignity and with her people decided not to ride segregated buses, and who responded with ungrammatical profundity to one who inquired about her weariness: "My feets
is tired, but my soul is at rest." They will be the young high school and
college students, the young ministers of the gospel and a host of their
elders, courageously and nonviolently sitting in at lunch counters and

willingly going to jail for conscience sake. One day the South will know that when these disinherited children of God sat down at lunch counters, they were in reality standing up for what is best in the American dream and for the most sacred values in our Judaeo-Christian heritage, thereby bringing our nation back to those great wells of democracy which were dug deep by the founding fathers in their formulation of the Constitution and the Declaration of Independence.

Never before have I written so long a letter. I'm afraid it is much too long to take your precious time. I can assure you that it would have been much shorter if I had been writing from a comfortable desk, but what else can one do when he is alone in a narrow jail cell, other than write long letters, think long thoughts, and pray long prayers? **48**

If I have said anything in this letter that overstates the truth and indicates an unreasonable impatience, I beg you to forgive me. If I have said anything that understates the truth and indicates my having a patience that allows me to settle for anything less than brotherhood, I beg God to forgive me. **49**

I hope this letter finds you strong in the faith. I also hope that circumstances will soon make it possible for me to meet each of you, not as an integrationist or a civil-rights leader, but as a fellow clergyman and a Christian brother. Let us all hope that the dark clouds of racial prejudice will soon pass away and the deep fog of misunderstanding will be lifted from our fear-drenched communities, and in some not too distant tomorrow the radiant stars of love and brotherhood will shine over our great nation with all their scintillating beauty. **50**

Yours for the cause of Peace and Brotherhood,
Martin Luther King, Jr.

 ## QUESTIONS FOR CRITICAL THINKING

THINKING CRITICALLY ABOUT CONTENT

1. Why do you think Martin Luther King, Jr., cited the words of philosophers and Christian founders in his letter? Is this an effective technique? Explain your answer.

2. What is King's main point about civil disobedience?

THINKING CRITICALLY ABOUT PURPOSE

3. What do you think Martin Luther King, Jr.'s purpose is in writing this essay?

4. This letter has been reprinted thousands of times because it is an extraordinary example of persuasion. Which parts of the letter appeal to you most strongly? Explain your answer in detail.

THINKING CRITICALLY ABOUT AUDIENCE

5.   This letter was written in 1963 and addressed to eight Southern clergymen. Are there other groups of people who would benefit from reading it today? Who are they? Explain your answer.

6.   An essential ingredient in writing an effective persuading essay is to avoid alienating or offending the reader. Does King accomplish this? Explain your answer.

THINKING CRITICALLY ABOUT POINT OF VIEW

7.   Describe in a complete sentence King's point of view, including the tone and mood he communicates. Does the letter sound as if it were originally written in a jail cell?

8.   Imagine that you are one of the Christian clergymen who received this letter. Write a paragraph responding to Martin Luther King, Jr.

Arguing a Position

Another form of **persuading** involves taking a supporting position (pro, meaning "for") or dissenting position (con, meaning "against") on an issue. The next two essays present pro and con arguments on condom use and its relation to the spread of AIDS. Both essays were written soon after basketball hero Magic Johnson announced that he was HIV-positive. The first essay, written by Sara Nelson and published in *Glamour* magazine in 1992, argues that using condoms will help prevent AIDS. The second essay, written by Ray Kerrison and published in *Human Events* magazine in 1991, claims the opposite viewpoint — that condoms will not help prevent AIDS. Both essays were adapted and reprinted in 1992 in *Opposing Viewpoints*, a series of essays on controversial issues.

Before You Read

Focusing Your Attention

Before you read these essays, take a few moments to answer the following questions in your journal:

1.   If you were asked to take a pro or con position on a topic of great importance to you and to society, what are some of the topics you would consider?

2.   In the two essays that you will be reading, one writer tries to persuade the readers that condoms will help prevent AIDS while the other writer tries to persuade the readers that condoms will not help prevent AIDS. Although you have not yet read the essays, which one do you think you will agree with? Why?

Expanding Your Vocabulary

Here are some words and their meanings from Sara Nelson's pro (in support of) essay that are important to your understanding of this reading. You might want to review them before you begin to read.

"dangerous **dichotomy** [division into two contradictory positions]" (paragraph 1)

"**savvy** [up-to-date, informed] women" (paragraph 2)

"**unleashed** [released] some powerful anger" (paragraph 4)

"bring out the **Neanderthal** [caveman] in some men" (paragraph 5)

"the emotional **ramifications** [developments] of those earlier relationships" (paragraph 9)

"condoms limit **spontaneity** [acting on the spur of the moment]" (paragraph 11)

"**backsliding** [returning to old habits] is practically **inevitable** [guaranteed to happen]" (paragraph 14)

"**accessible** [easily available], well-stocked condom machines" (paragraph 15)

Sara Nelson

Condom Use Will Help Prevent AIDS*

Now, more than ten years into the AIDS epidemic, it seems that smart women are making foolish choices when it comes to AIDS prevention. "I always use condoms the first time with someone new," says one woman. "Sure, I keep condoms in the bedside drawer," says another, as if their mere presence is all that's required. A recent study confirms this dangerous dichotomy: *Knowing about safer sex and practicing it are all too often separate matters.* In a survey of 5,500 Canadian college students, researchers found that, despite high levels of AIDS awareness, fewer than 16 percent of the women studied said they always have their partner use condoms. Another study revealed that only one-fifth of the sexually active students at the University of Florida always use condoms during intercourse. More encouraging is a study suggesting that condom use among college students at one university increased from 12 percent in 1975 to 41 percent in 1989.

1

*Sara Nelson, "Condom Use Will Help Prevent AIDS" from "Talking Smart, Acting Stupid about AIDS" from *Glamour* (February 1992).

Though that's a notable, heartening leap, it isn't the whole picture; a survey conducted during the 1988–1989 school year found that two in one thousand college students tested positive for HIV. A follow-up study conducted one year later showed similar results.

Women and AIDS

Why are so many savvy women not doing all they can to protect themselves from what is still an incurable disease? "Every group has its own reasons for not admitting AIDS risk," says Mindy Fullilove, M.D., of the HIV Center for Clinical and Behavioral Studies at Columbia University. "Women, for example, don't perceive themselves to be at risk. Even if they understand that there are dangerous behaviors, they haven't translated those dangers to themselves. Women use the fact that more men than women have gotten AIDS so far as an excuse. They say, 'I'm not at risk because AIDS is something men get.'"

What can explain this irrational response? "The idea of having to get a man to use a condom goes against everything that women have fought for," says Anke Ehrhardt, Ph.D., also of Columbia's HIV Center for Clinical and Behavioral Studies. "The development of the birth control pill made women more independent. But since condoms have to be worn by men, women have to depend on men to take action. Many aren't confident that men will take that responsibility, and they resent that a part of their sexuality—which they've fought so hard to embrace—is now in men's hands."

It's no wonder, then, that the whole issue of AIDS prevention has unleashed some powerful anger between the sexes. "I'd been dating a guy for a couple of weeks," says Nancy, a 28-year-old lawyer. "We hadn't slept together yet, but it was going in that direction. We'd gone to see *Pretty Woman,* and you know that scene where she pulls out a bunch of brightly colored condoms? I said something afterward about how they looked so silly, but it was good that movies were now addressing the issue of AIDS and condoms. I thought this was kind of an unthreatening, impersonal way to broach the subject. You know what the guy did? He laughed and said, 'Yeah, but she was a *hooker.* You've never been a hooker, have you?' I felt completely dismissed, that he wasn't taking the subject or me seriously—that if I insisted he use a condom, I'd be saying that I was some kind of slut."

Having a woman introduce the idea of using a condom does bring out the Neanderthal in some men. "I know I'm not supposed to feel that it's weird when a woman reveals that she carries them around

2

3

4

5

with her," says Bob, 28, "but, well, it makes me think she's the kind of person who has sex on the run. I've had that kind of encounter, but it's not an encounter I'm proud of. Besides, it still feels different to me for a *woman* to be that casual about sex." If you point out to Bob that his attitude is just a tad old-fashioned and that it reveals, at best, some hostility toward women, he'll deny it. "I like women," he says. "But they don't think like us about sex. Or, at least, I want the woman I'm with to take sex seriously. If she's carrying around condoms, she gives the impression of being a party girl."

Self-Preservation

You'd think, though, that self-preservation would win out with men—that if they wouldn't use condoms to protect women from AIDS, they'd use them to protect themselves. But heterosexual men are just as capable of denying their own risk as women are. "I'm married now," says Paul, 29, "but I don't think I'd be worried about it if I were single. I'd *know* I hadn't slept with a man who might have been bisexual. But women can't know that, so aren't they more at risk? I think they have more at stake in insisting on condoms." And some men feel that the issue of condoms—like most issues of birth control and sexual health—is the woman's responsibility. "I'd use a condom if a woman would just ask," says 30-year-old Mark. "It's not a big deal to me." But would he ever bring up the subject? "I guess I just don't worry about AIDS very much," he says. "Wearing a condom is something I'd do only if a woman felt strongly about it."

6

That's just the kind of attitude that makes some women furious. "Sex and everything related to it is supposed to be a mutual decision, right?" asks 31-year-old Dorothy. "But it never is. Men expect women to plan for these things and then when we do, we get criticized for it. We're loose, they claim, or too clinical or *something*. Why do I have to say or do anything? Why don't men care enough about women? The sexual revolution was great—for men. They could sleep with whomever they wanted, assume the woman was on the Pill, and not worry at all. They've gotten this false sense of security that women will always take care of everything, that they *should* take care of everything. It makes me sick."

7

Changing Behavior

Early in the epidemic, many experts advocated a "talk to your partner" strategy, stressing the importance of communicating with your

8

partner nearly as much as using condoms. "Research indicates that 'Know your partner' was very dangerous advice to focus on," says Rebecca Welch Cline, Ph.D., associate professor of communication studies at the University of Florida, and author of that school's AIDS awareness study. For one thing, you can't "know" if your partner has been infected with HIV just by looking at him or even asking about it. A study released in May 1991 by the National Center for Health Statistics (NCHS) found that 29 percent of the unmarried women participants did not think or weren't sure whether a symptomless, healthy-seeming man could even transmit the virus. (He can.) For another, "We've discovered that there is no relationship between people talking to their partners about AIDS and their using condoms," says Dr. Cline. "It seems that most of us, when faced with two pieces of health advice, will feel pretty good if we put into practice one of them at least part of the time. And obviously, we'll choose the one that's easier. But talking is not a substitute for condom use; the two pieces of advice are not of the same weight." The NCHS study showed that the most frequent change single women are making in their sexual conduct is limiting their sexual partners to one man; while that's certainly a step in the right direction, simply shifting to fewer partners may not significantly alter one's risk of contracting HIV. "This 'Know your partner' business makes no sense since most people with HIV don't even know they have it themselves," says Karen Hein, M.D., who directs the Adolescent AIDS Program at the Albert Einstein College of Medicine/Montefiore Hospital in New York City. "To prevent HIV infection, women have to insist that their partners use condoms."

Intimate conversations with a partner may, in fact, do more harm **9** than good, because they can be misleading. "What it comes down to," says Dr. Cline, "is that because women are socialized to be attracted to men who will talk to them, particularly about intimate topics, they will likely be attracted to men who will talk to them about AIDS. They'll think they may be safer than men who don't talk." But Dr. Cline's study revealed just the opposite: The men who said they talked to their partners about AIDS, but only sometimes or never used condoms, had had nearly 50 percent more partners than men who said they didn't talk about AIDS. Besides, says Tim Edgar, Ph.D., assistant professor of speech communication at the University of Maryland, "When people say they've talked to their partners about sexual history, very often they mean they've talked to them about a specific relationship. They're not asking questions or getting answers about AIDS-risk behavior; they're discussing the emotional ramifications of those earlier relationships." . . .

Condoms Are a Complication

Elizabeth, 28, has found that it's much easier to present condoms as **10** a birth control device than as a means of preventing sexually transmitted diseases (STDs). "I have been pregnant twice and had two abortions," she says. "I even got pregnant when I had an IUD (intrauterine device). So now I only trust condoms: At least I can see them and understand how they work. Men don't always want to talk about AIDS, but they usually will ask about birth control, and I just say, 'I want to use condoms.' Some men look surprised—my new boyfriend said, 'I haven't used a condom in 20 years'—but they usually respect my choice."

Both men and women agree that condoms limit spontaneity. **11** "There are already enough complications in my life," says Lisa, 33. "I don't want sex to be one of them. Using condoms is definitely a complication."

You could argue that AIDS, too, is something of a "complication." **12** But Lisa, like many others, doesn't directly feel the threat of AIDS in her life. Like 81 percent of the women surveyed by the NCHS who believe they have "no chance at all" or "not much chance" of contracting AIDS, Lisa's knowledge about AIDS stays impersonal. "I don't want to die," she says, "but I know lots of women who've slept with more men than I have, and they're not getting AIDS. I think I have a greater chance of getting killed by a terrorist than dying from AIDS."

Even those who say they *are* worried, that they do see AIDS as a **13** serious life-and-death question, occasionally "forget" their fears. "I'm in a serious relationship now," says Barbara, 30. "At the beginning, we were very careful to always use condoms. But after a while, we both were having a pretty hard time insisting on using them every single time. A couple of months into a relationship, you both start to feel like 'Hey, we're in this for the long haul. We might even want to get married and have children someday.' Forgetting about condoms becomes an unspoken statement about the level of trust and commitment you have toward the relationship. You're telling the other person that you know that he or she will be there for you, come what may."

Institutional Changes Are Needed

Margaret Reinfeld, director of education at the American Founda- 14
tion for AIDS Research in New York City, agrees that backsliding is
practically inevitable because, she says, "People cannot live in a continual state of crisis. If you look at people who have been through
floods and tornadoes, life begins to normalize in the trailers and shel-
ters. People have as much of a crisis as they can handle; then they
'normalize' their life. This is not an intellectual decision, it's an emotional one."

So the trick, say the experts, is to achieve the state of mind in 15
which safer sex is no longer a conscious decision at all but rather the
norm of behavior. "You can't pass laws making it illegal to have sex
without a condom," says Dr. Cline, "but you can work to change attitudes; in much the same way, public opinion has shifted through increased awareness of the dangers of cigarette smoking. Pro-condom
advertising (like the banning of cigarette advertising on television) is
a subtle, long-range tactic for changing societal attitudes; so are accessible, well-stocked condom machines. Changes in attitude often
result from institutional changes."

Some of those changes have already begun on many college 16
campuses. "My school gave out free condoms, which was great because then nobody had to be embarrassed by going out and buying
them," says Kathie, 21, a recent graduate of an Ivy League university. "Everyone I know uses condoms—for birth control,
too."

A Serious Problem

Despite terrifying forecasts of growing numbers of people with 17
AIDS, despite the well-publicized fact that women constitute one
of the fastest-growing groups of persons with AIDS, many middle-
class heterosexuals still do not accept AIDS as a life-and-death issue. As one woman who has worked as a volunteer at an AIDS
clinic for gays puts it: "It doesn't come home to you until people
you know are dying." But suddenly that's happening; Magic Johnson's admission that he's HIV positive may finally make us all realize that this disease knows no gender, racial, or class boundaries.
Maybe we'll finally recognize that all the talk and excuses are no
longer enough.

Expanding Your Vocabulary

Here are some words and their meanings from Ray Kerrison's con (against) essay that are important to your understanding of this reading. You might want to review them before you begin to read.

"**melancholy revelation** [sad telling of something not previously known]" (paragraph 1)

"**bizarre** [ridiculous, absurd] position" (paragraph 2)

"a 10-cent rubber **sheath** [cover, referring to a condom]" (paragraph 2)

"ever the **opportunist** [one who takes advantage of every opportunity]" (paragraph 3)

"The message is **fatally flawed** [contains a deadly error]" (paragraph 4)

"end this **plague** [severe epidemic disease]" (paragraph 4)

"Behavior has not figured **prominently** [noticeably]" (paragraph 6)

"reveal his background with a **candor** [honesty] not yet evident" (paragraph 6)

"a **promiscuous** [having sex indiscriminately, with many partners] life" (paragraph 7)

"Virtue, chastity, **monogamy** [having sexual relations with only one partner] were labeled **Victorian** [prim and hypocritical, referring to nineteenth-century British society]" (paragraph 8)

"**false prophets** [people who falsely say they speak the will of God] are . . . **asserting** [claiming] it can be fixed" (paragraph 11)

"This is Magic Johnson's **unprecedented** [never previously occurred] opportunity." (paragraph 17)

Ray Kerrison

Condom Use Will Not Help Prevent AIDS*

If first reactions to the melancholy revelation of Magic Johnson's   1
HIV-virus infection are any guide, the United States is going to rush
headlong into condom-mania under the national banner of Safe Sex.

We are about to adopt the utterly bizarre position that the dead-   2

*Ray Kerrison, "Condom Use Will Not Help Prevent AIDS" from "Condoms No Cure for AIDS Epidemic" from *Human Events* (November 23, 1991).

liest disease of the age can be beaten with a 10-cent rubber sheath. Johnson himself promised to launch a national crusade for condoms. "I want everybody to practice safe sex and wear condoms," he said.

Health experts, activists, educators, the media, and others joined the chorus, including New York City school Chancellor Joseph Fernandez, ever the opportunist, who invited Johnson to come to New York to warn kids they must rubber-up.   **3**

The message is fatally flawed. No one put it so bluntly as Larry Kramer, the militant homosexual activist, who said on "Nightline": "Drugs are useless. Magic Johnson is not going to beat it. I would make this plea to him. He said he is going out to talk to kids about safe sex. It's a waste of time. There is no amount of education that is going to end this plague. The only thing that is going to end it is a cure."   **4**

Dr. James Curran of the Centers for Disease Control put it another way: "If you can control behavior you can control the spread of this disease and save lives."   **5**

Changing Behavior

Behavior has not figured prominently in the national discussion so far. But it's coming. Randall Pope, the AIDS-prevention chief in Michigan's Department of Health, says that if Johnson wants to help the young he will have to reveal his background with a candor not yet evident. "This is a time for complete honesty, complete frankness about how he acquired his infection," said Pope.   **6**

In his autobiography, Wilt Chamberlain, the former basketball marvel, brags of a promiscuous life of mind-boggling dimensions. He claims he has had sex with 20,000 women, the equivalent of a different partner every single day for more than 54 years. Chamberlain explained, "If the milk's free, why buy the cow?"   **7**

Chamberlain is a product of the Sexual Revolution, which began in the '60's and tore down nearly every protective moral restraint. The pitch was, "You can have it all, baby, without cost." Virtue, chastity, monogamy were labeled Victorian and junked. Today, the tab is in. It's staggering and still climbing.   **8**

According to the Centers for Disease Control, 45 million Americans are infected with incurable, sexually transmitted diseases—and that does not include AIDS. The CDC adds another 1.5 million for HIV and AIDS.   **9**

Sexual Excess

Larry Kramer thinks the HIV count is closer to six million. Sexual excess—homosexual to heterosexual—has taken a horrendous toll in the United States. We are now counting the dead in tens of thousands.   **10**

Yet false prophets are all over TV asserting it can be fixed with a condom. This is the greatest threat of all because children are being fed the lie that sex is safe with condoms.   **11**

In a report on contraception, the Alan Guttmacher Institute said that condoms have a 14 percent failure rate in pregnancy. (Among homosexuals, the condom failure rate is 18 percent.)   **12**

Dr. Allan Rosenfield of the Columbia University School of Public Health told a Planned Parenthood conference that half of the three million unintended pregnancies in this country each year are due to contraceptive failure. So much for safe condoms.   **13**

The *New England Journal of Medicine* revealed that in married couples in which one partner was HIV-infected and condoms were used, 10 percent of the healthy became infected within two years.   **14**

Dr. Harold Jaffe, chief of epidemiology at the Centers for Disease Control in Atlanta, says "You just can't tell people it's all right to do whatever you want so long as you wear a condom. It's just too dangerous a disease to say that."   **15**

Dr. Theresa Crenshaw, former president of the American Association of Sex Educators, Counselors and Therapists and a member of the Presidential AIDS Commission, told a House Subcommittee on Health, "Saying that the use of condoms is 'safe sex' is, in fact, playing Russian roulette. A lot of people will die in this dangerous game."   **16**

This is Magic Johnson's unprecedented opportunity. He can use his heart-breaking ordeal to persuade society to change behavior or become just another public advocate for condoms.   **17**

 QUESTIONS FOR CRITICAL THINKING

THINKING CRITICALLY ABOUT CONTENT

1. Are the statistics equally effective in both essays? If not, which essay contains the most convincing statistics? Explain your answer.

2. Are the testimonies equally effective in both essays, or does one essay contain more convincing testimony than the other? Explain your answer.

THINKING CRITICALLY ABOUT PURPOSE

3. What do you think Sara Nelson's and Ray Kerrison's separate purposes were in writing these essays?

4. Which essay did you agree with? Did you agree with that position *before* you read the essay? If you changed your mind as a result of reading one of these essays, which part of the essay made you change your mind? Explain your answer.

THINKING CRITICALLY ABOUT AUDIENCE

5. What type of audience do you think would be most interested in the topic of these two essays? Explain your answer.

6. Why do you think each author quotes experts and cites the results of research and studies? Explain your reasoning.

THINKING CRITICALLY ABOUT POINT OF VIEW

7. State in separate sentences each writer's point of view.

8. Write a paragraph explaining some of the ideas and facts that both writers agree on.

LEARNING FROM YOUR PEERS

As people living in a society that allows us to voice our opinions freely, many of us strive to learn how to express our disagreement in a polite and reasoned way. As a student, your life may be affected by unreasonable school policies; you may be asked to participate in debates or class discussions; or you may be assigned a particular point of view when writing about an important social or historical issue. At home, you may want to write a letter to a public official or an employer to explain your views on a certain topic, or you may want to write to a store or a manufacturer to ask for your money back on a recent purchase. In short, American life is filled with opportunities to try to persuade others of your point of view. Learning how to persuade others effectively and respectfully is a valuable skill that will always be useful. To see how to excel at this skill, we are going to follow the writing process of a student named Melinda Jackson.

Melinda's Writing Assignment: Persuading

This is the topic Melinda's instructor assigned:

No one is born with the skill to persuade another person to change his or her way of thinking; it is a skill we develop. Some combination of emotional and logical arguments is probably the most effective formula when trying to convince another person to see a situation from your point of view. For this assignment, choose a controversial topic that you are familiar with. Then take one side, and try to convince your readers that your stand on the issue is the correct one.

Melinda goes through the process as outlined in Chapter 1: *thinking, planning, developing, organizing, drafting, revising,* and *editing.*

Thinking

After receiving this assignment, Melinda explains to her writing group that she doesn't feel like thinking of a topic today. She is upset because her brother, who is still in high school, was beaten up by one of his best friends at a school event yesterday. The friend had come to school after several hours of drinking, and his behavior was alarming to his friends. Melinda's brother confronted his friend and tried to get him to leave the school grounds so the school officials wouldn't notice he was drunk. The friend responded by hitting Melinda's brother repeatedly in the face, knocking him to the ground, and almost choking him before help arrived. The school officials called the drunk boy's parents, but there were no consequences for his bad behavior. Her brother, the innocent victim, had to go to the hospital for stitches and other necessary medical attention. Her writing group tells her how sorry they feel for her brother, and they encourage her to think about her topic later.

The next day comes, and Melinda is still upset about her brother's situation. He is home from the hospital but still in pain. She decides to write about her anger. At least she will have a journal entry for class. This is what she writes:

I am really mad about what happened to Scott. It is not fair. He is a good kid, and he was just trying to keep his friend out of trouble. Well, he sure succeeded at that. That kid probably didn't even remember what he did while he was drunk. The school didn't do anything to him. Who knows what his parents did. Knowing them, the worst thing they can think of is to take his car away for a week. Of course, they will let him drive to school. He just won't be able to drive at night.

And poor Scott. He might have permanent damage to his eyes. He wouldn't press charges because he said his friend was out of his mind and didn't know who Scott was or what he was doing to him. What is it with these people? They all seem to be helping the drunk. Who is helping Scott?

Melinda meets with her group the next day. They suggest that she write about the alcohol policy at her brother's high school. Maybe she can write a letter to someone in authority there and suggest a change in the policy or in the enforcement of the policy.

Planning

That evening, Melinda asks her brother for his school handbook. There she finds the current policy on drug and alcohol abuse. She sees that the policy is designed to be enforced only if the school authorities think it needs to be enforced. The policy has no "teeth" in it; there is no guaranteed punishment for offenders.

Melinda starts writing about possible policy changes at the school. This is what she writes:

> Innocent people are being hurt. Guilty people suffer no consequences.
> Everyone knows that drug and alcohol abuse is rampant, but no one
> does anything about it.
> There is no penalty for breaking the rules at that school. I think
> students could get away with murder as long as the parents would agree
> to pick them up and get them off the school grounds.
> The policy says that kids could get expelled from school. Not likely. Not
> in my experience. Maybe the school will suggest that Susie or William
> should go to a rehab program.
> Kids come to school events wasted all the time. They think they can't
> have any fun without some chemical high.
> So do mandatory drug tests. That might get rid of the problem for a
> while. A drastic solution, maybe. But what's the alternative?

Developing

Melinda knows she needs to do a little more research so that she can develop a few of her ideas more thoroughly before writing her first draft. First of all, she wants to make sure she quotes the actual school policy on drug and alcohol use: "School policy prohibits the unlawful use, manufacture, possession, distribution, or dispensing of controlled substances and alcohol on school grounds or at school-sponsored events." The wording of the penalty for breaking this rule ("may result in expulsion from school") is vague and tentative, and Melinda believes this is part of the problem.

In fact, there are several different aspects of this problem that Melinda feels the school isn't dealing with, so she records some more of these:

1. Students using drugs and alcohol at school
2. Students coming to school or school events under the influence of drugs or alcohol
3. Students not being punished at school or at home for substance abuse

Melinda believes there are several reasons for substance abuse among high school students. She thinks these might be important additions to her essay:

1. Students are reckless and experimental at this age
2. Peer pressure
3. Some students don't feel they can have fun without drugs or alcohol

Finally, Melinda has some ideas for punishments that might control substance abuse in high school:

1. Required drug tests for all students with results sent to parents
2. Random sobriety tests by security officers on campus
3. Random drug tests at school events

Melinda also believes that once evidence of drug and alcohol use is found, students should be punished further. She feels, however, that students should not be expelled or suspended because they will fall too far behind in their studies. Here are some additional forms of punishment Melinda has come up with:

1. Students should be barred from extracurricular activities for one month for their first offense.
2. Students should be barred from extracurricular activities for the rest of the school year--including all the big events, like the prom and football games, for their second offense.

Organizing

At the next class meeting, Melinda shows her notes to her writing group. They tell her that she has a good topic and some good ideas to support her point of view. They tell her to list the arguments that would be most convincing to the school board and to write her thoughts in a letter addressed specifically to that group. Once her audience and purpose are clear to her, she can decide on the tone that would be most effective.

Melinda goes home and talks to her parents, who are just as upset about Scott as Melinda is. They tell her that she has some good ideas and that she should address her letter to the school board.

Melinda goes over her notes and lists the most important points she wants to make. This is what her list looks like:

1. This school needs a stronger policy about drug and alcohol abuse.

2. Existing rules need to be enforced more strictly.

3. If students do not have drugs or alcohol on them, there is no problem. I think if drugs or alcohol are <u>in</u> them, the problem should not be ignored. Students have seen over and over again that being intoxicated is no problem. They can just claim they are silly teenagers, and their behavior will be overlooked.

4. Parents should be willing to give permission for their children to be tested for drugs or alcohol. If they care about their kids, they will want to know if there is a problem. Ignoring it will not make it go away.

5. There should be punishments for being drunk, but students should still be able to go to school. Knowing they will miss an important game if they are caught drunk may stop them from taking that drink before coming to school.

6. If the school board decided to change the policy, there should be lots of hoopla. Television, news conferences. The works. Everyone should know about it and stand behind it.

7. Maybe there are other solutions. I don't know. I just know too many people are being hurt. Innocent people.

Melinda decides that she is ready to write her draft. She knows that she is still angry and that she will need to concentrate on being reasonable in her essay. Too much emotion could get in the way of her good ideas and encourage her audience to respond emotionally instead of listen to her logic.

Drafting

Here is Melinda's draft.

Melinda's Essay: First Draft ....

Main Idea: We need to enforce the drug and alcohol policy at the high school.

Dear School Board Members:

I am a recent graduate of Sunnydale High School, and my experiences there tell me that you need to have a more stringent policy in regard to the drug and alcohol abuse that runs rampant throughout the student body. For too long, the attitude that reigns at our school has been one of tolerance and denial. It is high time to enforce existing rules more strictly and perhaps to add more drastic penalties to the Student Code of Conduct. We have been beating around the bush too long.

The current code states, "School policy prohibits the unlawful use, manafacture, posession, distribution, or dispenseing of controled substances and alcohol on school grounds or at school-sponsored events." Due to the fact that there is no specific penalty stated in the Code, it is my opinion that problems could arise. Although it falls in a category of behaviors that "may result in expulsion from school," who decides the penalties and if they will be given out fairly? The policy also has a vague statement which says the school has a responsibility to take all appropriate actions against violators, including referral to drug use/alcohol abuse assistance or rehabilitation programs. The problem with this rule, as I see it, is that students drink or use drugs before school or before coming to school-sponsored activitys. By coming to school already under the influence of the substances, students do not risk being expelled. To remedy or correct this problem, it is my opinion that the school should allow drug and alcohol testing in cases where students are suspected of being intoxicated.

Some people may argue that drug testing is a drastic measure that violates there individual rights. However, it seems to me that a large amount of parents are concerned about the welfare of their children and would sign release forms allowing their children to be tested. Reports of all kinds of tests should then be sent to the student's parents and teachers. This would have several affects. Students would know that their behavier at school and school-sponsored events is being watched, and they cannot claim that they are just being silly. If they are suspected of using drugs or alcohol, the test can be made as soon as a teacher or administrator suspects a problem. Students who feel pressured by their friends to use substances such as alcohol and drugs can use the threat of drug testing as a way to avoid drinking or drugging in the first place. Other students who stand by helplessly and see their friends become intoxicated everyday can hope that adults will use their authority to force the drinkers and druggers to abstain from their habits.

When evidence of drug or alcohol use is found, I believe that students should be excused from extracurricular activities for a period of one month. If the big dance or football game is coming up in the future, I myself believe students will not be so tempted to start celebrating with chemicals in advance of the event. If there is a second offense, I believe th student should be baned from all extracurricular activities for the remainder of the school year, includeing events such as the senior prom and gradaution. Under no circumstances should the school board give those students a break.

I do not believe that students should be expelled from classes for these offenses. Based on my experiences, students I know who were expelled from classes at school ended up getting behind in schoolwork and abusing substances even more than ever. If students are to be responsible adults, they need to learn to meet their obligations when they are students.

I think that these new policies should be implemented with a lot of fanfare. There oughta be a school-wide assembly with films or speakers from organizations like SADD (Students Against Drunk Driving) or AA (Alcoholics Anonymous) or the Council on Alcoholism. Students should be made aware that the policy will be strictly enforced if there is any sign that students is intoxicated.

I am sure that there are many solutions to the substance abuse problem at our school that I have not mentioned in this letter. Perhaps security officers at school events should be given permission to give students a sobriety test. Perhaps there should be random tests allowed. I do not know what the perfect solution is. I just know that the School Board needs to step on it. I just know that the four years I spent at Sunnydale High School were mared by many incidence at parties and football games that could have been avoided if students had not been drinking or drugging. Fights, fender benders, and verbal abuse may seem like normal parts of high school events, but many of those I observed were because of alcohol and drug abuse.

It is sometimes the responsibility of the school board to create policies that protect students from theirselves. It is clear as a bell that high school students are naturally reckless and take many unnecessary risks. By setting a firm and realistic policy that strongly discourages students from using drugs and alcohol, the school board will help these students succeed in school and in life. What is more important?

Revising

Melinda feels that she has made a worthwhile plea in her essay. Instead of just going through the motions to complete this assignment, she has spent her time writing about something she really believes in. Now her instructor wants each student to look closely at the effectiveness of his or her whole essay—paying special attention to the focus of the essay, its unity, its organization, and its support for the essay's main ideas.

Melinda is excited about revising this essay because she might actually send her letter to the school board. She reviews the Checklist for Writing Effective Essays at the beginning of the Tips for Revising section of this chapter. Melinda quickly sees how these guidelines are all related to one another, and she begins to restructure parts of her essay. As she rewrites her thesis statement and reorganizes several of her paragraphs, she realizes that her essay needs a lot more work than she originally thought, but the checklist gives her a focus for her revision. She reads the Tips for Revising section and does the exercises her instructor assigns.

Now Melinda goes back over each paragraph, thinking of each as an integral part of the whole essay. After she checks to see that each paragraph is fully developed, she reads her essay again to ensure that its paragraphs fit together smoothly and logically.

COLLABORATIVE WORK

PEER GROUP ACTIVITY

After you read the portions of the Tips for Revising your instructor assigns, turn to Melinda's first draft (pp. 380–382), and complete the following tasks in small groups:

A.   Underline the thesis statement (for a definition, see p. 392) of the essay.

B.   Put brackets around any of Melinda's paragraphs that your group believes are not directly related to the thesis statement.

C.   Write the number 2 beside any paragraph that contains more than one main idea.

D.   Put a question mark next to any paragraph that seems out of place; then draw an arrow to a better location for the paragraph.

Compare the marks your group made to those your instructor will show you. Where do your marks differ from your instructor's? What do you need to review before writing your own essay?

CLASS ACTIVITY

As an entire class, look at the underlined portions of Melinda's revised draft (pp. 385–388) to see how she changed each sentence.

A.   Did you identify the **revision** problems that Melinda corrected?

B.   Do you think her changes are good ones? Discuss her changes.

Editing

Now that the essay says what Melinda wants it to say, she needs to do some final proofreading and editing before handing it in. The instructor emphasizes that all the students in the class need to have a working knowledge of diction and spelling. So Melinda shifts her focus from the organization and development of her essay to specific points of grammar. She reads the Tips for Editing section in this chapter to learn about diction and spelling. After she finishes the exercises her instructor assigns, she takes the questions in the Checklist for Correcting Diction and Spelling one by one and makes changes in her draft to reflect the most appropriate word choices.

 ## COLLABORATIVE WORK

PEER GROUP ACTIVITY

After you read the portions of the Tips for Editing your instructor assigns, turn to Melinda's first draft (pp. 380–382), and complete the following tasks in small groups:

A.   Circle any problems with incorrect level of language, technical language, or slang (for definitions, see pp. 401–404, 404–405, and 405–406).

B.   Put an X through any nonstandard English words (see pp. 406–411).

C.   Underline any words that are not used accurately (see pp. 411–425).

D.   Write *SP* over any spelling errors.

Compare your marks with those your instructor will show you. Where do your circles differ from your instructor's? What do you need to review before writing your own essay?

CLASS ACTIVITY

As an entire class, look at the underlined portions of Melinda's revised draft (pp. 385–388) to see how she changed each sentence.

A.   Did you identify the **editing** problems that Melinda corrected?

B.   Do you think her changes are good ones? Discuss her changes.

Melinda's Revised Essay ....

Dear School Board Members:

I am a recent graduate of Sunnydale High School, and my experiences there tell me that you need to have a more stringent policy in regard to the drug and alcohol abuse that ~~runs~~ is rampant through~~out~~ the student body. For too long, the attitude that reigns at our school has been one of tolerance and denial. It is high time to clarify and then enforce existing rules more strictly and perhaps to add more drastic penalties to the Student Code of Conduct. But in order to make these changes, we must have a sure way to find out who the offenders are. To remedy and correct this problem, it is my opinion that the school should allow drug or alcohol testing in cases where students are suspected of being intoxicated. ~~We have been beating around the bush too long.~~ We need to take action now.

~~The current code states, "School policy prohibits the unlawful use, manafacture, posession, distribution, or dispenseing of controled substances and alcohol on school grounds or at school-sponsored events." Due to the fact that there is no specific penalty stated in the Code, it is my opinion that problems could arise. Although it falls in a category of behaviors that "may result in expulsion from school," who decides the penalties and if they will be given out fairly? The policy also has a vague statement which says the school has a responsibility to take all appropriate actions against violators, including referral to drug use/alcohol abuse assistance or rehabilitation programs. The problem with this rule, as I see it, is that students drink or use drugs before school or before coming to school-sponsored activitys. By coming to school already under the influence of the substances, students do not risk being expelled. To remedy or correct this problem, it is my opinion that the school should allow drug and~~

~~alcohol testing in cases where students are suspected of being~~
~~intoxicated.~~

Some ~~people~~ <u>students and others</u> may argue that drug testing is a drastic measure that violates ~~there~~ <u>their</u> individual rights. However, it seems to me that a large ~~amount~~ <u>number</u> of parents are concerned about the welfare of their children and would sign release forms allowing their children to be tested. ~~Reports of all kinds of tests~~ <u>All test reports</u> should then be sent to the ~~student's~~ <u>students'</u> parents and teachers. <u>Knowing that parents and teachers would receive reports of drug tests would encourage many students to give up alcohol and drugs.</u>

~~This~~ <u>The reports</u> would have several ~~affects~~ <u>effects</u>. Since s~~S~~tudents would know that their ~~behavier~~ <u>behavior</u> at school and school-sponsored events is being watched <u>by a teacher or administrator for signs of intoxication and those exhibiting this behavior are being tested,</u> ~~and~~ they cannot, <u>as some have done in the past,</u> claim that they are just being silly <u>when they are actually high or intoxicated.</u> ~~If they are suspected of using drugs or alcohol, the test can be made as soon as a teacher or administrator suspects a problem.~~ Also, s~~S~~tudents who feel pressured by their friends to use substances such as alcohol and drugs can use the threat of drug testing as a way to avoid ~~drinking or drugging~~ <u>such behavior</u> in the first place. Other students who stand by helplessly and see their friends become intoxicated ~~everyday~~ <u>every day</u> can hope that adults will use their authority to force the drinkers and ~~druggers~~ <u>drug users</u> to abstain from their habits.

<u>The current code has two flaws that make it ineffective in controlling alcohol and drug abuse: It is ambiguous about punishment, and it does not take into account drug use away from the school. The</u> ~~current~~ code states, "School policy prohibits the unlawful use, ~~manafacture,~~ <u>manufacture,</u> ~~posession,~~ <u>possession,</u> distribution, or

~~dispenseing~~ dispensing of ~~controled~~ controlled substances and alcohol on school grounds or at school-sponsored events." ~~Due to the fact that~~ Because there is no specific penalty stated in the ~~Code,~~ code, ~~it is my~~ ~~opinion that~~ I think problems could arise. Although ~~it~~ drug and alcohol use falls in a category of behaviors that "may result in expulsion from school," who decides the penalties and if they will be given out fairly? ~~The policy also has a vague statement which says the school~~ ~~has a responsibility to take all appropriate actions against violators,~~ ~~including referral to drug use/alcohol abuse assistance or~~ ~~rehabilitation programs.~~ The second problem with this rule, as I see it, is that students drink or use drugs before school or before ~~comeing~~ coming to school-sponsored ~~activitys~~ activities, but this problem could be avoided with drug testing. ~~By coming to school already under the~~ ~~influence of the substances, students do not risk being expelled. To~~ ~~remedy or correct this problem, it is my opinion that the school~~ ~~should allow drug and alcohol testing in cases where students are~~ ~~suspected of being intoxicated.~~

When evidence of drug or alcohol use is found, I believe that students should be ~~excused~~ banned from extracurricular activities for a period of one month. If the big dance or football game is coming up ~~in the future~~, I ~~myself~~ believe students will not be so tempted to start celebrating with chemicals in advance ~~of the event~~. If there is a second offense, I believe ~~th~~ the student should be ~~baned~~ banned from all extracurricular activities for the remainder of the school year, ~~includeing~~ including events such as the senior prom and ~~gradaution~~ graduation. Under no circumstances should the school board give those students a break.

I do not believe that students should be expelled from classes for these offenses. ~~Based on my experiences,~~ S~~s~~tudents I know who were expelled from classes at school ended up getting behind in their schoolwork and abusing substances even more than ever. For example, a friend of mine was expelled for other reasons, and she fell so far behind in her schoolwork that she ended up dropping out of school completely. As a result of her school problems, she is now on welfare and making very little money working for a janitorial service. If students like my friend are to be responsible, self-supporting adults, they need to learn to meet their obligations when they are students.

I think that these new policies should be implemented with ~~a lot of~~ great fanfare. There ~~oughta~~ should be a school-wide assembly with films or speakers from organizations like SADD (Students Against Drunk Driving) or AA (Alcoholics Anonymous) or the Council on Alcoholism. Students should be made aware that the policy will be strictly enforced if there is any sign that students ~~is~~ are intoxicated.

I am sure that there are many solutions to the substance abuse problem at our school that I have not mentioned ~~in this letter~~. Perhaps security officers at school events should be given permission to give students ~~a~~ sobriety tests. Perhaps there should be random tests allowed. I do not know what the perfect solution is. I just know that the ~~s~~School ~~b~~Board needs to ~~step on it~~ take action now. I ~~just~~ also know that the four years I spent at Sunnydale High School were ~~mared~~ marred by many ~~incidence~~ incidents at parties and football games that could have been avoided if students had not been drinking or ~~drugging~~ using drugs. Fights, fender benders, and verbal abuse may seem like normal parts of high school events, but many of ~~those~~ the incidents I observed ~~were~~ occurred because of alcohol and drug abuse.

It is sometimes the responsibility of the school board to create policies that protect students from ~~theirselves~~ themselves. ~~It is clear as a bell that~~ Clearly high school students are ~~natrually~~ naturally reckless and take many unnecessary risks. By setting a firm and realistic policy that strongly discourages students from using drugs and alcohol, the school board will help these students succeed in school and in life. What is more important?

WRITING YOUR OWN PERSUADING ESSAY

So far, you have seen three professional writers and a fellow student at work trying to persuade you to take some action or adopt a position on an issue. As you read the published essay and followed the writing process of another student from first to final draft, you absorbed ideas and ways of giving those ideas a form of their own. These reading and writing activities have prepared you to write your own persuading essay on a topic that is meaningful to you.

What Have You Discovered?

Before you begin your own writing task, let's review what you have learned in this chapter so far:

- In a persuading essay, you should choose a topic that is important to you, gather as much information as possible, and use this information to convince your readers to agree with you.

- Evidence is probably the most important factor in writing a persuasive essay.

- To present your persuading essay effectively, you need to organize your ideas.

- To help you shape your essay, you should learn as much as possible about your readers.

- Before you write a draft, you need to decide on a point of view toward your subject.

- After you write a draft, you should revise your essay for meaning and organization.

- After you revise your essay, you should edit its grammar, usage, and sentence structure.

Your Writing Topic

Choose one of the following topics for your persuading essay:

1. In "Letter from Birmingham Jail" (pp. 349–364), Dr. Martin Luther King, Jr., persuades his readers of the necessity of conducting demonstrations in order to end racism and segregation in Birmingham, Alabama. Choose an unjust practice, rule, activity, or policy that exists in your family, your school, your community, or society, and write an essay to persuade whoever is responsible to change or abolish the practice, rule, activity, or policy.

2. Write a letter trying to persuade an administrator at your college that a course requirement should be changed.

3. Write an essay trying to persuade your classmates to devote some of their time to doing volunteer work in your community.

4. Create your own persuading essay topic (with the assistance of your instructor), and write a response to it.

When you have selected one of these topics, you may begin your writing process in the same way Melinda did. (You may find her experience helpful in giving you ideas.) This time your purpose is to write your own persuading essay. If some tasks occur out of order, that adjustment is probably part of your personal writing ritual. Follow your instincts, and let them mold your own writing process. But make sure you've worked through all the stages to your final draft.

YOUR WRITING PROCESS

THINKING   Generate as many ideas on your subject as you can in as many different ways as possible: rereading, listing, freewriting, brainstorming, clustering, discussing, and questioning.

PLANNING   Begin to give your ideas shape by deciding on your approach to your topic (your content, your purpose, your audience, and your point of view). Make a list of points you want to include in your essay.

DEVELOPING   Add more details on three or four specific, focused topics that you have chosen from your list of general points.

ORGANIZING   Organize your material in a way that will be most interesting to your audience.

DRAFTING   Write a working draft of your essay in complete sentences.

REVISING   Consulting the Tips for Revising in this chapter (pp. 392–400), revise your first draft—paying special attention to the unity and logic of your essay.

EDITING   Consulting the Tips for Editing in this chapter (pp. 401–432), edit your draft for grammar and correctness—paying special attention to diction and spelling.

Turn in your revised draft to your instructor.

Some Final Thoughts

When you have completed your own essay, answer these four questions in your journal:

1. What was most difficult about this assignment?
2. What was easiest?
3. What did I learn about persuading by completing this assignment?
4. What did I learn about my own writing process from this assignment—how I prepared to write, how I wrote the first draft, how I revised, and how I edited?

Writing Effective Essays

Checklist for Writing Effective Essays

✓ Does the essay have a single controlling idea expressed in a **thesis statement**?
✓ Are all **topic sentences** in the essay related to the essay's thesis statement?
✓ Does each **body paragraph** develop only one main idea?
✓ Are **body paragraphs** arranged in the most logical order?

When medical researchers are working on large projects that require them to re-peat the same experiment many times, they develop a set procedure or "protocol" for laboratory assistants to follow so that the experiments remain focused on the same goal and the results remain reliable and valid. This protocol leads the assistant step by step through the experiment to ensure that each repetition is conducted in ex-actly the same manner. If you follow a revising plan similar to a protocol, it will lead you to produce essays that are effective because they are focused, unified, logically organized, and well supported.

In no other type of essay are these qualities—focus, unity, organization, and sup-port—as important as they are in a persuading essay. By establishing the focus or purpose of your persuading essay, clearing the essay and individual paragraphs of un-related ideas, making sure the essay's organization is logical, and including sufficient support for your ideas, you may be able to convince an audience to consider and per-haps adopt your position on a particular issue.

Focus

Especially in a persuasive essay, writers need to make sure their essays are focused on a single controlling idea or purpose. In other words, you should determine whether the essay contains a **thesis statement** (or sentence about the essay's general topic). Having a clear focus is crucial in a persuasive essay, because you are trying to con-vince your audience that your position on a particular issue is valid and worthy of consideration.

In "Letter from Birmingham Jail," Martin Luther King, Jr., provides a thesis state-ment at the end of his first paragraph that guides us through the rest of his essay: "But since I feel that you are men of genuine good will and that your criticisms are sincerely set forth, I want to try to answer your statement [their criticism that his present activities are 'unwise and untimely'] in what I hope will be patient and rea-sonable terms." The rest of King's essay addresses their concerns as thoroughly as he can.

When Melinda Jackson began to revise the letter she had written to the school board suggesting ways to better control alcohol and drug use in her brother's school and at extracurricular activities, she first needed to determine whether the focus of her essay—to persuade the school board to initiate drug and alcohol testing for students and then to enforce stricter punishments—was clear. Melinda read her first draft again and realized that she didn't really state her thesis until paragraph 2, and even then the statement was too broad. Here is her original introductory paragraph:

First Draft:

I am a recent graduate of Sunnydale High School, and my experiences there tell me that you need to have a more stringent policy in regard to the drug and alcohol abuse that runs rampant throughout the student body. For too long, the attitude that reigns at our school has been one of tolerance and denial. It is high time to enforce existing rules more strictly and perhaps to add more drastic penalties to the Student Code of Conduct. We have been beating around the bush too long.

As Melinda reread what she had written, she realized she needed to focus on her major suggestions for the school board: instituting drug testing at Sunnydale, clarifying and enforcing school rules related to drug and alcohol use, and adding more drastic penalties. Here is her revised paragraph:

Revision:

I am a recent graduate of Sunnydale High School, and my experiences there tell me that you need to have a more stringent policy in regard to the drug and alcohol abuse that is rampant through the student body. For too long, the attitude that reigns at our school has been one of tolerance and denial. It is high time to **clarify and then** enforce existing rules more strictly and perhaps to add more drastic penalties to the Student Code of Conduct. **But in order to make these changes, we must have a sure way to find out who the offenders are. To remedy and correct this problem, it is my opinion that the school should allow drug or alcohol testing in cases where students are suspected of being intoxicated.** ~~We have been beating around the bush too long.~~ **We need to take action now.**

Now Melinda's essay is clearly focused on her plan to reduce alcohol and drug abuse at her school, and she has established the best way to proceed with her essay. First, she will try to persuade her audience that drug testing is necessary to the process of reducing drug and alcohol abuse on campus. Then she needs to focus on the idea of enforcing the existing school rules after offenders are identified. Next she will argue for more drastic punishments and conclude her letter with a word about acting immediately. (Melinda corrected her diction errors when she began the editing stage in her writing process; see the Tips for Editing in this chapter.)

Exercise R8-1

Find and underline the thesis statement in "Condom Use Will Help Prevent AIDS" (pp. 366–367).

Exercise R8-2

Draft a thesis statement for Melinda's essay (pp. 380–382) that suggests ways other than drug testing to control the abuse of drugs and alcohol by high school students.

Exercise R8-3

Draft a thesis statement that takes a position or makes a statement about each of the following broad topics.

1. Making divorces harder or easier to obtain
2. Raising or lowering the speed limit on interstate highways
3. Requiring all U.S. students to become fluent in a foreign language
4. Requiring computer instruction for all U.S. students
5. Limiting the amount of time children can watch television

Exercise R8-4

Read the following introductory paragraph, and write a thesis statement for it.

Many cars today are equipped with safety devices such as seat belts, child protective seats, and air bags. However, too many people don't use this equipment correctly or at all. Many highway patrol officers witness the senseless injuries and deaths of people in auto accidents that could have been prevented.

Unity

In a **unified** essay, each body paragraph is focused on one controlling idea that contributes to the essay's purpose and relates directly to the thesis statement. Usually this idea is stated in a topic sentence at the beginning of the paragraph. Only details that contribute to that topic sentence should be included in that paragraph.

In the following paragraph from "Condom Use Will Help Prevent AIDS," Sara Nelson is careful to relate each body paragraph to her general thesis statement. The author's subheadings help keep the essay unified, and each paragraph is related to the essay's main controlling idea (the advantages of condom use). Take paragraph 2 as an example. It considers why women don't protect themselves from AIDS in a section titled "Women and AIDS."

> Why are so many savvy women not doing all they can to protect themselves from what is still an incurable disease? "Every group has its own reasons for not admitting AIDS risk," says Mindy Fullilove, M.D., of the HIV Center for Clinical and Behavioral Studies at Columbia University. "Women, for example, don't perceive themselves to be at risk. Even if they understand that there are dangerous behaviors, they haven't translated those dangers to themselves. Women use the fact that more men than women have gotten AIDS so far as an excuse. They say, 'I'm not at risk because AIDS is something men get.'"

This paragraph explains the reasoning of women as part of the larger essay arguing how important condoms are in the fight against AIDS. Furthermore, it helps establish some of the problems involved in making condoms a permanent part of sexual activity.

Another problem that threatens the unity of an essay is a body paragraph with more than one main idea. In the first draft of her essay, Melinda discovered that paragraph 3 dealt with two related but separate ideas: (1) the objections to drug testing and (2) the beneficial effects that she believed should outweigh the objections to drug testing.

First Draft: Some people may argue that drug testing is a drastic measure that violates there individual rights. However, it seems to me that a large amount of parents are concerned about the welfare of their children and would sign release forms allowing their children to be tested. Reports of all kinds of tests should then be sent to the student's parents and teachers. This would have several affects. Students would know that their behavier at school and school-sponsored events is being watched, and they cannot claim that they are just being silly. If they are suspected of using drugs or alcohol, the test can be made as soon as a teacher or administrator suspects a problem. Students who feel pressured by their friends to use substances such as alcohol and drugs can use the threat of drug testing as a way to avoid drinking or drugging in the first place. Other students who stand by helplessly and see their friends become intoxicated everyday can hope that adults will use their authority to force the drinkers and druggers to abstain from their habits.

After studying this paragraph, Melinda divided it into two separate paragraphs, one focused on why she thinks many parents would support drug testing and another that explained the benefits that she thought would come about from drug testing:

Revision:

Some ~~people~~ **students and others** may argue that drug testing is a drastic measure that violates their individual rights. However, it seems to me that a large number of parents are concerned about the welfare of their children and would sign release forms allowing their children to be tested. ~~Reports of all kinds of tests~~ **All test reports** should then be sent to the students' parents and teachers. **Knowing that parents and teachers would receive reports of drug tests would encourage many students to give up alcohol and drugs.**

~~This~~ **The reports** would have several effects. **Since** s~~S~~tudents would know that their behavior at school and school-sponsored events is being watched **by a teacher or administrator for signs of intoxication and those exhibiting this behavior are being tested,** ~~and~~ they cannot, **as some have done in the past,** claim that they are just being silly **when they are actually high or intoxicated**. ~~If they are suspected of using drugs or alcohol, the test can be made as soon as a teacher or administrator suspects a problem.~~ **Also,** s~~S~~tudents who feel pressured by their friends to use substances such as alcohol and drugs can use the threat of drug testing as a way to avoid ~~drinking or drugging~~ **such behavior** in the first place. Other students who stand by helplessly and see their friends become intoxicated every day can hope that adults will use their authority to force the drinkers and ~~druggers~~ **drug users** to abstain from their habits.

Now each of these paragraphs develops a single topic that is directly related to the essay's thesis statement. (Melinda corrected her spelling and diction errors when she began the editing stage in her writing process; see the Tips for Editing in this chapter.)

Exercise R8-5

Write out the topic sentence for paragraph 6 in "Condom Use Will Help Prevent AIDS" (p. 368).

Exercise R8-6

Identify the two ideas in paragraph 2 of Melinda's first draft (p. 368). Rewrite the paragraph by dividing it into two separate paragraphs with their own topic sentences.

Exercise R8-7

Read the following group of sentences and decide which ones contribute to the following thesis statement: "Most students are not particularly aware of political issues that affect their lives, such as proposed cuts in financial aid."

1. In my political science class, not a single student is aware of current proposed legislation that will severely limit the amount of student aid available.
2. Many students need to have outside jobs to stay in college.
3. The bill before Congress would affect 90 percent of the students who receive federal financial aid.
4. Nobody is proposing cuts in state aid programs.
5. We all need more education in the Information Age.

Exercise R8-8

Read the following paragraph and revise it, deleting all irrelevant material so that the paragraph focuses on one main idea.

Small children need good role models in television programs that are produced for a very young audience. I really liked *Kukla, Fran, and Ollie* when I was growing up. For instance, cartoon programs that feature violence should be eliminated. Also, programs that contain dangerous actions that the children might try to imitate should not be allowed. I had to read for 30 minutes before bedtime every night when I was in elementary school. In their television programs, children need to observe characters who are solving problems in nonviolent ways and practicing safety measures.

Logical Organization

Logical essays present information to their audiences in the most reasonable way possible. This means that logical essays follow a plan marked by the fact that one idea develops out of the previous idea.

In his essay "Condom Use Will Not Prevent AIDS," Ray Kerrison proceeds step by step to build his case against counseling people that condoms ensure safe sex. Kerrison proposes the alternative course of changing sexual behavior patterns. First, he argues that those recommending condom use to prevent AIDS have not taken into account the "changing behavior" that results in the proliferation of AIDS. Then he claims that "sexual excess" has led to possibly 6 million people being infected. Last, he points out that condoms have a 10 percent failure rate in preventing AIDS. In other words, Kerrison has given a step-by-step presentation of the material that allows his audience to proceed to each new phase of his persuasive essay.

As Melinda worked on her revision, she observed that paragraph 2 of her essay, which dealt with the school's policy on alcohol and drug abuse, was out of place, especially since she had moved her call for drug testing into her introduction. Her audience would need the information on drug testing first. Here is the order of her main ideas in her first draft:

Explanation of problem/Introduction

School policy on drug and alcohol use

Drug testing

Punishment for offenders

Expulsion

Implementation of new policies

Other solutions

Summary/Conclusion

Her revised plan for the essay places her arguments for drug testing earlier in the essay, puts the topic of the effects of testing (originally in the drug-testing paragraph) in a paragraph of its own, and places the paragraph on the school policy after drug testing and its effects, as paragraph 4:

Explanation of problem/Introduction

Drug testing

Effects of drug testing

School policy on drug and alcohol use

Punishment for offenders

Expulsion

Implementation of new policies

Other solutions

Summary/Conclusion

After she reorganizes these paragraphs, Melinda's essay becomes more logical and easier to follow.

Then Melinda makes several internal revisions in the paragraph on school policy connected to drug and alcohol use so that it fits more logically into its new location as paragraph 4. So Melinda not only moves the paragraph but develops its main idea more fully in the new location.

Exercise R8-9

List the main ideas in Sara Nelson's essay (pp. 366–371), and discuss the logic of their order.

Exercise R8-10

Outline the main ideas and details of Melinda's revised essay (pp. 385–388), and discuss the logic of her order.

Exercise R8-11

Arrange the following topic sentences in the most logical order. Then explain the reasoning for your arrangement.

1. Tendons, ligaments, and bones may not always hold up under the stress of professional sports, but an education lasts forever.
2. More and more college athletes are entering the professional sports drafts before they have completed their college eligibility because that is where the big bucks are.
3. Many athletes who have played only one or two years in college are a big disappointment to the professional teams that draft them.
4. The NCAA, NFL, and NBA need to take action to protect college athletics, athletes, and professional teams.
5. Colleges need to be realistic about their athletes' needs.

Exercise R8-12

Read the following thesis statement, and plan the most logical way to develop it. Then make a list of main ideas that might support it if you were to develop it into an essay.

The images of extremely thin young women that are so prominent in magazines, films, and television productions contribute to the proliferation of eating disorders, low self-esteem, and the failure to mature.

COLLABORATIVE WORK

After writing a draft or your own persuading essay, exchange papers with a classmate, and do the following tasks:

A.   Underline the essay's thesis statement.

B.   Put brackets around any topic sentences that are not directly related to the essay's thesis statement.

C.   Mark each body paragraph that contains more than one idea with a paragraph symbol in front of the sentence where the paragraph should be divided.

D.   List the main idea of each paragraph, and make sure the paragraphs are in the most logical order for what the writer is trying to accomplish.

Then return the paper to its writer, and use the information in this section to revise your draft.

Diction and Spelling

Checklist for Correcting Diction and Spelling

✓ Have you chosen a **language level** that is appropriate for your message, your purpose, and your audience?

✓ Does your writing use **formal and informal language** appropriately?

✓ Does your writing include **jargon or technical language**? If so, is jargon necessary in communicating your message?

✓ Does your writing include **slang**? If so, is slang appropriate in each instance?

✓ Have you avoided **nonstandard English**?

✓ Have you chosen your words carefully, taking into consideration **denotation/connotation**, **idiomatic usage**, and **clichés**?

✓ Are your sentences **free of word usage errors**, involving words that are easily confused with one another?

✓ Are your words **spelled correctly**?

Every day you find yourself in a variety of communication situations. While you prepare for the day, you interact with your family, your roommates, and maybe even your pets, sending and receiving a variety of messages. Then, as you enter the educational arena at your college campus, you communicate with classmates and instructors. You may even present a speech or participate in a discussion in which expressing yourself clearly is extremely important. Closing your books, you rush off to work, where your communication skills are essential and perhaps even critical, depending on the nature of your job. Finally at home after your busy day, you unwind, catch up on your studies—and then remember that the scholarship application you picked up last month is due tomorrow. Only after you complete the forms and write a letter to the selection committee do you put your communication skills away for the night and fall asleep, dreaming of a less hectic life.

The situation you are in at any given moment determines the type of language you should use to express yourself clearly and efficiently. In a typical day, you are constantly adjusting your **diction** or word choice to many different social groups and communication tasks. In this section, you will learn about different levels of language and how to adapt them to your own writing style and to the communication challenges you undertake.

Levels of Language

English can be divided into **standard** (grammatically correct) usage and **nonstandard** (incorrect) usage. All grammatically correct language falls into one of two distinct categories: *formal* or *informal* English. Even though both formal and informal language are correct, they vary greatly in style, in tone, and in the word choices for crafting clear, specific messages. The level you use depends on your message, your purpose, and your audience.

Standard English

Standard American English includes all grammatically correct usage, which can then be divided into formal and informal. **Formal English** is reserved for serious situations, while **informal English**, including jargon and slang, is used for all other communication.

Formal English

Writers use **formal English** for serious communication, such as speeches; some academic essays and assignments; business letters and reports; and scientific, historical, and literary texts. Formal English should not be stuffy or pretentious; it should send the message that the writer or speaker is educated and is adept at using the language with some level of skill and confidence. Vocabulary is on a higher plane, made up of words that you as a reader or listener may find unfamiliar. Sentences offer wide variations in form, ranging from simple to more complex structures that rely on phrases and dependent clauses for details and depth. Formal English is grammatically correct language that follows conventional guidelines for usage; it is a communication mode that excludes contractions, and everyday, faddish expressions. In essence, formal English is reserved, precise, and concerned about using the right word in the right context.

Melinda's letter to the school board relies on informal English to state her case about tightening rules concerning alcohol and drug use in her school. The following version of the first paragraph of her revised draft has been rewritten as formal English to demonstrate the difference between the two levels:

> Sunnydale High School urgently requires the implementation of drug and alcohol abuse policies considerably more stringent than those currently in place. For too long the reigning attitude here has been one of tolerance and denial. To address the substance abuse problems that currently plague the school, existing rules should be enforced more strictly than before, and further penalties should be added to the Student Code of Conduct.

Even though a few words here would send some readers running to a dictionary, the paragraph depends on well-crafted sentences, and it does not use the informal "I" but is framed as an objective statement. Notice also that it contains no contractions or errors. Finally, it has an air of authority, a self-assured, educated tone that comes across in the writer's command of the language and its conventions. Just as Melinda asks the members of the school board to pay attention, formal language does the same. Even though readers and listeners may have to concentrate closely, they will benefit from the messages that well-written formal English sends.

Informal English

Writing and speaking would be frustrating tasks if formal English were our only means of expressing ourselves. Communication would be too labored and slow in a world that values freedom and the expression of honest thoughts and feelings. That is why we have informal language—to give us an alternative to the seriousness and rigidity of formal English.

Logically, any language that is not formal is **informal.** That category covers a large territory, ranging from class notes and lists about things you have to do to essays and exams for your college classes. If you look around, you will find yourself surrounded by informal language: It leaps off the pages of newspapers and magazines; it carries messages on billboards, televisions, and radios; and it even thrives in some of your textbooks. Informal language, however, is not ungrammatical. Like formal English, well-written informal language communicates messages that are clear and grammatically correct. The words are more familiar than those used in formal English; however, the sentences are simpler, the tone is more relaxed, and contractions and popular expressions are allowed.

Melinda's entire letter to the Sunnydale school board is written in informal language. Her subject is serious, but Melinda explains the issues in everyday expressions and relatively simple sentence structures.

Exercise E8-1

Rewrite the following sentences from "Letter from Birmingham Jail," replacing formal words and expressions with informal ones.

1. If I sought to answer all the criticisms that cross my desk, my secretaries would have little time for anything other than such correspondence in the course of the day, and I would have no time for constructive work.
2. Several months ago the affiliate here in Birmingham asked us to be on call to engage in a nonviolent direct-action program if such were deemed necessary.
3. Moreover, I am cognizant of the interrelatedness of all communities and states.
4. There can be no gainsaying the fact that racial injustice engulfs this community.
5. There comes a time when the cup of endurance runs over, and men are no longer willing to be plunged into the abyss of despair.

Exercise E8-2

Using formal language, rewrite paragraphs 4 and 5 of Melinda's revised letter (pp. 386–387).

Exercise E8-3

Rewrite the following paragraph using formal language.

The figures show that most automobile accidents happen close to people's homes, within five miles of their houses. So what can drivers do? Stay home? That's probably impossible. But I believe that drivers should wear their safety belts. Every time you get behind the wheel, you should buckle up. Usually, it's pretty easy to remember since most cars have shoulder harnesses that automatically move into place. However, even if you have to buckle up yourself, it is worth the effort. Seat belts aren't guaranteed to keep you alive, but wearing them certainly won't hurt your chances.

Exercise E8-4

Write original sentences using the following formal words and phrases. Then rewrite each sentence, replacing the formal words and expressions with informal ones.

1. a brief respite from mundane concerns
2. deemed
3. a resounding affirmative reply
4. mediated on the dire possibilities
5. an obtuse but vociferous individual
6. conflagration
7. rekindle smoldering desires
8. consider with careful introspection
9. dreadful deed
10. aspiration

Jargon or Technical Language

Jargon, a subdivision of informal English, is employed by people sharing the same profession, hobby, or interest. You might think of jargon as trade language, dependent on highly technical terms that hold little meaning for those outside that particular profession or area of interest. For example, avid tennis players certainly know the terms *volley, lob, forehand,* and *love,* but people who have never picked up a tennis racket may not know the *head* from the *grip.* Thus, the terms of the tennis world hold meaning for those who are in this special interest group, excluding large numbers of people.

Sometimes textbooks, operations manuals, scientific and business journals, and academic reports and research papers are so overly technical that the general reader has a difficult time understanding the writer's message. Consider this excerpt from Sigmund Freud's landmark book *The Interpretation of Dreams:*

> Advances in psycho-analytic experience have brought to our notice patients who have shown a direct understanding of dream-symbolism of this kind to a surprising extent. They were often sufferers from dementia praecox, so that for a time there was an inclination to suspect every dreamer who had this grasp of symbols of being a victim of that disease. But such is not the case. It is a question of a personal gift or peculiarity which has no visible pathological significance.

Of course, psychology students might understand such terms as *dementia praecox* and *pathological significance.* However, general readers might have to depend on footnotes or a dictionary to fully comprehend the passage.

Jargon should be used only if it is necessary in communicating your message. When you use jargon or technical language, keep your audience in mind. If you are writing for people who are members of a specific profession or interest group who share your knowledge of a particular subject, you can use jargon and technical language with confidence. If you are writing for a general audience, however, you must be sure to define terms that readers are likely to misunderstand. Perhaps the best strategy is to use jargon and technical language sparingly so that you can reach the widest possible audience.

Slang

Certain words and expressions are as faddish as the trendy designs we snatch from the clothing racks. This special type of informal language is called **slang**—words and expressions that move quickly in and out of usage in different subcultures. Some slang words and expressions have their origin in movies (*Gumpisms*), advertisements (*Where's the beef?*), music (*Deadhead*), and fashion (*in drag*)—while other slang terms are coined from current events and newsmakers of the day (*Newtspeak and Reagonomics*). Some influential individuals and entire social groups take great pleasure in forming their own slang expressions. Think of the "gangspeak" of the 1990s, vivid language that varies as widely as the colors the gang members wear (*I was just kicking back at the crib with my homies*).

Some slang terms and expressions have been used long enough to gain widespread acceptance. Words such as *cool* and *neat* have taken on additional meanings. Most slang terms, however, have very short lives, so understanding and using this type of language can be difficult. The best strategy is to avoid slang unless you are writing dialogue, trying to capture a particular time period, or describing a certain group that uses specific slang words and expressions. Instead of using slang, you should rely on formal and informal diction that conveys a more precise message to a wider audience.

Exercise E8-5

Underline the slang words and expressions in the following sentences taken from "Condom Use Will Help Prevent AIDS," and explain their meanings.

1.   "I know I'm not supposed to feel that it's weird when a woman reveals that she carries them around with her," says Bob, 28, "but, well, it makes me think she's the kind of person who has sex on the run."
2.   "If she's carrying around condoms, she gives the impression of being a party girl."
3.   "I'd use a condom if a woman would just ask," says 30-year-old Mark. "It's not a big deal to me."
4.   "Men expect women to plan for these things and then when we do, we get criticized for it. We're loose, they claim, or too clinical or *something*."
5.   "A couple of months into a relationship, you both start to feel like 'Hey, we're in this for the long haul.'"

Exercise E8-6

List examples of jargon and technical language in the following paragraph.

My grandmother collects costume jewelry, and because I am her only grand-child, I have taken up the hobby. She mainly looks for marked pieces, particu-larly Eisenberg Originals that use Swarovski crystals. At last count, she had 14 dress clips and 21 parures, some dating to the early 1930s. She also likes pins with colored cabochon stones. While I also like Eisenbergs and other rhinestone pieces, I also collect bakelite and celluloid, particularly bracelets. In addition, I have an extensive collection of lucite purses, most of them dating from the 1950s.

Exercise E8-7

Choose an activity, field, career, or course of study in which you have knowledge or ex-pertise. List five examples of jargon or technical language, and use each word or expres-sion in an original sentence. Following are some areas you might want to consider for this exercise:

medicine	weight lifting	biology	cooking
sewing	accounting	aerobics	psychology
economics	nursing	basketball	journalism
football	cars	soccer	volleyball
computers	electronics	motorcycles	sociology

Exercise E8-8

List five slang words or expressions of your own, and use them in original sentences. If you have trouble thinking of your own slang terms, ask your parents, grandparents, or instruc-tors for examples of slang words and expressions.

Nonstandard English

Quite simply, **nonstandard English** is language that is not standard, communica-tion that doesn't follow the rules of usage generally observed in both formal and in-formal language. Nonstandard English lies beyond the sphere of widespread accept-ability, finding its use in small subsections of society. Not surprisingly, some of these mini-societies have developed languages of their own featuring unique words, ex-pressions, and usage patterns that serve as stumbling blocks when communicating with outsiders.

Because much of nonstandard English is restricted to certain groups, the educated general public uses such communication rarely. Moreover, because nonstandard words and expressions are often ungrammatical, educated speakers and writers avoid them unless the communication situation calls for such language. Certainly, in an ever-changing, fast-paced world, speakers and writers find themselves faced with myriad communication opportunities. The best strategy may be to arm yourself with knowledge so you can participate in dialogues with diverse groups, all the while knowing that there is a way to send more grammatically correct messages that communicate to larger numbers of people.

Sometimes words and expressions that find their origins in certain regions become popular beyond their original circles. When this occurs, there is often confusion concerning the grammatical correctness of the word or expression in question. Here is a list of common nonstandard words that speakers and writers sometimes mistakenly accept as grammatically correct:

ain't: My economics professor **ain't** giving us the test today.

Correction: My economics professor **isn't** giving us the test today.

alright: Melinda felt **alright** after she took a short nap.

Correction: Melinda felt **all right** after she took a short nap.

and etc. We bought all the things we needed to make a pie (flour, sugar, eggs, milk, **and etc.**).

Correction: We bought all the things we needed to make pie (flour, sugar, eggs, milk, **etc.**).

anyways: I did not plan to go with Yee Ming **anyways**.

Correction: I did not plan to go with Yee Ming **anyway**.

anywheres: Lashawn buys her clothes **anywheres** she can find a sale.

Correction: Lashawn buys her clothes **anywhere** she can find a sale.

awful, awfully: The movie's script was **awful**.

Correction: The movie's script was **terrible**.

We were **awfully** tired after skiing all day.

Correction: We were **extremely** tired after skiing all day.

be: I **be** so happy.

Correction: I **am** so happy.

being as, being that: Emilio will not get to go home over the Labor Day weekend, **being as** he has to work.

Correction: Emilio will not get to go home over the Labor Day weekend **because** he has to work.

TIPS FOR EDITING

bursted, busted: Mary Ann **busted** the cake-mix package when she dropped it on the floor.

Correction: Mary Ann **burst** the cake-mix package when she dropped it on the floor.

but that, but what: Even with the icy roads, we expect **but that** classes will continue.

Correction: Even with the icy roads, we **expect** classes to continue.

coulda, could of, musta, must of, shoulda, should of, woulda, would of: I *could of* made a better grade on my essay. I really **should of** spent more time revising.

Correction: I **could have** (or **could've**) made a better grade on my essay. I really **should have** (or **should've**) spent more time revising.

different than: Sandy Beach is no **different than** Marble Beach when it comes to facilities.

Correction: Sandy Beach is no **different from** Marble Beach when it comes to facilities.

don't: Jamie **don't** listen well because he daydreams too much.

Correction: Jamie **doesn't** listen well because he daydreams too much.

enthused: Jeff was **enthused** about the letter he received from the financial aid office.

Correction: Jeff was **enthusiastic** about the letter he received from the financial aid office.

everywheres: Trouble seems to follow Tony **everywheres** he goes.

Correction: Trouble seems to follow Tony **everywhere** he goes.

firstly, secondly, thirdly: Firstly, find the number's square root.

Correction: **First**, find the number's square root.

goes: When I told Ernie that we weren't ready, he **goes** "So what's new?"

Correction: When I told Ernie that we weren't ready, he **said,** "So what's new?"

gonna: Melinda said she is **gonna** apply for a part-time job at Pizza Palace.

Correction: Melinda said she is **going to** apply for a part-time job at Pizza Palace.

has got/have got: Mara **has got** nine sick days that she needs to use.

Correction: Mara **has** nine sick days that she needs to use.

hisself: Jim forced **hisself** to save money by having $100 withheld from each of his checks.

Correction: Jim forced **himself** to save money by having $100 withheld from each of his checks.

in regards to: We received a letter **in regards to** our complaint about the company's poor service.

Correction: We received a letter **in regard to** our complaint about the company's poor service.

inside of, outside of: The hostages are still **inside of** the building.

Correction: The hostages are still **inside** the building.

irregardless: Irregardless of how much time you spent on your paper, it still needs work.

Correction: **Regardless** of how much time you spent on your paper, it still needs work.

kinda, kind of, sorta, sort of: My English professor was **kinda** upset when she discovered that just a few people had read the assignment.

Correction: My English professor was **rather** upset when she discovered that just a few people had read the assignment.

learn: My brother says his English teacher didn't **learn** him anything.

Correction: My brother says his English teacher didn't **teach** him anything.

off of: The grasshopper jumped **off of** the lawn chair and onto a rose bush.

Correction: The grasshopper jumped **off** the lawn chair and onto a rose bush.

OK/O.K./okay: All three are acceptable spellings for informal usage. However, avoid using these expressions in formal writing.
My teacher said it was **okay** to turn in our papers late.

Correction: My teacher said it was **all right** to turn in our papers late.

oughta: You really **oughta** put more time into your studies.

Correction: You really **should** put more time into your studies.

rarely ever: Serena **rarely ever** watches television.

Correction: Serena **rarely** watches television.

real: The last ten questions on the test were **real** difficult.

Correction: The last ten questions on the test were **really** difficult.

somewheres: Your jeans are **somewheres** in that pile of clothes.

Correction: Your jeans are **somewhere** in that pile of clothes.

suppose: Seth was **suppose** to pay the phone bill yesterday, but he forgot.

Correction: Seth was **supposed** to pay the phone bill yesterday, but he forgot.

sure and: Please remember to be **sure** *and* lock the doors before you go to sleep.

Correction: Please remember to be **sure to** lock the doors before you go to sleep.

theirselves: The guests helped **theirselves** to the food in the buffet line.

Correction: The guests helped **themselves** to the food in the buffet line.

use: Our family car **use** to be a huge station wagon with wood-grain panels.

Correction: Our family car **used** to be a huge station wagon with wood-grain panels.

ways: When Kara's car broke down, she was a long **ways** from home.

Correction: When Kara's car broke down, she was a long **way** from home.

where . . . at: Does anyone know **where** the nearest bakery is *at?*

Correction: Does anyone know **where** the nearest bakery is?

while: Someone from the bank called **while** ago and asked for Beth.

Correction: Someone from the bank called **a while** ago and asked for Beth.

Exercise E8-9

Identify examples of nonstandard usage in these sentences from Melinda's first draft, and provide standard English alternatives.

1. Some people may argue that drug testing is a drastic measure that violates there individual rights.
2. This would have several affects.
3. I think that these new policies should be implemented with a lot of fanfare.

4. There oughta be a school-wide assembly with films or speakers from organizations like SADD (Students Against Drunk Driving) or AA (Alcoholics Anonymous) or the Council on Alcoholism.

5. It is sometimes the responsibility of the school board to create policies that protect students from theirselves.

Exercise E8-10

Rewrite the following paragraph in standard English.

After my best friend Larry filled out my tax returns, I was real enthused to find out that I would be getting a $432 refund. I immediately began thinking how I'd spend the money, irregardless of how many pressing bills I had to pay. My first though was to blow it all on a trip, maybe somewheres like Las Vegas. But then I would have to find someone to go with me, and all my friends are busted. Then I thought being as I watch television a lot, I would buy a new remote-control TV with a built-in VCR. My brother bought hisself one last year, and he loves it. But then I looked inside of my closet and realized I rarely ever buy any clothes. I mean, all I could see was torn jeans, baggy sweatshirts, T-shirts, and baseball caps. So I decided to go on a spending spree for a new wardrobe, which made my girlfriend real happy. She likes me, my physical looks and personality, but she don't like anything I wear.

Choosing the Right Word

Writing is a process of putting words together to form complete thoughts that fully express the writer's message. Sometimes the right words escape the author, making writing a frustrating endeavor. However, choosing words with care—looking at words and their many meanings from different perspectives—will make choosing the right word an exercise in precision as you strive to communicate exactly what you mean.

Denotation and Connotation

Most words in our language have a denotative meaning and a connotative meaning. The **denotative meaning** of a word is its actual dictionary definition. The **connotative meaning** is the feelings or emotions that the word arouses or any associations you make with the word. Usually the connotations of words carry either positive or negative implications.

For example, consider the word *grass*. *Grass* is defined by the *American Heritage Dictionary* as "any of various plants having slender leaves characteristic of the grass family." Reading the word *grass*, however, may make you think of a soft, green field where you lie down to forget about your troubles. Or the word *grass* may produce a negative reaction because you have an allergy to nature's handiwork that makes you break out in red spots. You might even think of marijuana because *grass* is a slang term for this drug. Whatever the case, *grass*—like all words—has a range of connotations; some are known to everyone and some are personal for the individual reader.

You should choose the correct word depending on your purpose, your subject matter, and your audience. If the word does not seem appropriate, you should make another choice. For example, Melinda changed a word in the first sentence of paragraph 4 of her letter because her original choice had the wrong connotation:

First Draft:	When evidence of drug or alcohol use is found, I believe that students should be excused from extracurricular activities for a period of one month.
Revised Draft:	When evidence of drug or alcohol use is found, I believe that students should be ~~excused~~ **banned** from extracurricular activities for a period of one month.

Excused carries the connotation of obtaining permission to miss an activity. *Banned* is a better word choice because the connotation is taking away privileges. The denotations (dictionary definitions) of these two words are very similar, but their connotations make *banned* a better choice in this context than *excused*.

Idioms

Idioms are groups of words that work together to create a single meaning. For example, if you plan to *get hold of* a counselor to help set up your schedule next semester, you plan to *contact* a counselor. The phrase *get hold of* cannot be defined or translated word for word, but it can be defined as a unit: *contact or obtain.* Idioms are difficult to translate, so they often cause problems for nonnative speakers of English. By consulting a dictionary, however, you will find definitions of expressions like the following:

Idioms	
agree with	on sale
cut it out	plan to
give me a break	step on it
hit the road	sure to
intend to do	try to
little does he know	

These words have to be learned as units because it is their special combination that gives them their meaning.

Clichés

Like idioms, clichés are phrases. However, **clichés** are phrases that have been used so often that they have lost some of their original meaning (*pretty as a picture, out of the frying pan and into the fire*). These expressions lack impact because speakers and writers over the years have worn them out. Since clichés lack originality and force, you should avoid them in written communication. For example, your baby sister may be *cute as a bug's ear,* but it is more interesting to write that your sister is as *cute as a Christmas package.* New, creative expressions will bring your writing to life, producing new images for your readers.

Exercise E8-11

Explain the connotation of the italicized words in the following sentences from Dr. Martin Luther King's "Letter from Birmingham Jail."

1. A just law is a man-made code that *squares* with the moral law or the law of God.
2. All segregation statutes are unjust because segregation *distorts* the soul and damages the personality.
3. Is not segregation an existential expression of man's *tragic* separation, his awful estrangement, his terrible sinfulness?
4. Throughout Alabama all sorts of *devious* methods are used to prevent Negroes from becoming registered voters, and there are some counties in which, even though Negroes constitute a majority of the population, not a single Negro is registered.
5. Sometimes a law is just on its *face* and unjust in its application.

Exercise E8-12

List any idioms or clichés in the following sentences from Melinda's first draft.

1. It is high time to enforce existing rules more strictly and perhaps to add more drastic penalties to the Student Code of Conduct.
2. We have been beating around the bush too long.
3. Under no circumstances should the School Board give those students a break.
4. I just know that the School Board needs to step on it.
5. It is clear as a bell that high school students are naturally reckless and take many unnecessary risks.

Exercise E8-13

Complete the idioms in the following paragraph by filling in the blanks with the missing words.

My friend Stacy is putting her car up (1) _____ sale. She used

(2) _____ like her yellow Sunbird, but it has given her

nothing (3) _____ trouble lately. In fact, she thinks it's ready

to (4) _____ the dust any day now. I agree

(5) _____ Stacy because I've seen it and ridden in it recently.

I had a mind (6) _____ tell Stacy that I would walk. The car

sputtered and chugged and put out the most awful fumes. I told Stacy then that she

had better quit fooling (7) _____ and put an ad in the paper.

Finally, she got on (8) _____ . I'm not sure if the car will

meet (9) _____ anyone's approval because the fact

(10) _____ , the Sunbird is a big lemon.

Exercise E8-14

Write original expressions to replace the following clichés.

1. dead as a doornail
2. selling like hotcakes
3. plain as the nose on your face
4. dog tired
5. skinny as a rail

Confusing Words

In editing their writing, writers are more often concerned with making sure each *i* is dotted, appropriate words are capitalized, and the commas are in the right places rather than with choosing their words carefully. Because they are focused on punctuation and mechanics, they often overlook usage errors.

When words look alike, sound alike, or have similar meanings, choosing the right one can be tricky. You will find that some words and phrases are acceptable in formal academic writing, while others are more appropriate in informal situations. The best strategy is to analyze each writing situation, including the paper's purpose and audience, as you choose the correct word. The following list will help you decide between the most easily confused words and phrases:

a/an: A and *an* are two of the three articles, adjectives that indicate a specific person, place, or thing. Use *a* before words that begin with a consonant or a consonant sound plus a *y* sound, and use *an* before words that begin with vowels or vowel sounds:

a street, **a** problem, **a** unit

an egg, **an** orange, **an** emergency

accept/except: *Accept* is a verb that means "to receive." *Except* is a preposition meaning "without" or "other than."

> We will **accept** all of the applicants **except** the one who lacks a college degree.

advice/advise: The noun *advice* means "guidance or helpful information." The verb *advise* is the act of giving advice.

> My career counselor **advised** me to consider social work, good **advice** for someone who has a strong desire to help others.

adapt/adopt: Both words are verbs. *Adapt* means "to adjust." *Adopt* means "to take into a relationship or to use as one's own."

> We **adopted** a kitten from the animal shelter. It took just a couple of days for our new pet to **adapt** to its new surroundings.

affect/effect: *Affect* usually functions as a verb meaning "to influence" or "to move emotionally." *Effect* can function as a verb ("to bring about or make happen") or as a noun ("a result").

> The movie **affected** me greatly, and I could think of little else for days after I saw it.

> The board's recommendations should **effect** positive changes in the quality of education.

> The **effect** of drinking too much is often a headache.

a lot/allot: *A lot* is a slang expression that means "a great deal" and should be avoided in formal writing. *Allot* is a verb meaning "to set aside."

> My brother paid **a lot** of money for his new leather jacket.

> Shawna **allots** $15 each week for gasoline.

allude/elude: Both words are verbs. *Allude* means "to refer to something indirectly." *Elude* means "to avoid or escape."

> The poet **alludes** to the Civil War in line 13 when he mentions "the Blue and the Gray."

> Hiding in the dense underbrush, the fox **eluded** its pursuers.

allusion/illusion: Both words are nouns. *Allusion* means "an indirect reference." *Illusion* refers to a misconception or a mistaken image.

> I don't believe most people understood the speaker's **allusion** to King Lear.

> The magician specializes in creating optical **illusions**.

already/all ready: *Already* is an adverb indicating "previously." *All ready* is a phrase meaning "completely prepared."

Hope has **already** registered for the spring semester.

We were **all ready** to go when a small emergency made us leave late.

altogether/all together: *Altogether* is an adverb meaning "completely" or "thoroughly." *All together* is a phrase meaning "gathered in one place."

Ahmad was **altogether** confused when we told him to meet us at Grant Park.

After 15 years my dad's brothers and sisters were **all together** at the reunion.

among/between: Use *among* to refer to three or more persons or items, *between* to refer to only two individuals or things.

Among all the students in the design class, Sharla is the most talented.

When they went car shopping, my parents had a hard time deciding **between** a Neon and a Lumina.

amount/number: *Amount* refers to quantities that cannot be counted. *Number* refers to quantities that can be counted.

You need to check the **amount** of air you have in your tires.

A small **number** of students have preregistered for the literature class.

awhile/a while: *Awhile* is an adverb meaning "a short period of time." *A while* is a noun phrase referring to a short time span and usually functions as an object of a preposition.

Mario and Pete decided to stay **awhile** in Hannibal to tour Mark Twain's home.

Our teacher let us discuss in groups for **a while** before she began lecturing.

bad/badly: *Bad* is an adjective meaning "not good." *Badly* is an adverb meaning "performing in an unacceptable manner."

In the play Kevin plays a **bad** character who is constantly scheming.

My nieces and nephews behaved **badly** when I took them to the movie.

beside, besides: Both words function as prepositions. *Beside* means "at the side of or next to," and *besides* means "other than or in addition." *Besides* sometimes appears as an adverb meaning "furthermore."

Shanice sat **beside** Ronald at lunch.

Besides sleeping, I can think of nothing else I want to do.

Clint collected $250 for the fund-raising drive; **besides**, he kicked in $25 himself.

bring/take: Use *bring* when the action comes toward the speaker and *take* when the action moves away from the speaker.

Luz said she will **bring** me a serape from her visit to her homeland of Mexico.

Rick plans to **take** the leftover clothes to the Goodwill store this afternoon.

can, may: According to traditional usage, *can* refers to ability and *may* refers to permission or a possibility.

Tracy **can** juggle four balls at once.

Diana **may** let Binky go outside for a while this afternoon.

The forecast says that the weather **may** turn colder this afternoon.

capital/capitol: As a noun, *capital* refers to a city, money, or upper-case letters. *Capital* as an adjective means "important or major." *Capitol* refers to a building where lawmakers conduct business.

Tallahassee is the **capital** of Florida and should begin with a **capital** letter.

The business venture will require an initial investment of $55,000 in **capital**.

A new heating system is considered a **capital** expenditure.

The **capitol** building in Tallahassee is located downtown.

choose/chose: The verb *choose* means "to select." *Chose* is the past tense of *choose*.

It is Greg's turn to **choose** a card.

Keith **chose** last time.

cite/site: The verb *cite* means "to quote"; the noun *site* refers to a place or scene.

Our instructor said we had to **cite** at least five different sources in our paper.

Phoenix was the **site** for the 1996 Super Bowl.

complement/compliment: *Complement* can function as a verb ("to complete or go with") or as a noun ("something that completes"). *Compliment* can function as a verb ("to praise or flatter") or as a noun ("an expression of praise or flattery").

Sasha found the neatest pair of shoes to **complement** her outfit.

Mom's necklace is the perfect **complement** for my new dress.

People should **compliment** others when praise is due because **compliments** put a smile on people's faces.

conscience/conscious: The noun *conscience* refers to "a sense of morality or what is right or wrong." *Conscious* is an adjective meaning "acting alert or aware."

Many people would argue that murderers have no **conscience**.

When Will passed out, he was not **conscious** of his surroundings.

continual/continuous: Both words are adjectives. *Continual* refers to something that recurs or happens repeatedly. *Continuous* refers to something that happens over time without being interrupted.

The **continual** leaks in our roof finally made us spend $1,200 in repairs.

The alarm clock produced a **continuous** high-pitched screech until John pulled its plug.

disinterested/uninterested: Both words are adjectives. *Disinterested* means "impartial" or "objective." *Uninterested* means "showing no interest at all."

The union sought a **disinterested** mediator to settle the contract dispute.

Nerissa is **uninterested** in going to school right now because she is making good money at her job.

due to/because of: *Due to* should be used after a linking verb but not as a substitute for *because of*.

Rob's low grade was **due to** his careless errors.

When they sold their houses, many people suffered losses **because of** the nuclear power plant being built nearby.

emigrate/immigrate: *Emigrate* means "to leave one country to settle in another." *Immigrate* means "to enter one country from another, taking up residence."

Chu's parents **emigrated** from Laos almost 20 years ago.

Many Jews **immigrated** to the United States after World War II.

eminent/imminent: Both words are adjectives. *Eminent* means "important or distinguished." *Imminent* means "about to happen."

The speaker is an **eminent** scholar who earned a doctorate from Oxford.

I am afraid that because of her absences, Shanequa's dismissal is **imminent**.

everyday/every day: *Everyday* is an adjective meaning "usual" or "ordinary." The phrase *every day* can function as a noun phrase or as an adverb referring to how often.

Walking his Irish setter is an **everyday** ritual for Niles.

I try to greet **every day** with a positive attitude.

Carl runs five miles **every day**, even when it's raining or snowing.

farther/further: *Farther* refers to physical distance. *Further* means "additional" or "to a certain degree."

Maria lives **farther** from school than Emilio does.

After today we will have no **further** discussions about my habits, I hope.

fewer/less: Both words are adjectives. *Fewer* refers to things that can be counted; *less* refers to things that cannot be counted.

February has **fewer** days than March.

I admit that I have **less** respect for Mr. Adams after he was arrested for not paying child support.

formally/formerly: Both words are adverbs. *Formally* describes the manner in which something is done. *Formerly* means "previously."

The people in line **formally** greeted the ambassador.

The ambassador was **formerly** a congresswoman.

former/latter: *Former* refers to the first of two people or items. *Latter* refers to the second. The adjectives should be used only when referring to two people or items, no more.

Cathy and Claudia are two of my first cousins; the **former** is a student at Northwestern, and the **latter** is a lawyer in Philadelphia.

good/well: *Good*, usually an adjective, means "pleasing." *Well*, usually an adverb, refers to how something is done. However, when *well* refers to a state of health, it functions as an adjective.

Even though Brady didn't feel **well,** we still had a **good** time at the movie.

Because the team arrived late and didn't get much rest, they didn't play **well.**

its, it's: *Its* is a possessive pronoun, and *it's* is the contraction for *it is* or *it has.*

We think the tornado will lose **its** momentum once **it's** moved across Union County.

lay/lie: *Lay* is a transitive verb that means "to place or set"; its principal parts are *lay, laid, laid*. *Lie* is an intransitive verb that means "to recline or to rest"; its principal parts are *lie, lay, lain*.

Lay your shoes at the foot of the bed before you **lie** down to take a nap.

leave/let: Both are verbs. *Leave* means "to depart"; *let* means "to allow."

If we **leave** the arena, the gatekeepers will not **let** us come back in.

liable/likely: *Liable* means "tending toward something" or "responsible for" in legal terms. The adjective *likely* means "probable."

It's **likely** that Dan is **liable** for damages because he failed to yield the right of way.

like/as: *Like* is a preposition, and *as* is a subordinating conjunction. Informally, you may use *like* as a conjunction in certain instances. However, in formal usage use *as* or *as if*.

He looks **like** he is exhausted. (Informal)

He looks **as if** he is exhausted. (Formal)

loose/lose: *Loose* can function as an adjective ("free or unfastened") or as a verb ("to release"). The verb *lose* means "to misplace or fail to win."

Hal's pants are **loose**; they hang on his hips.

The wildlife agents plan to **loose** the alligators in the swamp next week.

Matt **loses** his keys quite often.

maybe, may be: *Maybe* is an adverb meaning "possibly." *May be* is a verb phrase.

Maybe we will go to the beach tomorrow if the sun is shining.

There **may be** more layoffs if the economy does not improve.

moral/morale: *Moral* can function as a noun ("the lesson of a story") or as an adjective ("referring to ethics"). *Morale* is a noun meaning "the mental condition of a person or group of people."

I believe the **moral** of the story is that people should choose their friends with care.

The abortion issue is a **moral** question that people must answer for themselves.

The employees' **morale** sank after Mr. Sanders announced his resignation.

TIPS FOR EDITING

perspective/prospective: *Perspective* is a noun meaning "from one's viewpoint." *Prospective* is an adjective meaning "potential."

Looking at the issue from Mara's **perspective**, I agree with her decision.

The man getting into the truck is our **prospective** tenant.

precede/proceed: Both words are verbs. *Precede* means "to come or go before"; *proceed* means "to move forward."

The table of contents **precedes** the preface in most books.

The long line of graduates **proceeded** slowly across the gym floor.

principal/principle: *Principal* is either an adjective ("first" or "most important") or a noun ("head of a school" or "sum of money"). *Principle* is a noun meaning "a basic law, truth, or rule of conduct."

Mr. Reed, the **principal** of our school, is the **principal** decision maker when it comes to closing school for weather-related reasons.

Our criminal courts rest on the **principle** that people are innocent until proven guilty.

quotation/quote: *Quotation* is a noun; *quote* is a verb.

Luther's indented **quotation** takes up most of the page.

Tad likes to **quote** philosophers in an attempt to impress people.

raise/rise: *Raise* is a transitive verb meaning "to increase" or "to lift upward." *Rise* is an intransitive verb that means "to go up."

Why don't you **raise** the windows so we can feel the breeze?

My grandmother **rises** every morning at 5:30.

respectfully/respectively: *Respectfully* is an adverb meaning "showing admiration"; *respectively* refers to the specific order in which things are listed.

You would expect people, including teenagers, to act **respectfully** at a family member's funeral.

Sara, Janet, and Mindy went to Harvard, Columbia, and Princeton, **respectively**.

set/sit: *Set* is a transitive verb meaning "to put"; *sit* is an intransitive verb meaning "to put the body in a seated position."

Please **set** the pitcher on the counter before you **sit** down at the table.

stationary/stationery: The adjective *stationary* means "not moving"; the noun *stationery* refers to materials used in writing and sending letters.

The meteorologist says a **stationary** front will keep temperatures low.

Lawanda bought five sets of **stationery** at the going-out-of-business sale.

sometime/some time/sometimes: The adverb *sometime* means "at some future, unspecified time." *Some time* is a noun phrase referring to a period of time. *Sometimes* is an adverb meaning "now and then."

Jackie says she will spend **some time** with Martin **sometime** in the future, but she **sometimes** stretches the truth.

sure/surely: *Sure* is an adjective meaning "certain"; *surely* is an adverb meaning "without doubt."

Brad is **sure** that the front door was open when he arrived.

Surely you believe him, don't you?

than/then: *Than* is a conjunction used in making comparisons; *then* is an adverb of time.

If you think you are stronger **than** Mike, **then** show us.

I revised my essay more **than** you did; **then** I wrote a final draft.

that/which/who: *That* introduces essential dependent clauses. *Which* introduces nonessential dependent clauses. *Who* can introduce either an essential or nonessential clause, but keep in mind that *who* always refers to people (or sometimes animals).

The book **that** I bought yesterday is about model trains, **which** is a hobby that I have enjoyed since I was a child.

Lana is the girl **who** spoke to me at the jewelry store.

their/there/they're: *Their* is a possessive pronoun; *there* is used as an expletive or as an adverb indicating location. *They're* is simply the contraction for *they are*.

They're so happy because **there** are extra tickets to see **their** favorite team in action—the Bulls!

to/too/two: *To* is a preposition that means "toward"; it can also begin an infinitive. *Too* is an adverb that means "also" or "very." *Two* is the numeral following one.

Two of my friends went **to** the Pearl Jam concert **too**.

toward/towards: Both spellings are acceptable, although *toward* is preferred in standard American English.

> Tyler says he has no hard feelings **toward** his father, who abandoned the family years ago.

weather/whether: *Weather* is a noun referring to the condition of the atmosphere or a verb meaning "to endure." *Whether* is a conjunction referring to a possibility.

> Many people are wondering **whether** the **weather** will change and grow colder.

> Will she be able to **weather** the criticism from her family?

were/where: *Were* is the past tense of the verb *to be; where* is a subordinating conjunction and an adverb.

> **Where were** you yesterday?

> They **were** in the city **where** you live.

who/whom, whoever/whomever: Use *who* and *whoever* as subjects and subject complements; use *whom* and *whomever* as objects.

> **Whoever** ordered the pizza has to go pick it up. **Who** disagrees?

> To **whom** do you owe your musical talent? To **whomever** will take credit.

who's/whose: *Who's* is the contraction for *who is*, and *whose* is a possessive pronoun.

> **Who's** going to decide **whose** plan is the best?

your/you're: *Your* is a possessive pronoun, and *you're* is the contraction for *you are*.

> **Your** attendance at the conference is proof that **you're** serious about a real estate career.

Exercise E8-15

Find the usage errors in the following sentences, which appear in their correct forms in "Condom Use Will Help Prevent AIDS" by Sara Nelson (pp. 366–371).

1.   In a survey of 5,500 Canadian college students, researchers found that, despite high levels of AIDS awareness, less than 16 percent of the women studied said they always have there partner use condoms.
2.   They could sleep with whoever they wanted, assume the woman was on the Pill and not worry at all.
3.   Early in the epidemic, many experts advocated a "talk to your partner" strategy, stressing the importance of communicating with you're partner nearly as much as using condoms.

4. But Dr. Cline's study revealed just the opposite: The men that said they talked to their partners about AIDS, but only sometimes or never used condoms, had had nearly 50 percent more partners than men that said they didn't talk about AIDS.
5. This is not a intellectual decision, its an emotional one.

Exercise E8-16

Find the usage errors in the following sentences, which appear in the first draft of Melinda's persuading essay (pp. 380–382).

1. The policy also has a vague statement which says the school has a responsibility to precede with appropriate actions against violators, including referral to drug use/alcohol abuse assistance or rehabilitation programs.
2. Some people may argue that drug testing is a drastic measure that violates there individual rights.
3. However, it seems to me that a large amount of parents are concerned about the welfare of their children and would sign release forms allowing their children to be tested.
4. Other students who stand by helplessly and see their friends become intoxicated everyday can hope that adults will use their authority to force the drinkers and druggers to abstain from their habits.
5. Fights, fender benders, and verbal abuse may seem like normal parts of high school events, but many of those I observed were because of alcohol and drug abuse.

Exercise E8-17

Choose the correct word in parentheses to complete each sentence in the following paragraph.

Journalists are often faced with (1) (*moral, morale*) issues as they go about their jobs of covering the news. Some ethical questions are more serious than others and may cause a reporter to seek (2) (*advice, advise*) from a superior or someone with more insight and experience. For example, (3) (*a while, awhile*) ago I read about a television reporter who was fired because he accepted bribes from a local business-man. That's just a minor instance. When journalists are caught in lies and stretch the truth to gain viewers and readers, the public (4) (*loses, looses*) its trust in the me-dia. From my (5) (*perspective, prospective*), upholding the highest ethical standards should be a primary goal for anyone who reports the news to the public.

Exercise E8-18

Write original sentences using the following words.

1. conscious
2. fewer
3. lie

4. principle
5. their

Spelling

Remembering how letters are arranged to form certain words can be frustrating. The best advice for improving your spelling skills is to follow some general guidelines and refer to a dictionary when questions arise.

1. *Learn to distinguish between words that sound alike.* Some of the most common spelling errors occur with **homonyms** or **homophones**, words that sound alike but are spelled differently (*mail/male, to/too/two,* etc.). When you are determining the correct spelling, you should analyze the sentence closely to determine which meaning is needed (We are going *to* the play *too*). *To* is the first correct spelling because the word functions with a noun; *too* is the correct second spelling because it means "also." You should try to isolate those homonyms that cause you trouble and then pay close attention to them as you edit and revise your papers. The following list includes the most common English homonyms you will encounter.

Common Homonyms		
accept . . . except	decent . . . descent	knew . . . new
access . . . excess	device . . . devise	know . . . no
aid . . . aide	dual . . . duel	
air . . . heir		lead . . . led
altar . . . alter	elicit . . . illicit	lessen . . . lesson
ascent . . . assent	exercise . . . exorcise	loan . . . lone
ate . . . eight		
	fair . . . fare	made . . . maid
bare . . . bear	flour . . . flower	mail . . . male
berry . . . bury	for . . . four	main . . . mane
berth . . . birth	forth . . . fourth	meat . . . meet
board . . . bored		medal . . . metal
born . . . borne	gorilla . . . guerrilla	miner . . . minor
brake . . . break		
bread . . . bred	hair . . . hare	one . . . won
buy . . . by	hear . . . here	
	heard . . . herd	pain . . . pane
cell . . . sell	heroin . . . heroine	pair . . . pear
cereal . . . serial	higher . . . hire	peace . . . piece
coarse . . . course	hoarse . . . horse	peak . . . peek
council . . . counsel	hole . . . whole	peer . . . pier
		personal . . . personnel
dairy . . . diary	idle . . . idol	plain . . . plane
dear . . . deer	in . . . inn	

Common Homonyms		
pray . . . prey	seam . . . seem	their . . . there . . . they're
rain . . . reign	shone . . . shown	tide . . . tied
read . . . red	sole . . . soul	waist . . . waste
right . . . rite . . . write	stake . . . steak	wander . . . wonder
road . . . rode	steal . . . steel	weak . . . week
role . . . roll		were . . . where
sail . . . sale	tail . . . tale	which . . . witch
scene . . . seen	taught . . . taut	wood . . . would
	team . . . teem	

2. *Learn the main spelling rules, such as "i before* e *except after* c *or when sounded like* ay, *as in* neighbor *and* weigh."

Examples:	believe, fierce, relief (*i* before *e*)
	receive, eight, neighbor (*e* before *i*)
Exceptions to the Rule:	either, foreign, weird

3. *Review rules for adding suffixes to words.*   Prefixes such as *mis-*, *pre-*, and *pro-* never change the spelling of the root or base word (*misinformed, premeditated, profile*). However, suffixes often cause problems because the last letter of the root word changes. The following chart summarizes the spelling shifts that occur when suffixes are added.

Spelling Changes with Suffixes

Word Ending	Suffix	Rule	Examples
Vowel + consonant onto one-syllable words: *bet* and *got*	Beginning with a vowel (*-en, –ed, -ing, -able*)	Double the final consonant	*betting gotten*
Vowel + consonant onto two-syllable words, accent on the last syllable: *begin, regret*	Beginning with a vowel (*-en, –ed, -able, -ing*)	Double the final consonant	*beginning regretting, regrettable*
Vowel + consonant onto two-syllable words, the last syllable unaccented: *open, final, deliver*	Beginning with a vowel (*-en, –ed, -able, -ing*)	No change	*opened, opening finalist delivering, deliverable*

Spelling Changes with Suffixes

Word Ending	Suffix	Rule	Examples
Consonant + *y*: *happy, pretty*	Any suffix	Change *y* to *i*	*happiness prettiest*
Vowel + *y*: *toy, play*	Any suffix	No change	*toying playful, playing*
Silent *e*: *assure, drive, late*	Beginning with a vowel (-en−ed, -ing, -able, -est)	Drop the *e**	*assuring drivable latest*
Silent *e*: *pure, excite*	Beginning with a consonant (-ly, -ment)	No change*	*purely excitement*

*Words such as *advantageous, changeable, judgment, noticeable,* and *truly* are exceptions to the "silent *e*" general rules.

4. *Learn how to form plurals.* For most nouns, simply add *-s* or *-es*. For compound words such as *father-in-law* and *editor-in-chief*, add the plural ending to the first word: *fathers-in-law, editors-in-chief.* Otherwise, use the information summarized in the following chart.

Plural Endings for Nouns

Noun Ending	Rule	Examples	Exceptions
-ch,-s, -sh, -x, -z: *match, mass, bush, box, waltz*	Add *-es*	*matches, masses, bushes, boxes, waltzes*	
f: *leaf, knife*	Change *f* to *v* and add *-es*	*leaves, knives*	*beliefs, roofs, safes*
y preceded by a consonant: *baby, diary*	Change *y* to *i* and add *-es*	*babies, diaries*	
y preceded by a vowel: *day, monkey, joy*	Add *-s*	*days, monkeys joys*	
o preceded by a consonant: *tomato, hero*	Add *-es*	*tomatoes, heroes*	*pianos, solos*
o preceded by a vowel: *video, radio*	Add *-s*	*videos, radios*	

5. *Pay close attention to difficult spellings.*   As you write, try to focus on the words that give you trouble. A good idea is to make a customized list in your journal of the words that cause you trouble. Then commit your problem words to memory, or use your journal list as a handy reference tool. Use the following list of commonly misspelled words to help isolate your problems.

Commonly Misspelled Words

abbreviate	autumn	cemetery	cozy
absence	auxiliary	census	criticize
accelerate	avenue	certain	curiosity
accessible	awkward	certificate	curious
accompany		challenge	curriculum
accomplish	baggage	champion	cylinder
accumulate	balloon	character	
accurate	banana	chief	dairy
ache	bankrupt	children	dangerous
achievement	banquet	chimney	dealt
acknowledgment	beautiful	coffee	deceive
acre	beggar	collar	decision
actual	beginning	college	definition
address	behavior	column	delicious
adequate	benefited	commit	descend
advertisement	bicycle	committee	describe
afraid	biscuit	communicate	description
aggravate	bought	community	deteriorate
aisle	boundary	comparison	determine
although	brilliant	competent	development
aluminum	brought	competition	dictionary
amateur	buoyant	complexion	difficulty
ambulance	bureau	conceive	diploma
ancient	burglar	concession	disappear
anonymous	business	concrete	disastrous
anxiety		condemn	discipline
anxious	cabbage	conference	disease
appreciate	cafeteria	congratulate	dissatisfied
appropriate	calendar	conscience	division
approximate	campaign	continuous	dormitory
architect	canoe	convenience	
arithmetic	canyon	cooperate	economy
artificial	captain	corporation	efficiency
assassin	career	correspond	eighth
athletic	carriage	cough	elaborate
attach	cashier	counterfeit	electricity
audience	catastrophe	courageous	eligible
authority	caterpillar	courteous	embarrass
	ceiling		emphasize

Commonly Misspelled Words

employee
encourage
enormous
enough
enthusiastic
envelope
environment
equipment
equivalent
especially
essential
establish
exaggerate
excellent
exceptionally
excessive
exhaust
exhilarating
existence
explanation
extinct
extraordinary

familiar
famous
fascinate
fashion
fatigue
faucet
February
fiery
financial
foreign
forfeit
fortunate
freight
fundamental

gauge
genius
genuine
geography
gnaw
government
graduation

grammar
grief
grocery
gruesome
guarantee
guess
guidance

handkerchief
handsome
haphazard
happiness
harass
height
hesitate
humorous
hygiene
hymn

icicle
illustrate
imaginary
immediately
immortal
impossible
inconve-
nience
incredible
independence
indispensable
individual
inferior
infinite
influential
initial
initiation
innocence
installation
intelligence
interfere
interrupt
invitation
irrelevant
irrigate
issue

jealous
jewelry
journalism
judgment

kindergarten
knife
knowledge
knuckles

laboratory
laborious
language
laugh
laundry
league
legible
legislature
leisure
length
library
license
lieutenant
lightning
likable
liquid
listen
literature

machinery
magazine
magnificent
majority
manufacture
marriage
material
mathematics
maximum
mayor
meant
medicine
message
mileage
miniature
minimum

minute
mirror
miscellaneous
mischievous
miserable
misspell
monotonous
mortgage
mysterious

necessary
neighbor-
hood
niece
nineteen
ninety
noticeable
nuisance

obedience
obstacle
occasion
occurred
official
omission
omitted
opponent
opportunity
opposite
original
outrageous

pamphlet
paragraph
parallel
parentheses
partial
particular
pastime
patience
peculiar
permanent
persistent
personnel
persuade

Commonly Misspelled Words			
physician	responsibility	subtle	vacuum
pitcher	restaurant	succeed	valuable
pneumonia	rhyme	success	various
politician	rhythm	sufficient	vegetable
possess		surprise	vehicle
prairie	salary	syllable	vicinity
precede	satisfactory	symptom	villain
precious	scarcity		visible
preferred	scenery	technique	volunteer
prejudice	schedule	temperature	
previous	science	temporary	weather
privilege	scissors	terrible	Wednesday
procedure	secretary	theater	weigh
pronounce	seize	thief	weird
psychology	separate	thorough	whose
	significant	tobacco	width
questionnaire	similar	tomorrow	worst
quotient	skiing	tongue	wreckage
	soldier	tournament	writing
realize	souvenir	tragedy	
receipt	sovereign	truly	yacht
recipe	spaghetti		yearn
recommend	squirrel	unanimous	yield
reign	statue	unique	
religious	stomach	university	zealous
representative	strength	usable	zoology
reservoir		usually	

Exercise E8-19

Correct the spelling errors that have been added to the following sentences from "Letter from Birmingham Jail."

1. I submit that an individuel who breaks a law that consciense tells him is unjust, and who willingly accepts the penalty of imprisonment in order to arouse the consciense of the comunity over its injustice, is in reality expressing the highest respect for the law.

2. But though I was initially dissapointed at being categoryzed as an extremist, as I continued to think about the matter I gradualy gained a mesaure of satisfaction from the label.

3. Instead, some have been outright oponnents, refusing to understand the freedom movment and misrepresenting its leaders; all too many others have been more cautiuos than couragous and have remained silent behind the anesthetizing security of stained-glass windows.

4. If today's church does not recapture the sacrificial spirit of the early church, it will lose its authenticity, forfit the loyalty of millions, and be dismissed as an irrelevant social club with no meaning for the twentyeth century.

5. Let us all hope that the dark clouds of racial prejudgice will soon pass away and the deep fog of misunderstanding will be lifted from our fear-drenched communitys, and in some not too distant tommorow the radiant stars of love and brotherhood will shine over our great nation with all their sintillating beauty.

Exercise E8-20

Correct the spelling errors in the following sentences from the first draft of Melinda's persuading essay (pp. 380–382).

1. The current code states: "School policy prohibits the unlawful use, manafacture, posession, distribution, or dispenseing of controled substances and alcohol on school grounds or at school-sponsored events."
2. The problem with this rule, as I see it, is that students drink or use drugs before school or before coming to school-sponsored activitys.
3. Students would know that their behavier at school and school-sponsored events is being watched, and they cannot claim that they are just being silly.
4. If there is a second offense, I believe that students should be baned from all extracurricular activities for the remainder of the school year, includeing events such as the senior prom and gradaution.
5. I just know that the four years I spent at Sunnydale High School were mared by many incidence at parties and football games that could have been avoided if students had not been drinking or drugging.

Exercise E8-21

Correct the misspelled words in the following paragraphs.

Do you have friends who like to exagerrate? I have one friend, Joey, who stretches the truth every chance he gets. He doesn't really set out to willfully decieve people. But he definitly believes that he has to impress people with tall tales to get them to like him.

Joey likes to make up stories about his acomplishments. For example, he said he had run a marathon this past summer, certainly a big achievement for anyone, much less a guy who hasn't been working out that long. He did take part in a walkathon. But a marathon? I guess he thinks it's easier to manafacture daring feats than actually preform them.

Sometimes Joey just tells stories about extrordinary things he's done just to add to the conversation. One time he also said he'd gone on tour as a stage hand for the Grateful Dead. Sure, he went to a couple of their concerts. But telling people he toured with them was an unnecesary untruth.

We, as his friends, certainly haven't benefitted from his made-up experiences. We constantly take up for him and defend him because he's truely a nice guy. And we've talked to him, too. But every now and then he gets a mischievous twinkle in his eye, and we know his mouth will be off and running.

Exercise E8-22

Write the plural forms for the following words.

1. topaz
2. ditch
3. carriage
4. baby
5. wharf

Exercise E8-23

Add the following suffixes as indicated, and use each new word in an original sentence.

1. retire + ment
2. irrigate + tion
3. finance + ial
4. mystery + ous
5. responsible + ity

 ## COLLABORATIVE WORK

After you revise your persuading essay, exchange papers with a classmate, and do the following tasks:

A. Determine the language level of the essay.

B. Underline any jargon or slang.

C. Put any nonstandard words in squares.

D. Circle any words that are used incorrectly or misspelled.

Then return the paper to its writer, and use the information in this section to edit your draft.

CHAPTER NINE

Problem Solving
Reading and Writing for a Reason

**The shrewd guess, the fertile hypothesis, the courageous leap
to a tentative conclusion—these are the most valuable coins of
the thinker at work.**

—JEROME BRUNER

We all encounter problems in our lives, ranging in seriousness from mild irritants (a car that won't start) to grave personal problems (an unhappy relationship) to overwhelming social problems (world hunger). One reason we write about difficulties is to organize our thoughts and experiences in relation to a specific problem or series of problems so we can understand them better. In fact, **problem solving** is an especially satisfying form of essay writing because it helps us identify what is wrong in our lives, in our communities, in our country, or in our world and then discover and present solutions to these problems so that others can benefit from them.

In her memoir *Dead Man Walking* (recently made into a motion picture), Sister Helen Prejean describes the dilemma she faced when the members of her religious community decided to leave the field of teaching in order to "stand on the side of the poor." At first, Sister Helen was unhappy with this decision, but she went through a problem-solving process in her own mind:

> I didn't want to struggle with politics and economics. . . . Even Jesus Christ himself had said, "The poor you will always have with you." Besides, it was all so complex and confusing—the mess the world was in—with one social problem meshed with other problems. . . . Enlightenment had come in June 1980. I can remember the moment because it changed my life. My community had assembled . . . and the chief speaker was Sister Marie Augusta Neal. A sociologist, she described glaring inequities in the world: two thirds of the peoples of the world live at or below subsistence level while one third live in affluence. . . . I found myself mentally pitting my arguments against her challenge—*we were nuns, not social workers, not political.* But it's as if she knew what I was thinking. She pointed out that to claim to be . . . neutral in the face of such injustices would be, in actuality, . . . on the side of the oppressors.

But it was the way she presented the message of Jesus that caused the most radical shift in my perspective. "The Gospels record that Jesus preached good news to the poor," she said, "and an essential part of that good news was that they were to be poor no longer." Something in me must have been building toward this moment because there was a flash and I realized that my spiritual life had been . . . too disconnected. I left the meeting and began seeking out the poor.

Soon after this meeting, Sister Helen Prejean began to minister to the needs of the prisoners on death row in Louisiana. What first seemed to be a major conflict in her spiritual vocation became her life's work.

LEARNING FROM PUBLISHED WRITERS

The following problem-solving essay is of particular importance to you as a college student. This essay, "Battling Bigotry on Campus," appeared in *USA Today Magazine* in March 1992. The writer, Kenneth Stern, works for the American Jewish Committee in New York and is a specialist on anti-Semitism (hatred of Jewish people) and extremism (advocating extreme measures, often illegal and immoral).

Before You Read

Focusing Your Attention

Before you read this problem-solving essay, take a few moments to answer the following questions in your journal:

1. Have you ever been the victim of bigotry? Have you ever felt prejudiced against others? What are some of the causes of prejudice?

2. The essay you are about to read describes some terrible instances of bigotry on America's college campuses. How is your college dealing with the issue of bigotry? If you were a victim of bigotry on your campus, how would you deal with it?

Expanding Your Vocabulary

Here are some words and their meanings that are important to your understanding of the essay. You might want to review them before you begin to read.

"**Swastikas** [symbols of Hitler's Nazi party]" (paragraph 1)

"T-shirts with **homophobic** [showing hatred of homosexuals] slurs" (paragraph 1)

"**degenerate** [morally or physically inferior] race" (paragraph 1)

"a **kaffiyeh-clad** [wearing an Arab headdress] woman" (paragraph 1) "acts of **ethnoviolence** [violence against people in a given ethnic group]" (paragraph 2)

"the **perpetrator** [person who commits a crime]" (paragraph 4)

"their **predecessors** [those who came before]" (paragraph 6)

"**institutionalized** [tolerated or caused by the institution itself] discrimination" (paragraph 6)

"**poll taxes and literacy tests** [methods to keep African Americans from voting] and *de jure* [approved by law] segregation" (paragraph 8)

"the **abrasive** [rough, irritating] disruption of bigotry" (paragraph 10)

"*ad hoc* [Latin legal term meaning, 'for this case only'] response" (paragraph 11)

"**Conflicting** [disagreeing] accounts must be **weighed** [considered] and **reconciled** [made to match]" (paragraph 12)

"The **alleged** [accused but not yet tried in court] bigot" (paragraph 12)

"the **deliberative** [decision-making] process" (paragraph 13)

"**unredressed ills** [uncorrected problems]" (paragraph 14)

"**chaos** [disorder]" (paragraph 15)

"much can be **distilled** [gathered and learned] from the . . . incidents that have occurred" (paragraph 17)

"to **effectuate** [put into effect]" (paragraph 18)

"an **escalating** [increasing, worsening] crisis" (paragraph 18)

"The president's statement should be **transcribed** [put in written form] and **disseminated** [distributed] throughout the community" (paragraph 19)

"**predesignated** [already selected], well-rehearsed . . . team" (paragraph 20)

"an award for information resulting in **apprehension** [capture]" (paragraph 20)

"**presidentially instigated** [called by the president] rally will **diffuse** [lessen, cause to dissolve] anger" (paragraph 22)

"strong **stances** [positions]" (paragraph 25)

"**prospective** [likely in the future] students" (paragraph 25)

"**manifests** [shows] itself through a **sanctionable** [punishable] act" (paragraph 26)

"the disciplinary code allows for **summary** [immediate] suspension" (paragraph 27)

"**circumscribed** [prohibited] by law" (paragraph 28)

"Fear is **engendered** [caused]" (paragraph 31)

" a **backlash** [negative reactions to a previously accepted trend] . . . could jeopardize their education" (paragraph 32) "offenders are **deterred** [prevented from acting]" (paragraph 35)

"regulations to **proscribe** [forbid]" (paragraph 39)

"**egregious** [extremely bad] use of hateful words" (paragraph 44)

"a racial **epithet** [abrasive term]" (paragraph 44)

"no perfect **definitional** [clear boundary] line can be drawn" (paragraph 47)

"a **functional** [workable] code" (paragraph 47)

"community **ostracism** [rejection or exclusion] will be punishment enough" (paragraph 47)

"students who feel . . . **maligned** [spoken unfairly of]" (paragraph 51)

"two **polarized** [separated by opposing beliefs] campus groups" (paragraph 53)

"**Infringing** [trespassing] on . . . rights" (paragraph 54)

"the right to invite speakers would remain **inviolate** [untampered with]" (paragraph 56)

"**exacerbate** [make worse] them" (paragraph 59)

"the campus is in **turmoil** [total confusion]" (paragraph 62)

"a **blatantly** [obviously] prejudiced remark" (paragraph 64)

"to **exploit** [take advantage of] incidents" (paragraph 66)

"**articulate** [speak clearly] a commitment" (paragraph 69)

"persuaded by example rather than **fiat** [arbitrary rule]" (paragraph 70)

"an educational mission that **saturates** [completely fills] the campus" (paragraph 74)

"**myopic** [short-sighted]" (paragraph 74)

Kenneth S. Stern

Battling Bigotry on Campus*

Swastikas. Cross burnings. Date rape. Assaults motivated by racial   1
hatred. T-shirts with homophobic slurs. Shouts of "JAP! . . . JAP!
. . . JAP!" from a crowd as a Jewish student walked to her seat at a
sporting event. Whispers of "nigger" by a member of the board of
trustees. KKK literature. Campus security checking African-Ameri-

*Kenneth S. Stern, "Battling Bigotry on Campus" from *USA Today Magazine* March 1992,
pp. 58–82.

can male, but not white male, identification at a school dance. A faculty member using the term "Jap test" to describe a surprise exam. A note with the word "Spic!" slid under a student's door. Hate mail: "Custer should have finished off your entire degenerate race." A picture in a school newspaper showing African-American students at a concert, with the caption "Music soothes the savage beast." Palestinian students displaying a poster of a kaffiyeh-clad woman protruding through the center of a yellow Star of David, her legs spread, her sandals untied, blood dripping from her thighs. The Black Student Union inviting Minister Louis Farrakhan to speak. A professor asking Ku Klux Klan members to address his class. Incidents like these are charged with racial, religious, sexist, homophobic, and ethnic tension. They tear at the tranquility of academic institutions.

Incidents of bigotry are becoming commonplace on college campuses. According to the National Institute Against Prejudice and Violence, more than 250 of the nation's 3,300 colleges and universities have reported acts of ethnoviolence since 1986. Many more have gone unreported.   **2**

Campus officials say they don't know what to do. Incidents vary in origin and burst on the scene unpredictably. Some are very complex, as, for example, when a faculty member says something that some people interpret as bigoted, while others do not; or when pressures from the outside community come into play, dividing the campus along previously unobserved seams, all under the watchful eyes of the media. Incidents also raise different institutional concerns and passions, frequently challenging the university's self-image, pitting academic freedom against the need for a campus free from ethnic and racial hostility.   **3**

Why is this happening? What should officials do when such an incident occurs? More importantly, what should they do *before* an incident occurs? How effective are the codes against bigoted behavior? These, and other related questions, are difficult to answer. What if the professor who invited KKK members wanted to teach his students how to sharpen their interview skills so they could expose bigots? If a student can be expelled for engraving a swastika on a Jewish student's door in the dead of night (this is vandalism), what about the student who distributes a swastika-covered leaflet to Jewish students (First Amendment right)? What should the university do if the perpetrator is never found? Or if found, how do the perpetrator's due process rights limit the administration's response?   **4**

What is the underlying, everyday level of bigotry on campus, and how does this relate to the explosions? Even if there are no explo-   **5** sions, what could campuses be doing to help students enjoy healthy intergroup relations? What should universities be doing to prepare students for life in an increasingly diverse society?

Bigotry always has been on campus. Whereas some of today's university administrators may be insensitive to problems of intergroup hatred, their predecessors practiced it. Jews were tolerated, but only in small numbers. African-Americans—and, on many campuses, women—weren't welcome at all. This institutionalized discrimination almost has disappeared. Certainly, it is better that an African-American or Hispanic or Asian or Jew or woman be called an offensive name than not be allowed into the university at all.   **6**

Years ago, slurs were confined to scribblings on bathroom walls. Today's graffiti have overflowed the bounds of propriety and, at many institutions, become part of campus life. They appear in classrooms and dorms, at sporting events, and in casual conversation.   **7**

This trend is disturbing because campuses mirror society. In the 1950s, when so many school policies discriminated against African-Americans, it was not coincidental that some states had poll taxes and literacy tests and *de jure* segregation. Today's campus bigotry reflects the larger society as well, with all its injustices and racial, ethnic, sexist, religious, homophobic, and class tensions. Overtly hateful incidents, groups, and individuals in power, while still a minor phenomenon, are on the rise.   **8**

Colleges attract our brightest youngsters. If our young people finish their educations without learning to respect each other's differences and cherish their own backgrounds, the future will be a troubled one. Our leaders-to-be will be bigots or, perhaps more disturbing, people who tolerate a bigoted society.   **9**

Some students will come to campus with bigoted or intolerant attitudes. Knowing this, the universities must strive to make every student feel welcome. They need an environment free from the abrasive disruption of bigotry in which to study. Colleges must adopt programs and plans to make their community as bias-free as possible. As leaders in the educational field, they should direct changes in high and elementary school programs, so that their future students are better prepared to live peaceably with each other.   **10**

Responding to Incidents

Many universities assume they never will have to respond to an act of bigotry. An incident occurs, then administration officials wonder   **11** what they should do. It is a rare *ad hoc* response that is effective. Most make a difficult situation worse.

Assume, as has happened, that a professor called a student a "black bitch." Students are angry and want action. Yet, which administration member has prime responsibility to act? That may not be certain. A decision takes time. What happened may not be clear. Facts need to be found. Conflicting accounts must be weighed and reconciled where possible. People's reputations can be destroyed. The alleged bigot may be a colleague or friend. The tension grows. **12**

The administration official put in charge wants any response to be completely accurate and fair. Two days pass. The students don't understand the deliberative process. All they know is that some bigoted sexist called one of his students a "black bitch," and the administration hasn't said a word. The university apparently doesn't care. It never did anything about the everyday low-visibility bigotry that students endure. **13**

"Look at how few minority faculty members there are," students will point out, "how few blacks are incorporated into the curriculum, as if no black person ever contributed to art or literature or science. . . ." A wide range of unredressed ills will be thrown onto the stage, not as something important to be discussed rationally and planned with a long-term perspective, but as demands in the midst of a tension-filled, media-monitored eruption. Two words from one mouth have paralyzed an entire campus. **14**

To avoid this chaos, universities must have two types of plan. First, they need a response plan. Basic decisions about what to do, and who should do it, should be made before a crisis erupts. Once an incident occurs, the response will be quicker and more effective. Second, they must have a plan to reduce the level of bigotry on campus, not only so there will be fewer and less explosive incidents, but also because students deserve an environment that makes them feel welcome. **15**

As any administration official who has had to do it can attest, responding to an incident is a complex affair. Passions are high, and each incident has a new wrinkle not previously thought through. The institution's view of itself and its commitment to free speech are challenged. **16**

Yet, much can be distilled from the hundreds of distinct incidents that have occurred. Some principles are specific to types of incidents—*e.g.,* graffiti, slurs, speakers, assaults—but the most important lessons apply regardless of the particular circumstances. **17**

The most important rule is the simplest to effectuate. When an in- **18** cident occurs, the university, at its highest level, must respond immediately and strongly. Presidents must make themselves as public as possible and say—in the most powerful words—that bigotry has no place on campus. Failure to act quickly with a clear statement will create an escalating crisis. Wishy-washy, delayed, or low-level pronouncements indicate that bigotry is not a serious problem, that the hurt students feel is somehow invalid. That invites further, and longer-lasting, explosions.

Sometimes the facts are known, and action can be taken quickly—   **19**
for example, when a student assaults someone while yelling ethnic slurs. If that student can be suspended immediately, before a hearing, he or she should be. Even if disciplinary codes do not provide for pre-hearing suspensions, the facts justifying such action are not apparent, or the perpetrator is unknown or beyond the scope of the disciplinary code (*e.g.*, faculty, staff, or from outside the campus family), immediate, visible, clear action by the head of the institution is still possible, and necessary. The president's statement should be transcribed and disseminated throughout the community and, where appropriate, mailed to parents and alumni as well.

Second, a predesignated, well-rehearsed "bigotry team" should   **20**
meet immediately. This should include the university president, appropriate deans, campus security, and representatives from students and faculty. The group can assess the incident better and plan appropriate action. For example, if a culprit has not been found, the team can mobilize the campus. The president can announce an award for information resulting in apprehension.

Other responses can be pre-planned as well. Regardless of the na-   **21**
ture of the incident, rumors abound. A hotline should be in place, so that there is one central controlled source of information. (Hotlines also allow people to know where to report incidents and encourage reporting of incidents that, but for an easily understood reporting mechanism, would be suffered in silence.)

If the incident is serious, students are likely to protest. The univer-   **22**
sity president should call a rally, before the students do. The entire community should be invited. A presidentially instigated rally will diffuse anger and make students perceive a real commitment to their security.

Other prepared responses can be crafted for the particular commu-   **23**
nity, given its size, location, population, and history. The purpose is always to remind the victimized students that they truly are wanted and that bigotry has no place on campus.

To make these actions work, however, they have to be sincere. **24**
Public statements have risks. When presidents of universities speak,
newspaper articles follow. The school's reputation for harmony may
be tarnished. Minority students, whom the university are trying to attract, may be less inclined to attend if they know that KKK literature
was distributed or an African-American student was beaten up and
called "nigger."

Yet, the short-term risks from drawing attention to incidents will **25**
pay off in the long run. The university will benefit from strong
stances which end the crisis quicker. Prospective students will know
that the administration really cares.

A university's commitment to free speech complicates the desire to **26**
discipline students who engage in bigotry. Universities work best
when students and faculty feel free to say whatever they think.
Whereas students should be aware that their words can hurt others,
they should not be forced to weigh their thoughts against the admin-
istration-imposed limits of political correctness. Higher education is
at its best when the clash between ideas is heated, not chilled. Yet,
bigotry many times manifests itself through a sanctionable act. Free
speech issues diminish, and acts can be punished promptly and force-
fully.

If a student commits an assault, burglary, arson, or other serious of- **27**
fense and the disciplinary code allows for summary suspension, and
the known facts warrant it, he or she should be suspended immediately, pending a hearing. If there are questions about what happened
or who did what, summary suspension should not be used, regardless
of any pressure to do so. The response to critics who call for immediate suspension is to have a realistic "fast track" disciplinary hearing
procedure established, so that a full due process hearing can be held
quickly.

While the university cannot punish bigoted thoughts or words, it **28**
can do so for bigoted behavior. As in the larger society, acts which are
already circumscribed by law can and should be punished more severely if committed with a bigoted motive.

Punishment must be fair. When there are many students involved, **29**
each should be disciplined according to the seriousness of his or her
act and prior history. Other factors that can inflame a campus—such
as treating the star athlete differently from others—should be re-
jected, despite institutional pressure.

Schools have a real interest in separating people who commit vio- **30**
lent acts from their community, especially when such an act is against

gays, women, Jews, African-Americans, Asians, Indians, or anyone else just because of who they are. Swift clear action can be a deterrent and reaffirm the school's commitment to make the victimized group truly welcome.

However, that is only half the task. Regardless of what the admin-   **31**
istration does, the student who has been traumatized still hurts. The effects of any bias assault—whether physical or verbal—are devastating. Fear is engendered "far beyond what the average person would imagine," according to Joan Weiss, executive director of the National Institute Against Prejudice and Violence.

The trauma is long-lasting and frequently affects family, friends,   **32**
the entire campus, and sometimes the community beyond. Some victims even abandon their college plans and leave. Others are too afraid to report incidents, fearing a backlash that could jeopardize their education.

Universities must help victims recover. A specially trained victims'   **33**
advocate should be available to counsel students and direct them to therapists and lawyers where appropriate. The advocate also can help shape the university's plans and institutions to meet the needs of bias victims. Otherwise, they feel increasingly isolated, bouncing from one unprepared campus service to another without receiving any help.

Disciplinary Codes

Acts of bigotry, even when not physically violent, are psychologi-   **34**
cally distressing. Ethnic slurs, whether yelled, painted on a sign, printed in a leaflet are emotional assaults. People have their identity and self-worth shattered. Bigotry injures. Everyone wants justice. Someone should be punished.

Some universities seem to think that all their bigotry problems can   **35**
be solved through strong disciplinary codes. In theory, offenders are punished and would-be offenders are deterred. However, institutions that see codes as "magic cures" are deceiving themselves.

First, many bigots are not caught. As one Berkeley student said, "If   **36**
I call you a name to your face or do damage to your person or your property, then it's easy to pursue someone. But if in the dark of night I throw a stone through your window and vanish, then how do you pursue the culprit?"

Second, even if found, the person may be beyond the disciplinary   **37**
code. Faculty members and university officials are subject to different

standards. Outsiders, like Ku Klux Klan members who paint swastikas and Skinheads who beat up gay students, are also beyond the code's jurisdiction.

Third, rules that punish assault, arson, vandalism, burglary, harass- **38**
ment, threats or intimidation are effective on their own. Codes need not be changed to punish bigots who hit, burn, burgle, or harass.

When universities speak of codes against bigotry, they mean regu- **39**
lations to proscribe students from what is, essentially, verbal or symbolic expression. The arguments in favor of such codes are attractive at first blush. What better way to demonstrate that the institution will not tolerate bigotry? If the school can punish a person who spray paints the word "nigger" on the wall of a predominately African-American dorm in the middle of the night (that is vandalism), why shouldn't it be able to punish another student who, in broad daylight, walks up to a particular African-American student and yells, "I hate niggers!" Certainly, the hurt caused by a personally directed scream exceeds that from the written slur.

One suggested rationalization for punishing the vandal, but not **40**
the screamer, is that the school has an interest in knowing who its bigots are. This rationale fails when the comparison is between a spray-painted swastika and one drawn on paper and taped to the dorm wall. The harm is practically the same, but the former, as destruction of property, can result in expulsion; the latter may be protected speech.

That result seems, and is, unsatisfactory. Yet, it is better to draw **41**
the line here—between action that is punishable regardless of its bigoted character and action that is not punishable precisely because it has no character beyond being an expression of bigotry.

Justice can not always be found in laws. Laws are imperfect. Results **42**
may be unsatisfactory, but it is nonetheless true that attempts to punish the expression of words simply don't work. Codes designed to outlaw bigotry—such as the University of Michigan's and the University of Connecticut's—have been found violative of the First Amendment. No lawyer can draft language precise enough to punish the person who says "nigger" only when he or she *really* means it.

Attempts at broad codes have backfired. Students at the Univer- **43**
sity of Michigan—which adopted different standards of speech for the classroom, dorm, etc.—had a grand time making fun of the entire effort with "free speech zones" written in broad chalk strokes around the campus. What is the deterrent effect of that ridiculed rule or any code when acts of bigotry are likely to be spontaneous, frequently

committed under the influence of alcohol? No drunk about to yell "nigger!" at a passing African-American student weighs his words against the finely drawn limits of a disciplinary code.

Egregious use of hateful words can be punished under most existing codes that proscribe harassment, intimidation, or threats of violence. Codes that would punish a student who repeatedly calls another at 3:00 a.m. and says, "I hate your mother" also would punish a student whose harassing phone calls are racist. Codes that prohibit one student from threatening and intimidating another (*e.g.*, "You go out with Peggy Sue again and I'll slash your face") also apply when the student warned to stay away from Peggy Sue is called a racial epithet.   **44**

Even narrowly drawn anti-bigotry codes tarnish the schools' reputation for academic freedom and open inquiry. Punishing a student for using bigoted words or printing bigoted articles drapes the bigot, instead of the school, in the First Amendment. The bigot becomes the victim, even a martyr, as the real victim disappears, a casualty of a fight that has become one for free speech instead of against bigotry.   **45**

The practical limits of codes are difficult to accept. Some people who should be disciplined will not be. Nevertheless, the university will benefit from a narrow code. A student's suspension for writing "Gays should die of AIDS," or "I kill Jews, therefore I am," or "Puerto Ricans are scum" can not outweigh the damage of months of disruption, legal proceedings, and constitutional debate that continue to open wounds. There are other ways to respond to such cases.   **46**

While no perfect definitional line can be drawn, a functional code that punishes action and not words is preferable to an unacceptably fuzzy one that tries to legislate morality. If the campus develops a real commitment to fighting bigotry, community ostracism will be punishment enough.   **47**

Controversial Speakers

Outside speakers with reputations for bigotry who come to campus, and then leave, often create traumatic moments that take years to undo. The problem is not as much what the speaker says (usually the address is tamer than people expect), but the tension that precedes and follows the event.   **48**

Universities are places for open inquiry. No idea should be barred. On most campuses, student groups and faculty members have the absolute right to invite anyone they want. However, what happens when someone invites a member of the Ku Klux Klan; or Louis Far-   **49** rakhan, who peppers his words of African-American political action with gross anti-Semitism (Judaism is a "gutter religion"); or the late Meir Kahane, whose views on Arabs were akin to Farrakhan's on Jews or the KKK's on African-Americans?

The students who are the targets of the speaker's hatred feel inse- **50** cure, misunderstood, and powerless. The protestation that "we want to hear about the good things [the speaker] has done," or "everyone has a right to speak—ask him questions and expose him, if you can" are wholly inadequate. "Why should our student fees be used to bring someone here who would kill us if he could?" some ask.

The greatest pain for the students who feel unfairly maligned may **51** be that their fellow classmates cannot—or will not—understand why they feel so hurt. Lines are drawn, and victimized students react angrily—in protest if they are strong enough numerically; in silence if they are too few.

The inviting group also feels misunderstood. African-American **52** students who invite Farrakhan can't comprehend why Jewish groups are so upset. He speaks strongly for empowering African-Americans. "Can it be that the Jewish students are afraid of such a strong leader?" they may ask themselves. "So what if Farrakhan said some nasty things. That's not important. His message of power for African-American people is. Who are they to tell us we can't listen to him, anyway?"

Administration officials—committed to free speech—are caught **53** in the middle between two polarized campus groups that desire pun-ishment, even victory. It is not easy to hold the community together as the conflict heats up. Sometimes the cost of additional security is prohibitive and the speaker does not come, but usually he or she does, and the campus is paralyzed in anticipation of what may hap-pen.

The group opposed to the speaker may protest and seek faculty and **54** community support for their own exercise of First Amendment rights. Officials may fear hecklers. Many times, speakers cannot be heard over screams. Infringing on other students' free speech rights may vi-olate disciplinary rules.

The administration's priorities in the weeks before and after the **55** crisis peaks should be twofold. The commitment to free speech must be ironclad, and so must be the commitment to intergroup sensitivity. While the tension between these two principles cannot be elimi-nated, it can be reduced with planning.

On campuses where the polarization is not extreme, the adminis- **56** tration might invite student groups to submit the names of contemplated speakers to each other before an invitation is extended. Such a procedure would be voluntary and, regardless of any opposition, the right to invite speakers would remain inviolate.

A voluntary pre-invitation notice to other groups would allow discussion and decision before "saving face" issues, such as how to uninvite an invited speaker, come into play. Jewish students, for example, could let African-American students know why having Farrakhan on campus is hurtful. The point might be made at a meeting (coordinated by an intergroup professional) with role plays, transposing Farrakhan's words, substituting the words "African-American" for "Jew," so that the African-American students can understand the hurt better. Jewish students, meanwhile, could begin to understand the isolation African-Americans feel on a white campus with white values and why an African-American speaker who talks of power is important to them.   **57**

Even with the implementation of procedures to make people more sensitive to others' feelings, controversial speakers still will come to campus—as they should. The administration must ensure that students pro and con can exercise their First Amendment rights with minimal interference. Hecklers should not be allowed, but protests should be accommodated. Innovative protests that show respect for fellow students should be encouraged. At Oberlin College, for example, Jewish students protested an anti-Semitic African-American speaker silently. They attended the speech, sitting patiently in their white T-shirts with the Star of David on the back. At the speaker's first anti-Semitic words, they stood and turned their backs to the stage. Their silent protest was dramatic and effective. Other people in the audience stood and joined them in sympathy.   **58**

Campus Police Bias

Campus police forces frequently are a source of tension on campus. Sometimes they instigate incidents. Frequently, they exacerbate them. In many universities, male minority students complain that campus police officials are more likely to stop and question them than they do whites or women. Sometimes, campus police use racial slurs, and false detention cases (*e.g.*, presuming the African-American student in an interracial brawl is the culprit) have resulted in lawsuits.   **59**

One problem is that many low-paid guards bring with them bigoted attitudes exacerbated by economic resentment. Administrators,   **60**

or the agencies with whom they contract, should try to weed out bigots before they are hired. Guidelines for relating to and detaining students should be clear, and the color-blindness of the rules reasserted.
They can be screened and educated to act more sensitively. They
should know that swastikas and racial and sexual assaults are not
pranks, be able to ensure that no evidence is destroyed, and make
sure that the victim is treated with sympathy.

Larger universities should have one better-trained and higher-paid   **61**
special campus security team on duty, or on call, at all times. This
group should be trained to respond to every type of bias incident. It
can soothe the victims and help prevent incidents from turning into
riots. Also, the presence of a better-paid anti-bias group provides the
regular security guards with an option for advancement. If they want
this better job, they know they have to be sensitive to all students to
get it.

During and after an explosion of bigotry, the campus is in turmoil.   **62**
Emotions and anger run high. Rational thought is sometimes difficult.

Students forced to confront ethnic conflict and other potentially   **63**
divisive issues can react defensively and lash out, or withdraw. There
are practitioners in the field of intergroup relations who go to campuses and cultivate ethnic pride and understanding. They also help
the university community develop structures and procedures for managing diversity. The American Jewish Committee's Institute for
American Pluralism and the National Coalition Building Institute
are but two of many. These groups provide valuable assistance to
schools even in calm times. Certainly, they should be contacted before, and invited to campus after, any incident of bigotry.

Specialists also train faculty members to deal with the difficult sit-   **64**
uations in their classrooms that nothing in their education has prepared them for. Even faculty members who know what to do when a
student utters a blatantly prejudiced remark may have no idea what
to do when student A says something from which student B infers a
hidden prejudiced agenda.

The university president must encourage students and faculty to   **65**
develop their own anti-bigotry institutions. Anti-bias student groups
can distribute anti-racist literature and buttons (such as one with a
slash through the encircled word "bias"), organize rallies, empower
victims, initiate discussion, and form coalitions with the students on
other campuses. The more involved students are in developing their
own programs, the better they will succeed.

Faculty groups can lend intellectual credibility to the fight against bias. Professors can teach about bigotry both in their classes and at specially designed forums, including freshman orientation. They also can pre-plan ways to exploit incidents for their educational value.   66

There is much that can be planned before the onset of the unpredictable, but inevitable, crisis. The suggestions given here are certainly not all the possible responses. Experience, experimentation, and changing personnel and circumstances will dictate the details of any particular response plan.   67

Hotlines, response teams, training, a "fast track" for disciplinary cases, improving campus security, and many other practical things can be done so that the administration doesn't grope or give the impression of negligence or insensitivity.   68

The most important thing is that university presidents articulate a commitment to creating a campus community with zero tolerance for bigotry. This should be communicated not only after an incident, but also at calmer times. It must be demonstrated with actions that build structures so the campus community can manage conflict better. The commitment must include plans not only for responding to bigotry, but for reducing it.   69

Change is a long process, best achieved when people are persuaded by example rather than fiat. A faculty member may see a suggestion to include James Baldwin in his literature class as an invasion of academic freedom. If others he or she respects are seen changing their courses and the faculty member allowed the time and access to outside help to make similar curriculum modifications, he or she may do so enthusiastically.   70

While some changes take time, others can be made while the university studies itself and encourages change gently. First, every way it can, the school must make students, faculty, staff and alumni know that it is committed to eradicating bigotry while upholding academic freedom and free speech. The president has to lead, but others must follow.   71

All members of the incoming freshman class should undergo intergroup training workshops as part of their orientation. Faculty, administration, and other staff—including janitors, telephone operators, and secretaries—should receive this training as well. Everyone should be encouraged and empowered to take a stand when they encounter bigotry.   72

Since it will take years to integrate examples of the contribution of all groups into the everyday curriculum, ethnic studies courses should   73 be offered and promoted. Students and faculty alike should learn that people interpret their own realities differently, that there is no one perspective that necessarily defines truth.

Teaching diversity should be an educational mission that saturates the campus. Programs that help different student groups achieve a healthy group identity and feel that they can have a real role in campus life should be encouraged, as long as they are not myopic. Others should be developed that draw students from different backgrounds together to work on common goals. **74**

Our universities must teach our students how to live in the America that will be. That nation will be multiethnic and multicultural, and will demand citizens who understand, appreciate, and respect pluralism. The institutional changes needed to meet this future must have the support of an enthusiastic and forward-looking board of trustees. **75**

The entire institution must be energized. It is not enough that faculty and students survey themselves or begin to recognize bigotry as an issue. That is only the first step. Chaplains, deans of students, staff, administration, faculty, and students must become involved in the process of change. They all have to be encouraged through forums, presidential statements, and campus debate to remold the institution into one that will be stimulating, relevant, and comfortable for all its members. **76**

 ## QUESTIONS FOR CRITICAL THINKING

THINKING CRITICALLY ABOUT CONTENT

1. Is Kenneth Stern solving a problem in this essay, or is he suggesting ways for others to solve a problem? Are the solutions he suggests clearly stated and explained?

2. Why do you think Stern began his essay with a series of one- and two-word phrases? Is this opening paragraph effective? Explain your reaction.

THINKING CRITICALLY ABOUT PURPOSE

3. What do you think Stern's purpose is in writing this essay?

4. Why do you think he places so much importance on the behavior and actions of college presidents?

THINKING CRITICALLY ABOUT AUDIENCE

5. Would this be an effective essay for every entering student at your college to read? Explain your answer.

6. What other groups of people would benefit from reading this essay? Explain your answer.

THINKING CRITICALLY ABOUT POINT OF VIEW

7. Describe in a complete sentence the writer's point of view.

8. Write a paragraph explaining whether you think a bigoted student would change his or her attitude as a result of reading this essay.

LEARNING FROM YOUR PEERS

In our lives, we face problems every day. Some problems have obvious solutions (finding things we need), and we handle them quickly. Others are more complicated (deciding where to go to college), and we may not be able to find a solution unless someone helps us. Sometimes we find that we are experiencing the same problem with minor variations over and over. Maybe we always seem to choose unreliable friends or loan money to the wrong people. Maybe we procrastinate whenever we are faced with a lot of work to do. Maybe we would rather rent a video than go to the library. Learning to analyze and solve problems is a valuable skill that we can develop throughout life if we are open to possibilities. In response to a problem-solving assignment, we are going to follow the writing process of a student named Sarah Chen.

Sarah's Writing Assignment: Problem Solving

This is the topic Sarah's instructor assigned:

Most of us will never find the solutions to overwhelming social problems or the cures for devastating diseases, but we do manage to solve the smaller problems in life every day. Sometimes we can learn from people around us who have faced the same problems in their lives. Think of a problem you are trying to solve. Then talk to at least three people who have successfully solved a similar problem. Write an essay explaining how the people you talked to identified their problems and carried out their solutions.

Sarah goes through the process as outlined in Chapter 1: *thinking, planning, developing, organizing, drafting, revising,* and *editing.*

Thinking

Sarah sits in the campus Student Center staring blankly at the newspaper in front of her. She realizes that she has been sitting there for 20 minutes—and she does not remember a single image that has passed from her eyes to her brain. She knows that she should go to the library and start her homework, but she cannot seem to force herself to get up and walk across the street. Just as she thinks she is definitely ready to leave, her friend Marsie walks over to Sarah's table, plunks down her bookbag, and starts talking.

Sarah explains that she has to start working on her next essay, but she doesn't know what she wants to write about. She says that she is still wasting more time worrying about her work than doing it. Marsie tells her that she should stop worrying and just do her work. As Sarah gets up from the table, she says, "Easier said than done."

Marsie says that she would be glad to talk about how she manages her time. Sarah sits back down and listens as Marsie talks about scheduling classes, work, and family responsibilities.

Finally Sarah says, "You've been very helpful, but now I feel more guilty than ever. I'd better be getting to the library."

Planning

At the library, Sarah writes in her notebook:

I need to write about solutions to problems. Sometimes I think I have problems that have no solutions. Everyone else is so busy studying that I hate to ask them anything. And I don't even know for sure what I want to write about.

Logically, I guess I could write about time management since that seems to be one of my biggest problems. I don't have to have solved the problem personally. I just have to talk to some people who think they are in control of their schedules. How long can that list be? I know exactly one person who claims to be on top of this: Marsie.

And she says that the answer is to read all assignments before going to class. She reads everything when she gets up at four in the morning. I can just see that. My alarm clock would go off, and the next thing I would know the sun would be shining and the birds would be singing. I know I can't do that. Marsie just has more self-discipline than I do.

I know that coming to the library is a good idea. Theoretically, at least. As long as I use my time productively. But sometimes I just sit and stare into space, just like I do in the cafeteria, so I might as well sit in the library.

Perhaps there is something to be said for being in a certain place. Maybe that helps. But four hours of reading at one sitting! I don't think so.

Well, I certainly didn't solve that problem.

Sarah puts her notebook in her bookbag and is about to take out a reading assignment for her history class. Just then, her friend Mike comes over and asks how she is doing. She tells him about the essay she is trying to develop. Mike tells her that he was fairly disorganized when he first started college, but since then he has developed habits that work for him.

Sarah stands up and says, "Great. Let's go to the cafeteria, and I'll buy you a cup of coffee while you tell me all about your great time-management skills. Then I can ignore my terrible ones and not feel guilty about them."

Developing

During the next week, Sarah has several conversations with friends and friends of friends who give her tips for organizing her time. She finds that she has several pages of notes when she goes to her next writing class.

Friends in her writing group ask about her topic. She tells them that now she has so many ideas that she doesn't know where to start. Her classmates tell her to keep asking people questions until she thinks she understands exactly how they manage their time. They tell her she has been asking too much about how they study and not enough about how they manage to do everything else in their lives.

Sarah goes back to the cafeteria armed with a new set of questions and ready to ask anyone who will answer them. This is her list:

1. When do you do your laundry?

2. Do you buy groceries? If so, when?

3. Do you go to the bank during daytime hours? If not, do you use teller machines?

4. What habits have you developed that save you time and help you do other things you need to do, like studying?

5. Do you have a clean house or apartment? How do you keep the Health Department away from your door?

Sarah is surprised that so many of her friends take her questions seriously and are willing to take the time to answer them.

Organizing

Sarah takes her notes and attempts to find some patterns. She notices that a few ideas are repeated over and over. She makes a list she labels "Often-repeated advice." This is the list:

> Go to class, every class.
>
> Read your assignments before going to class.
>
> Block out four or five hours at a time to study. You can't study for 10 minutes or half an hour unless you're just trying to memorize a list of definitions or words or something like that.
>
> Find a place that is comfortable for you, and make an appointment with yourself on your calendar. For example: Saturday, 10-12, second floor of library. Reading.

Then Sarah takes out another piece of paper and labels it "List 2: How much time do Real Students spend studying?":

> Most everyone says they study at least 20 hours a week, and they schedule their study time. They don't leave it to luck. (Plan for success, yes?)
>
> A few people spend 10-12 hours every Saturday and Sunday hitting the books--the pre-med contingent, no doubt.

Sarah takes out another piece of paper and labels it "List 3: The School–Is–My–Career Syndrome":

> 8:00 to 5:00; two 10-minute coffee breaks and a half hour for lunch. My friend Terry.
>
> Let's not talk about people who get up and read at 4 a.m.
>
> If you have a goal, you have to work at it every day.

Sarah then gets out another sheet of paper and labels it "List 4: The Get–a–Job (It Makes You More Efficient) School of Thought":

> Some people think the more you work, the more you should study.
>
> If they work during the week, they study on weekends, and vice versa.
>
> Then again, some study all day and work all night.

Sarah looks over the papers spread in front of her and concludes that she actually does have enough information to start writing her essay. She is familiar with her notes, and the four lists have helped her see the main ideas that have emerged from her numerous interviews. As she begins her draft, she decides to choose certain people to represent the groups she has created.

Drafting

This is Sarah's draft.

Sarah's Essay: First Draft ....

Main Idea: After talking with some successful students at my college, I have some good ideas for managing my time as a student.

When I started college, managing my time effectively was very important to me, but I did not have any idea how to do it. Constantly behind in my reading, every test and paper produced fear and trembling. During my first semester, I observed successful students and ask them what they did to keep up with all of their assignments and other obligations. All of the students I talked to called themselves extremely busy people, but everyone had made graduating from college their first priority. The one universal recommendation was to attend absolutely all classes and labs. In high school I never went to all of them. Nevertheless, since I have completed my interviews and collected students' experiences, I can confidently offer their advice to you.

Almost every person suggested reading through all assignments prior to attending class. In a study guide I bought at the bookstore, it said that keeping up with assigned reading is critical if you want to succeed. By reading the assignments ahead of time, students claimed that they have to take fewer notes and are able to ask more intelligent questions. You can really develop more confidence. They also calim that they spend less time reviewing for their classes and studying for tests. One student said that he spends the first week of classes skimming his textbooks to get an overview of each course. Then, if a class seems boring or too difficult, he can change to another class before it is too late.

Some students said every day that they study and make sure they spend a certain amount of time reading, writing, or doing research. Most of the students who do this blocked out four or five hours to study. Some prefer to study for no more than an hour or two at a time. Some people like to spend the entire time in the library while others like to study in a place where there are no distractions, like an empty classroom. Then they can do quick research, if necessary. Some students like to spend more time studying during the week and less time on weekends. However, I was surprised that several have jobs in the afternoons and evenings during the week and spend 10-12 hours every Saturday and Sunday reading and studying. All the students I talked to spend at least 20 hours a week in scheduled study sessions. They emphasize that they do not allow themselves to do anything else during that time. One woman said that she considers her time at school to be her most important job and that she does not waste time during the day. That way, she says, she can study and attend classes from 8 a.m. to 5 p.m. and spend her evenings earning money as a waitress. This schedule works out well for her, and she does any extra studying she needs to do during the weekend.

Other students schedule their classes in blocks of time that allow them to do their studying and research in large blocks of time. For instance, one student spends almost all day on Tuesdays and Thursdays in class. Reading all his assignments for the week on Mondays, some weeks this takes 12-15 hours. On Wednesdays, he spends the day in the library or in a study room at the Student Center. To keep on track, Friday is for writing. This schedule works for him because he takes several classes that require library research and lengthy papers. On the weekends, he works at the mall and earns enough money so he does not have to work during the week.

I talked to one student who is a pre-med student in the library and spends many hours a week in laboratory classes. He said every morning that he reads for four hours before he comes to campus. Then, between classes and labs he works on lab reports and homework is completed. These tasks do not require as much concentration as reading does for him. Working on Friday and Saturday nights at a restaurant, the job is about as much social life as his schedule will allow him right now.

One woman that I interviewed is married and has two small children. She does not take a full load of classes. She and a friend who works part time take care of each other's children. She worked in a bank for several years. She says that she does all her reading and homework before leaving campus. She wants to give all her attention to her family and her home when she is at home. She and her husband split all the usual chores like grocery shopping and laundry and cooking. She says that she would rather take a few more years to finish college than neglect them. If her children are ill, she might miss a class to take them to the doctor. She makes it a practice not to miss classes unless it is an emergency.

All of these students told me that they plan their study time and that they do not wait until they are given assignments or homework. They try to learn as much as possible from every class and to read supplementary material as often as possible. One political science major told me that she reads the newspaper every morning and clips articles that are interesting to her, making a note of the date and jotting down the page numbers. Then, when she needs to do library research, she already has files full of them. She still goes to the library and reads other sources, but her basic footwork is done. She says that she enjoys reading the newspaper, and it helps you feel less guilty if you can say that you're doing research at the same time.

 Talking to these students has made me appreciate their self-discipline and dedication to their studies and has inspired me to commit to a specific schedule. I now know how to manage my time effectively by listening to the trials and tribulations of other students with complicated lives.

Revising

Now that Sarah has written her draft, she knows it's time to revise. Her instructor wants the class to look at the conclusions of their essays, paying special attention to how their conclusions relate to their thesis statements and to the main ideas in their essays. At this point in the course, the students know that every part of an essay has its own place and should be related to other parts of the essay.

 Sarah reviews the Checklist for Writing Conclusions at the beginning of the Tips for Revising section of this chapter. Her instructor explains that at this stage, the revising process for students involves rethinking their conclusions and making sure their final paragraphs are as effective as possible. The checklist asks students to compare their conclusions to their introductions and then check to see that the conclusion actually brings the essay to a close.

 Sarah takes these guidelines seriously as she uses them to check the content and structure of her conclusion. She reads the Tips for Revising and completes the exercises her instructor assigns. She rereads her introduction and writes her thesis statement on a separate piece of paper. Then she checks to see that her conclusion mirrors her introduction and summarizes her essay. She finds several parts of her conclusion that she wants to change. After rewriting her conclusion, she looks at her essay a second time and feels that it fulfills the revision guidelines and is much more coherent.

Collaborative Work

Peer Group Activity

After you read the portions of the Tips for Revising your instructor assigns, turn to Sarah's first draft (pp. 454–457), and complete the following tasks in small groups:

A.   Highlight the essay's thesis statement (for a definition, see p. 392) and each topic sentence (for a definition, see p. 394) with colored markers.

B.   Circle any main ideas that are not represented in the conclusion.

C.   Suggest other ways she might end her essay.

Compare the marks your group came up with to those your instructor will show you. Where do your marks differ from your instructor's? What do you need to review before writing your own essay?

CLASS ACTIVITY

As an entire class, look at the underlined portions of Sarah's revised draft (pp. 459–462) to see how she changed each sentence.

A.   Did you identify the **revision** problems that Sarah corrected?

B.   Do you think her changes are good ones? Discuss her changes.

Editing

Now that the sentences say what Sarah wants them to say, she needs to do some final proofreading and editing before handing in her essay. The instructor tells the class they need to know more about pronoun reference, modifiers, parallelism, and sentence variety. So Sarah shifts her focus from the content of her essay to specific points of grammar. She reads the Tips for Editing section in this chapter to learn about pronouns and antecedents, new modifier problems, the importance of parallel structure within sentences, and the value of varying her sentence structure. After she finishes the assigned exercises, she takes the questions in the Checklist for Writing Successful Sentences one by one and makes changes so that her revised draft fulfills all these requirements.

 ## COLLABORATIVE WORK

PEER GROUP ACTIVITY

After you read the portions of the Tips for Editing your instructor assigns, turn to Sarah's first draft (pp. 454–457), and complete the following tasks in small groups:

A.   Draw an arrow from each pronoun (for a definition, see p. 470) in the essay to its antecedent (for a definition, see p. 470), and circle any pronouns that are not clearly related to a specific pronoun or that could be closer to their antecedents.

B.   Draw an arrow from each modifier (for a definition, see p. 474) in the essay to the word it modifies, and circle any modifiers that not are placed properly.

C.   Underline any items in a series, and circle any words at the beginning of those items that are not grammatically parallel (for a definition, see p. 477).

D.   Put brackets around any awkward shifts within sentences (for a definition, see p. 480).

E.   Underline any sentences that are monotonous in their structure and should be varied (for a definition, see pp. 485–487).

Compare your marks to those your instructor will show you. Where do your marks differ from your instructor's? What do you need to review before writing your own essay?

CLASS ACTIVITY

As an entire class, look at the underlined portions of Sarah's revised draft (pp. 459–462) to see how she changed each sentence.

A.   Did you identify the editing problems that Sarah corrected?

B.   Do you think her changes are good ones? Discuss her changes.

Sarah's Revised Essay

Time Management for College Students

When I started college, managing my time effectively was very important to me, but I did not have any idea how to do it. Constantly behind in my reading, I faced every test and paper ~~produced~~ with fear and trembling. During my first semester, I observed successful students, and ~~ask~~ I often asked them what they did to keep up with all of their assignments and other obligations. All of the students I talked to called themselves extremely busy people, but ~~everyone~~ they had made graduating from college their first priority. The one universal recommendation was to attend absolutely all classes and labs/, something I never did i/n high school. ~~I never went to all of them.~~ Nevertheless, since I have completed my interviews and collected students' experiences, I can confidently offer their advice to you.

Almost every person suggested reading through all assignments prior to attending class. ~~In a~~ A study guide I bought at the bookstore/ ~~it~~ said that keeping up with assigned reading is critical if ~~you~~ students want to succeed. By reading the assignments ahead of time, students claimed that they ~~have~~ had to take fewer notes and ~~are~~ were able to ask more intelligent questions. ~~You~~ Students can really develop more confidence. They also ~~calim~~ claim that they spend less time reviewing for their classes and studying for tests. One student said that he spends the first week of classes skimming his textbooks to get an overview of each course. Then, if a class seems boring or too difficult, he can change to another class before it is too late.

Some students said ~~every day~~ that they study every day and make sure they spend a certain amount of time reading, writing, or doing research. Most of the students who do this blockⒺ out four or five hours to study. Some prefer to study for no more than an hour or two at a time. Some people like to spend the entire time in the library so they can do quick research, if necessary, while others like to study in a place where there are no distractions, like an empty classroom. ~~Then they can do quick research, if necessary.~~ Some students like to spend more time studying during the week and less time on weekends. However, I was surprised that several have jobs in the afternoons and evenings during the week and spend 10-12 hours every Saturday and Sunday reading and studying. All the students I talked to spend at least 20 hours a week in scheduled study sessions. They emphasize that they do not allow themselves to do anything else during that time. One woman said that she considers her time at school to be her most important job and that she does not waste time during the day. That way, she says, she can study and attend classes from 8 a.m. to 5 p.m. and spend her evenings earning money as a waitress. This schedule works out well for her, and she does any extra studying she needs to do during the weekend.

Other students schedule their classes ~~in blocks of time~~ so that ~~allow them to~~ <u>they can</u> do their studying and research in large blocks of time. For instance, one student spends almost all day on Tuesdays and Thursdays in class. Reading all his assignments for the week on Mondays/ ~~some weeks this~~ takes 12-15 hours <u>some weeks</u>. On Wednesdays, he spends the day in the library or in a study room at the Student Center. To keep on track, <u>he sets aside</u> Friday ~~is~~ for writing. This schedule works for him because he takes several classes that require library research and lengthy papers. On the weekends, he works at the mall and earns enough money so he does not have to work during the week.

I talked to one ~~student who is a~~ pre-med student in the library ~~and~~ <u>who</u> spends many hours a week in laboratory classes. He said ~~every morning~~ that he reads <u>every morning</u> for four hours before he comes to campus. Then, between classes and labs<u>,</u> he works on lab reports and <u>completes his</u> homework ~~is completed~~. These tasks do not require as much concentration as reading does for him. Working on Friday and Saturday nights at a restaurant, <u>he says</u> <u>that his</u> ~~the~~ job is ~~about as much~~ <u>his only</u> social life ~~as his schedule will allow him right now~~. <u>He knows that he will be a student for several years to come, and he thinks that should be his first priority for now.</u>

One woman that I interviewed is married and has two small children. She does not take a full load of classes. She and a friend who works part time take care of each other's children/ <u>, so she is able to go to class.</u> Even though s$~~S~~he worked in a bank for several years/<u>, going to college is much harder for her because of the homework.</u> She says that she does all her reading and homework before leaving campus. <u>When she is at home,</u> s$~~S~~he wants to give all her attention to her family and her home ~~when she is at home~~. She and her husband split all the usual chores like grocery shopping and laundry and cooking/, but s~~S~~he says that she would rather take a few more years to finish college than neglect ~~them~~ her family. If her children are ill, she might miss a class to take them to the doctor/, but s~~S~~he makes it a practice not to miss classes unless it is an emergency.

All of these students told me that they plan their study time and that they do not wait until they are given assignments or homework. They try to learn as much as possible from every class and to read supplementary material as often as possible. One political science major told me that she reads the newspaper every morning and clips articles that are interesting to her, making a note of the date and jotting down the page numbers. Then, when she needs to do library research, she already has files full of ~~them~~ material. She still goes to the library and reads other sources, but her basic footwork is done. She says that she enjoys reading the newspaper, and it helps ~~you~~ her feel less guilty if ~~you~~ she can say that ~~you're~~ she's doing research at the same time.

Talking to these students has made me appreciate their self-discipline and dedication to their studies and has inspired me to commit to a specific schedule. I now know how to manage my time effectively ~~by~~ after listening to the trials and tribulations of other students with complicated lives. Instead of spending so much time drinking coffee and thinking about studying, I plan to do some reading while I drink that coffee. Maybe I'll stop at the newsstand in the morning and start my research in the cafeteria. Maybe all of you, my classmates, might want to think about doing the same thing.

WRITING YOUR OWN PROBLEM-SOLVING ESSAY

So far, you have seen a professional writer and a fellow student at work trying to solve a problem they feel is worth resolving. As you read the published essay and followed the writing process of another student from first to final draft, you absorbed ideas and ways of giving those thoughts a form of their own. These reading and writing activities have prepared you to write your own problem-solving essay on a topic that is meaningful to you.

What Have You Discovered

Before you begin your own writing task, let's review what you have learned in this chapter so far:

- In a problem-solving essay, you identify a problem, determine whether it has a solution, and present the solution.

- Problem-solving essays are especially satisfying because they force you to think through a problem that is important to you.

- To present your problem-solving essay effectively, you need to organize your ideas.

- To help you shape your essay, you should learn as much as possible about your readers.

- Before you write a draft, you need to decide on a point of view toward your subject.

- After you write a draft, you should revise your essay for meaning and organization.

- After you revise your essay, you should edit its grammar, usage, and sentence structure.

Your Writing Topic

Choose one of the following topics for your problem-solving essay:

1. In "Battling Bigotry on Campus" (pp. 436–449), the writer describes the many ways in which bigotry can be controlled, and even abolished, on college campuses. Choose a problem that exists in your life today, and write an essay in which you consider the options available to you for solving it.
2. Your school newspaper has announced a competition focusing on campus problems and possible solutions to those problems. Write an essay for the competition that describes a problem on campus and proposes a solution to it.
3. Write a letter to a past or present supervisor that describes a problem where you work (or have worked in the past), and propose a solution to that problem.
4. Create your own problem-solving essay topic (with the assistance of your instructor), and write a response to it.

When you have selected one of these topics, you may begin your writing process in the same way Sarah did. (You may find rereading her experience helpful in giving you ideas.) This time your purpose is to write your own problem-solving essay. If some tasks occur out of order, that adjustment is probably part of your personal writing ritual. Follow your instincts, and let them mold your own writing process. But make sure you've worked through all the stages to your final draft.

YOUR WRITING PROCESS

THINKING   Generate as many ideas on your subject as you can in as many different ways as possible: rereading, listing, freewriting, brainstorming, clustering, discussing, and questioning.

PLANNING   Begin to give your ideas shape by deciding on your approach to your topic (your content, your purpose, your audience, and your point of view). Make a list of points you want to include in your essay.

DEVELOPING   Add more details on three or four specific, focused topics you have chosen from your list of general points.

ORGANIZING   Organize your material in a way that will be most interesting to your audience.

DRAFTING   Write a working draft of your essay in complete sentences.

REVISING   Consulting the Tips for Revising in this chapter (pp. 465–469), revise your first draft—paying special attention to your conclusion and how it relates to your thesis statement and to your essay as a whole.

EDITING   Consulting the Tips for Editing in this chapter (pp. 470–494), edit your draft for grammar and correctness—paying special attention to pronoun reference, modifiers, parallelism, and sentence variety.

Turn in your revised draft to your instructor.

Some Final Thoughts

When you have completed your own essay, answer these four questions in your journal:

1. What was most difficult about this assignment?
2. What was easiest?
3. What did I learn about problem solving by completing this assignment?
4. What did I learn about my own writing process from this assignment—how I prepared to write, how I wrote the first draft, how I revised, and how I edited?

Writing Conclusions

Checklist for Writing Conclusions

✓ Does the conclusion **mirror** the introduction?
✓ Does the conclusion **summarize** the main ideas of the essay, not adding any new material?
✓ Does the conclusion actually bring the essay to a **close**?

The writer of a mystery concludes a novel by tying up all the loose ends of the plot in some realistic and logical manner. At the close, the readers should have all their questions answered and feel satisfied that the plot is complete. An essay is like a mystery novel in that it presents several main ideas that need to be tied up at the end. So conclusions are just as important to essays as they are to novels.

Concluding paragraphs can be structured in several different ways, but the most effective ones follow some basic requirements that provide a clear, stimulating summary of the essay's main points. Beyond certain necessary features, writers can add a variety of options to their concluding paragraphs, each of which produces a different effect.

Basic Requirements

A **summary** of the main points of your essay is one of the basic ingredients of any conclusion. Not only should a summary highlight the main points of an essay, but it should also remind the readers of the thesis statement from the introduction and the topic sentences from each body paragraph in the paper.

In the last paragraph of "Battling Bigotry on Campus" (p. 449), Kenneth Stern touches on the primary points he makes in the essay:

1. The entire campus—faculty, students, staff, and administration—must recognize and deal with bigotry.
2. To stop bigotry on campus, the entire institution must be committed to change.
3. The campus needs to take some proactive steps in confronting bigotry.
4. A campus should try to make all of its members comfortable.

> The entire institution must be energized. It is not enough that faculty and students survey themselves or begin to recognize bigotry as an issue. That is only the first step. Chaplains, deans of students, staff, administration, faculty, and students must become involved in the process of change. They all have to be encouraged through forums, presidential statements, and campus debate to remold the institution into one that will be stimulating, relevant, and comfortable for all its members.

465

In this paragraph, the writer summarizes his main points and concludes his essay by stressing the importance of comfort for everyone in a campus community.

Additional Options

Some writers like to do a little more in their conclusions than summarize their main points. In addition to summarizing, you might consider ending your essay with a question, a prediction about the future, a suggested solution, or a call to action. Each of these options sends a specific message and creates a slightly different effect at the end of an essay.

One way to conclude an essay effectively after your summary is to leave your audience with a final **question** to mull over. This approach at the end of an essay leaves the readers with something to think about beyond the confines of the essay. It is especially effective for a complex topic that invites many perspectives. Student writer Melinda Jackson (in Chapter 8) uses this strategy to end her revised essay on drug and alcohol abuse at her old high school:

> It is sometimes the responsibility of the school board to create policies that protect students from themselves. Clearly high school students are naturally reckless and take many unnecessary risks. By setting a firm and realistic policy that strongly discourages students from using drugs and alcohol, the school board will help these students succeed in school and in life. What is more important?

The question at the end of Melinda's essay makes the readers think about the importance of succeeding in school and in life. This strategy is very effective for Melinda's purpose and audience.

Another option for ending your essays effectively is to add a **prediction** to your summary. Such a conclusion might be just what your readers need to capture their long-term interest in your topic. In Chapter 5, David Gardner and his co-authors find that a prediction along with a summary is an effective way to end "A Nation at Risk":

> Despite the obstacles and difficulties that inhibit the pursuit of superior educational attainment, we are confident, with history as our guide, that we can meet our goal. The American educational system has responded to previous challenges with remarkable success. In the 19th century our land-grant colleges and universities provided the research and training that developed our Nation's natural resources and the rich agricultural bounty of the American farm. From the late 1800s through mid-20th century, American schools provided the educated workforce needed to seal the success of the Industrial Revolution and to provide the margin

of victory in two world wars. In the early part of this century and continuing to this very day, our schools have absorbed vast waves of immigrants and educated them and their children to productive citizenship. Similarly, the Nation's Black colleges have provided opportunity and undergraduate education to be the vast majority of college-educated Black Americans.

. . .

We are the inheritors of a past that gives us every reason to believe that we will succeed.

This conclusion not only summarizes some of the most important points in the essay but also predicts that America will survive this crisis as it has many other crises in the past.

In other essays, **suggesting a solution** is a good way to conclude, especially for a problem-solving essay. Such an approach leaves the readers with a positive suggestion to consider after you lay out a problem or conflict. Sara Nelson, in Chapter 8 ends her essay on condoms and AIDS with an emphasis on what she believes is the first stage of a solution to the AIDS epidemic:

Despite terrifying forecasts of growing numbers of people with AIDS, despite the well-publicized fact that women constitute one of the fastest-growing groups of persons with AIDS, many middle-class heterosexuals still do not accept AIDS as a life-and-death issue. As one woman who has worked as a volunteer at an AIDS clinic for gays puts it: "It doesn't come home to you until people you know are dying." But suddenly that's happening: Magic Johnson's admission that he's HIV positive may finally make us all realize that this disease knows no gender, racial, or class boundaries. Maybe we'll finally recognize that all the talk and excuses are no longer enough.

Her last sentence adds a specific suggestion to the summary that brings the essay to an exciting close.

A frequent device used to conclude both problem-solving and persuasive essays is a **call to action.** Such an approach makes one last attempt to stir up the emotions and energy of the readers as the essay comes to a close. In this example from "Condom Use Will Not Help Prevent AIDS" in Chapter 8, the call to action is actually directed to Magic Johnson:

This is Magic Johnson's unprecedented opportunity. He can use his heart-breaking ordeal to persuade society to change behavior or become just another public advocate for condoms.

With this plea, the author makes his readers aware of the seriousness of the issues connected with the AIDS epidemic and indirectly calls us all to action.

Sometimes a combination of these techniques will effectively conclude an essay.

As Sarah Chen studied her first draft, she decided her conclusion needed strengthening in two ways. She needed a clearer summary of her main points and a concrete proposal for solving her time-management problems as a student. To accomplish this, she realized she needed to add a few sentences to her existing conclusion:

First Draft: Talking to these students has made me appreciate their self-discipline and dedication to their studies and has inspired me to commit to a specific schedule. I now know how to manage my time effectively by listening to the trials and tribulations of other students with complicated lives.

Revision: Talking to these students has made me appreciate their self-discipline and dedication to their studies and has inspired me to commit to a specific schedule. I now know how to manage my time effectively ~~by~~ **after** listening to the trials and tribulations of other students with complicated lives. **Instead of spending so much time drinking coffee and thinking about studying, I plan to do some reading while I drink that coffee. Maybe I'll stop at the newsstand in the morning and start my research in the cafeteria. Maybe all of you, my classmates, might want to think about doing the same thing.**

Sarah's conclusion now offers a more concrete solution to her time-management problems, and in the last sentence, she calls her classmates to action. Her revised conclusion gives her readers additional information, and it is much more engaging. Now Sarah's essay is complete with both a summary and a proposed plan for solving her time-management problems.

Exercise R9-1

Look again at Stern's concluding paragraph in "Battling Bigotry on Campus" (p. 449). Write an alternative conclusion, using another method of bringing his essay to a close.

Exercise R9-2

Can you think of other ways Sarah could have concluded her essay? Write a new conclusion using another method or a combination of the methods discussed in this section.

Exercise R9-3

Go back to the essays on controlling AIDS in Chapter 8 (pp. 366–371 and 372–374). Write an alternative conclusion for each essay, using a different strategy in each case.

Exercise R9-4

Write a conclusion for an essay on the topic of using your free time. Use a combination of the strategies you have studied in this section.

 ## COLLABORATIVE WORK

After writing a draft of your own problem-solving essay, exchange papers with a classmate, and do the following tasks:

A. Decide whether the essay's conclusion is effective; if it is not, suggest revisions.

B. Survey the class and list all the different strategies your classmates used to conclude their problem-solving essays.

Then return the paper to its writer, and use the information in this section to revise your draft.

TIPS FOR REVISING

Successful Sentences

Checklist for Writing Successful Sentences

✓ Is each **pronoun** located **near its antecedent**?
✓ Does each **pronoun** clearly refer to only **one antecedent**?
✓ Do **pronouns** refer to **specific antecedents**?
✓ Does each **modifier** have an **antecedent**?
✓ Are **modifiers** as close as possible to their **antecedents**?
✓ Are items in a series and in comparisons **grammatically parallel**?
✓ Are sentences **consistent in tense, voice, person, and number**?
✓ Do sentences **vary** according to beginning elements, structure, and type?

You learned in Chapter 3 that only two things are necessary for a sentence to exist: a subject and a verb. But you have also learned from this book that to be successful in communicating a meaningful message, a sentence often needs more than just a subject and a verb. The best sentences are usually packed with a variety of sentence parts—words, phrases, and clauses—spelled and punctuated correctly.

While spelling, grammar, and punctuation errors may be the most obvious problems as you edit your writing, you may fail to notice other problems that keep your sentences from communicating clearly. These fine points in writing—such as pronoun reference, modifiers, parallelism, consistency, and sentence variety—deserve close attention. Following the guidelines in this section will help your essays flow better and will engage your audience with the lively prose that experienced writers produce.

Pronoun Reference

Do you remember from Chapter 2 that pronouns replace nouns or other pronouns in the same sentence or in nearby sentences? The noun (or pronoun) being replaced is called the **antecedent.** Sometimes problems with antecedents occur that result in vagueness and ambiguity.

Remote Reference

An antecedent should be as close as possible to the noun or pronoun it refers to. When we begin expanding sentences—adding descriptive words, phrases, and clauses—antecedents sometimes get pushed far away from the words they refer to. Look at the following sentences from paragraph 3 of the first draft of Sarah's problem-solving essay:

Remote:	Some **people** like to spend the entire time in the library while others like to study in a place where there are no distractions, like an empty classroom. Then **they** can do quick research, if necessary.

They in the second sentence refers to *people* in the first sentence, the people who study in the library. Therefore, Sarah should revise the two sentences, making sure *they* is located closer to its antecedent.

Revision:	Some **people** like to spend the entire time in the library **so they can do quick research, if necessary,** while others like to study in a place where there are no distractions, like an empty classroom. ~~Then they can do quick research, if necessary.~~

Unclear Reference

Sometimes a pronoun may appear to have more than one antecedent. The reference may be clear to you, but the reader may have difficulty deciphering your intentions. Look at this example from paragraph 1 of Sarah's first draft:

Unclear:	The one universal recommendation was to attend absolutely all **classes** and **labs**. In high school I never went to all of **them**.

Them in the second sentence could refer to *classes,* to *labs,* or to both *classes* and *labs.* If you let the sentences remain as written, *them* would refer to both *classes* and *labs.* However, other revisions are possible, including eliminating *them* altogether:

Revision:	The one universal recommendation was to attend absolutely all classes and labs/**, something I never did i~~I~~n high school.** ~~I never went to all of them.~~
Revision:	The one universal recommendation was to attend absolutely all classes and labs. In high school I never ~~went to all of them~~ **attended all of my classes or all of my lab sessions**.

The references are clear in both revisions. We now understand that Sarah's attendance in both classes and labs was not perfect in high school.

Here's another example of an unclear pronoun reference that is confusing for readers:

Unclear:	**Beth** argued with **Sarah** about how **she** should spend her spare time.

The way this sentence is structured, we cannot determine who has the spare time—Beth or Sarah. In this instance, *she* should be replaced with a noun that will make the reference clear:

Revisions:	**Beth** argued with **Sarah** about how **Beth** should spend her spare time.
	Beth argued with **Sarah** about how **Sarah** should spend her spare time.

Sometimes a pronoun may have no antecedent at all. In these cases, an antecedent must be added, or the pronoun itself should be replaced with a specific noun:

Unclear:	Sarah went to school yesterday to preregister, and **they** said she had to take another math class.
Revisions:	Sarah went to school yesterday to preregister and talk with **counselors,** and **they** said she had to take another math class.
	Sarah went to school yesterday to preregister, and the counselors said she had to take another math class.

When these references are clear, the writer's message becomes easier to understand in each case.

Broad Reference

The pronouns *you* and *it* often cause communication difficulties because they can re-fer to broad groups of people, places, things, or ideas. But even a broad group does not include everyone or everything. Writers should avoid general references when possible and focus on making antecedents clear, concrete, and easily identifiable. Look at these examples from paragraph 2 of Sarah's essay:

Broad:	**You** can really develop more confidence.
Revision:	**Students** can really develop more confidence.
Broad:	In a study guide I bought at the bookstore, **it** said that keeping up with reading is critical if **you** want to succeed.

Revision: ~~In a~~A **study guide** I bought at the bookstore/ ~~it~~ said that

keeping up with reading is critical if ~~you~~ **students** want to

succeed.

A good rule to follow is to avoid using *you* and *it* unless they have specific antecedents.

Exercise E9-1

List the pronouns and their antecedents in paragraphs 3 and 4 of "Battling Bigotry on Campus" (p. 437). (Do not include pronouns that function as adjectives, such as <u>some</u> people.)

Exercise E9-2

Correct the faulty pronoun references in paragraphs 6 and 7 of Sarah's first draft (pp. 456–457).

Exercise E9-3

Correct the faulty pronoun references in the following paragraphs.

    I decided to get up at 8 a.m. Saturday. It said in an advertisement in Friday's paper that a local furniture store was going out of business. Since I would be moving into an apartment this fall, I needed to find to some bargain furniture items. You can always use an extra chair or two or a bookshelf.

    When I arrived at the store at 8:45, the line in front of the door was long and it was covered entirely with brown paper. I don't know why they did that, unless they didn't want people to see inside the store. I took my place in line. You weren't supposed to leave the line, but several people did and came back about five minutes before nine. Then when they opened the doors, people rushed forward past the employees, forging ahead for the bargains.

    I searched quickly and spotted a pair of end tables and matching wicker chairs that I liked. They were reasonable priced — $40. The chairs were more—$60 for both, still a good deal. Then, I saw two customers battling over a couch and a loveseat. Two women sat on it and refused to move. The red-haired lady told the blonde lady that she was there first. A store manager came and told her that she was going to have to move. I felt like I was eavesdropping, so I moved along, paid for my purchases, and escaped that madhouse.

Exercise E9-4

Write a short paragraph (6–8 sentences) in which you describe either an embarrassing moment or a proud accomplishment. Use as many pronouns as you can. After proofreading your work, underline each pronoun and draw an arrow to its antecedent.

Modifier Problems

Modifiers are adjectives and adverbs that describe other words in a sentence. Without words, phrases, and clauses that function as modifiers, our writing would be lifeless and uninteresting.

Usually modifiers pose few problems. However, writers sometimes find that their modifiers describe the wrong word or have no word to refer to at all. We call these common errors *misplaced* and *dangling modifiers*.

Misplaced Modifiers

As the name implies, a **misplaced modifier** finds itself in the wrong place in its sentence. As a result, it describes or enhances the meaning of the wrong word. Sarah has a misplaced adverb in paragraph 3 of her first draft (p. 455):

Misplaced Modifier:	Some students **said every day** that they study and make sure that they spend a certain amount of time reading, writing, or doing research.

The adverb *every day* appears to modify the word *said*. However, the context of the sentence suggests that the students did not make this statement every day; rather they said that they *studied* every day. Thus, the adverb should be moved closer to the verb *study:*

Revision:	Some students said ~~everyday~~ that they **study every day** and make sure that they spend a certain amount of time reading, writing, or doing research.

Phrases can also be misplaced, particularly prepositional phrases and participial phrases. Look at the following examples:

Misplaced Phrase:	Marianna **decided in New York** that she would try to model during the summer months when she was out of school.
Revision:	Marianna decided that she would try **to model in New York** during the summer months when she was out of school.
Misplaced Phrase:	Listening to her pep talk about Las Vegas, the travel agent convinced my parents to book a trip over the Labor Day weekend.

Revision: Listening to the travel agent's pep talk about Las Vegas, my **parents** were convinced to book a trip over the Labor Day weekend.

Misplaced clauses are usually easy to correct once you find them. Here are some examples:

Misplaced Clause: We bought a peach at a roadside **fruit stand that had worms in it**.

Revision: At a roadside fruit stand, we bought a **peach that had worms in it**.

Misplaced Clause: **When he got home,** Rinaldo **said** he would call me.

Revision: Rinaldo said he would **call** me **when he got home**.

Occasionally a modifier may appear to refer to more than one word or sentence element. We call this type of misplaced modifier a **squinting modifier** because it is wedged between two possible antecedents, producing an unclear sentence:

Squinting Modifier: Sarah **decided today** that she **would quit** her job.

Revisions: **Today** Sarah **decided** that she would quit her job.

Sarah decided that she **would quit** her job **today**.

Dangling Modifiers

Sometimes modifiers have no word to describe or refer to, and the reader is left puzzled and confused. When this occurs, we say that the modifier **dangles;** it literally hangs by itself, with no real connection to the rest of the sentence. Look at this example from paragraph 1 of Sarah's first draft:

Dangling Modifier: **Constantly behind in my reading**, every **test and paper** produced fear and trembling.

The way this sentence is constructed, *constantly behind in my reading* modifies *test and paper*, which is not logical. Who was constantly behind? Of course, since Sarah is writing in the first person, *I* is the person who is constantly behind:

Revision: **Constantly behind in my reading**, **I** faced every test and paper ~~produced~~ with fear and trembling.

Another option is to rewrite the modifier, rewording so that it makes sense where it is located in the sentence. Usually you will have to make the modifier a dependent clause:

Revisions: **Because I was constantly behind in my reading**, every test

and paper produced fear and trembling.

Every test and paper produced fear and trembling

because I was constantly behind in my reading.

Dangling modifiers usually appear as introductory elements in sentences. If the dangling modifier has nothing to refer to, you can either add the correct word or rewrite the modifier, as these additional examples illustrate:

Dangling
Modifier: While walking through the mall yesterday, my **wallet** was lost.

Revisions: While walking through the mall yesterday, **I** lost my wallet.

While **I** was walking through the mall yesterday, my wallet was lost.

Dangling
Modifier: To compete in the race, the **application** has to be submitted by Friday at noon.

Revisions: To compete in the race, **you** must submit the application by Friday at noon.

If you want to compete in the race, submit the application by Friday at noon.

You can avoid modifier problems if you make sure the word each modifier refers to is clear to the reader.

Exercise E9-5

Identify and correct any modifier problems in the following sentences, which appear in their correct form in "Battling Bigotry on Campus."

1. Finishing their educations without learning to respect each other's differences and cherish their own backgrounds, the future will be a troubled one for our young people.
2. To avoid this chaos, two types of plans are needed by universities.
3. Other prepared responses, given its size, location, population, and history, can be crafted for the particular community.
4. The response to critics who call for immediate suspension is to have a realistic "fast track" disciplinary hearing procedure established, so that quickly a full due process hearing can be held.

5. Fearing a backlash that could jeopardize their education, incidents cause others to be too afraid to come forward.

Exercise E9-6

Identify and correct the modifier problems found in paragraphs 4 and 5 of the first draft of Sarah's problem-solving essay (pp. 455–456).

Exercise E9-7

Correct the modifier errors in the following paragraph.

Deciding which school I want to transfer to has been a hard choice. I have narrowed my choices down to two—a small liberal arts college located a thousand miles from my home and a large university just an hour's drive away. Traveling to Woodhouse College last spring, the campus impressed me tremendously. It is quiet, peaceful, wooded, and serene, a beautiful place steeped in tradition. After staying there two days, the trip back home was a letdown, since it was dreary, cold, and in the dead of winter. As far as the state university goes, it would offer some advantages. There would be so many activities, so many people to meet. Being much closer to home, my parents and family could keep in close contact. I will make a decision about where I will go to college tomorrow. Then my final transcripts will be sent, and I'll be off.

Exercise E9-8

Write a short paragraph (6–8 sentences) in which you describe yourself or someone else. Then underline all modifiers—any words, phrases, or clauses that describe other sentence elements.

Parallelism

Many things can be parallel—lines, gymnastic bars, telephone wires—that is, they run in the same direction and never intersect. In English, words, phrases, and clauses must be **parallel** when they appear in a series, particularly when they are connected by a coordinating conjunction (*for, and, nor, but, or, yet,* or *so*). Look at these sentences from Sarah's revised draft that illustrate parallel structures:

Parallel Words:	Constantly behind in my reading, I faced every test and paper with **fear** and **trembling**.
Parallel Phrases:	They also claim that they spend less time **reviewing for their classes** and **studying for tests**.
Parallel Clauses:	All of these students told me **that they plan their study time** and **that they do not wait until they are given assignments or homework**.

Items in a series should begin with the same grammatical structure. Adjectives should be paired with adjectives, verbal phrases with verbal phrases, dependent clauses with dependent clauses, and so on. If dissimilar elements are joined, faulty parallelism occurs, making the sentence awkward and unclear. Editing sentences with unparallel elements is a simple process of "matching up" words, phrases, and clauses and making sure they are equal in structure and in form. Look at the following examples of faulty parallelism in a series:

Faulty:	Ben likes *lifting* weights, *jogging* at the bike path, and *basketball* to keep in shape.
Revision:	Ben likes *lifting* weights, *jogging* at the bike path, and *playing* basketball to keep in shape.
Faulty:	Embarrassment is *locking* your keys in your car, *calling* your mom to bring an extra set, and then *to find* that you had an extra set in your purse.
Revision:	Embarrassment is *locking* your keys in your car, *calling* your mom to bring an extra set, and then *finding* that you had an extra set in your purse.
Faulty:	Sarah decided to open a savings account *because she wanted* to buy a 10-speed bike and *for an emergency fund*.
Revision:	Sarah decided to open a savings account *because she wanted* to buy a ten-speed bike and *because she needed* an emergency fund.

Items in a comparison should also begin with the same grammatical structure. Look at the following examples:

Faulty:	When he gets ready to study, Ron prefers *settling* down in his bed to *the library*.
Revision:	When he gets ready to study, Ron prefers *settling* down in his bed to *going* to the library.
Faulty:	*Having* a few classic blazers and suits is much more economical than *a closetful* of trendy outfits.
Revision:	*Having* a few classic blazers and suits is much more economical than *having* a closetful of trendy outfits.
Faulty:	*When you left* the party is less important than *the reason*.
Revision:	*When you left* the party is less important than *why you left*.

Words, phrases, and clauses connected by correlative conjunctions, such as *either . . . or* and *neither . . . nor*, should also be grammatically parallel, beginning with similar elements. Here are some examples:

Faulty:	Neither *going* to the beach nor *a trip* to the Field Museum was Sarah's choice for our Saturday getaway.
Revision:	Neither *going* to the beach nor *taking* a trip to the Field Museum was Sarah's choice for our Saturday getaway.
Faulty:	Either *you try* to work out your problems on your own, or *telling* us what is bothering you is an option.
Revision:	Either *you try* to work out the problems on your own, or *you tell* us what is bothering you.

Parallel constructions make your sentences clear and easy to read.

Exercise E9-9

Each of the following sentences containing faulty parallelism appears in its correct form in Kenneth Stern's essay "Battling Bigotry on Campus." Identify and correct each error.

1. They appear in classrooms and dorms, going to sporting events, and in casual conversation.
2. Second, they must have a plan to reduce the level of bigotry on campus, not only so there will be fewer and less explosive incidents, but also students deserve an environment that makes them feel welcome.
3. This should include the university president, appropriate deans, campus security, and to elect representatives from student and faculty.
4. Other prepared responses can be crafted for the particular community, given its size, where it is located, population, and history.
5. The purpose is always to remind the victimized students that they truly are wanted and displaying bigoted behavior has no place on campus.

Exercise E9-10

Underline the parallel elements in the following sentences from Sarah's first draft. Circle the first word in each element, and correct any errors that you find.

1. One woman said that she considers her time at school to be her most important job and that she does not waste time during the day.
2. That way, she says, she can study and attend classes from eight to five and spend her evenings earning money as a waitress.
3. On Wednesdays, he spends the day in the library or in a study room at the Student Center.
4. They try to learn as much as possible from every class and to read supplementary material as often as possible.

5.   One political science major told me that she reads the newspaper every morning and clips articles that are interesting to her, making a note of the date and jotting down the page numbers.

Exercise E9-11

Underline and correct the faulty parallelism in the following paragraph.

To act and sing on Broadway and appearing in a movie are goals that my sister has had since she was three years old. I remember her singing "Row Your Boat" endlessly, sometimes at the top of her lungs. Honestly, at that age I would rather have watched her act rather than singing during her every waking hour. Of course, as she got older her voice got better. She wanted to take voice lessons when she was eight, but no teacher would take her as a student until she got older. When she turned 13, she signed up for acting lessons at the local theater and going to the community college for Saturday classes. She finally began studying voice, which really produced quick results and giving her extra confidence. During her high school career, she has been in countless musical theater productions in our city. She is now ready to attend college to continue her studies and getting closer to her dream.

Exercise E9-12

Follow the directions here for writing sentences using parallel constructions.

1.   Use three parallel nouns as objects.
2.   Write a sentence using two parallel prepositional phrases.
3.   Write a sentence using *neither . . . nor.*
4.   Write a sentence using two adverb clauses.
5.   Compare two things using *more than.*

Unnecessary Shifts

When a shift occurs, things become unbalanced, whether it's a stack of books, a packed moving van, or a bag of groceries. The same is true of sentences. Sudden shifts keep sentences from flowing smoothly, often jarring readers and confusing them. Unnecessary shifts—occurring in tense, voice, person, and number—are simple to recognize and correct. Eliminating them will help you produce clear and engaging prose.

Shifts in Tense

As you learned in Chapter 2, tense refers to the time of the verb's action—present, past, and future. Unless the message you are sending actually refers to different times, in most instances the verbs within a sentence should be in the same tense:

                Present   **Present**
Sarah **begins** writing her rough draft after she **brainstorms**

     Present
and **jots** down notes and a brief outline.

        Future   **Present**
We **will get** our deposit back when the landlord **comes**

     Present
and **inspects** the apartment.

The first sentence here is all in the present tense. But notice that the second sentence uses verbs in the future and present tenses. In this case, the two tenses are necessary to communicate the sentence's message.

Sometimes in our haste we mix tenses illogically. Most commonly, the shift occurs from present to past or from past to present. Just remember that verb tenses should be consistent in your writing. If they aren't, change the faulty verb to help your sentence make sense. Look at these sentences from Sarah's first draft:

Shift in Tense:	**Past** During my first semester, I **observed** successful students **Present** and **ask** them what they did to keep up with all of their assignments and other obligations.
Revision:	**Past** During my first semester, I **observed** successful students, **Past** and ~~ask~~ I often **asked** them what they did to keep up with all of their assignments and other obligations.
Shift in Tense:	**Present** **Past** Most of the students who **do** this **blocked** out four or five hours to study.
Revision:	**Present** **Present** Most of the students who **do** this ~~blocked~~ out four or five hours to study.

The verbs in the revised sentences are all in the same tense. You can see that the sentences are easier to understand without the shifts between present and past tense.

Shifts in Voice

Another shift dealing with verbs may occur in voice. You may recall from Chapter 6 that there are two voices: active and passive. The **active voice** means the subject performs the verb's action (*Sarah* took the test). The passive voice occurs when the receiver of the action becomes the subject (The test was taken *by Sarah*).

Just as tenses should be consistent, so should voices. Once you begin writing in one voice, you should not suddenly shift to another. If you do, an awkward, confusing sentence will result:

Shift in Voice:
                  Active
Sarah **spent** two hours last night completing her financial

                  Active
aid forms. Then she **checked** them again this morning

                  Passive
before the information **was mailed**.

Revision:
                  Active
Sarah **spent** two hours last night completing her financial

                  Active
aid forms.Then she **checked** them again this morning

                  Active
before she **mailed** the information.

Shift in Voice:
             Passive   **Passive**
The answers **were** quickly **determined** without a calcula-

                  Active
tor, which was surprising because I usually **rely** on the miracle machine every step of the way.

Revision:
                  Active
I quickly **determined** the answers without a calculator,

                  Active
which was surprising because I usually **rely** on the miracle machine every step of the way.

These revisions show how the same voice throughout a sentence makes the message clear and easy to read.

Shifts in Person

As you may remember, personal pronouns have three *persons* (see p. 42). **First person** is the person(s) speaking, *I* or *we;* **second person** is the person spoken to, *you;* and **third person** is the person spoken about—*he, she, it, they.*

Just as writers should keep verb tenses consistent, they should also keep person references logical. Unnecessary shifts in sentences occur most often between first person and second person, usually when the writer attempts to make a generalization by referring to a large group of people. The following sentences illustrate the confusion that can result:

	First .... **First**
Shift in Person:	When **I** interviewed for the job, **I** first took a skills test.
	Second
	Then **you** had to complete a personality profile.
	First .... **First**
Revision:	When **I** interviewed for the job, **I** first took a skills test.
	First
	Then **I** had to complete a personality profile.
	First .... **First**
Shift in Person:	**We** need to shuffle the starting lineup for **our** softball
	Third
	team because **they** always need more power at the plate.
	First .... **First**
Revision:	**We** need to shuffle the starting lineup for **our** softball
	First
	team because **we** always need more power at the plate.

Consistency in person is important to good writing, as you can see in these examples.

Shifts in Number

While tense and voice refer to verbs and person relates to pronouns, **number** refers simply to whether nouns and pronouns are singular or plural. Determining a noun's or pronoun's number is not a difficult task. When collective nouns and indefinite pronouns are concerned, however, number shifts may occur more frequently.

Problems with collective nouns often happen when they serve as antecedents. Since collective nouns such as *audience* or *squad* can be singular or plural, choosing the proper pronoun to refer to these nouns can be tricky. To solve these number problems, determine whether the noun is functioning as a single unit or the members of the group are acting individually:

	Plural .... **Singular**
Shift in Number:	The **audience** jumped to **its** feet after Greg Louganis finisshed his speech.

> **Plural**   **Plural**
>
> **Revision:**   The **audience** jumped to **their** feet after Greg Louganis finished his speech.

> **Singular**   **Plural**
>
> **Shift in Number:**   The **audience** listened attentively as **their** final vote tally was announced.

> **Singular**   **Singular**
>
> **Revision:**   The **audience** listened attentively as **its** final vote tally was announced.

Probably more confusing is the case in which indefinite pronouns serve as antecedents for other pronouns. Some indefinite pronouns, such as *everyone, everybody,* and *everything,* seem contradictory in number; they appear to be plural grammatically, but are really singular (see p. 43). The best advice is to remember which pronouns are singular and which are plural. Remember also that some pronouns, such as *all* and *some,* can be singular or plural. Then make sure that all pronouns agree in number:

> **Singular**   **Plural**
>
> **Shift in Number:**   **Everybody** shut down **their** computer when the lightning flashed.

> **Singular**   **Singular**
>
> **Revision:**   **Everybody** shut down **his or her** computer when the lightning flashed.

If *his or her* seems awkward to you, another revision option is to change the singular references to plural.

> **Plural**   **Plural**
>
> **Revision:**   The **students** shut down **their** computers when the lightning flashed.

Making singular and plural references consistent is worth spending time on because clarity is essential to good writing.

Exercise E9-13

Underline the unnecessary shifts in the following sentences, whose correct versions appear in "Battling Bigotry on Campus." Label them as shifts in tense, voice, person, or number.

1. If the incident is serious, students were likely to protest.
2. The purpose is always to remind the victimized student that they are truly wanted and that bigotry has no place on campus.

3. If a student commits an assault, burglary, arson, or other serious offense and summary suspension was allowed by the disciplinary code, and the known facts warrant it, he or she should be suspended immediately, pending a hearing.
4. Punishing a student for using bigoted words or printing bigoted articles drapes you, instead of the school, in the First Amendment.
5. Sometimes the cost of additional security is prohibitive and the speaker does not come, but usually they do, and the campus is paralyzed in anticipation of what may happen.

Exercise E9-14

Correct the unnecessary shifts in the following sentences adapted from Sarah's first draft, and indicate whether the shifts are in tense, voice, person, or number.

1. All students I talked to called themselves extremely busy people, but everyone had made graduating from college their first priority.
2. By reading the assignments ahead of time, students claimed that they have to take fewer notes and were able to ask more intelligent questions.
3. Then, between classes and labs he works on lab reports and homework is completed.
4. In a study guide I bought at the bookstore, it said that keeping up with reading is critical if you want to succeed.
5. She says that she enjoys reading the newspaper, and it helps you feel less guilty if you can say that you're doing research at the same time.

Exercise E9-15

Underline and correct the unnecessary shifts in the following paragraph.

Are professional athletes paid too much? I am sure that everyone has their own opinion about this question. But I think salaries have gotten out of hand. Certainly I believe that athletes are gifted and adequate compensation should be given to them by the teams' owners. But $15 million or more a year is a bit much. I think these outrageous figures send the wrong messages to young people that they can make it big in sports one day, that you don't have to complete your education. But the big dreamers forget that he faces astronomical odds of reaching the professional level of any sport. Maybe that's a reason to justify the big money paid to pro athletes, a huge reward for "making it."

Exercise E9-16

Correct the unnecessary shifts in Exercise E9-13.

Sentence Variety

Producing good writing is hard work. Getting ideas, brainstorming, organizing, adding details, revising, and editing take time and concentrated effort. But sometimes these activities are not enough to make your prose as polished as it could be. Why? The answer is simple. Many writers rely too heavily on the basic subject-verb-object sentence pattern, sometimes referred to as a sentence's *natural order.* For instance, every sentence in the following paragraph is grammatically and mechanically correct. But these sentences offer little variation in structure:

                  S   **V**   **S** **V**

Many **people collect** things as a hobby. **I have** a friend who collects

                S   **V**   **S**   **V**

baseball cards. **He must have** about 5000. **They are stored** in shoeboxes

                                  S **V**

in his closet and in the garage. **They are** probably worth at least $20,000

                             S   **V**

in his opinion. Another **friend collects** matchbooks from all over the

                S   **S**   **V**

world. His **parents** and **grandparents gave** him most of them from their

              S **V**   **S**   **V**

travels. **He gets** matchbooks wherever he goes. My **mom collects** com-

                                S **V**

pacts, particularly old ones from the 1930s to 1960s. **She has** about 25 of

         S **V**   **V**

them. **I don't collect** anything right now except bills, which is another

story.

In this paragraph, every sentence is structured in S-V-O order, so the paragraph is a string of starts and stops. This makes for bumpy, choppy reading that is likely to lose the readers' interest. By shifting sentence patterns, combining structures, and adding words, we can greatly improve the paragraph's flow:

                  S   **V**   **S** **V**

Many **people collect** things as a hobby. *For example,* **I have** a friend

who collects baseball cards, *amassing over* 5,000 cards *that* **he stores in**

                                     S   **V**

shoeboxes in his closet and in the garage. *In his opinion,* his **collection is**

                         S   **V**

probably worth at least $20,000. Another **friend collects** matchbooks from

all overthe world. *If it weren't for his parents' and grandparents' travels,*

S   V   V   S V

he wouldn't have as many items in his collection. *But* he gets matchbooks

                               S   V

wherever he goes. **Mom collects** compacts, mainly from the 1930s to the

                   S V   S V   V

1960s. *Currently* **she has** about 25. *As for me,* **I don't collect** anything

                              S   V

right now—except bills. *But* **that's** another story.

In this revised paragraph, the main subjects and verbs appear in different locations in their sentences. Producing a variety of sentences like the ones in this example paragraph takes extra time and effort. But as you work with your sentences, you will find that with practice you will automatically make them more varied.

Varied Beginnings

A quick fix for choppy sentences is to vary their beginnings. Often adding a word, phrase, or clause before the subject and verb will break up a monotonous pattern. Look again at the revised paragraph about collecting. Words, phrases, and clauses appear before the subject and verb in several sentences.

Word:	**Currently** she has about 25.
Phrase:	**In his opinion,** his collection is probably worth about $20,000.
Clause:	**If it weren't for his parents' and grandparents' travels,** he wouldn't have as many items in his collection.

Sometimes you can move words, phrases, and clauses from the middle or end of a sentence to the beginning. When you combine sentences, you will also discover opportunities to vary their beginnings. On other occasions, you may have to add words and phrases to the beginnings of your sentences in order to make smooth transitions from sentence to sentence.

As an example, let's use a simple sentence that begins with a subject and a verb: *Sarah juggles school, work, and her social life with amazing skill.* The following sentences illustrate the many choices you have when it comes to starting sentences with words, phrases, and clauses instead of with a subject and verb:

Adverb:	**Amazingly,** Sarah juggles school, work, and her social life with skill.
One-word Transition:	**Also,** Sarah juggles school, work, and her social life with amazing skill.
Transitional Phrase:	**On the other hand,** Sarah juggles school, work, and her social life with amazing skill.

Prepositional Phrase:	**With amazing skill,** Sarah juggles school, work, and her social life.
Appositive Phrase:	**A busy young woman,** Sarah juggles school, work, and her social life with amazing skill.
Participial Phrase:	**Keeping her cool at all times,** Sarah juggles school, work, and her social life with amazing skill.
Infinitive Phrase:	**To meet her parents' expectations,** Sarah juggles school, work, and her social life with amazing skill.
Dependent Clause:	**Because she is mature and responsible,** Sarah juggles school, work, and her social life with amazing skill.

Notice that the introductory element in each of these examples adds a different emphasis and varies the sentence structure slightly. Also note that each introductory element is set off by commas. If you need help in making sure your sentence beginnings are punctuated correctly, see page 313.

Exercise E9-17

Explain how Kenneth Stern begins each of the following sentences from his essay "Battling Bigotry on Campus."

1. According to the National Institute Against Prejudice and Violence, more than 250 of the nation's 3,300 colleges and universities have reported acts of ethnoviolence since 1986.
2. Whereas some of today's university administrators may be insensitive to problems of intergroup hatred, their predecessors practiced it.
3. Knowing this, the universities must strive to make every student feel welcome.
4. To avoid this chaos, universities must have two types of plans.
5. If that student can be suspended immediately, before a hearing, he or she should be.

Exercise E9-18

Explain how Sarah begins each of the following sentences from her revised draft of "Time Management for College Students."

1. When I started college, managing my time effectively was very important to me, but I did not have any idea how to do it.
2. By reading the assignments ahead of time, students claimed that they had to take fewer notes and were able to ask more intelligent questions.
3. However, I was surprised that several have jobs in the afternoon and evenings during the week and spend 10–12 hours every Saturday and Sunday reading and studying.

4. Working on Friday and Saturday nights at a restaurant, he says that his job is his only social life.

5. Instead of spending so much time drinking coffee and thinking about studying, I plan to do some reading while I drink that coffee.

Exercise E9-19

Rewrite at least five sentences in the following paragraph, making sure that they do not be-gin with a subject and a verb. You may shift sentence elements, combine sentences, or add words, phrases, and clauses of your own.

My best friend Amy has twin brothers. Their names are Randy and Ricky. They weighed only three pounds each when they were born. You would never know it be-cause today they stand over six feet tall, 200 pounds of solid muscle. Amy has told me quite often about the stunts her brothers pull. She says they have always been mischievous. Trouble has followed them wherever they have gone. She says that they have never done anything too serious, mostly just pranks and playful gags. They like to switch places, especially when they are out on dates. Randy once went out with a girl that Ricky had been dating for three months. She didn't know it until the date was over and Randy told her. She was mad at first, but she got over it. She and Ricky are still dating.

Exercise E9-20

Add two introductory elements to each of the following independent clauses, making six dif-ferent sentences.

1. We sailed for several days.
2. Kelly slipped on a patch of ice.
3. The professor lectured for almost an hour.

Varied Structure

You could say that the simple sentence—one independent clause with one subject-verb pair—is the most important sentence structure. After all, it provides the basis of the three other sentence structures: compound, complex, and compound-complex (see pp. 103–110). The simple sentence is also the most overworked sentence struc-ture. Because it is the first kind of sentence we learn to speak and write, we grow up relying on simple sentences to communicate most of our messages.

Good writers use simple sentences with skill, varying beginnings and separating subjects and verbs without interfering with the main idea. Good writers also use the other three sentence structures along with simple sentences. In fact, most writers work very hard to avoid repeating the same structures. Look at the opening para-graph of Sarah's revised draft. Can you determine each sentence's structure without referring to the list at the end of the paragraph?

(1) When I started college, managing my time effectively was very

important to me, but I did not have any idea how to do it. (2) Constantly behind in my reading, I faced every test and paper with fear and trembling. (3) During my first semester, I observed successful students, and I often asked them what they did to keep up with all of their assignments and other obligations. (4) All of the students I talked to called themselves extremely busy people, but they had made graduating from college their first priority. (5) The one universal recommendation was to attend absolutely all classes and labs, something I never did in high school. (6) Nevertheless, since I have completed my interviews and collected students' experiences, I can confidently offer their advice to you.

1. compound-complex
2. simple
3. compound-complex
4. compound
5. complex
6. complex

Notice that this example uses all four sentence structures. Repeating sentence structures in moderation is fine as long as the repetition isn't noticeable or irritating. Just remember not to overuse any one of the sentence structures. If you alternate structures throughout your paragraphs, your readers will be swept along with free-flowing prose and won't be bored or annoyed by needless repetition.

Varying the form of your sentences—like changing sentence beginnings—takes time and energy. However, you will find that with a little practice you will be composing sentences with interesting structures. For example, look at how Sarah revised paragraph 6 of her essay. The subjects and verbs of all clauses are in bold type:

(1) One **woman** that **I interviewed is married** and **has** two small children. (2) **She does** not **take** a full load of classes. (3) **She** and a **friend who works** part time **take care** of each other's children. (4) **She worked** in a bank for several years. (5) **She says** that **she does** all her reading and homework before leaving campus. (6) **She wants** to give all her attention to her family and her home when **she is** at home. (7) **She** and her **husband split** all the usual chores like grocery shopping and laundry and cooking. (8) **She says** that **she would** rather **take** a few more years to finish college than **neglect** them. (9) If her **children are**

ill, **she might miss** a class to take them to the doctor. (10) **She makes** it

a practice not to miss classes unless **it is** an emergency.

Here is a list of sentence structures in this paragraph:

1.	complex	6.	complex
2.	simple	7.	simple
3.	complex	8.	complex
4.	simple	9.	complex
5.	complex	10.	complex

Sarah depends almost entirely on two sentence structures (simple and complex). The structures become monotonous because her main subjects and verbs are almost always located at the beginnings of sentences. By combining sentences and shifting or adding words, phrases, and clauses, Sarah produces a much better mix of structures that communicates a clearer, more interesting message (The additions are in italics.):

(1) One **woman** that I **interviewed is married** and **has** two small children. (2) **She does** not **take** a full load of classes. (3) **She** and a **friend who works** part time **take care** of each other's children, *so she is able to go to class*. (4) *Even though* **she worked** in a bank for several years, *going to college is much harder for her because of the homework*. (5) **She says** that **she does** all her reading and homework before leaving campus. (6) *When she is at home*, **she wants** to give all her attention to her family and her home. (7) **She** and her **husband split** all the usual chores like grocery shopping and laundry and cooking, *but* **she says** that **she would** rather **take** a few more years to finish college than **neglect** her family. (8) If her **children are** ill, **she might miss** a class to take them to the doctor, *but* **she makes** it a practice not to miss classes unless **it is** an emergency.

This revised paragraph contains a variety of sentence structues:

1. complex (same as the first draft)
2. simple (same as the first draft)
3. compound-complex (an independent clause was added)
4. complex (a subordinating conjunction and an independent clause were added)
5. complex (same as the first draft)
6. complex (dependent clause shifted to the beginning of the sentence)
7. compound-complex (combination of original sentences 7 and 8)
8. compound-complex (combination of original sentences 9 and 10)

Of course, these revisions are not the only options for improving sentence variety. Virtually an endless number of choices is available to you. Countless combinations of clauses and phrases make improving sentence structure a challenging and productive proposition. If you need any further review of the four sentence structures, look again at the Tips for Editing in Chapter 3.

Exercise E9-21

List the structure (simple, compound, complex, or compound-complex) of each sentence in paragraphs 26 and 27 of Stern's "Battling Bigotry on Campus" (p. 441).

Exercise E9-22

List the structure (simple, compound, complex, or compound-complex) of each sentence in paragraph 6 of Sarah's revised draft (pp. 461–462).

Exercise E9-23

Rewrite paragraph 3 of Sarah's first draft (p. 455), using different sentence structures. Then identify the structure of each new sentence.

Exercise E9-24

Choose one of the following topics, and write a short paragraph (6–8 sentences). Then edit your paragraph by varying your sentence structure. After you finish editing your paragraph, label the structure of each sentence in your paragraph.

1. Explain how you relax.
2. Describe your room.
3. Tell about something you did that got you into trouble.
4. Explain why you chose your major or career.

Varied Types

All sentences contain at least one subject and verb and express a complete thought. But all sentences do not function in the same way. Some sentences express ideas, while others ask questions or make requests. Whatever the case, changing the sentence's pattern or type may help express an idea more vividly or clearly while adding variety to your writing.

The most common type of sentence is the **declarative sentence,** a statement that ends with a period. Declarative sentences simply express or declare ideas. The great majority of the sentences in Sarah's essay "Time Management for College Students" are declarative:

Declarative: When I started college, managing my time effectively was very important to me, but I did not have any idea how do it.

To keep on track, he sets aside Friday for writing.

Another type of sentence that begins with a capital letter and ends with a period is the **imperative sentence.** This kind of sentence states a command or gives orders or directions. The subject of an imperative sentence is often the understood *you:*

Imperative: (You) Drop off those clothes at the cleaners on your way to school.

Don't (you) forget to call home when you arrive at the hotel.

An **interrogative sentence,** or question, ends with a question mark. Interrogative sentences are normally inverted, with part or all of the verb appearing before the subject:

Interrogative: How much did your books cost?

Did Sarah turn in her paper on time?

An **exclamatory sentence,** or exclamation, ends with an exclamation point because it expresses strong emotion:

Exclamatory: Sarah wrote a great paper!

She got an A!

We depend heavily on declarative statements in our writing, sometimes forgetting about imperative, interrogative, and exclamatory sentences. Try restructuring some of the declarative sentences in your own writing to prevent monotony. You will find that a variety of sentence types will make your prose more engaging than it already is.

Exercise E9-25

Choose five declarative sentences from Kenneth S. Stern's essay "Battling Bigotry on Campus" (pp. 436–449). Then rewrite each sentence, making it a question, a command, or an exclamation. Write at least one of every type of sentence.

Exercise E9-26

Using the paragraph you wrote in Exercise E9-24 on page 492, vary the sentence types, including at least one question, one command, and one exclamation. You may need to add sentences and transitions to accomplish this task.

 ## COLLABORATIVE WORK

After you revise your problem-solving essay, exchange papers with a classmate, and do the following tasks:

A. Underline any problems in pronoun usage, especially pronouns that are not close to their antecedents or do not agree with their antecedents.

B.   Circle any errors in modifier usage.

C.   Put brackets around any series or comparisons that are not grammatically parallel.

D.   Put an X through any inconsistencies in tense, voice, person, and number.

E.   Choose one paragraph and label each sentence according to structure and type.

Then return the paper to its writer, and use the information in this section to edit your draft.

CHAPTER 2

Lynda Barry, "The Sanctuary of School" from The New York Times (January 5, 1992), "Educational Life" section. Copyright © 1992 by The New York Times Company. Reprinted with the permission of The New York Times.

CHAPTER 3

N. Scott Momaday, "The Way to Rainy Mountain" from *The Way to Rainy Mountain*. First published in The Reporter (January 26, 1967). Copyright © 1967, 1969 by The University of New Mexico Press. Reprinted with the permission of the publishers.

CHAPTER 4

William Zinsser, "Words" from *On Writing Well, Fifth Edition* (New York: Harper-Collins Publishers, 1994). Copyright © 1976, 1980, 1985, 1988, 1990, 1994 by William Zinsser. Reprinted with the permission of the author and Carol Brissie.

CHAPTER 6

Duane P. Schultz and Sidney Ellen Schultz, "The Challenge of Fair Employment" from *Psychology and Industry Today, Fifth Edition*. Copyright © 1990 by Macmillan Publishing Company. Reprinted with the permission of Prentice-Hall, Inc. This selection contains a table: "Pre-Employment Questionnaire" adapted from R. L. Minter, "Human Rights Laws and Pre-Employment Inquiries," Personnel Journal 51 (1972). Reprinted with the permission of the publishers.

Table: "Black Representation Within Occupations" from Andrew Hacker, *Two Nations: Black and White, Separate, Hostile, Unequal*. Copyright © 1992 by Andrew Hacker. Reprinted with the permission of Scribner, a division of Simon & Schuster, Inc.

"The Financial Payoff of Higher Education for Women" from "Campus News" from The Monthly Forum on Women in Higher Education 1, no. 3 (December 1995). Copyright © 1995. Reprinted with the permission of the publishers.

INDEX